ArtScroll Judaica Classics®

הגות בפרשיות התורה

STUDIES

Published by

Mesorah Publications, ltd

ARTSCROLL / ארטסקרול / ירושלים בע"מ
Jerusalem, ltd.

IN THE WEEKLY PARASHAH

The classical interpretations of major
topics and themes in the Torah

by
Yehuda Nachshoni

translated from the Hebrew by
Raphael Blumberg

FIRST EDITION
First Impression . . . December 1988
Second Impression . . . December 1989
Third Impression . . . January 1992

Published and Distributed by
MESORAH PUBLICATIONS, Ltd.
Brooklyn, New York 11232

Distributed in Israel by
MESORAH MAFITZIM / J. GROSSMAN
Rechov Harav Uziel 117
Jerusalem, Israel

Distributed in Australia & New Zealand by
GOLD'S BOOK & GIFT CO.
36 William Street
Balaclava 3183, Vic., Australia

Distributed in Europe by
J. LEHMANN HEBREW BOOKSELLERS
20 Cambridge Terrace
Gateshead, Tyne and Wear
England NE8 1RP

Distributed in South Africa by
KOLLEL BOOKSHOP
22 Muller Street
Yeoville 2198
Johannesburg, South Africa

THE ARTSCROLL JUDAICA CLASSICS®
STUDIES IN THE WEEKLY PARASHAH
Vol II: Sh'mos
© Copyright 1988, by MESORAH PUBLICATIONS, Ltd.
4401 Second Avenue / Brooklyn, N.Y. 11232 / (718) 921-9000

ISBN:
0-89906-935-5 (hard cover)
0-89906-936-3 (paperback)

Typography by CompuScribe at ArtScroll Studios, Ltd.
4401 Second Avenue / Brooklyn, N.Y. 11232 / (718) 921-9000

Printed in the United States of America by Noble Book Press Corp.
Bound by Sefercraft Inc., Quality Bookbinders, Brooklyn, N.Y.

❧ Table of Contents

הגות בפרשיות התורה

STUDIES
IN THE
WEEKLY
PARASHAH

ספר שמות

Sh'mos

Sh'mos – שמות

I.
Moshe's Sense of Justice:
Prerequisite for Prophet and Redeemer

he Torah tells little about the life of Moshe, redeemer of Israel, before his rise to greatness. Yet, how ripe with meaning are those first few words, dealing with the marriage of his parents: "A man of the house of Levi went and married Levi's daughter" (*Sh'mos* 2:1). In *Parashas Va'eira* the Torah will elaborate on his lineage, but for now, a single point is emphasized: Moshe was born of a woman, hence he is different from all those mythological heroes claiming descent from the gods, and from those founders of later faiths to whom superhuman births are likewise attributed. With this, the Torah stresses the root and essence of Judaism — man's spiritual development proceeds from earth towards heaven, and not the reverse. Born naturally, his mission is to raise nature to a Divine level, i.e., to establish the Torah in control over life.

Another fundamental principle is stressed here: Torah cannot be acquired through inheritance. Moshe's greatness does not stem from his lineage, but from his spiritually elevating himself (Barshover Gaon: *Michtav LeDavid*). These interpretations may sound abstract and homiletical. However, they are embodied in an incident narrated by the Torah: "A man of the house of Levi went and married Levi's daughter." This incident has little significance as narrative, and can only have meaning in terms of the deeper ideas perceived in it by profound thinkers.

Chazal and the *rishonim* try to fathom what purpose there is to the expression "a man of the house of Levi went." Where did Amram go? The Talmud (*Sotah* 12a) relates that after Pharaoh's decree to kill every male baby, Amram, in despair, divorced his wife. Verse 2:1 tells of

Amram's taking his daughter's advice and remarrying Yocheved. Hence, Amram "went" after his daughter's advice.

Ibn Ezra explains that with the Israelites living in different cities, Amram left his own city and went elsewhere to find a wife. *Ramban* rightly questions the Torah's need to tell us this. His own explanation differs: The Torah is stressing that Amram took a wife in order to bear children, despite Pharaoh's decree to drown the male babies that will be born of this marriage.

Really, all the ideas mentioned should be attributed to the verse. Brief and vague, it is our only introduction to the birth of Moshe, redeemer of Israel, and surely embodies every relatable idea of significance.

Likewise noteworthy is Moshe's having been raised and educated in Pharaoh's house. While the Torah does relate how this happened, it does not explain why. R' Sorotzkin (*Oznayim LaTorah*) states that the Torah here wishes to show that Hashem's will always prevails. Pharaoh decrees the drowning of all male Israelites in the river. Hashem orchestrates events so that Israel's redeemer is educated in Pharaoh's house, having been saved by Pharaoh's daughter. From here he later goes out to his brethren, becoming their national redeemer and lawgiver.

This understanding, the source of which is *Akeidas Yitzchak* on our *parashah*, is an independent truth, an archetypical lesson applying not just to our *parashah*, but to all of history: We can only see the present. No man can predict what the future will bring.

Ibn Ezra culls yet another lesson from the events of our *parashah*. He begins by stressing that Hashem's plans are profound and unfathomable, and that events can truly be understood by Hashem alone. Yet, allowing for the limitations of human understanding, he offers the following theory to explain why Moshe grew up in Pharaoh's house:

> Perhaps Hashem caused Moshe to grow up in a royal palace, so that his soul would be on a high level of study and behavior, rather than the low expectations of a slave. Had things been otherwise, would Moshe have killed the Egyptian for his violent act, or saved Yisro's daughters from the shepherds who were stealing their water?

Ibn Ezra makes an interesting point. Had Moshe grown up and been educated in a Jewish home, he would have displayed an "exile syndrome" and been incapable of brave acts. Therefore Hashem arranged for him to grow up in a house where there was no fear of flesh and blood, so that he would develop the self-confidence to carry out great, miraculous acts. Ibn Ezra then adds: "Had Moshe grown up among his brethren, and been familiar to them from his youth, they would not have revered him, for they would have considered him one of them."

This explanation as well has a psychological basis, taken from real life. Those familiar with someone cannot afford him the full honor he deserves, for he is one of them, and they are unwilling to accept his authority. Not so a leader who comes from afar, unfamiliar to all.

Abarbanel embellishes this idea:

> Why are the murder of the Egyptian (v. 2:12), the quarrel of the two Israelites (v. 2:13) and the rescue of Yisro's daughters (v. 2:17) mentioned immediately after we are told that Moshe grew up in Pharaoh's house? It is not to tell us that they chronologically followed one after the other, but to inform us of Moshe's spiritual greatness. He was first exiled to Pharaoh's palace so that he could learn the tactics of leadership and monarchy, which would cause him to develop courage and spiritual greatness. All of this ultimately made him a heroic, fearless individual, unwilling to tolerate evil either in Egypt or in Midian, even though in the latter place he was a stranger and fugitive. These episodes teach us of Moshe's inherent righteousness, honesty and generosity of spirit. These are *mitzvos* worthy of a prophet. In fact, such traits lead to prophecy.

Abarbanel's words are in harmony with our original remarks. The events narrated here serve as an introduction, enabling us to understand the background of Moshe's emergence as a man of valor, psychologically prepared for his great mission and destined by Providence to be Israel's prophet and redeemer. He required a setting unmarked by exile, so his spiritual traits could be developed and revealed, unimpeded by his surroundings.

◆§ Moshe Went out to His Brethren and Saw Their Travail

The Torah does not tell us just when Moshe became aware of his Jewishness nor how his feelings for his people became so magnified that he came to their aid. *Rashi's* comment is neutral: "Moshe devoted his attentions to sharing in their trouble." For *Rashi*, the word וַיַּרְא, "he saw," refers not to physical seeing, but to reflection. Moshe's unwillingness to tolerate injustice or violence preceded even his feeling of brotherhood, and may have been what led to it. Feeling Israel's pain, he devoted himself to alleviating it.

Ramban explains similarly, but understands וַיַּרְא literally. After

Moshe became aware that he was Jewish, he went out to observe and become familiar with his brethren. Shocked by their harsh suffering, he killed an Egyptian attacker.

According to Abarbanel, Moshe became attached to Yocheved his nursemaid and to her children. When he grew up, he found out from them that he was their son and brother. He then left the royal palace to observe his Hebrew brethren working on the royal construction outside the city, and there he saw what he saw.

The Torah says, "And it came to pass in those days that Moshe grew up, and he went out to his brethren and saw their suffering." (ibid.). *Chasam Sofer* sees this verse as clarifying the way in which Moshe became so great in Hashem's eyes as to become an agent of redemption. It was a reward for his having shared in their pain and having observed their suffering. Interestingly, this explanation is presented, albeit not as the plain meaning of the text, by *Chazal* in *Bereishis Rabbah*:

> Hashem said, "You have set aside your personal affairs and gone to observe the suffering of Israel, treating them like brothers: Therefore, I shall set aside the beings of both Heaven and earth to speak to you:" This is the meaning of the verse, 'Hashem saw that he turned aside to see' (ibid. 3:4). Hashem saw Moshe turn aside from his own affairs to see their suffering. Hence: "He called to him from within the bush" (ibid.)

Indeed, this idea parallels another idea of *Chazal*. Hashem's revealing His Divine Presence to Moshe hints at His being "with us in trouble" (*Tehillim* 91:15). Hashem shows Moshe that even He, as it were, suffers Israel's suffering. His words at the burning bush are well explained by the author of *Shevet Sofer* of Pressburg:

> "This is the sign that I sent you" (*Sh'mos* 3:12): Hashem wished to instill in Moshe an awareness of his mission, to help him understand that he and he alone was right for it, having sympathized with Israel's trouble. He therefore said, "This is the sign," i.e., "Let My appearance in the burning bush, symbolizing My sharing in Israel's trouble, be a sign that 'I sent you' — specifically you, who personify sharing in Israel's trouble." This is related to *Chasam Sofer's* idea that Moshe's greatness stemmed from his observing Israel's suffering.

The Torah says, "Moshe went out to his brethren, and saw their travail" (*Sh'mos* 2:11). Ibn Ezra writes: "his brethren; i.e., the Egyptians." I cannot understand Ibn Ezra's seeing this verse as referring to Egyptian brethren, while when Moshe sees the Egyptian smite אִישׁ עִבְרִי מֵאֶחָיו —

an Israelite, one of his brethren" (ibid.), Ibn Ezra explains this as referring to his fellow Jews.

[Atypically, Rabbi Nachshoni does not explain Ibn Ezra's words here. He merely suggests that a scribal error may have entered the manuscript copy from which our printed editions were taken. Obviously, he was unaware that the supercommentaries on Ibn Ezra explain that by the phrase "the Egyptians," Ibn Ezra means the Jews who were living in Egypt. Since the words "Moshe went out to his brethren" could be misinterpreted to mean that Moshe left Egypt to see his brethren who dwelled elsewhere, Ibn Ezra emphasizes that Moshe went out to see the Jews who were living in Egypt. And "went out" refers to Moshe's leaving the royal palace, not Egypt. — Ed.]

ঙ§ First Stage of Prophecy

"Moshe went out to his brethren and observed their suffering" (Sh'mos 2:11). With this verse the Torah emphasizes the aspect of Moshe's personality that was decisive in his development as redeemer of Israel. Other traits of Moshe are later described, but all stem from his fierce longing for justice and his active efforts to implement it against the common will, despite clear risks.

The Torah describes three events in Moshe's life that occurred before his emergence as the redeemer of the Jewish people. All involve his efforts for justice, be it personal, national or universal: (a) Moshe saw an Egyptian smiting a Jew and came to the victim's aid, killing the Egyptian despite the risks involved; (b) two Jews quarreled, and once more Moshe rose to the aid of the weak, strongly admonishing the guilty party (ibid. 2:13), "וַיֹּאמֶר לָרָשָׁע לָמָּה תַכֶּה רֵעֶךָ" — He said to the evildoer, 'Why do you beat your brother?' "; (c) the previous events became known to Pharaoh through informers and Moshe having to flee before Pharaoh's anger, went to Midian; although newly arrived and a stranger, he came to the aid of Yisro's daughters who were being harassed by the shepherds of Midian.

The three events just described serve to highlight the elements of the personality of Moshe, who was destined to redeem Israel and humanity from their low spiritual level through the Torah given at Sinai. Why does the Torah specifically choose justice as the criterion for testing the worthiness of Moshe to be Israel's shepherd?

A famous secular writer wrote an essay about Moshe, in which he maintained that absolute justice is the key element in prophecy, inseparable from the prophet's personality. The essence of his idea was taken or plagiarized from Rambam's Moreh Nevuchim (2:45), with one substantive difference. *Rambam* counts this trait as only a first step, and a minor one, in the attainment of prophecy, while the secular writer sees it as the entire essence of prophecy. The following are the words of *Rambam*:

> Prophecy begins when a man is Divinely guided in the performance of a major good deed such as delivering a large group of people from attack, saving a highly important person or influencing many persons towards righteousness. When an individual is inspired in this way, and finds within himself the impetus to act, we say that he has been "cloaked in" or "invested with" a Divine spirit. Be aware that such inspiration never departed from Moshe once he reached manhood. Through it, he was aroused to kill the Egyptian and to deter the wrongdoer in the quarrel of the two Jews. So strong was it in him that even after he fled to Midian, frightened stranger though he was, he could not bear the sight of injustice, neither could he desist from removing it, as it is written (*Sh'mos* 2:17), "Moshe rose to their aid."

Rambam goes on to make clear that not everyone who has this capacity is a prophet. Rather, whomever Hashem chooses is seen to have this capacity, which is the first of eleven levels of prophecy, each higher than that preceding. Moshe merited the highest rank of prophecy, that of conversing with Hashem (*Sh'mos* 33:11) פָּנִים אֶל פָּנִים — "face to face." God's spirit began to beat in Moshe once that first evidence of prophecy, active pursuit of justice, was revealed in him.

Akeidas Yitzchak elaborates as well on this fundamental trait in the psyche of Moshe, Israel's redeemer. He finds it equally associated with the *Mashiach*, of whom King David said (*Tehillim* 72:4), "He shall judge the poor, rescue the needy and break the oppressor." These three elements were discovered in Moshe with his emergence upon the scene. His smiting the Egyptian corresponds to "he shall break the oppressor." His reproach of the evildoer, "Why are you beating your brother?" parallels "He shall judge the poor," and his rescue of Yisro's daughters, where "Moshe got up and came to their aid," is similar to "He shall rescue the needy." The prophet Gidon, too, revealed corresponding traits when he appeared, at which time Hashem commanded him (*Shoftim* 6:14), "Go with this virtue of yours and save Israel." In this vein, *Akeidah* concludes:

> The Torah related these notable events in the life of Moshe to inform the compassionate that God had found a man after His own heart. Supervised by Hashem, Moshe was able to punish the Egyptians, who tyrannized the Jewish people with slave labor. He

saved that poor nation from its tormenters, and gave them Torah and *mitzvos*, which enabled them to conduct all their affairs according to Divine justice. Who besides Moshe was worthy to perform all of these acts?

The aforementioned secular article was simply a plagiarism of Torah sources with the author's own heretical ideas superimposed. Interestingly, what was true in the article had been previously expressed, more concisely and to the point, by *Chasam Sofer*, in the holy spirit of his predecessors:

> Even at first glance, Moshe is a man who cannot tolerate injustice. On the first day he goes out to his brethren, he witnesses an Egyptian committing a wicked deed, and kills him. Although the Egyptians ruled over the Jews, Moshe, who possessed a proud love of truth, could not stand the sight of oppression. On the second day as well, he proved himself in the realm of injustice even where his own brethren were involved. Finally he acted even to stop local Midianite shepherds from mistreating Yisro's daughters. Although Moshe at the time was a wandering stranger fleeing for his life, he still rose to save them. He asked no recompense, going on his way until summoned to eat with Yisro's family. Moshe loved truth and uprightness above all else.

According to *Ramban*, a belief in justice for all oppressed, whatever their national origin, is the first and foremost step in the attainment of prophecy. The commentaries consider it essential for a redeemer of Israel. It is this the Torah wished to underscore in its preface to the mission of Moshe.

II.

Consecration of Moshe as Redeemer

he section devoted to the consecration of Moshe as prophet and redeemer is brief. Yet *rishonim* and *acharonim* have something to say about every word. In the scope of this work we shall deal with three points: (a) Moshe's preparation for prophecy; (b) the site of Hashem's revelation to him; and (c) Hashem's purpose in revealing Himself, and Moshe's reaction.

Later in this *parashah* we shall dwell on justice as an aspect of Moshe's personality in his protection of the weak and downtrodden, whether Jew or non-Jew. This trait is a prerequisite of prophecy. We will deal with the phenomena of isolation and withdrawal from normal life, which Moshe experienced as a shepherd on the verge of prophetic inspiration.

In the Midrash, *Chazal* interpret Moshe's shepherd experience either as a basic point or as a vision for the future. Hashem examined Moshe's fitness as leader based on the way he treated his flocks. His mercy, which assumed concrete form when he was a shepherd, served as the standard by which his leadership abilities were tested. The desert was his testing ground, for that was where all the events of his leadership career were destined to occur.

The early commentaries follow the path taken by *Chazal*, yet penetrate more deeply the spiritual significance of herding sheep. "Prophecy does not rest upon Moshe," says Abarbanel, "when he is in Pharaoh's house, nor when he goes out to his brethren, nor when he reigns in the land of Kush, for power and pride deter the onset of prophecy." Abarbanel adds that, according to *Rambam* in *Moreh Nevuchim* (2:36), a prophet must possess three fundamental virtues: (a) scholastic excellence; (b) exemplary character; and (c) superb intuition. Parallel to this, *Chazal* speak of a prophet requiring "wisdom," "bravery" and "wealth."

The three traits mentioned by *Chazal* carry unconventional connotations (see *Rambam's Shemoneh Perakim* which elaborates). "Rich," for example, refers to "he who is happy with his lot." Possibly, however, these fundamentals are all prerequisites not for prophecy, but for achieving influence. The conditions for prophetic revelation would then be those of our *parashah*: seclusion within nature and simple living. Through these an individual can achieve perfect character, the cornerstone of prophetic virtue.

Rabbenu Bachya views the simple life of the shepherd as psychological preparation for spiritual elevation. Hevel, the Patriarchs and the twelve sons of Yaakov were all shepherds. Thus engaged, they could guard themselves from committing theft and achieve considerable spiritual advancement. In this way, Moshe attained increasingly greater levels of prophecy, achieving visions of greater and greater depth. First he saw the burning bush, a concrete object, discernible to the human eye. Then he saw an angel on a Divine mission, and finally the glory of Hashem Himself. Hashem wished to accustom Moshe to prophecy, step by step. When a man leaves a dark house, his eyes must adapt to sunlight. The mind, like the body, must adapt as well.

Obviously, we cannot examine what is too wondrous to understand, neither can we explain in logical terms the loftiness of Moshe, Father of the Prophets, or the nature of his visions. Nonetheless, *rishonim* find in the Biblical descriptions of prophetic revelation the fundamental principles leading to every kind of spiritual elevation. *Torah Sheleimah* cites *Midrash HaGadol* that the Torah aims to teach that a life of physical labor leads to spiritual elevation, just as Moshe, at the time of his revelation, was a shepherd.

Kli Yakar focuses on the process whereby the candidate for prophecy secludes himself, communing with nature and reflecting on Hashem's works until Hashem pours forth His spirit upon him from above, as in *Tehillim* (8:4), "I behold Your heavens, the work of Your fingers."

Chasam Sofer sees in the preparation for prophecy through identification with Israel's suffering the way that one achieves a sublime understanding of the destructive forces that threaten the Jewish people. The verse indicates that, "Moshe pondered the destruction of the Temple." Through such reflection Moshe merited to become an emissary of Hashem, like Gidon, who merited this for the same virtue (*Shoftim* 6:14), "Go with this virtue of yours and save Israel."

Alternatively, Chassidic thought and medieval philosophy are both preoccupied with understanding the psychology of Moshe's actions. When Moshe sees the burning bush, he says (*Sh'mos* 3:3), "I must go over there and investigate." This illustrates the Divine intention of having Moshe reflect actively on what he saw. Also his walking through the desert is a stage in this process of observation. *Toaliyus Ralbag* concludes from the above that, "a person should strive to his utmost to examine why things happen." Moshe, having shown that such was his custom, i.e., that he was eager to know the reason behind things, merited an awesome spiritual level.

There are countless other interpretations and explanations of the prerequisites for prophetic consecration. *Kol Simchah* finds an allusion that Moshe will be our future redeemer as well. The Torah says (*Sh'mos* 3:1), "He led the flock beyond the desert." The letters of the alphabet following [i.e., that lie "beyond"] each of the letters of מִדְבָּר — "desert" are ג, ה, נ and ש. [These same letters appear on the Chanukah *dreidel*, representing "A great miracle happened there."] Their numerical value is 358, equal to מָשִׁיחַ (*Mashiach*).

If you reflect on the words of the *rishonim* and *acharonim* in this *parashah*, you will find the key to the various lessons and secrets it contains.

It is no coincidence that Hashem revealed Himself to Moshe from a burning bush. *Chazal* in the Midrash saw this as evoking a broad range of symbolic themes and prophetic visions. The commentaries add almost nothing to the multi-faceted explanations of *Chazal*, although they occasionally uncover a new secret in their words.

Rabbenu Bachya regards the burning bush as a revelation that our nation, despite its hardships, is eternal: "The burning bush conjures up the image of a lowly nation in iron fetters, constantly aflame with suffering. Threatened on all sides, yet worthy of relief, the Jewish people continue to endure miraculously among their enemies."

This interpretation is found in *Midrash Sh'mos*, regarding the Exile in Egypt: "Just as the bush burns but is not consumed, so too, Egypt cannot destroy the Jewish people."

Yet, another explanation of Rabbenu Bachya follows the line of the medieval philosophers. Moshe's seeing the burning bush represented his striving to conceptualize Hashem, which led to his achieving prophecy. According to Rabbenu Bachya, the burning bush represents matter in the universe, which remains unconsumed even though it is cloaked in Heavenly fire. Moshe investigated the way that form and matter combine to produce innovation in the universe, and he found Hashem the Creator to be the root of all existence.

This interpretation is embodied in the Midrash as well (*Sh'mos Rabbah* 1:9): "From the burning bush we learn that no place, even a bush, is devoid of the Divine Presence." Nonetheless, here various Jewish schools of thought branch out in familiar directions. The Chassidism of the *Ba'al Shem Tov* understands this idea as meaning simply that the Divine Presence can be as easily cloaked in evil as in good, and that no place is devoid of it in any sense. This idea finds clear expression in *Degel Machaneh Ephraim* on *Ki Seitzei* regarding the verse, "If you come across a bird's nest" (*Devarim* 22:6):

> I heard from my grandfather and master [the *Ba'al Shem Tov*] that the *Shechinah* descends from the highest to the lowest level. And that this is the meaning of the verse (*Nechemiah* 9:6), "You sustain them all." Even when an individual sins, he is still surrounded by the *Shechinah*, without which no person would have the power to perform any act, even to move a muscle. It is that which sustains him, investing him with energy and life. This is, as it were, the *Shechinah* in Exile.

This idea aroused vociferous opposition from the Vilna Gaon, and is one of the factors that led to the persecution and excommunication of Chassidism. At the end of *Metzaref Ha'Avodah* we find quoted a letter from the *Ba'al HaTanya* who offers an in-depth analysis of the two views. He explains the view of the Vilna Gaon that one should not interpret "No place is devoid of Him" literally, but rather in the sense of (*Yeshayahu* 6:3) "The whole Earth is full of His glory," meaning that *hashgachah* — Divine Providence — is everywhere. He notes that as a result of this contention, the Chassidic works *Toldos* and *Shivchei Ba'al Shem Tov* were burnt.

Sefas Emes clarifies this sublime idea in various ways. For him, the statement "no place is devoid of the *Shechinah*" points to the purpose of *galus* — exile — namely, that Israel must everywhere reveal the Divine light. *Galus* is from the same root as *hisgalus* — revelation. Through the dispersion of the Jewish people, Hashem's will becomes revealed everywhere and concerning every matter.

Elsewhere he says that the burning bush symbolizes holiness burning brightly despite the presence of the "thorns," i.e., the profane. Moshe was puzzled by the holy fire's endurance in the face of these "thorns," yet Heaven wished to demonstrate that even within the very depths of darkness is stored a great light, as in the verse (*Sh'mos* 1:12), "The more the Egyptians oppressed them, the more the Israelites proliferated and spread."

Chazal, interpreting the burning bush, state that just as a rosebush produces both flowers and thorns, so too do the Jewish people possess both great saints and awful sinners.

Maharal views the bush as symbolizing Jewish stubbornness. Through this trait are produced both personality types mentioned. As each draws his vital essence from stubbornness, transition between the two extremes is easy for a Jew, despite their being polar opposites.

The vision of the burning bush therefore makes clear the historic and spiritual essence of Israel, the phenomenon of good and evil confronting each other, and Hashem's promise (*Vayikra* 26:44), "I will not grow so disgusted with them nor so tired of them that I would destroy them."

Moshe was impressed by the greatness of the vision and he said (*Sh'mos* 3:3), "I will turn aside to see this great sight." The burning bush, representing Moshe's mission, was a harbinger of its future success. Similarly, *Rashi* interprets the verse (ibid. 3:12) "This shall be a sign for you," as referring to the burning bush, for through it, his mission became clear to him.

⋖§ This Shall Be a Sign That I Have Sent You

Rashi, *Rashbam* and Ibn Ezra each explain how the burning bush represents such a "sign." All three treat the continuation of the above verse as a separate sentence, dealing with a separate question. The verse continues, "When you take the people out of Egypt, you will all serve Hashem on this mountain." This is seen as answering either, "By what merit will the Jewish people be redeemed?" (*Rashi's* second understanding) or, "Just how will Pharaoh allow such a large nation to leave?" (*Rashbam*).

Hashem's solution to taking out the nation is to disguise His real intent by telling Pharaoh that the Jewish people wish to go serve Hashem in the desert. This Moshe does later when he pleads with Pharaoh (ibid. 5:8), "Let us go and sacrifice to our God."

Ibn Ezra, however, explains arriving at Mount Sinai to serve Hashem as the objective for leaving Egypt. Hashem chose to inform Moshe of this now, since He was not appointing him at this time to take the Jewish people directly into *Eretz Yisrael*. According to *Akeidah* and Abarbanel, Moshe expresses his puzzlement by asking (3:11), "Shall I take out the Children of Israel?" i.e., to what end is the Exodus if not that we may enter the Land of our Forefathers?

Ramban shifts the focus of concern to Israel's psychological state and their relative willingness to leave the country they are in for a strange land. For him, Moshe's question means, "If liberation were to occur within Egypt itself all would be well and good, but if the aim is for me to take them out, who will listen to me?" Hence Hashem replies that the Jewish people will now undergo a process of education and spiritual elevation at Mount Sinai. Then, they will believe everything Moshe says.

Kli Yakar relates Moshe's question to his hopes of elevating the Jewish people from their impure state, a precondition for redemption. Moshe asks how it is possible to raise them from their spiritual level and separate them from the Egyptians. Therefore Hashem promises that at Mount Sinai their defilement will cease, and a true separation between them and the Egyptians will be established.

Sefas Emes takes this idea a step further, saying that their defilement will abate the moment they leave Egypt. At that point, they will already be on a different spiritual plane, yearning to serve Hashem. That is the meaning of the verse (*Sh'mos* 11:1), "When he lets you leave, he will actually drive you out of here." As soon as Pharaoh drives them out, it will become clear that they have been liberated from every other servitude as well, and that they no longer have any connection or attachment to Egypt. *Divrei Shaul* follows this direction as well.

HaKesav VeHaKabalah states that when the Jewish people left Egypt, it was so they could serve Hashem forever. This involved no one-time act, but rather an everlasting process of spiritual inspiration. Note that *Sh'mos* 3:12 employs not תַּעַבְדוּ for "you will serve," but תַּעַבְדוּן. We find that usage in הַמַּעֲשֶׂה אֲשֶׁר יַעֲשׂוּן — "Show them the things they must do" (*Sh'mos* 18:20), which refers to *mitzvos* commanded for eternity. This everlasting devotion required our breaking the yoke of *galus*, and being liberated from the persecution of Egypt. As *Chazal* said, "You are slaves to Hashem, not slaves to other slaves." The purpose of the Exodus from Egypt was for us to become servants of Hashem. This is the purpose for which Moshe was sent.

Chasam Sofer, however, holds that liberation from Egypt was not conditioned on the Jewish people accepting the Torah:

> We do not find concerning any of the miracles of the Exodus that Hashem mentions the condition of the giving of the Torah or the acceptance of the *mitzvos*. Rather, a few *mitzvos* were commanded at Marah, and after they had all been performed, Hashem sent His emissary, Moshe, for the Jewish people to accept if they wished. The Jewish people responded (*Sh'mos* 19:8), "We will do" before "We will hear," and in our prayers we say, "Hashem's children beheld His might; they gave praise and thanks to His name, and willingly accepted His sovereignty."

This acceptance was voluntary, without precondition. When Moshe expressed puzzlement over his mission, Hashem mentioned this virtue to him: "You are going to take out a nation that will accept Torah and *mitzvos* voluntarily."

Rambam is the only one who explains the verse, "This shall be a sign for you," as implying that the Torah, rather than any miraculous sign, would be the basis of Israel's faith. According to *Rambam's* view, Moshe was hesitant to undertake Israel's redemption through signs and wonders, for complete faith cannot be attained in this manner. Hashem therefore told him that these signs were only a temporary measure until Sinai; from then on, faith would be based exclusively on *Torah* (*Yad HaChazakah*):

> Moshe knew that whoever bases his belief on signs and wonders suffers from an imperfect, calculating faith, hence he declined to undertake the mission, saying, "They will not believe me." Finally, Hashem informed him that these signs would only apply prior to the Exodus from Egypt. When the Jewish people would stand before Sinai, all their sinful calculations would leave them ... From

here we deduce that our faith in the prophets who follow Moshe is not only because they do signs and wonders, but because of the *mitzvah* commanded by Moshe in the Torah.

Such is Hashem's calming message to Moshe from the burning bush. Only temporarily did He wish to influence the nation with signs and wonders. For the future, Hashem wished the Torah to guide the nation and to confirm the mission of Hashem's prophets with its command that the Jewish people accept them.

III.
The Rod with Which You Shall Perform the Signs

Numerous questions confront the reader of the *parashah* before us. Can Moshe truly doubt that the Children of Israel will believe him and listen to his voice after Hashem's clear promise that they will do so? What is the nature of the three wonders Hashem shows Moshe, each more persuasive than that preceding? If it is the Jewish people who need proof, why does Hashem show the wonders to *Moshe*, making it seem as if he himself needs encouragement and persuasion? How does Moshe sin, according to *Chazal*, in suspecting the Jewish people of disbelief? Does not Hashem Himself say, "And if they do not believe you . . ."?

Ramban expresses puzzlement at Hashem's performing the wonders in Moshe's presence rather than having Moshe hurl his rod before the Jewish people. He agrees therefore with the definition of *Chazal* that the signs that Hashem showed Moshe are punishments. The first wonder, a rod transformed into a serpent, is meant to remind Moshe that he has spoken *lashon hara* — slander — about the Jewish people in suspecting them of disbelief. Moshe feared the snake and bolted lest it bite him for defaming the Children of Israel. The second wonder, *tzora'as* — "leprosy," serves to punish him and cleanse him of sin.

Ramban also offers another explanation. Hashem wished to instill in Moshe the belief that, through him, new acts of creation would take place in the world, and Hashem proved this by means of two signs. As for the third wonder, water being transformed into blood, Hashem commanded Moshe to perform this in the presence of the people of Israel because that was where water was available.

Ibn Ezra states that Hashem performed the wonders in Moshe's presence so he would know what to show the people. The people — not Moshe — needed persuading, hence Hashem's conclusion, "in order that they may believe."

The first wonder was performed by means of Moshe's ever-present rod, an implement the elderly use for support. When Hashem said, "If they do not believe you," He was just communicating in human terms. Hashem knew in advance whether the Children of Israel would believe Moshe or not, and He was only expressing Moshe's doubts. Similarly, Hashem said, "If they do not hearken to the voice of the first wonder." Can a wonder have a voice? Here too Hashem was just employing normal idiom.

Abarbanel, however, declares that these signs and wonders serve to verify Moshe's role as emissary. Actions contrary to the laws of nature, performed by an emissary, demonstrate that the emissary acts on the Sender's authority. Such acts of verification are quite common, because circumstances generally make them necessary.

Rambam, in *Moreh Nevuchim* (1:63), similarly explains Moshe's doubts, expressed in the words: "They will not believe me." Moshe was now appearing as a prophet presenting his mission before the public. Avraham, Yitzchak and Yaakov had preceded him as prophets, yet their task had consisted solely of perfecting themselves and their offspring, and educating the masses. Although they had imbued the masses with faith, they had employed no prophetic vision. Moshe was the first to prophesy to the masses in Hashem's name. His appearance demanded verification through signs and wonders. Moshe argued, "They will not believe me" without signs and wonders, for I am a prophet on a mission from Hashem. If I am to demonstrate through wisdom and logic that a Prime Being exists, I can only do this aided by signs, for I myself am an emissary of that Prime Being. Hence the inclusion of signs and wonders.

৵৳ Suspicions of Disbelief

Rashi, quoting *Chazal*, explains that the first two wonders serve to emphasize that Moshe spoke *lashon hara* about the Children of Israel in suspecting them of disbelief. Only the third sign, water turning to blood, deals with the future, indicating that the Nile — an Egyptian divinity — will be smitten with the first plague.

The Midrash (*Devarim Rabbah* 9) plays on the word הֵן which can mean either "behold" or "they":

> When Hashem announced to Moshe (*Devarim* 31:14), "Behold
> (הֵן), your day is nearing to die," Moshe protested saying (*Devarim
> Rabbah* 9), "With the word הֵן — behold — I praised You as it is
> written (ibid. 10:14), "Behold (הֵן), the Heavens, even the Supreme
> Heavens, belong to Hashem your God." Hashem replied, "Yet, you
> said as well, 'They (הֵן) will not believe me.' "

Chafetz Chaim explains as follows. It is hard to understand why
Moshe was punished for saying, "They will not believe me." Was it not
important for him to know what would happen if they exhibited
disbelief? In truth, he was punished for speaking with certainty, implied
by the word הֵן, as if he was sure from the start that he would not be
believed. Such certainty constituted *lashon hara*. Had he employed אִם
— "if," he would not have been punished.

This is what *Chazal* meant in *Devarim Rabbah*. Moshe was puzzled
by Hashem's saying, "Behold, your day is nearing to die," so Hashem
responded that His words were fitting punishment: "You too used the
word הֵן, proclaiming with certainty that the Jewish people would surely
doubt you. Your punishment is therefore to hear your approaching
death proclaimed with equal certainty."

Michtam LeDavid explains Moshe's words in similar fashion. Moshe
says, "They (הֵן) will not believe me," while Hashem says, "If (אִם) they
do not believe you . . ." Moshe decisively determines that they will not
believe, while Hashem says that if at first they do not believe Moshe, in
the end they will. The Jewish people are the faithful descendants of the
faithful, destined to have belief. Nonetheless, efficient measure must be
employed to arouse in them the spark of faith. Anyone rebuking his
fellow Jew for wrongdoing must strive and strive again in this regard
until his words have an effect. He must not lose hope on seeing his
words make no impression, for if his words do not register on his first
attempt, they will have an impact on some later attempt.

In addition, *Michtam LeDavid* explains the reason for Hashem
saying, "If they do not believe you . . ." Hashem suspected that Moshe's
words would leave their impression and cause the people not to believe
because Moshe had said that they would not. This conforms to the
principle that an emissary on a mission to perform a *mitzvah* must have
no doubts that his mission will succeed. Doubt creates a negative
impression, and has a counterproductive influence.

Nonetheless, *HaKesav VeHaKabalah* interprets the expression
"They (הֵן) will not believe me," as if Moshe had said, "If (אִם) they do
not believe me." He is supported by *Yirmiyahu* (2:10), הֵן הָיְתָה כָּזֹאת,

which *Rashi* reads as, "If there had been such a thing." In accordance with this, Moshe, too, was not making a decisive statement, but expressing suspicion that they might not believe him.

⋖§ Moshe's Hesitation

The commentaries have much to say concerning Moshe's doubts about whether the Jewish people would believe in his mission. *Ramban*, Abarbanel and S'forno explain these doubts in term of Hashem's having told him that Pharaoh would not let the Jewish people leave Egypt. This would be enough to cause the Jewish people to jeer at Moshe, saying, "How could Hashem have appeared to you with promises of rescue? Even now Pharaoh trespasses His word and ignores His command. Did not Hashem create the world?" Alternatively, *Ramban* suggests that they could have argued with Moshe that "Hashem did not offer as much mercy as you claim. You are no greater than the forefathers, hence Pharaoh did not listen to your voice."

According to Abarbanel, Moshe complained to Hashem: "You have promised me (*Sh'mos* 3:18), 'They will listen to your voice' because they will find the news of their exodus from suffering and slavery pleasant. Yet, once Pharaoh rebukes them, they will be bitterly disappointed. They will no longer believe in my mission, calling me a liar to whom Hashem did not truly appear."

Ibn Ezra and other commentaries hold that Moshe's hesitation stemmed from Hashem's promise that the elders of the Jewish people would listen to him, while He did not assure him that the people would believe him.

Ramban says that Moshe suspected that "they will listen to your voice" was not a promise but an order. He thought that the Jewish people were being compelled to listen to him. This is in keeping with the later verse (ibid. 4:8), "If they ... do not heed the first sign, it will be proper for them to heed the second." This constitutes no assurance that they will heed Moshe.

Furthermore, we have Hashem's message to Pharaoh prior to the first plague (ibid. 7:17), "This should make you aware that I am Hashem." There is no certainty that this will happen, for Pharaoh, even at a later stage, refused to acknowledge Hashem's existence, hence Moshe's doubts about the Jewish people as well.

Ma'asei Hashem expresses an idea similar to that of *Ramban*. Moshe feared that "they will listen to your voice" was not a promise, but only a precondition for what follows in the verse (ibid. 3:18), "You and the elders of Israel shall approach the King of Egypt." In other words, if they listen to your voice they will go with you, otherwise they will not. This is in fact what happened, for Moshe and Aharon approached Pharaoh alone, unaccompanied by the elders.

Or HaChaim explains that Moshe's hesitation was due to his humility, which was unbefitting to his mission. *Rambam* in *Hilchos Yesodei HaTorah* says, "The gift of prophecy rests only upon a great scholar . . . who is physically perfect." Moshe, in his great humility, did not consider himself a great scholar, and he said, "They will not believe me," for I lack the virtues expected of a prophet. Furthermore, "They will not listen to my voice," for I find it difficult to speak and express myself. Hence I lack physical perfection, a prerequisite for prophecy.

The Lutzker Gaon quotes *Koheles Rabbah* (21) regarding the generation of the Prophet Amos, which complained: "How could Hashem pass over everyone else, investing his Divine Presence upon that disabled tongue?" Similarly, Moshe was afraid that his contemporaries would make a similar complaint, saying, "Hashem could not have appeared to you, for you are slow of speech."

The Dubno Magid says that Moshe feared that the Jewish people would say that what he saw was not of Hashem, but from the *sitra achara* — Satan's camp.

Rabbenu Sa'adiah Gaon says that false prophecy can take two forms. Either the individual intentionally fabricates a false vision or his eye misleads him so he sees something without knowing what he saw. Moshe feared both possibilities. On the one hand, he was afraid the Jewish people would suspect him of inventing the mission in his own mind, and on the other hand, that they would believe he saw something, but that it was not Hashem who appeared to him. To dispel these two fears, Hashem entrusted Moshe with two wonders. One involved transforming an inanimate object (rod) into an animate one (serpent) and then back again. This was to signify that he had been sent by a higher power; Moshe could not perform these wonders on his own. The purpose of the second wonder (leprosy), a punishment to Moshe for speaking *lashon hara* about the Jewish people, was to demonstrate that his mission originated with Hashem. Satan would not punish him for speaking evil of the Jewish people, for the task of the *sitra achara* is to denounce Israel.

Sefas Emes invests Chassidic content into the discussion. When Moshe complained about disbelief among the Jews, he was referring not to his own time, but to future generations. Moshe knew that the Egyptian exile was the prototype for all future exiles, just as the redemption from Egypt was the key to future redemption. Through his words he wished to establish that even if Israel is not strong in its faith it will be redeemed. He wished to hear Hashem promise to redeem the nation even after his prediction that the Jewish people would not listen to him.

Tiferes Shlomo takes a slightly different path. Moshe said to Hashem: "Your people Israel are so decadent that they will be unable to raise themselves up and believe. Therefore, You must arouse them with Your holy spirit to make them worthy of believing me and listening to my voice." Hashem responded that Moshe was mistaken regarding the essence of Israel; that he was unaware of the great depths of faith at their disposal. He showed Moshe that even his Divine staff, on which was carved Hashem's Ineffable Name, could become a serpent, and that even water from the Nile, one of four rivers running out of Eden, could be transformed into blood.

This demonstrates that even something of holy origin can look as if it had been turned into something else, as stated (*Sh'mos* 4:4), "Stretch forth your hand and take it by its tail ... and it became a rod in his hand." The *tzaddik* must transform reality. He must take every Jew by the hand and bring him close, so he becomes once more מַטֶּה בֵּית אֲבוֹתָם — "a staff of his father's house" [playing on the word מַטֶּה which can mean either "staff" or "tribe"]. The roots of the Jewish people are holy and their foundation is based on faith. They must be returned to their root and source.

◄§ Nature of the Signs

Our commentaries attempt to decipher the symbolism of the three miraculous signs. Not all commentaries deal with all three, yet, from the sum total of explanations, it emerges that one way or another, Hashem is offering Moshe a window on the future, and teaching him Divine conduct.

S'forno sees as the purpose of the rod turned serpent and of the leprous hand, to instill in us an awareness that Hashem grants life and death. A rod is inanimate, yet through Hashem's will it can be given life. Conversely, a hand holds life within, yet if Hashem wills it, it can be put to death. Moshe fled the serpent because it was alive and harmful. The serpents created by the Egyptian magicians, however, possessed no living spirit. As *Chazal* say in *Sanhedrin, Perek Arba Misos*, "The magicians of Egypt could not even create an ant." For this reason, the being created by means of the Divine staff was called a נָחָשׁ, while that created by the magicians of Egypt was called a תַּנִּין.

These two creatures are unalike. Moshe created a real snake while the magicians created only an illusion. Yet, even if the Jewish people did not believe the first sign, there was still the second one, the cure of leprosy, which represented a greater natural wonder.

Ma'asei Hashem explains the signs similarly but in greater depth. The signs function as proof that Hashem and not an angel will redeem Israel. This is so because *Chazal* teach us that no angel performs two missions, whereas here Hashem's powers are revealed in dual form as in the verse (*Devarim* 32:39), "I crush and I heal." This verse found in the Song of *Ha'azinu* incorporates the three signs. The Torah says, "See now that I, even I, am He. There is no god with Me. I kill and give life. I crush and I heal, yet there is no protection from My power."

"I kill and give life" refers to the first sign, involving an inanimate object given life and then deprived of it.

"I crush and I heal" refers to the second sign, a hand turned leprous, then restored to health.

"There is no protection from My power" refers to the water that turns to blood and then remains irrevocably transformed.

Abarbanel regards the three wonders as responses to three questions asked by Moshe, allusions to which we find solely in the responses themselves: (a) How can we be saved from a tyrannical despot whose land is a crucible of affliction? (b) How shall the Children of Israel be purged of their sins so they merit redemption? (c) How shall they be saved from the Egyptian people, who attack them, thirsting for their blood?

To these three questions, the three wonders offer concise answers. The first wonder of the rod and serpent symbolizes Pharaoh's downfall. Historians tell us that Pharaoh was not of the royal line. However, he overcame his predecessors and usurped the kingdom. Like the rod turned into a snake from which Moshe fled, but which ultimately again became a rod, Pharaoh's end is that he would be destroyed forever.

The hand that became leprous when removed from the bosom symbolizes the destiny of the Jewish people. As long as they are in the bosom of their native land, they remain clean and pure. Yet, once they are uprooted from their homeland and transported to the exile, they become leprous and flawed. When the Jewish people return to their native land, they will once more become pure as before. Finally, the water transformed to blood symbolizes the fate of Egypt, who will ultimately drown in the Sea of Reeds.

Chasam Sofer, as well, sees in the wonders, specifically the first one, a symbol of Israel's destiny. Israel, the staff of Hashem's strength, was thrown to the ground and subjugated by foreign powers, and this made its people what they are. Through their long-suffering patience they developed humility, and a loving acceptance of their yoke. Moshe is directed to make his brethren aware of how holy is their lineage, so that they may ascend once more to the pinnacle of glory. He is told (*Sh'mos* 4:4), "Take it by its tail!" i.e., focus on their modesty and humility. By dint of these they will once more become the staff of Hashem's strength and glory.

Akeidah sees in the wonders three types of marvelous phenomena, each greater than that preceding it. The first category consists of a phenomenon that is impossible under normal circumstances, yet possible under others. For example, all things being equal, wheat cannot be transformed into a baby chick. It is possible, however, that a chick will consume some of the wheat, and the food within will be transformed into an egg, from which a baby chick will be born. The rod transformed to a serpent is on a par with that. Under normal circumstances it is an impossible phenomenon. Yet, the rod can be transformed to dust, and snakes consume dust.

The second category concerns normal phenomena of nature whose uniqueness lies in their happening to only half of an object. Out of a chicken egg can come a baby chick. Yet it is impossible for there to be an object which is half chick and half egg, as in the case of the second sign, in which Moshe's hand becomes half leprous. A man can be smitten with leprosy, but he cannot be partially leprous and partially well.

The third category involves something totally removed from reality. Iron cannot become either wool or a baby chick under any circumstances, yet such is the nature of the water transformed to blood.

Binah L'Itim finds still other miraculous aspects. Hashem wished to demonstrate for Moshe that all innovation has a Divine source. Hashem of His own volition transforms good to evil and evil to good. Therefore, He showed Moshe three miraculous actions involving innovations in essence, location and time.

The rod turned staff involves a change in essence. It was transformed from good to evil and from evil to good. The second wonder involves location. In one part of the body there is goodness, an absence of leprosy, and in another part there is evil. Contact with the bosom causes leprosy, yet cures it as well. The third wonder involves time. Water and blood exist at the same time in the water itself.

Some commentaries, however, regard the essence of the wonders as a metaphor for tactics of leadership. *Pardes Yosef* understands (*Sh'mos* 4:2), "What is this in your hand?" as constituting Hashem's probe of Moshe, "Just how shall you conduct communal leadership?"

Moshe answers, "A staff," by which he means, "I shall rule by an iron staff." Yet, Hashem responds that such leadership will become a "serpent," and the nation will flee in rebellion.

On the other hand, Hashem tells Moshe not to totally evade such conduct. Rather, Hashem says, "Take it by its tail!" Be prudent in your application of such tactics. Apply a little of each. In just the same way the Torah commands that a king may not exalt himself in his heart above his brethren. Even so, a king is forbidden to forgo his honor.

Likutei Basar Likutei perceives the verse, "Stretch forth your hand and take it by its tail," as enjoining the leader to sacrifice himself for the good of the Jewish people. It is exceedingly dangerous to grasp a serpent by its tail. Yet, the good leader must be oblivious to danger when he assumes control of a nation and the responsibility of leading it to rest and security.

IV.

He Met Him and Sought to Kill Him

The five verses involving the return of Moshe from Midian to Egypt (*Sh'mos* 4:24-28) are the most obscure in the entire Book of *Sh'mos*. Hashem sends Moshe to redeem Israel, and suddenly, surprising him on the way, desires to kill him. What reason could Hashem have had? Later we shall enlist the words of *Chazal* who say that Moshe deserved death for not having circumcised his son Eliezer. If so, however, why was he specifically confronted with his death sentence in the place where they spent the night? Also, if Moshe and his wife had already concluded that they must circumcise him, why then did Tzipporah perform the task and not Moshe, especially since there is one view in the Talmud that invalidates a woman from performing circumcision?

Before circumcising her son, Tzipporah said (*Sh'mos* 4:25), "You are a bloody bridegroom to *me*." Furthermore, when the angel finally desisted from them she said (verse 26), "You are a bloody bridegroom because of the circumcision." Neither does the Torah explain just who the angel wished to kill — Moshe or the child.

Whoever ponders these verses will find that without the assistance of *Chazal* it is not possible to understand the text.

✥ Why the Negligence in Circumcising Eliezer

Rashi quoting *Chazal*, as well as the other Torah commentators, notes that Moshe brought the wrath of Heaven upon himself for not having circumcised his son Eliezer. Nevertheless, *Chazal* in Tractate *Nedarim*, 31 say that Moshe was not negligent in his failure to perform the *mitzvah*. Rather, he saw himself as obligated to go on Hashem's mission and redeem Israel. Had he circumcised his son he would have been obligated to wait at least three days until his son was out of danger. Only then would he have been able to take him and start out on the way. He therefore hastened to leave so he could fulfill his mission. Yet, when Hashem saw that he tarried in his resting place, unafraid of delaying Israel's redemption, Moshe was punished for not circumcising his son at that moment. Although there was still the trip to Egypt and the resulting danger to the circumcised child, R' Eliahu Mizrachi explains that only one more day was involved and such a short journey would do the child no harm.

Ramban says that Eliezer was born only after Moshe returned from the burning bush to Yisro, his father-in-law. Eliezer's eighth day occurred, therefore, while Moshe was on the road, and it was then that Hashem stopped him.

Ibn Ezra concurs that the eighth day occurred when they were traveling. Moshe possessed an oral tradition that one must not circumcise a child in a place of danger and the open road represents such a place. Therefore, Hashem sent Moshe an angel to advise him that the child could be circumcised and left with its mother at their lodging place until fully recovered.

According to Ibn Ezra, the word וַיִּפְגְּשֵׁהוּ — "he met him" — implies that a serious disease struck Moshe, bringing with it such severe trembling that Moshe could not circumcise Eliezer himself, hence Tzipporah performed the act.

Tur states that in the place they had slept, Tzipporah said to Moshe, "Let us tarry here and circumcise the child," and the angel compelled Moshe to listen to Tzipporah's voice. Through *gematria* we find an allusion to this. The Torah says, אָז אָמְרָה — "then she said ..." אָז has the numerical value of eight. Tzipporah told Moshe that the eighth day of Eliezer's life had arrived, and he must be circumcised.

✥ Punished for Bringing His Wife and Children

Rashbam holds that Hashem wished to kill Moshe for delaying his mission by bringing along his wife and child. They were a tedious burden that impeded his journey from Midian to Egypt. Then, Tzipporah made the decision to circumcise her son, and the blood from the circumcision functioned as a *korban* — "an offering," as it did for Gidon and Manoach when the angel appeared before them (*Shoftim* 13).

Chazal have Yisro express the severity of Moshe's bringing along his wife and children (*Sh'mos Rabbah* 4):

> "Moshe went and returned to Yisro his father-in-law." Where did he go? To bring along his wife and sons. Yisro asked him, "Where are you taking them?" and he answered, "To Egypt." Yisro then said, "The Jews in Egypt are trying to leave. How can you take them there?" The next day Moshe answered, "The Jewish people are destined to stand before Mount Sinai and hear the Torah from Hashem's lips. Shall my children not hear it as well?" Immediately Yisro responded, "Go in peace."

This Midrash justifies Moshe's act. Wishing his family to be with the Jewish people for the Sinai Revelation, he brought them to Egypt.

Ralbag and *Ramban* see psychological merit in Moshe bringing his wife and sons along. The Jewish people, sighing under a heavy burden, would believe redemption near on seeing Moshe unafraid to bring along his family.

Meshech Chochmah, as well, sees Moshe's bringing his wife and children to Egypt as a ruse on his part to instill faith in the Jewish people. Still, he holds that Moshe was punished for this. Hashem granted Moshe signs and wonders with which to persuade them of the truth of his mission and he had no need of further proofs, which were, in fact, forbidden. Therefore, Moshe's being an emissary to perform a *mitzvah* did not protect him, and he was almost punished.

Interestingly, *Akeidah* interprets the phrase "in the lodging place" as a reference to Moshe having occupied himself with his wife. Lodging infers affairs of the home, so that Moshe attended to his own affairs rather than having devoted himself entirely to the redemption of Israel. Therefore, Hashem sought to kill him and would have done so if not for the merit of the *mitzvah* he was going to perform.

⋖ He Met Him and Sought to Kill Him

The commentaries interpret this verse as, "an angel of Hashem met him." Previously, we quoted Ibn Ezra that "He met him" indicates that a severe illness struck Moshe on his journey. *Ralbag*, too, understood that because Moshe had not circumcised his son, Hashem punished him in this way.

Up to that point Moshe thought himself exempt from circumcising Eliezer because he had to hasten with his mission. He also considered it proper to bring his family along to Egypt. He hoped, thereby, to gain the trust of the Jewish people and to avoid the ridicule he would suffer if they thought him afraid of introducing his family to the Egyptian crucible of suffering. Yet, Hashem knew that the signs would be sufficient to instill such faith in the Jewish people. Therefore, Hashem waited for Moshe to reach a resting spot, a place where he could leave his wife and circumcised son. Moshe, in fact, did this. He left his family there and told them to return to Yisro's home after the child recovered from his circumcision. Hence the words (Sh'mos 18:2) "after he had sent her back."

According to *Paneach Raza*, Tzipporah first thought that the angel wished to kill Moshe for having taken a Midianite wife. Therefore she said, "You are a bloody bridegroom to 'me,' " i.e., I see that I am at fault for your coming to kill my husband. However, after she circumcised her son and saw that the angel had desisted from Moshe, she became aware that Moshe was "a bloody bridegroom." The angel had come only because Eliezer had not been circumcised: Once the child was circumcised, the angel left Moshe alone.

The interpretation of R' Samson Raphael Hirsch differs only slightly. *Chazal* say that Tzipporah exacted from Moshe an agreement that her first son would be consecrated to idol worship. When she saw that Moshe was punished, she first thought that the punishment came as a result of this condition: "You are a bloody bridegroom to me." Yet, she later became convinced that he was a "bloody bridegroom" because of lack of circumcision.

S'forno explains the words "and Hashem met him" in an entirely different manner. This was not a negative confrontation. Rather, Hashem's Divine Presence appeared because the date of circumcision had arrived. Once Hashem's Glory appeared and the circumcision did not take place, the appointed angel sought to kill Moshe. At that point Tzipporah said to Moshe, "When you took me for a wife, you exacted my agreement that my children would be circumcised." She spoke these words in defense of Moshe, before the angel who wished to kill him. Then, she took the flint stone and performed the act.

◄§ Why Tzipporah and Not Moshe?

The question of why Tzipporah performed the circumcision, and not Moshe, is puzzling. As we find in *Rashbam*, this circumcision was merely an appeasement to the looming angel, similar to the act performed by Manoach when he sought to appease the angel in his day. Tzipporah performed the act only because Moshe was frightened by the angel's threat.

Ibn Ezra holds that Moshe was seized by trembling and could not perform the circumcision alone. *Tur* deduces from Tzipporah and not Moshe performing the act, that "He sought to kill him," refers to Moshe, not the child. Otherwise, Moshe would have performed the circumcision himself. Nonetheless, this question had been dealt with previously in *Nedarim* 32: "R' Shimon ben Gamliel says, 'Satan did not wish to kill Moshe, but the baby: "You are a bloody bridegroom (חֲתַן דָּמִים) to me." Consider this. Who would be called חֲתַן — a bridegroom? I would say it is the baby.' "

Similarly, Ibn Ezra, quoting R' Shmuel ben Chofni, says, "God forbid that Hashem should wish to kill Moshe who was on a Divine mission. It was Eliezer whom Hashem wished to kill."

Nonetheless, *Chazal* in *Midrash Rabbah* (22) see no contradiction between Hashem having said (*Sh'mos* 3:12), "I will be with you," and Hashem seeking to kill him. They simply conclude that there are no guarantees in this world, even to the righteous, i.e., even Hashem's promises do not protect them if they place themselves into danger.

Maharsha as well (*Nedarim* 31) reads "and He sought to kill him" as a sign that Hashem submits the righteous to exceedingly strict scrutiny. Legally, Moshe would not have deserved death even had he left his son uncircumcised, for one who transgresses a positive commandment does not incur a death sentence.

Factually, the precepts observed here are not in keeping with *halachah* following the Sinai Revelation, since according to one Talmudic view women may not perform circumcision. Moreover, even according to those who permit a woman to circumcise, she may only do so when no man is available to perform the task. *Chazal* therefore read the word וַתִּכְרֹת — "and she (Tzipporah) cut off" her son's foreskin, as if it were vowelized וַתִּכָּרֵת — "and it was cut off," i.e., by someone else. Yet, *Chasam Sofer* says, if a woman is not sanctioned to perform circumcision, neither is a non-Jew. In which case, what value has this answer that Eliezer was circumcised by someone else?

Most feasible is *Rashbam*'s interpretation. The blood of circumcision in this situation served as an atonement, as with Temple offerings. Furthermore, *Chasam Sofer* answers that while through circumcision performed by a non-Jew the *mitzvah* was not fulfilled, Moshe's sentence was still mitigated, and he could complete the circumcision. Likewise, *Chazal* say (*Avodah Zarah* 27), "Tzipporah began it, Moshe completed it."

Tzofnas Paneach maintains that the "completion" here refers to פְּרִיעָה — "the uncovering of the corona." Hence, Tzipporah performed the מִילָה — "actual circumcision," and Moshe completed it through פְּרִיעָה.

Moreover, Rabbenu Bachya and S'forno state that both מִילָה and פְּרִיעָה were performed here, explaining the use of the plural לָמוּלֹת when Tzipporah exclaims, "a bloody bridegroom לָמוּלֹת," for the act was considered like two circumcisions.

Interestingly, the Jerusalem Talmud deduces from the use of לָמוּלֹת that פְּרִיעָה was not performed on Avraham (*Shabbos* 19:2; *Nedarim* 3:9). Yet, *Chazal* in *Yevamos* 71 learn this from *Yehoshua* 5:2, "Go and circumcise the Israelites a second time." The *Tosafists* there ask, "If פְּרִיעָה was not performed until the times of Yehoshua, what weight does it have as law? Do we not say that a prophet is unauthorized to create halachic innovations? The *Tosafists* answer that פְּרִיעָה is הֲלָכָה לְמשֶׁה מִסִּינַי — an oral tradition taught by Moshe at Sinai. But R' Avraham Lefkovitz in *Vayosef Avraham* (appended to *Revid HaZahav*) answers that in accordance with the Jerusalem Talmud just quoted, there is a Biblical allusion to פְּרִיעָה in the Torah, and we have no need here for the application of הֲלָכָה לְמשֶׁה מִסִּינַי.

Yerushalmi, Shabbos (19:2), lists another Biblical source for פְּרִיעָה. Hashem says to Avraham (*Bereishis* 17:13), הִמּוֹל יִמּוֹל, "[He that is born in your household] must be circumcised." *Chazal* comment, "From this (double expression), we deduce two acts: מִילָה and פְּרִיעָה." This is, however, contrary to the words of *Chazal* in *Yevamos* 71: "Rav said, פְּרִיעָה was not commanded to Avraham."

The *Yerushalmi* quoted above, whereby Avraham performed פְּרִיעָה, is based on the words of R' Akiva who (in reference to הִמּוֹל יִמּוֹל) said, "Double expressions serve to expand." On the other hand, according to the opinion that double expressions merely represent common usage, we learn the law of פְּרִיעָה from the verse, חֲתַן דָּמִים לַמּוּלֹת, whereby the plural form, לָמוּלֹת, serves to instruct us in both מִילָה and פְּרִיעָה.

In any event, this entire *parashah* is vague, and we have only the words of our *rishonim* to guide us.

Va'eira – וָאֵרָא

I.

I Was Not Known to Them by My Name ה'

All the commentaries view the beginning of this *parashah* as the continuation of the previous one, and a response to Moshe's grievance (*Sh'mos* 5:22), "Why did You mistreat this nation?" *Rashi* finds support for this view in the use of the word וַיְדַבֵּר — "and He spoke," which implies harsh speech, rebuke and penalty.

The commentaries are divided over the nature of God's Name. *Rashi* deduces that Moshe is rebuked for the lack of faith that he expresses by seeming to question Hashem's ability to fulfill His word. Hashem proclaims at the start, "I am Hashem," the One who faithfully rewards those who walk before Him. Thereafter, Hashem describes the reward He has in store for the Children of Israel in Egypt. This is to be the fulfillment of the promises made to the *Avos* — Patriarchs — but which have not yet been accomplished.

Hashem appeared to the *Avos* and made His promises to them as *El Shaddai*. He was not, however, known to them by His Ineffable Name [which will appear in this chapter in its abbreviated form — ה'] which attests to the truth of His promises and His ability to carry them out. Now the time had come for Him to be revealed by the Name that incorporates the Divine virtue of Truth, as verification of His ability to keep His word.

According to *Rashi*, "El Shaddai," as revealed to the *Avos*, and "My Name ה'," are both titles for the One who keeps His promise. Yet, it is the latter title that implies actual fulfillment of the promise. Other commentaries like *Ramban*, Ibn Ezra, and *Akeidas Yitzchak* follow *Rashi's* lead, assigning specific attributes to each of Hashem's Names. *Akeidah* states that "Hashem's titles are only important for the attributes they represent." But each of the *rishonim* has his own way of linking various attributes to Hashem's titles. This concept is not the innovation of the commentaries but is to be found in *Midrash Sh'mos* 3:

> R' Abba bar Mamal said, "Hashem said to Moshe, 'Is it My Name that you wish to know? I am called according to My deeds. I am called variously *El Shaddai*, *Tzevaos*, *Elohim* and 'ה. When I judge humanity I am called *Elohim*, when I wage war against the wicked I am called *Tzevaos*, when I suspend punishment I am called *El Shaddai*, and when I take pity upon My world I am called 'ה.' "

Verse two, with its harsh וַיְדַבֵּר, is therefore interpreted by *Chazal* as follows: Hashem rebukes Moshe as if he, personally, is harming Israel with his severe complaints, at a moment when Hashem is about to appear before them in His merciful attribute. As it is written (*Sh'mos* 6:5), "And I have also heard the groaning of the Children of Israel."

On the other hand, *Torah Temimah* cites a Midrash according to which the Name 'ה implies revenge upon an enemy. (There is no contradiction intended since revenge upon an enemy of Israel comprises a form of mercy. The latter, however, indicates that Hashem's mercy is not universal, but relates to the Jewish people alone.) The Midrash states:

> [Hashem said,] "I have performed many miracles for them under the Name *Shaddai*. I have saved them from their enemies without killing those enemies. I saved Avraham from Pharaoh, Yitzchak from Avimelech, and Yaakov from Lavan, but I was not known to them by My Name 'ה, i.e., I did not inflict vengeance upon Israel's enemies, although My Name 'ה is vengeance" — as it is written (*Yirmiyahu* 16:21), "Therefore, behold, I will make it known to them this once, and they shall know that My Name is 'ה." This refers to revenge. Hashem announced to His enemies, "I may have tolerated you in the days of the Prophets, but I shall now take revenge."

The Midrash and commentaries offer abundant explanations of the traits embodied in the Name 'ה. *S'forno* holds that *El Shaddai* refers to God as the First Cause, whereas 'ה refers to His causing what has already been created to endure (*Nechemiah* 9:6), "You sustain them all." Until now, Hashem had not changed reality. He had only manifested His existence during the times of the *Avos*. From now on He would also change reality. Thereafter it would become clear that not only is Hashem the Creator of reality, but that He sustains or changes it as He wishes.

Abarbanel summarizes and lists the questions that puzzle us concerning this *parashah*:

(a) The *parashah* begins, "God spoke to Moshe saying, 'I am 'ה.' " What information does this add? Did not Hashem already inform Moshe of His Name 'ה at the burning bush?

(b) Hashem tells Moshe that He spoke to the *Avos* as *El Shaddai* and not as 'ה. Yet, He had previously revealed Himself to Avraham in this way (*Bereishis* 15:7), "I am 'ה who took you out of Ur Kasdim." Furthermore, when Hashem came to visit Avraham after his circumcision, we find (ibid. 18:1), "And 'ה appeared to him."

(c) Why does it state here, "but I was not known to them by My Name 'ה?" Should He not have said, "but I did not make Myself known to them?" Furthermore, what do we add to our knowledge of Hashem with the phrases (*Sh'mos* 6:4-5), "I also made My covenant with them," and "I have also heard the groaning of the Children of Israel." Is there a connection between Hashem's appearing to the *Avos* exclusively as *El Shaddai*, and between the covenant and the groaning of the Children of Israel?

Abarbanel explains *Ramban* and Ibn Ezra's conception that *Shaddai* refers to natural conduct, whereas the Ineffable Name 'ה expresses supernatural conduct. In their view, Hashem revealed Himself to the *Avos* only in veiled miracles, cloaked in nature. He did not resort to the supernatural. Yet, Abarbanel rejects this view, pointing out that Hashem did, in fact, perform various supernatural miracles for the *Avos*. Avraham survived a fiery furnace unharmed. Pharaoh was smitten with a plague for what happened to Sarah. Sodom and Amorah were overturned, Lot was rescued, his wife was turned into a pillar of salt and countless other miracles occurred.

Abarbanel therefore suggests that the words, "and My Name 'ה," continue the phrase that preceded them. Hashem is telling Moshe that He had appeared to the *Avos* both as *El Shaddai* and as 'ה. Hashem had shown the *Avos* all sorts of miracles, both natural and supernatural. Even so, "I was not known to them by My Name 'ה." He had not communed with them face to face, but only in an unclear fashion that *Chazal* refer to as through a clouded lens (אַסְפַּקְלַרְיָא שֶׁאֵינָה מְאִירָה). Now Hashem wished to redeem the Jewish people, revealing Himself fully, addressing them face to face, as He in fact did later at the Splitting of the Sea and at the Sinai Revelation. In His appearance to Moshe He added *two* reasons for His wishing to redeem the Jewish people in the near future: (a) The time had arrived for Him to fulfill his promise of the Land of Israel as an inheritance. The *Avos* never inherited it, for it was inhabited by foreigners. Now, however, Hashem would keep His covenant and grant the Land to His children. (b) The measure of defilement of the Egyptians had reached its zenith. The Just Hashem would now punish them for oppressing His people (Sh'mos 6:5), "I have also heard the groaning of the Children of Israel." The time for their punishment had come, and Hashem would avenge His enemies.

Rashbam interprets, "I was not known to them by My Name ה׳," in the same way as Abarbanel. Hashem is saying: "I appeared to the *Avos* as *El Shaddai*. However, not *El Shaddai*, but ה׳ is My chief Name. My promises to the *Avos* did not concern the *present*. To you, Moshe, I have revealed Myself as ה׳, indicating the current relevance of My words. In your era I shall fulfill the promises I made to the *Avos*."

Interestingly, *Ta'amei HaMikra* also associates the words, "and My Name ה׳," with what precedes them. He is apparently sensitive to *Ramban*'s question: If these words are connected to what follows, Hashem should have said, "I did not make known," rather than, "I was not known." Yet, according to *Rashbam*'s grandfather *Rashi*, "I was not known" means, "I did not bring My promises to fulfillment." The Name ה׳ indicates Divine power to reward the good and punish the wicked. Yet, this power was not realized practically for the *Avos*. They heard Hashem's promises, but did not see them fulfilled. That would now follow.

⊷§ Revelation to Moshe and to the Avos

The Torah stresses that Hashem revealed Himself by separate titles or attributes to Moshe and the *Avos*. To the *Avos* He was *El Shaddai* and to Moshe He was ה׳. This distinction is puzzling, however, for God appeared as ה׳ not only to Moshe, but to the *Avos* as well. First He told Avraham (*Bereishis* 15:7), "I am ה׳ Who took you out of Ur Kasdim, to give you this land for an inheritance"; and then He told Yaakov (*Bereishis* 28:13), "I am ה׳, God of Avraham your father and God of Yitzchak. I will give to you and your descendants the land upon which you are lying."

Rashi apparently answers this question with his comment on the verse (*Sh'mos* 6:3), "I was not known to you by My Name ה׳": "Hashem does not say, 'I did not make known,' but rather 'I was not known,' for His true nature was unknown to them." Hashem did mention His Name ה׳ to the *Avos*, but they remained unaware of its implications. For *Rashi*, ה׳ means the fulfillment of promises, and ה׳ had not yet fulfilled those He made to the *Avos*. Only now would He do so.

The same answer applies for the other commentaries as well, though the Name ה׳ may imply different attributes for each. During the time of the *Avos*, Hashem did not concretely exercise any of these attributes.

Why was this the case? Was Moshe greater than the *Avos*? Was there no need in their times for these traits to be employed? According to *Chazal* in *Midrash Rabbah*, *Sh'mos* 6:4, not only was Moshe no greater than they, but Hashem even chastised Moshe for having weaker faith:

> What a pity they are gone and forgotten! Many times I appeared to Avraham, Yitzchak and Yaakov as *El Shaddai*. I did not inform them of My Name 'ה and they did not question My nature. You, however, asked Me My Name even before you began your mission, and when you completed it you said, "Since I came to Pharaoh to speak in Your Name, he has done evil to this people."

Yet, the commentaries say that viewing the text literally, Moshe merited greater revelation than the *Avos*. According to *Kuzari* (2:2), this was not due to any greatness on the part of Moshe's generation, but because they by then comprised a "multitude," plagued by doubt. Hashem unleashed His might in new ways sufficient to convince them of His identity. The *Avos*, on the other hand, were a small group of pure-hearted individuals, so sure of their faith that although they suffered all their lives, their belief in Hashem remained firm.

◄§ Moshe: Supreme Prophet

Chazal say in *Yevamos*: "How did the prophecy of Moshe differ from that of other prophets? Moshe saw through an אַסְפַּקְלַרְיָא הַמְּאִירָה — a clear lens; others through an unclear lens." Rabbenu Bachya explains אַסְפַּקְלַרְיָא הַמְּאִירָה as the open occurrence of miracles in our world. The *Avos* did not merit to see this. Hashem appeared to them as *El Shaddai*, capable of reordering what already existed. Yet, He did not appear to them by His special Name 'ה, through which all existence came into being. Hashem did not, through an open miracle, create anything new or esoteric. Furthermore, the *Avos'* visions came to them at night in dreams. Therefore Hashem says, וָאֵרָא — "I appeared." נוֹדַעְתִּי — "I was known" — refers to face-to-face acquaintance.

Rambam (in *Moreh Nevuchim*, 2:35 and in *Sefer HaMada*) lists the four differences between the prophecies of Moshe and other prophets: (a) Hashem appeared to other prophets in their dreams, but to Moshe in his waking hours (*Sh'mos* 34:34), "Whenever Moshe came before Hashem to speak to Him ..."; (b) Hashem spoke to other prophets through an angel, but to Moshe directly; (c) all other prophets would shudder and collapse during visions, whereas Moshe conversed with Hashem as with a neighbor; (d) other prophets were blessed with prophetic vision only at certain times, whereas Moshe could speak to Hashem whenever he wished (*Bamidbar* 9:8), "Wait here," replied Moshe. "I will hear what orders Hashem gives you."

In *Moreh Nevuchim*, *Rambam* adds:

> Proof that Moshe's visions differed from those of prophets who preceded him lies in the words (*Sh'mos* 6:3), "I appeared to Avraham ... yet I was not known to them by My Name 'ה." This in itself informs us that Moshe's visions not only equaled but exceeded in greatness those of the *Avos*, and surely those of others who preceded him. Yet, his superiority over all who followed is stated explicitly by the words (*Devarim* 34:10), "No other prophet like Moshe has arisen in Israel who knew Hashem face-to-face."

Ikarim (3:19), when explaining why no prophet may cancel any Torah law, says that only Moshe was entitled to cancel something from his predecessors. Moshe was greater than they, having been shown signs and wonders never before observed. Hashem states this explicitly (*Sh'mos* 6:3), "I appeared to Avraham ... yet I was not known to them by My Name 'ה."

Hashem revealed Himself to Moshe by His Great Name, altering nature. He had never done this for those who preceded him. To them, rather, He revealed Himself with hidden miracles, rescuing them from famine, death and war. Moshe outshone other prophets in one additional way: His conversations with Hashem were verified for all to see, for all of Israel heard Hashem's voice, as it is written (ibid. 19:9), "Behold, I will come to you in a thick cloud so the people will hear when I speak to you."

The commentaries and Kabbalists have offered various explanations of the "clear" and "unclear lens." Rabbenu Bachya and *Ikarim* comment that these expressions serve to distinguish between the revelation of open miracles and wonders to Moshe, and hidden miracles to his predecessors. This is also Ibn Ezra's explanation, as elaborated upon by *Ramban*:

> Hashem appeared to the *Avos* as *El Shaddai*, Who reorders what already exists. The miracles He showed them were hidden within nature, like reward and punishment here on Earth. But He did not appear to the *Avos* as 'ה, the Creator of supernatural innovation.

The Kabbalists, however, interpret אַסְפַּקְלַרְיָא הַמְּאִירָה literally. Moshe saw concretely what others could not. This is aptly explained in *Melo HaOmer*: Because Moshe was destined to give the Torah, it was necessary that his prophetic revelations be clear. Puzzles and riddles would not have enabled him to convey the Torah's message, for the Torah must be open and clear to all.

So does *Melo HaOmer* interpret the words, "And I appeared to Avraham, Yitzchak and Yaakov as *El Shaddai*." Hashem appeared to the *Avos* "through an unclear lens." He promised them the Land of Israel, but it was given only to their descendants. He said (*Bereishis* 15:13), "They shall enslave them and persecute them for four hundred years," but the Children of Israel left after only 210. Either the difficulty of their slavery compensated for the lost time, or the 400 years began with the birth of Yitzchak.

Whatever is seen through a "clear lens," however, appears with exact precision, requiring neither interpretation nor clarification. Moshe's prophetic visions leave no room for interpretation. Hashem says (*Sh'mos* 6:4), "I have also made My covenant with them, promising them the Land of Canaan." In reality, however, the Land was given only to their descendants. "Therefore, tell the Children of Israel that I am 'ה" (6:6) — loyal to keep My promise. Hashem is saying to Moshe, "For Me everything must occur concretely. Your visions are through a clear lens. I shall not converse with you in riddles."

Akeidas Yitzchak explains differently. For him, the Name 'ה encompasses all other Names (*Devarim* 10:17), "For 'ה your God is the God of all gods and the Master of all masters, (הַגָּדוֹל) the great, (הַגִּבּוֹר) the mighty and (הַנּוֹרָא) the awesome God."

הַגָּדוֹל — Creator of all, the greatest of all powers.

הַגִּבּוֹר — Supervisor and ruler over all through His great might.

הַנּוֹרָא — Awesome and imposing to all around Him, punishing all evildoers.

Hashem says, I at first appeared to the *Avos* by only one title: *El Shaddai* — Father of all beings. Yet, I made a covenant with them, thereby manifesting My title הַגִּבּוֹר. Now, I have heard the groaning of the Children of Israel, so that I shall exhibit My title הַנּוֹרָא as an indication of punishment and might. Ultimately, "you will know that I am 'ה encompassing all these titles together."

S'forno explains similarly. I became familiar to the *Avos* as אֵל שַׁדַּי (*El Shaddai*), Creator of all existence, the One who said to His world, (דַּי — *dai*) "Enough!" But My Name 'ה — indicating continued maintenance of what exists — I did not reveal to them. I broke no laws of nature for them. As the Children of Israel inherited no such belief from their ancestors, I must exhibit Myself to them in this way, so they will know and obey Me.

The second reason for My appearance in this form is the covenant I made with their ancestors, giving them the land of their destiny.

Therefore, tell them that I am 'ה, Who devised and created all existence. Responsible for all that exists, I constantly perform new acts of creation: "And you will know that I am 'ה".

Toldos Yitzchak intensifies this theme. Hashem revealed to the *Avos* His Ineffable Name, as we find in numerous places. Yet, while He informed them of His true nature, He did not exercise it. For Hashem to have been truly known to the *Avos*, He would have had to demonstrate before them the attributes inherent in that Name. This He never did. Now He wished to realize for them His true nature, by letting them see creation *ex nihilo*. He showed them the way Moshe's inanimate rod could become a real snake. The serpents of the Egyptian magicians were only an illusion. Moshe's rod consumed theirs, and the creation of new matter was fulfilled before them. The *Avos* never had such a revelation: "I was not known to them — actively and concretely — by My Name 'ה." Ultimately, however, the Jewish people would see that "I am 'ה," Creator of matter.

⋑ Ahavas Yisrael of Moshe and the Avos

Rashi begins by observing that Moshe was rebuked for having said to Hashem (*Sh'mos* 5:22), "Why did You mistreat this people?" *Rashi* enlists *Chazal* in *Sanhedrin* who say that Hashem rebuked Moshe for lack of faith compared to the *Avos*. The *Avos* trusted Hashem even though He had not yet fulfilled His promises.

One of the *acharonim* attributes the cause of Hashem's anger to Moshe's complaint (ibid. v. 23): וְהַצֵּל לֹא הִצַּלְתָּ — "You have done nothing to rescue them." *Chazal* say that the word הַצָּלָה — *hatzalah* — does not connote full redemption, but rather nullification of a decree. As such, Hashem asks Moshe: "If Pharaoh's decree that the Children of Israel must gather their own straw were abolished, would that have satisfied you? Would you and the Jewish people then adjust to a life of Egyptian servitude?"

Hashem spoke harshly to Moshe because a leader of the Jewish people must not be satisfied with partial salvation: Hashem told Moshe, "I am 'ה, Who will redeem and exalt you forever. How can you make do with mere rescue?"

Chazal, in the Midrash, clarify the reason for Hashem's anger, attributing to Him the following words:

> What a pity they are gone and forgotten! How often I revealed Myself to Avraham, Yitzchak and Yaakov as *El Shaddai*, yet they never asked Me My Name or questioned My nature. I said to

Avraham (*Bereishis* 13:17), "Rise! Walk throughout the length and width of the Land, for to you shall I give it." Yet, when he sought a place to bury Sarah he did not find one. Eventually he bought a plot for four hundred silver shekels.

A fine explanation of this source appears in *HaDrash VeHaIyun*: In our *piyut* (poetic liturgy) for the *parashah* of *Shekalim* we find,

> My beloved, I remember the *shekalim* of Efron,
> Weighed out by our father for Machpelah in Chevron.

We may ask what purpose is served by remembering the money that Avraham paid in exchange for the Cave of Machpelah. Yet, says R' Aharon Levin, the poet is alluding to the Midrash quoted. The *piyut* acknowledges Avraham's great faith in Hashem. Although the land had been promised to him, he did not question Hashem when he was compelled to pay an exorbitant price for Sarah's burial place.

A Chassidic treatise transforms Moshe's behavior from criticism to praise. At the beginning of the *parashah*, *Rashi* interprets וַיְדַבֵּר — "and He spoke," to mean that Hashem דִּבֶּר אִתּוֹ מִשְׁפָּט — "spoke harshly to Moshe." The word מִשְׁפָּט in this sense is understood to mean judgment. But R' Meir of Premishlan interprets מִשְׁפָּט as the quality of justice. Thus, Hashem says to Moshe, "You acted as the defender of Israel, asking Me, 'Why did You mistreat them?' You were not afraid of Me, because you are a pillar of justice and righteousness."

This direction appears in other Chassidic works too. For example, *Noam Elimelech* views as exemplary Moshe's having spoken insolently towards his Maker out of his love for the Jewish people. By virtue of Moshe's *ahavas Yisrael*, says *HaDrash VeHaIyun*, Hashem's strict justice was transformed to mercy (*Sh'mos* 6:2), "Elohim [connoting justice] spoke to Moshe and said to him, 'I am ה' [connoting mercy]."

Chasam Sofer makes a similar point. Moshe knew he was forbidden to speak harshly to Hashem. Nonetheless, he sacrificed himself for the sake of saving the Jewish people. Therefore, Hashem was immediately filled with compassion, and said, "I am ה'."

Chasam Sofer explains why Hashem needed to perform greater miracles now than in the time of the *Avos*. During Moshe's lifetime, the Children of Israel in Egypt sank to the forty-ninth level of impurity. Miracles such as occurred during Patriarchal times did not suffice to raise them from their defilement to lofty purity for the Sinai Revelation. Great, supernatural miracles were needed, as written (*Sh'mos* 6:6), "Then you will know that I am ה', your God, Who removes you from the labors of Egypt." This explains the change in Hashem's conduct from that of Patriarchal times. The Jewish people had sunk body and soul in the forced labor of Egypt, and could not be extricated without supernatural wonders.

The Ineffable Name ה׳ expresses that which transcends nature, God who is both past, present and future. In other words, the Prime Cause. On the other hand, *El Shaddai* expresses Hashem's rule within nature. The distinction between the two is provided by *HaKesav VeHaKabalah*:

> *Shaddai* represents the manner in which the Holy One, Blessed is He, sustains all beings and blesses them with such bounty that their lips tire of uttering דַּי (*dai*) — "It is enough!" *Shaddai* is also similar to *shadai'im* (breasts) that nurture and sustain a child. The Ineffable Name, on the other hand, is pronounced *Adonai*, for Hashem is אָדוֹן — *Adon* — Master of all worlds and beings, and His will cannot be denied. He can alter nature and events, canceling normal conduct and adjusting the behavior and essence of his living creatures however He wishes.

This aspect of His nature was revealed only at the time of the Exodus from Egypt.

Akeidas Yitzchak has an entirely different explanation. Being aware of the attributes inherent in the Name ה׳ is greater than merely knowing of Hashem's existence. The Torah relates that the *Avos* not only knew Hashem's Name, but were familiar with His attributes as well. Not so the Children of Israel in Egypt. They did not even know of Hashem's existence. The Torah says (*Sh'mos* 6:3), "I was not known to them by My Name ה׳. "Them" refers to the Children of Israel in Egypt. Therefore (*Sh'mos* 6:6), "you will know that I am ה׳." The Children of Israel in Egypt would have to be informed of Hashem's very existence, before learning the secrets embodied in His Ineffable Name.

Yet, *HaKesav VeHaKabalah* challenges this interpretation on the basis of the verse (*Yechezkel* 20:5), "I made Myself known to them in Egypt." This shows that the Children of Israel knew of Hashem's existence even before the advent of Moshe and Aharon. Furthermore, it is difficult to read "them" as referring to the Children of Israel and not the *Avos*. Instead, he offers an original and innovative interpretation of the text. He treats לָהֶם in the phrase לֹא נוֹדַעְתִּי לָהֶם — "I was never known to them"— as מֵהֶם (from them, through them, or of them) as in *Yechezkel* 1:6, וְאַרְבַּע כְּנָפַיִם לְאַחַת לָהֶם — "four wings to each one of them." Furthermore, the letter ל in לָהֶם can denote the cause of something (*Bereishis* 38:18): וַתַּהַר לוֹ — "She became pregnant of him." Hence the verse (*Sh'mos* 6:3), וּשְׁמִי ה׳ לֹא נוֹדַעְתִּי לָהֶם, translates as "They did not cause Hashem's Name to be publicized among the masses."

Only the *Avos* knew Hashem. The remainder of humanity remained sunken in idolatry. While Avraham did gather souls in Charan, these souls left no trace. No nation of Hashem was realized through them to announce God's existence in the world.

The Holy One, Blessed is He, informs Moshe of both the reasons for, and the results of, the Egyptian exile. It will result in all of humanity recognizing Hashem's existence (ibid. 7:5), "And Egypt will know that I am 'ה." Moshe, too, before bringing the fourth plague, arouses Pharaoh with this message (ibid. 8:18), "It is so you will know that I am 'ה in the midst of the land."

◄§ The Parashah of Divine Revelation

I believe this *parashah* to be independent of the preceding section, in which Moshe complains to Hashem. The Holy One, Blessed is He, has already answered Moshe's question (*Sh'mos* 5:22), "Why have You mistreated this nation?" with the words (v. 6:1), "Now you will see what I do to Pharaoh." Now begins the episode of revelation, preceding the set of plagues.

Hashem presents Himself by His full Name: "I am 'ה," stating that He never revealed Himself to the *Avos* in this way. He relates His promise to give them the Land of Canaan. Now, having heard the groaning of the Children of Israel, He recalls His covenant. He invokes His full Name in regard to saving his people and taking them out of Egypt (v. 6:6), "Tell the Children of Israel, therefore, that I am 'ה, and I shall remove you from the slave labor of Egypt."

He also invokes His Name regarding the selection of Israel as a chosen people (v. 6:7), "I shall adopt you as a nation and be for you a God, and you will know that I am 'ה." He also mentions His Name once more regarding the giving of the Land (v. 6:8), "I shall give it to you as a heritage. I am 'ה."

The main point of these verses is that Hashem reveals Himself by His full Name in regard to the rescue, the giving of the Torah and the dividing up of the Land of Israel. The Torah does not say what is meant by "I am 'ה" nor what it means when it says that this Name was not revealed to the *Avos*. We, however, may rely upon the explanations of the commentators I quoted earlier. I only wish to state that our present *parashah* is not a continuation of what precedes, but an independent description of Hashem's revealing Himself, creating a break between Hashem's answer above and the beginning of the rescue operation that follows. Hashem makes known that He will reveal Himself through His full Name in the three stated events: the Exodus, the Sinai Revelation and the inheritance of the Land.

We might also add the interpretation of *HaKesav VeHaKabalah* regarding the appearance of the statement (*Sh'mos* 6:7) אֲנִי ה׳ — "I am ה׳," in which, he says, אֲנִי — "I" — is not a general pronoun, but is itself a Name of Hashem, as *Zohar* comments on (*Vayikra* 11:44), "You should be holy, for I (אֲנִי) am holy. Who is אֲנִי? אֲנִי is the Holy One, Blessed is He."

HaKesav VeHaKabalah explains the reasoning behind this as well. The word אֲנִי derives from (*Sh'mos* 21:13), "But God caused (אִנָּה) it to happen." As Hashem is the Supreme, First Cause, He is known by the Name אֲנִי. Hence, (*Sh'mos* 6:6), "Then you will know that I am ה׳ your God," means the following: Know and understand that ה׳, the First Cause, is also Master of all. This is contrary to the opinion of those who mistakenly claim that even if a First Cause existed, once the world was created, it functioned on the power of that first act, without change.

The miracles and wonders of *yetzias Mitzraim* prove that the First Cause is also Master of All. Hashem the Creator is in constant control of all His handiwork, and He holds the power to change Creation, altering it every second according to His will. This is the meaning of (*Devarim* 29:5) "I am ה׳ your God," and (ibid. 32:39) "I, even I, am He, and there is no god with Me."

II.

The Gates of Repentance
Are Sealed Before Pharaoh

he "hardening of Pharaoh's heart," mentioned in our *parashah*, refers to a negation of Pharaoh's free will, and his being directed to evil. This seems contrary to the basic Jewish tenet that man is free to repent from sinning. Yet, here we see that not all evildoers possess this option.

Elisha ben Abuyah acquired the title אַחֵר — "*acher*" (i.e., different), after he turned heretic. *Chazal* portray him as hearing a Heavenly voice: "Return, rebellious children, except for Acher." Seemingly, the gates of repentance were sealed before him, as before Pharaoh. But the great figures of the *Mussar* movement explain that all that Elisha ben Abuyah lacked was a call to repentance. Heaven avoided appealing to his soul to change his ways since "when someone proceeds to defile himself, he is allowed to." Nonetheless, had he repented on his own, his repentance would have been accepted, as that of even greater sinners had been accepted before when they voluntarily repented.

Yet, concerning Pharaoh, the Torah states specifically that he was compelled not to repent (Sh'mos 7:3), "I will harden Pharaoh's heart." All the commentaries justifiably wonder how such a thing is possible. If Pharaoh's will was really overruled for the sake of Hashem's displaying many miraculous signs and wonders in Egypt, why did he deserve to be punished? Is not the entire principle of reward and punishment based on free will?

Chazal in Midrash Rabbah ask this difficult question, and answer quoting R' Yochanan: "Hashem does not jest regarding sin. He issues one, two or three warnings, and then makes good His word, closing the door on repentance so He can punish the sinner for his deed".

Ramban explains. Regarding the first five plagues, Pharaoh was punished solely for his crime, and could still have repented. Yet, Pharaoh made himself stubborn (v. 8:11), "he hardened his heart," and (v. 7:13) "he remained obstinate." Thus, Pharaoh willfully chose evil, despite his knowledge of what would result.

Later on he was forced by the severity of the plagues to submit against his will, and he decided to set the Jewish people free. Yet, he did so not to repent, but to save himself. Hashem therefore intervened so Pharaoh would hold to his evil course and not submit. When Hashem said to Moshe (v. 7:3), "I will harden Pharaoh's heart," that applied to the last five plagues, Pharaoh having demonstrated that his obstinacy was of his own making. He was unwilling to turn his heart to good, even after the plagues and the other trials he suffered.

Rashi expresses a similar idea, portraying Hashem saying the following: "Pharaoh wickedly defied Me. It is well known to Me that idolatrous nations like Egypt are incapable of full repentance. In this case, it is better Pharaoh should remain obstinate. Then at least I will have an opportunity to display great miracles . . ."

Rashi's intent is probably in line with what preceded. Hashem knew that Pharaoh would not willingly relent even after the first blows. Therefore, He hardened Pharaoh's heart and sent numerous plagues so that through Pharaoh, faith could be instilled in the Jewish people and the world. Pharaoh was not deprived of his free will. Rather, Hashem knew Pharaoh was wicked, even proving by means of the first plagues that Pharaoh would not willingly choose good. He therefore employed Pharaoh as a tool to demonstrate His own mighty, miraculous deeds to Israel and the world.

Meshech Chochmah develops and embellishes this idea. Pharaoh was so cruel and callous that the first plagues, intended to remove Pharaoh's stubbornness, had little effect. *Rambam* rules in *Yad HaChazakah*, *Hilchos Gittin*, that a Jew can be forced to follow Torah law. As a Jew by nature is good and seeks goodness, when he sins we assume that his Evil Impulse has overcome him, preventing him from doing what his heart desires. Therefore, when we force a Jew to do good, the tough outer shell preventing him from revealing his true nature falls away. He then regains equilibrium and chooses good, in accordance with the goodness in his soul.

Pharaoh, however, was evil to the core. The plagues did not help to remove his obstinacy, as the Torah states (*Sh'mos* 3:19), "The king of Egypt will not let you go except by a mighty hand." Even force, successful with any Jew, could not bring a change in Pharaoh's thinking. His mind and sub-conscience were so wicked he could not be improved. Therefore, Hashem toughened Pharaoh to bear physical suffering, so he could be a tool to sanctify Hashem's Name.

⋖§ Pharaoh is Fattened for the Kill

Rambam in *Hilchos Teshuvah* (6:3) presents the novel and surprising idea that Hashem does not allow some evildoers to repent, sealing the gates of repentance before them. He is supported in his outlook by Hashem's having hardened Pharaoh's heart. *Rambam* holds that for such an evildoer, and for all sinners who have committed numerous or severe crimes, repentance is impossible. They incur death, and there is no remedy for their sins.

The question is therefore asked: If the gates of repentance were sealed before Pharaoh, why did Moshe go to threaten him, demanding that he make amends? *Rambam* answers that Moshe, directed by Hashem, came to teach the world this very point: Not all sinners are eligible to repent. Some sinners are so steeped in sin that they may not repent until they receive their full punishment.

This view is greeted with amazement by the *rishonim*. How can there be a difference between the wicked in terms of repentance? The prophet states (*Yechezkel* 18:32,23): "Hashem does not desire the death of the wicked ... but that they repent and live." Is this not said regarding every evildoer, without distinction?

Akeidas Yitzchak brings proofs of this from Achav and Menashe who sinned more than anyone who preceded them, yet Hashem responded positively to their repentance. He therefore declares: "Truth be told, as corrupt as a sinner may be, when he comes, full of contrition and humility, in search of purification, and covers Hashem's destroyed altar with his bitter tears, the gates of tears will not close before him, for they close before no man." According to him, the gates of repentance do not close before any evildoer. Hence, when Hashem made Pharaoh obstinate, it was for a different reason. Pharaoh, in his wickedness, had incurred numerous punishments. Therefore, Hashem hardened his heart and toughened his body to enable him to withstand the many trials coming his way. When a criminal is being flogged, society allows him time between lashes, the better to endure his fate.

Akeidah offers yet another explanation. The hardening of Pharaoh's heart consisted of Hashem's allowing him to err, in accordance with the principle that "man is led along whichever path he wishes to take." Motivated by lame excuses, Pharaoh became increasingly obstinate. Hashem allowed this process to continue, offering him no opportunity for contrition.

Abarbanel offers an interesting theory. He, too, subscribes to the belief that no sin is beyond repentance. Yet, there are two paths of repentance. If an individual offends Hashem in matters of belief and faith, his repentance is a simple matter. If he chooses to return to the path of goodness he will be forgiven. If, however, he steals from his neighbor, repentance is of no benefit unless the sin itself is rectified. Likewise, the murderer, in order to repent, must pay with his life. Pharaoh and his nation spilled Jewish blood. They had to pay for their sin with their lives. Hashem hardened their hearts, not to deter them from repentance, but to lead Pharaoh and his nation to receive their full punishment, the only way they could truly atone.

Abarbanel's theory is essentially identical to that of *Akeidah*'s first opinion. Yet, he produces still another novel idea: Repentance exists for none but the Jewish people, for it belongs within the scope of mercy (*midas harachamim*), and not strict justice (*midas hadin*). Mercifully, Hashem does not judge us according to our behavior.

Why then was Nineveh allowed to repent? It was only so Assyria would be able later on to fulfill the role of "staff of My anger," acting as Hashem's agent to punish Israel (*Yeshayahu* 10:5). The prophet Yonah could not understand this, being unaware of Hashem's thoughts. Therefore, when he was sent to bring the citizens of Nineveh to repent, he fled.

Maharal in *Gevuros Hashem* explains that, logically, repentance cannot be an option for a man such as Pharaoh. Repentance is entirely based upon man being a creature of changing impulses and attributes, outlooks and opinions. It is therefore well suited to man's nature, for it involves a change in the soul. Nonetheless, a stubborn individual such as Pharaoh, unbending in thought or deed, who holds to his own ways even after threat and punishment, testifies that normal human vicissitudes do not apply to him. He is ineligible for repentance, for it involves fundamental change.

Furthermore, says *Maharal*, Pharaoh's punishment was well suited to his crime. Pharaoh publicly profaned Hashem's Name, arrogantly announcing (*Sh'mos* 5:2), "Who is Hashem that I should listen to His voice?" Fittingly, his punishment brought with it the sanctification of Hashem's Name.

Shalah HaKadosh also explains Hashem's hardening Pharaoh's heart as a means of preventing *chilul Hashem* — a profanation of Hashem's Name. Hashem hardened Pharaoh's heart so the nations would see he was unwilling to free the Children of Israel and therefore worthy of punishment. Hashem knew that in his heart, Pharaoh could never truly repent. The nations, however, seeing Pharaoh repent outwardly, without being answered, would say, "How cruel Hashem is to punish a sinner despite his repentance." Therefore, Hashem made Pharaoh obstinate so he would not repent. That way, no negative impression would be made.

◂§ The Influence of the Zodiac upon Man's Behavior

Regarding Hashem's making Pharaoh stubborn, Ibn Ezra states, "Hashem granted man the wisdom and good sense to use the higher powers to improve his fortune or lessen his misfortune." These words are unclear. Elaborating on this in *Sh'mos* 32:32, he explains that man possesses innate characteristics which are determined by the sign of the zodiac under which one is born. He can willfully alter these aspects of his personality to a small degree. When Hashem says He will harden Pharaoh's heart, this means He will make these innate characteristics central to Pharaoh's personality.

Michtav MeEliyahu remarks on "the obscurity" of Ibn Ezra's comment, and attempts to explain it. Man, he says, has the power to overcome his nature through his devotion to Hashem. Pharaoh was punished for not doing so.

Despite this explanation, Ibn Ezra's words remain difficult to understand, especially the original text we quoted. It seems possible to me, however, that he may be saying something simple. *Chazal* in Tractate *Shabbos* describe "butchers, blood letters and those who perform circumcision" as characteristic professions of those born under the sign of Mars, the red planet. *Chazal* go on to say that if these people did not use their natural traits for sacred purposes, they would become murderers.

This may be what Ibn Ezra has in mind. While man's nature is determined by the sign under which he is born, the choice of whether to employ his attributes for good or evil is his own. Pharaoh was born stubborn, as is the Jewish people. Yet, Pharaoh's stubbornness did not negate his free will. He could have used this trait for good, as do the Jewish people. Hashem implanted stubbornness in Pharaoh so that if he turned this trait towards evil, Hashem would be able to demonstrate His miraculous signs among the Egyptians. Pharaoh's free will was not taken from him, for he could have used his stubbornness for good.

Most commentaries view Hashem's hardening Pharaoh's heart as a means of deterring him from repentance. Interestingly, however, S'forno sees it as a way of bringing him close to Heaven to know the full power of Hashem. Had Pharaoh obeyed when first approached, without being convinced of Hashem's power, he would have remained unaware of Hashem's strength, and would never have repented. Hashem therefore hardened Pharaoh's heart to prove to him His omnipotence, so Pharaoh would submit wholeheartedly. Hashem wished to bring Pharaoh to repentance, yet Pharaoh remained defiantly unmoved. Hence, his punishment was justified.

S'forno's opinion is accepted in various ways by the great Chassidic personalities. All of them agree that the gates of repentance were open even to Pharaoh. Well known is the *Ba'al Shem Tov's* explanation of the Heavenly voice resounding from Mount Sinai calling (*Avos* 6:2), "Woe is to humanity for the shame of Torah." This voice represents man's soul. Every day, a person is inflamed with a Heavenly spark which may bring him to repent. But for the thoroughly evil, say the Chassidic works, one spark does not suffice. Such people are firmly entrenched in wickedness and require a powerful opposing force to arouse the goodness in them, so that a voice is heard and echoes in their hearts. This, according to the disciples of the *Ba'al Shem Tov*, is why Hashem hardened Pharaoh's heart. It was done in order to arouse a forceful and vigorous reaction from Pharaoh's *yetzer tov* — good impulse, which would enable him to repent.

◆§ Stubbornness Imposed to Enhance Free Will

It is possible to say that Hashem, in making Pharaoh stubborn, did not impinge upon the principle of free will. Whatever effect the Divinely imposed stubbornness had upon Pharaoh was counterbalanced by the plagues that were visited upon him. This made it possible for Pharaoh to act of his own choosing.

The Torah explains explicitly why Pharaoh was treated as he was. He was made stubborn (*Sh'mos* 10:1) so that Hashem could demonstrate His miraculous signs among the Egyptians. Those who have not been made stubborn do not need plagues. But Pharaoh, who had become stubbornly evil, needed the plagues, and these helped him to maintain his equilibrium and function as any other human being.

Traces of this idea appear in *Ikarim*. There it is noted that repentance following suffering and punishment is beneficial only if the smitten individual, through his suffering, undergoes some change in outlook. Fear of the whip is meaningless in itself. The smitten must recognize the one who punishes, not the punishment.

Pharaoh, according to *Ikarim*, was the type of sinner who reacts only to punishment, reverting to sin once the punishment ends. Even after ten plagues, when he had purportedly acknowledged the hand of Hashem, on seeing the Jewish people worship Egyptian idols he announced (*Sh'mos* 14:3), "They are lost in the land," and proceeded to follow them into the desert. All this proves that his only motive for repentance was fear of punishment, not true introspection. Therefore, Hashem removed this fear from his heart and made him stubborn, so his shame would be uncovered, and all would see that his pious repentance was just a facade.

R' Simcha Zisl of Kelm expresses in broad depth a similar idea. By making Pharaoh stubborn, Hashem established him on a par with all other evildoers who are aware of Hashem's existence yet spite Him. Nonetheless, since through the plagues Pharaoh knew his Maker more concretely than other evildoers, Hashem was compelled to harden his heart even more, so he would retain his free will.

In accordance with this he explains in his *Or Rashaz*, Part 2, the following pronouncement of *Chazal*: "The greater one is, the greater is one's temptation." Spiritual greatness means a greater impulse to do good, but this is always accompanied by a greater impulse to do evil as well. Hence, equilibrium is always maintained.

These views are the source of the idea I have developed in this essay which, simply put, is this: Hardening of the heart creates a need for strict punishment, and strict punishment dictates hardening of the heart. Hashem effects such a process with one goal in mind (*Sh'mos* 10:2), "Then you will be able to tell your children and grandchildren what I have done in Egypt so you may know that I am Hashem."

III.
Various Types of Redemption

Rashbam in his commentary on the first *mishnah* in the last chapter of Tractate *Pesachim*, quotes *Midrash Rabbah* (88) regarding the four cups of wine drunk on Pesach: "These correspond to the four לְשׁוֹנוֹת — idioms — of redemption uttered in regard to the Egyptian Exile (*Sh'mos* 6:6-7): וְהוֹצֵאתִי — 'I will remove you'; וְגָאַלְתִּי — 'I will redeem you'; וְלָקַחְתִּי — 'I will take you'; וְהִצַּלְתִּי — 'I will rescue you.'"

This Midrash also corresponds to the beginning of our *parashah*, and appears in the Jerusalem Talmud, *Pesachim* (10:1).

HaDrash VeHaIyun expresses puzzlement at *Rashbam's* having changed the order of these expressions from the order in which they appear in the text: First וְהוֹצֵאתִי, then וְהִצַּלְתִּי, then וְגָאַלְתִּי, and finally וְלָקַחְתִּי. He leaves the matter as a question.

I personally have wondered as well about the phrase "four idioms of redemption" appearing in *Rashbam*, *Rashi* and the other commentaries, when the wording in the Midrash and the Jerusalem Talmud is only "four redemptions."

While the terminology "idioms of redemption" does appear in *Yalkut Yirmiyah* 307, *Torah Temimah* on our *parashah* holds that the proper form is "four redemptions." He reasons that one redemption, even expressed in four phrases, would not provide sufficient cause to establish four cups of wine as thanksgiving. He therefore understands these expressions to refer to four different types of redemption, each requiring separate praise.

The first phrase, וְהוֹצֵאתִי — "I will remove you from the labors of Egypt" — means that their labor will be eased, but will not cease entirely. וְהִצַּלְתִּי — "I will rescue you from serving them"— promises a complete end to labor, although officially they will remain slaves. וְגָאַלְתִּי — "I will redeem you" — ensures complete redemption and departure from Egyptian control, while וְלָקַחְתִּי — "I will take you to Me as a nation and be for you a God"— guarantees spiritual redemption. What emerges are four stages of redemption, on the pattern of "not only X but Y." Each stage requires its cup of thanksgiving.

In the *rishonim* as well we find different meanings attributed to the various expressions of redemption. *Ramban* understands "I will remove you from the labors of Egypt" as promising a lightened burden and liberation from slave labor. "I will save you from serving them" means an end to their official status as slaves. "I will redeem you" refers to Hashem's inflicting such severe punishment upon the Egyptians that they say, "Be redeemed but let us live!" since the Hebrew word *"geulah"* implies a bargain struck. Finally, "I will take you to Me as a nation" refers to the Sinai Revelation.

S'forno holds that וְהוֹצֵאתִי promises an end to enslavement; this end will start to become manifest with the first plague. וְהִצַּלְתִּי refers to the day of their arrival at Rameses, when the Jewish people left the borders of Egypt. וְגָאַלְתִּי refers to the Splitting of the Sea of Reeds, where the Jewish people felt totally redeemed, fearless of any human master. וְלָקַחְתִּי refers to the Sinai Revelation. Hashem adds, וְהֵבֵאתִי — "I will bring you to the Land," meaning, that when you reflect on all this you will be worthy of inheriting the Land.

Every *rishon* and *acharon* has his own way of explaining the various terms so that they are not just interchangeable "idioms" of redemption, but separate stages thereof. All at least view "I will remove you from the labors of Egypt" as a first stage. *Chasam Sofer* therefore wonders why the section concludes (*Sh'mos* 6:7), "Then you will know that I am Hashem your God who removes you from the labors of Egypt." Why is knowledge of Hashem bound up with the lowest level of redemption?

Chasam Sofer explains that once their workload was lightened, the Jewish people no longer wished to leave Egypt. Likewise, we later find that they resented Moshe for taking them out, and suspected him of doing so on his own initiative, unbidden by Hashem. This was the chief sin of the spies. Therefore the Torah says, "Then you will know that I am Hashem your God Who removes you from the labors of Egypt," i.e., "Know and acknowledge that it was Hashem Who lightened your burden."

Lest the Jewish people attribute the later stages to Moshe, the Torah continues (v. 8), "I will bring you to the Land which I swore to give to Avraham, Yitzchak and Yaakov," i.e., "Not only am I removing you from the labors of Egypt, but I am preparing you for your entrance to the Land of Israel."

Acharonim wonder why no fifth cup was established out of gratitude for וְהֵבֵאתִי — "I will bring you to the Land." It seems to me that since the Torah separates the first four idioms of redemption from this fifth one with the words "Then you will know that I am Hashem your God," this may be a sign that the sum total of "redemptions" tied to the Exodus ends with the Sinai Revelation. Thereafter begins a new process, וְהֵבֵאתִי, unconnected to the redemption from Egypt.

To explain our not drinking a fifth cup, several *acharonim* answer that those redemptions tied to the Exodus and the Sinai Revelation were completed for all time, while the redemption of the Land of Israel would be interrupted and suspended in the course of time. It is for this reason that we have a fifth cup known as "Eliyahu's Cup," announcing that Hashem will bring even this fifth redemption to a conclusion. My own thought is that because those who left Egypt never entered *Eretz Yisrael*, and never merited more than four redemptions, only four cups were instituted.

Both *rishonim* and *acharonim* are puzzled by the promise of וְהֵבֵאתִי — "I will bring you to the Land", which was not fulfilled in any way for those to whom it was spoken. Hashem says (v. 8), "I will give it to you for a מוֹרָשָׁה — legacy." Many *rishonim* find in the use of מוֹרָשָׁה rather than יְרוּשָׁה — an inheritance — a message that the Land will be given only to the children of those being addressed, an opinion cited by *Chazal*.

Ibn Ezra holds that with their children inheriting the land, it is just as if they are inheriting it themselves. Nonetheless, *Or HaChaim* comments that the preceding verse, "Then you will know that I am Hashem your God," is a precondition for the promise of "I will bring you." Hashem is saying, "If rather than acknowledging that I am Hashem, you curse Me, then there is no promise."

This explanation actually appears in S'forno who states that Hashem said, "If you reflect on all that I have told you, you will be worthy of entering the Land." Yet, so impatient were they that they did not listen to Moshe or believe that Hashem would save them. Therefore, Hashem gave the Land not to them but to their children.

Chasam Sofer in his *Toras Moshe* makes a philosophical statement. The Torah links the redemption from Egypt and the entrance into *Eretz Yisrael* by means of the phrase, "You will know that I am Hashem." This informs us that Hashem is responsible for all occurrences, however they may appear to man. Man is normally unimpressed by small insects, but he is impressed by monkeys and elephants, animals to which he is unaccustomed. He is unimpressed by a stalk of wheat growing from a single kernel or a tree sprouting and growing forth from a single seed.

The Jewish people leaving Egypt knew Hashem's might through His miraculous signs and wonders, and from the manna and quail. Yet, the generation entering *Eretz Yisrael*, who had already become accustomed to manna and quail, saw Hashem's might in the planting of seed. For them, that was something new. Therefore, the Torah concludes its announcement of the entrance into the Land, with the words, I am Hashem. Hashem's existence is revealed in various ways, be they the miracles of the Exodus or those involving the Jewish people's possessing the Land.

◄§ Because of Impatience and Hard Labor

According to S'forno, cited earlier, the Torah attributes "lack of faith in, and refusal to reflect upon, Hashem," as the reason why the Children of Israel who left Egypt did not reach *Eretz Yisrael*. *Ramban* and *Rashbam*, however, regard the Torah's description here as an exoneration of the behavior of the Jewish people who were not ready to answer the call of redemption. They did believe in Hashem and His prophets, but did not heed Moshe, like a man so caught up in his labors that he cannot think about tomorrow.

Impatience, says *Ramban*, refers to their fear that Pharaoh would have them killed, as expressed in the taskmasters' grievance against Moshe and Aharon. Whereas, hard labor refers to the oppression inflicted upon them by the Egyptians, making it impossible for them to hear or to reflect upon Hashem's word.

Meshech Chochmah provides a fine explanation. A man whose life is difficult at present is psychologically unprepared to accept promises regarding the future. He wishes first to be rescued from his present plight. Therefore, Hashem returns and directs Moshe and Aharon exclusively concerning the present (*Sh'mos* 6:13), "to bring the Children of Israel out of the land of Egypt." This is a promise that they can better comprehend than one regarding *Eretz Yisrael*.

Pardes Yosef states that the Children of Israel did not believe the tidings of redemption, because they knew that only 210 years had passed of the 400 years anticipated. In truth, however, Hashem brought redemption early for two reasons:

(a) *Because of impatience* — Their spirit was already broken, and they could tarry no more. Had they been detained in Egypt any longer, they would have assimilated, and it would then have become impossible to extricate them.

(b) *Because of hard labor* — The harshness of their servitude compensated for what time was lacking.

Nonetheless, the Children of Israel were not prepared to acknowledge "impatience and the hard labor" as reasons for their early redemption while both conditions also prevented them from listening to Moshe.

Ralbag offers an interesting explanation. The Children of Israel did not listen to the tidings of redemption due to the impatience of Moshe. Moshe's vociferous protest to Hashem, "Why did You mistreat this nation?" served to demonstrate for them that Moshe himself was eaten up by doubt. A leader must be bold and fearless. The Children of Israel, seeing that Moshe lacked these attributes, did not believe he would succeed in completing his mission.

The *Mechilta* perceives the word *avodah* in עֲבֹדָה קָשָׁה (hard labor) as *avodah zarah* — foreign worship. In other words, it was hard for the Children of Israel to cease idol worship, hence they did not listen to Moshe. Likewise, *Targum Yonasan* translates the words עֲבֹדָה קָשָׁה to the Aramaic, פּוּלְחָנָא נוּכְרָאָה — "foreign worship."

It is also in connection to the verse (*Sh'mos* 6:13), "And He commanded [Moshe and Aharon] regarding the Children of Israel," that the Midrashic authorities comment that this was Hashem's command to them to forsake idolatry. Their interpretation follows from the relationship that this verse bears to the preceding verses related to the behavior of the Children of Israel who were suffering from "the hard labor," which *Chazal* interpret to mean idolatry. Nonetheless, *Tosefos Berachah* holds that the exposition of the Midrashic authorities is based on the Torah's very use of the word וַיְצַוֵּם — "And He commanded them." Here the Torah offers no indication regarding the nature of the command. But similar use of the word "to command" is found in (*Bereishis* 2:16), "And Hashem, God, commanded man." There (see *Sanhedrin* 56b), *Chazal* view the "command" as banning idolatry, as in (*Sh'mos* 32:8), "They have quickly strayed from the path I commanded to them, and made themselves a golden calf." That is why the Midrashic authorities here view the phrase, "And He commanded them," as pertaining to idolatry.

Previously Moshe said (*Sh'mos* 6:12), "Behold, if the Children of Israel did not listen to me, why should Pharaoh?" *Chasam Sofer* in his *Toras Moshe* explains the logic of this: "The Children of Israel did not listen to me, and they were merely drawn towards idolatry. How then will Pharaoh listen to me, when he is idolatry incarnate, viewing himself as a god?"

Rashi explains, "And He commanded [Moshe and Aharon] regarding the Children of Israel," as follows: "He commanded them to lead the Children of Israel gently and tolerantly." *Sifsei Kohen* comments that *Rashi*'s words are aligned with those of *Midrash Rabbah*, from which they are taken. The Holy One, Blessed is He, tells Moshe, "Consider how eager I am to redeem Israel despite their inability to break away from idolatry. You too, even if troubled by them, must learn My tolerance. They are My children even if idolaters." Similarly, the Prophet Yeshayahu (1:4) called the Jewish people, "corrupt children," and *Chazal* comment, "Although they deal corruptly, they are still called Hashem's children."

◆§ Behold, the Children of Israel
Did Not Listen to Me

The failure of the Children of Israel to listen to Moshe weakened his resolve. A leader, says *Sefas Emes*, draws his inspiration and strength from the people. If they do not wish to be redeemed, in whose name can he demand redemption? Moshe complains, "I have uncircumcised lips," i.e., "under present conditions I lack the impetus to express myself in the way I must."

Chasam Sofer here presents an engaging idea. Pharaoh confronts Moshe and Aharon, asking "What do you mean that 'I' must set the Children of Israel free? 'You' must first desire to leave. If I deter you, you must fight me as is customary for rebels seeking liberation. You, however, have expressed no desire to leave, so what logic is there in your demand that I free you?"

In truth, says *Chasam Sofer*, Pharaoh is right. The Children of Israel were low spirited, and afraid of war with Egypt (Ibn Ezra, beginning of *Beshalach*). Therefore, nothing could be gained by telling the Children of Israel to leave without Pharaoh first banishing them. Moshe had this in mind when he argued, "Behold, the Children of Israel did not listen to me." He meant that they had expressed no desire to leave, and he wondered why Pharaoh should be expected to listen to his request that they be sent away.

S'forno's explanation is somewhat similar. Moshe understood why the Children of Israel did not listen to him: Since he had first approached Pharaoh, their bondage had only become worse. With the Children of Israel not listening to him, why should Pharaoh have listened? Surely he was becoming more and more arrogant, thinking none could be saved from his hand.

By nature, says *Divrei Shaul*, man finds giving hard and taking easy. As the Children of Israel, who stood to receive freedom, did not heed Moshe, why should Pharaoh have heeded him when asked to grant that freedom?

Rashi, quoting *Midrash Rabbah*, declares Moshe's argument to be one of ten examples of *kal vachomer* — *a fortiori* — found in the Torah. "If the Children of Israel were not listening to Moshe, why would Pharaoh be expected to listen?" But both *rishonim* and *acharonim* question the validity of this argument as a *kal vachomer*. They note that earlier the Torah attributed the Children of Israel's failure to heed Moshe, to their "impatience." As impatience was not a problem for Pharaoh, the *kal vachomer* is insupportable. On the contrary, Pharaoh, who was not suffering from "impatience" as the Children of Israel were, should be expected at least to listen to Moshe.

The Tosafists in *Da'as Zekeinim*, however, answer that Moshe, by injecting the words, "I am slow of speech," reinforces the *kal vachomer*. As far as Pharaoh is concerned, Moshe's speech defect is an insult to the throne. Hence, Moshe was convinced that if for any reason the Children of Israel did not listen, Pharaoh surely would not.

Kesav Sofer adds to this. Moshe is described as (*Sh'mos* 4:10) "heavy of speech and tongue," i.e., he stuttered, and did not know the language of Egypt. Vis-a-vis the Children of Israel he had only one shortcoming, as he spoke their language. Regarding Pharaoh, however, both problems presented. This is the meaning of (v. 6:12), "And how then shall Pharaoh hear me (as I know not his language), and I am of uncircumcised lips (being also slow of speech and tongue)."

Interestingly, *Rashi* explains the end of verse 6:12, "and I am of uncircumcised lips," before explaining the words "Why should Pharaoh listen?" which precede. *Levush HaOrah* interprets *Rashi*'s intent in accordance with what we said before that the *kal vachomer* is based on Moshe's claim of a speech defect: "The Children of Israel, whom I addressed in their mother tongue, did not listen to me because of my speech defect. Pharaoh, whom I addressed in a language foreign to him, surely will not heed me." This *kal vachomer* cannot be contested, for we cannot dispute human nature. As for the "impatience" demonstrated by the Children of Israel, that, according to *Levush HaOrah*, was a consequence of Moshe's speech defect. They became impatient with him when they found it difficult to understand him.

Divrei David explains *Rashi* similarly. Logically, insulting a king by addressing him with a speech defect presents a greater impediment to communication than does "impatience."

We find an apt explanation of this matter in *Yismach Moshe* and other works, according to which Moshe's argument with Hashem is not related to any *kal vachomer*. Moshe says, "The Children of Israel have already ignored me. How will it be if Pharaoh obeys? I will have a 'speech impediment,' i.e., my complaints against Hashem will be silenced." *Paane'ach Raza* explains that Moshe feared for Hashem's honor. He was certain that Pharaoh would say, "If the Children of Israel did not listen to you, why should I?"

◄§ Hashem's Command to the Children of Israel

The Torah states (*Sh'mos* 6:13) that Hashem commanded Moshe and Aharon regarding the Children of Israel. We have already discussed the view that the Children of Israel were here commanded to cease idolatry. Alternatively, the Jerusalem Talmud, in harmony with the text, holds that Hashem commanded Moshe and Aharon to ensure that the Children of Israel free their own slaves. Such a command is highly understandable. Were they to approach Pharaoh to free the Children of Israel at a time when the Children of Israel held slaves, Pharaoh would retort, "Practice what you preach!"

Meshech Chochmah finds it likely that in Egypt there were prominent aristocrats and princes among the Jews themselves who had bought Jewish slaves from Egyptians. Therefore, they were first commanded to free their Jewish slaves, so that Moshe and Aharon might then ask such a thing of Pharaoh. The commentaries also quote *Midrash Shir HaShirim*, 4:15, "None of the tribes exercised dominion in Egypt except these (Reuven, Shimon and Levi)." They were therefore commanded to free their slaves once and for all.

The Jerusalem Talmud further confirms the view of R' Hila, who said: "The Children of Israel in Egypt were punished only because they broke the laws of freeing slaves, as it is written (*Yirmiyahu* 34:14), 'After seven years you must free your Jewish brother.'"

Torah Temimah explains that the above quotation from the Jerusalem Talmud hinges upon the preceding verse (ibid. vs. 13-14): "I forged a covenant with your ancestors on the day I took them out of the land of Egypt and the house of bondage, saying, 'After seven years you must free your Jewish brother.'"

Since no such command is mentioned in the Torah, but an unexplained order, וַיְצַוֵּם — "And He commanded," does appear in our *parashah*, we therefore attribute the latter to the details of the covenant in *Yirmiyahu*. The Jewish people were commanded to free their slaves and to live lives of social equality as a precondition for their exodus from Egypt.

IV.

The Educational Objective of the Ten Plagues

he differences between the various plagues catch the attention of many commentators. Some plagues influence Pharaoh to beg Moshe to have mercy and pray for him. Others have less effect. Regarding some, a warning is issued, and regarding others, none. In some cases Moshe is directed to rise early in the morning to warn Pharaoh, and in others he is told, "Go to Pharaoh." Regarding some, Hashem lays stress upon a goal: "So you will know that I am Hashem." Others have no such emphasis. Some are executed by Moshe; others by Aharon; still others by Hashem Himself. The first to categorize the plagues by types and groups is Abarbanel.

The Torah explicitly states that three plagues — עָרוֹב — wild beasts; דֶּבֶר — pestilence; and בָּרָד — hail — neither struck in Goshen nor harmed the Children of Israel. Why are only these mentioned? Were the Jews harmed by the others? Ibn Ezra holds that wherever no mention appears otherwise, the Children of Israel were, in fact, harmed. דָּם — blood, צְפַרְדֵּעַ — frogs and כְּנִים — lice were non-dangerous plagues, hence they struck all, Jew and non-Jew. שְׁחִין — boils and אַרְבֶּה — locusts struck all too, being plagues with no long-term effects. Only the mixture of wild animals, because of its severity, and pestilence and hail, which bring irrevocable harm to livestock, did not strike the Children of Israel. This explanation concurs with the words of *Chazal* who said, "The cabbage is smitten with the shrub," i.e., the good suffer with the bad (*Bava Kamma* 92a).

Ramban holds that the Children of Israel were not smitten by any plague. Regarding the first three, which were stationary, the Torah did not need to tell us that they remained outside of Goshen. The wild animals, however, consisted of a moving mass: "Lion and leopards, descending from their mountains and lairs to destroy the land of Egypt, should naturally have reached Goshen." The Torah therefore informs us that they did not.

Ramban's words must be explained, however. First of all, the second plague consisted of frogs, which are ambulatory. Could not the frogs have left their territory and entered Goshen? Second of all, since the seventh plague, hail, is a local phenomenon, why did the Torah have to stress its non-appearance in Goshen?

Ramban, sensing this problem, explains that since hail was induced by Moshe raising his hand to the sky, one might mistakenly think that it struck in Goshen, which shares the same atmosphere with the rest of Egypt. The Torah therefore emphasized that Goshen was spared.

Yet, this explanation is troublesome. Was not the plague of blood brought on by Moshe raising his hand? Why did the Torah not inform us that it did not occur in Goshen?

Chazal seem to provide added confirmation of Ibn Ezra's view. Yaakov, they say, commanded his children not to bury him in Egypt since its earth was destined to be infested with lice. Now if the plagues did not strike Goshen, where Yaakov resided, why could Yaakov not be buried there?

⇜ The Abbreviation of the Ten Plagues

We are all aware from the *Haggadah of Pesach* of R' Yehudah's having abbreviated the ten plagues as דְּצַ"ךְ (*Detzach*), עֲדַ"שׁ (*Adash*), בְּאַחַ"ב (*Be'achav*). Many have wondered what his point was. Abarbanel finds a surprising distinction between these three groups that emerge, and therefore attributes a special purpose to each. Let us examine their distinguishing traits.

Each of these groups has its own sort of introduction. Concerning the first of the trio, *Detzach* — blood, wild animals and hail — Moshe is told to rise early in the morning to threaten Pharaoh (the smiting of the firstborn is a special category). In the second, *Adash* — frog, pestilence and locusts — the threat is prefaced with Moshe being told, "Go to Pharaoh." Concerning the third, *Be'achav* — lice, boils and darkness — no threat is mentioned. This arrangement proves that the three groups are separate units performing unique functions.

Still another distinguishing trait stands out. At the beginning of each threesome a goal is stressed: that Pharaoh should realize Hashem's existence, as written, "in order that you know." Through these patterns, the division into three groups is crystallized, and this division finds expression in R' Yehudah's mnemonic.

How is each group unique? Credit goes to Abarbanel for working on this first. All who follow only clarify and extend his idea. Through his personality, Pharaoh comprised the consummate heretic, and his heresy expressed itself on three levels: (a) denial of Hashem's existence; (b) denial of Divine Providence; and (c) denial of Hashem's ability to alter nature.

The first group of plagues serves to challenge Pharaoh's denial of Hashem's existence, hence with the first plague Hashem says (*Sh'mos* 7:17), "Through this you will know that I am Hashem." This goal is achieved when the Egyptian magicians concede (v. 8:15), "It is the finger of God."

The second group serves to prove Divine Providence. Regarding this, the Children of Israel are treated more favorably than any other beings in Egypt, demonstrating that Hashem watches over and distinguishes between His creatures. Before the fourth plague, Hashem stresses His wish to publicize that (v. 8:18) "I am Hashem right here on earth," reminiscent of (*II Divrei HaYamim* 16:9), "Hashem's eyes roam throughout the earth."

The third group serve to demonstrate Hashem's ability to alter the laws of nature and to demonstrate might, power and acts of deterrence. Once this objective is fulfilled, Hashem says (*Sh'mos* 9:14), "There is none like Me throughout the earth," to the extent that none can match His supernatural power and might.

Abarbanel elaborates on the way this idea fits into the text. Moshe informs Pharaoh of these three axioms of faith (v. 5:1), "So said Hashem (Divine existence), God of the Hebrews (Divine Providence), 'Let my people go' (ultimatum backed by force)."

Pharaoh, however, confronts this with total denial and says (v. 5:2), "Who is Hashem (denial of Divine existence) that I should listen to His voice? (denial of Divine Providence) . . . Neither shall I let Israel go (force versus force)."

The three groups of plagues are intended to negate Pharaoh's hardness of heart, characterized by his perverse attitude towards the three principles of faith. In the tenth plague, the killing of the first-born, the three principles are mentioned together. Pharaoh is told (*Sh'mos* 11:4,7,6), "Around midnight I will go out into Egypt (Hashem's existence) . . . Hashem will differentiate between Egypt and Israel (Divine Providence) . . . There will be a great cry throughout the land of Egypt such as never was and never will be (Hashem's power and might)."

Akeidas Yitzchak and *Malbim* develop Abarbanel's ideas further. They add that the first plague was accompanied by a public warning at the river side, the second by a warning to Pharaoh alone, as written (*Sh'mos* 7:26), "Go to Pharaoh," and the third came without any warning.

Following Abarbanel's approach, it is possible to make another point. The third plague of each group delineated by R' Yehudah is directed against the human body, while the preceding two never are, indicating that two warnings precede each physical punishment. This implies that the first two plagues in each group are not meant to mete out physical punishment but to achieve an educational goal. Only when that goal has not been achieved is the body punished.

Meshech Chochmah states that in those days Egypt was the greatest culture in existence. It was therefore selected to have its views degraded with a view to advancing knowledge of Hashem. As *Meshech Chochmah* adds, the main educational goal was aimed at the Children of Israel in Egypt (v. 7:5), "I will stretch out My hand over Egypt and bring out the Children of Israel from among them." This means that every plague that befell the Egyptians redeemed the Children of Israel from Egyptian defilement, uprooting from their hearts the heretical views mentioned above.

The Kotzker Rebbe says that the ten phrases by which the world was created represent ten paths to knowledge, and correspond to the ten plagues. Each plague redeemed one phrase for the Jewish people. For example, from (v. 10:21), "Let there be darkness in Egypt" emerged (*Bereishis* 1:3), "Let there be light," in knowledge, outlook and deed.

◄§ Warning to What End?

Following Abarbanel's system, the reason that no warning precedes the third plague in each group is that the two earlier plagues serve this function. Alternatively, *Ramban* holds that only those plagues fatal to man were preceded by warnings. Therefore, lice, boils and darkness, non-fatal to man, carried none. Blood, as the first plague, carried a warning. In *Tehillim* 78:45 frogs are described by King David as fatal. There it is written that Hashem sent frogs which destroyed the Egyptians. This destruction literally means death. Moreover, wild beasts and hail are both potentially fatal, and locusts bring death through famine. As for the cattle epidemic, this was intended for man as well (*Sh'mos* 9:16), "The only reason I let you survive was to show you My strength."

According to *Ramban*, the warnings in the respective plagues represent Hashem's mercy for man (*Yechezkel* 33:9), "If you warn the evildoer to change his ways but he does not do so, he shall die for his sins but you have saved your life."

Chasam Sofer offers his own reason for the lack of warning before the plagues of lice, boils and darkness. The warnings served to allow Pharaoh the opportunity to prepare his magicians to demonstrate their alleged powers. It was clear from the start, however, that the magicians would be unable to confront these three plagues. Regarding lice, sorcery can create nothing smaller than a lentil. When the boils struck, the magicians were too ill to appear before Pharaoh. During the darkness, no one could move from his spot, besides which, they could not create more darkness than already existed. Hence, there was no benefit due Pharaoh from the warnings and they were entirely superfluous.

Other commentaries try their hand at interpreting the warnings in their own way, but no explanation is as all encompassing as Abarbanel's. *Paane'ach Raza* notes a source for two warnings followed by a punishment from the *Mishnah* (*Sanhedrin*, 9:5): "Whoever twice incurs flogging is imprisoned the third time." Although suggestive, this source certainly does not provide a halachic basis for our situation, since the *Mishnah* in *Sanhedrin* refers to the specific instance of an individual flogged in court for the repeated transgression of a sin involving *kares*, Divine punishment by premature death. Nonetheless, this explanation represents an attempt to find an additional reason for the strange division and the lack of a warning regarding the third plague in each of the groupings.

According to *Paane'ach Raza*, the reason the pattern of double warning before punishment must occur three times over the ten plagues is that each group of three was executed by a different party. The first three were performed by Aharon, the second by Hashem and the third (except for the firstborn) by Moshe.

S'forno as well finds a textual allusion to the double warning before punishment (*Iyov* 33:29), "Lo, Hashem does all these things twice or three times with a man." This is, however, nothing more than an allusion, for in Tractate *Yoma*, *Chazal* deduce from this verse that Hashem withholds punishment until the fourth time an individual commits a sin, as in *Amos* 2:4, "I shall withhold punishment for three sins of Yehudah, but not for a fourth." S'forno, however, wished only to point out that in the Book of *Iyov* we find a Biblical source for the difference between the second and third plague, as represented by the expression "twice or three times."

S'forno, following the division of R' Yehudah, classifies the plagues so they represent a directed effort to underscore Hashem's mastery over all Creation. *Detzach* — blood, frogs and lice are earthbound (blood and frogs appear in water, lice on the ground); *Adash* — wild beasts, pestilence and boils strike man and animal; *Be'achav* — hail, locusts and darkness take place in the sky while death of the first-born is the decisive plague in the liberation of the Children of Israel from Egypt.

⋖ Mastery Over Heaven and Earth

The plagues as a means of underscoring Hashem's mastery over heaven and earth is a widespread theme among the *rishonim*. Rabbenu Saadya Gaon divides the ten plagues among the four classic elements of nature. Boils, lice and wild beasts belong to earth (boils are the indirect result of furnace soot, lice regenerate in the earth, and of the wild beasts we read (*Sh'mos* 8:17), "And also the ground on which they are"). Blood, frogs and hail belong to water; pestilence, darkness and locusts belong to air, and the killing of the firstborn belongs to fire.

Tur similarly categorizes the plagues according to their nature and in accordance with those instrumental in performing them. The first three plagues relate to earthly elements of nature and are executed by Aharon. Hail, locusts and darkness are related to higher sources and are executed by Moshe. Wild beasts, pestilence and the smiting of the firstborn are executed by Hashem Himself.

Kuzari (1:83) broadens the extent to which the plagues eclipse nature, defining them in terms of their effect upon the "water, air, plant and animal life, bodies and souls" of the Egyptians. Pharaoh was meant to learn that "the plagues are the will of Hashem, Who performs His will when it suits Him, unaided by nature, the stars, sorcery or chance."

Ma'asei Hashem offers an interesting comment. The plagues represent a general eclipse of Hashem's handiwork since the time of Creation. The heavens were stricken (*Sh'mos* 9:22), "Stretch out your hand toward the heavens." The earth was stricken (v. 8:12), "Smite the dust of the land." The light was stricken (v. 10:21), "Let there be darkness." Water was stricken by the plague of blood. Trees were stricken by hail. The creatures swarming in water were stricken by the plague of frogs. Animals were stricken by the plagues of wild beasts and pestilence. Man was struck by boils, and so were the firstborn, as with all the plagues, in accordance with (*Yoel* 3:3), "I shall place My wonders in the heavens and in earth."

R' Samson Raphael Hirsch classifies the plagues in terms of the sins they served to punish. As he explains, the Egyptians were guilty of disenfranchisement, enslavement and torture, and measure for measure, the plagues correspond to these, thus assuming an educational function. With disenfranchisement he associates the plagues of blood, wild animals and hail [i.e., the first plague of each group]. Through the Egyptians the Jewish people were wrenched away from the source of their being, and made dependent upon others. The plague of blood therefore tore the Egyptians away from their deities, and diminished their spiritual support, i.e., the Nile. The plague of wild animals made beast mightier than man. Hail challenged the Egyptian faith in climate and nature.

With enslavement are associated the plagues of frogs, pestilence and locusts [i.e., the second plague of each group]. The master is carried away by feelings of his own greatness, and by arrogance over his wealth and power. These three plagues served to destroy this state of mind. The plague of frogs set the fear of the small amphibian upon the great ruler. Pestilence sapped the Egyptians' strength, and locusts their wealth, so that they were left naked of every element from which the feeling of mastery draws life.

Finally, the three plagues of lice, boils and darkness [i.e., the third plague of each group] served to torture them as they had others.

Bo – בא

I.

Let Them Ask . . .
Vessels of Gold and Silver

The commentaries pose several questions regarding Hashem's command to the Jewish people to ask their Egyptian neighbors for objects of gold and silver on the eve of the Exodus. *Chazal* say that the words דַּבֶּר נָא — "please speak," as employed by Hashem when instructing Moshe, denotes a sense of beseeching. Yet, why should the Jewish people have needed prodding? Did they have reason to object to receiving silver and gold?

According to Tractate *Berachos* 7, Hashem's request included an admonishment:

> So that this righteous man Avraham should not say, "Hashem fulfilled His word (*Bereishis* 15:13), 'they (the Egyptians) will enslave and torture them,' but He did not fulfill His promise (ibid. 15:14), 'and afterwards they will go out with great wealth.' "

Yet, if Hashem wished to keep His promise, what did it matter what Avraham might say? Would not Hashem have to fulfill His promise in any event? Furthermore, if Hashem promised that the Jewish people would go out with great wealth, could He not have fulfilled this promise without their having to borrow gold and silver objects from the Egyptians?

Many commentaries also are concerned about the ethics of borrowing articles from non-Jews with no intention of returning them. *Chazal* deal with this in *Sanhedrin* 91. In the times of Alexander of Macedonia, the Egyptians took the Jewish people to court, suing them for the gold and silver they had borrowed during the Exodus but had not returned, and it was Gaviah ben Pasisa who served as the defense attorney. This account, provided by *Chazal*, attests to the need to explain this incident despite the extensive passage of time.

It is no surprise that in later generations as well, *Tanach* commentaries took pains to clarify this. Ibn Ezra on our *parashah* explains that borrowing the gold and silver was simply Hashem's will, no questions asked: "Hashem created all, and all belongs to Him, hence He can grant wealth to whomever He wishes, remove it and give it to another."

Others remain unsatisfied by this explanation. True, Hashem can do as He wishes, yet, does He not treat man as he deserves, and in ethical terms that man can understand? In this instance, Hashem's command seems ethically incomprehensible.

⋘ A Sense of Beseeching

According to S'forno, the Children of Israel feared that taking the gold and silver would cause the Egyptians to pursue them. Hashem promised them they had nothing to fear. They were not only permitted but commanded to borrow these articles from the Egyptians, and doing so would mean their salvation.

Chasam Sofer explains that Hashem's beseeching was aimed not at the Jewish people, but at Moshe. Moshe wanted them to occupy themselves with removing the bones of Yosef from Egypt, not with borrowing silver and gold. Yet, Hashem wished them to deal with material matters as well (*Berachos* 7), "So that this righteous man Avraham should not say ..."

Chazal hold that the Jewish people had to be pressured to borrow the silver and gold. They did not consider anything more important than freedom and an end to exile. *Chazal* liken this to the prison inmate who, when told that he will be freed tomorrow and given a large stipend, prefers to be freed now and given nothing. The Jewish people wished only to leave the house of bondage.

Nonetheless, Hashem had promised that they would go out with great wealth. It was in Hashem's interest to have this promise fulfilled and, according to one view in *Berachos* 9, even "against Israel's will." Moshe was compelled to lure them into requesting of their neighbors articles they considered a physical and psychological "burden," something unwanted and unacceptable.

Radak, however, shows that the word נָא — usually translated "please"— can also be translated "now." Thus the verse reads, "Speak *now* to the people that they should borrow silver and gold articles."

Sifsei Kohen explains why all of this had to be now. During the plague of darkness the Jewish people could have taken from the homes of the Egyptians whatever they wished, but did not do so. Therefore, the Egyptians would now trust them when they came requesting these articles, and would not refuse their request.

Oznayim LaTorah sees a contemporary parallel, in the events following the Holocaust, for the Jewish people's refusal to take the Egyptian silver and gold. Like many of the refugees of World War II, the Jewish people in Egypt did not want to accept compensation for the murders committed against their parents and their children. They did not wish to cleanse or soothe the consciences of the Egyptians through such reparations.

Nonetheless, Hashem had promised Avraham that his descendants would leave Egypt with great wealth. Hashem did not view this as a "cleansing" of Egypt but as the fulfillment of His promise to the *Avos*. This "forced" acceptance of the Egyptians' wealth later served Moshe as an argument following the incident of the Golden Calf, when he told Hashem (*Berachos* 32), "The silver and gold that You bestowed upon them caused them to fashion the calf."

The author of this narrative in *Berachos* is from the school of R' Yannai, and he is also the author of the interpretation quoted above that (ibid. 9), "נָא denotes a sense of beseeching." According to the school of R' Yannai, Moshe argued that the Jewish people had not wanted the silver and gold, but Hashem compelled them to possess it. Therefore, it was not their fault that this gold later served as material for the Golden Calf.

◂§ Loan or Gift?

Most commentaries hold that the borrowing referred to in the Torah (v. 11:2) is not a loan but a gift, and they cite sources where the root שאל is used to refer to a gift. Rabbenu Saadya Gaon cites (*I Shmuel* 1:28), הוּא שָׁאוּל לַה׳ — "He shall be handed over to Hashem," whereby the term שָׁאוּל describes the permanent dedication of the prophet Shmuel by his mother to Hashem.

Rashbam quotes (*Tehillim* 2:8) "שְׁאַל — Ask of Me, and I shall give these nations as your inheritance." Other commentaries bring other verses. *Mechilta* (*Bo* 12) quotes R' Yishmael's explicit statement: "Before even they had a chance to say, הַשְׁאִילֵנִי [from the root שאל], the Egyptians would give it to them." Also, Rabbenu Bachya quotes R' Chananel:

Heaven forbid that Hashem should have permitted them to deceive their fellow man by borrowing silver and gold articles with no intention of returning them. Rather (*Sh'mos* 3:22), וְשָׁאֲלָה

— "and let them ask," refers to their requesting these items as gifts. Gidon says (*Shoftim* 8:24), "I would make a request — שְׁאֵלָה — of you, that you would give every man the earnings of his spoils," and Bas Sheva addresses King David (*I Melachim* 2:20), "I have שְׁאֵלָה אַחַת קְטַנָּה — one small request to ask you . . . Let Adoniah your brother have Avishag the Shunamis as a wife." We see therefore that gifts can be referred to by שְׁאֵלָה — something requested.

Josephus Flavius presents the same idea in his *Jewish Antiquities* (*II*:14): "The Egyptians bestowed gifts upon them so they would hasten to leave, and they accepted these gifts as a show of neighborliness. As they left, the Egyptians wept, contrite over their evil treatment." The presumed intention of Josephus here is to justify before the nations the Jews' having taken the gold and silver articles, concerning which our enemies have slandered us from time immemorial.

Others view the transaction as one of mutual exchange, whereby the Egyptians were remunerated for their losses through the property which the Children of Israel left behind upon their exodus from Egypt.

Malbim, following the path of earlier commentators, states:

> As they were leaving they asked their neighbors and boarders to take their homes and property in exchange for silver and gold articles of equal value, which would be easier to carry in transit. In doing so they fulfilled the verse (*Sh'mos* 3:22), וְנִצַּלְתֶּם אֶת מִצְרָיִם — "And you will save [i.e., save your property from] the Egyptians." The word "save" means that the Jewish people leaving Egypt would be able to save their property in this way [through exchange not theft], as in the verse (*Bereishis* 31:9), "And God saved [וַיַּצֵּל, from the same root as וְנִצַּלְתֶּם] the flock of your father."

Earlier, as well, *Malbim* writes, regarding the verse (ibid. 31:21), "I will give this people favor in the sight of the Egyptians":

> The Children of Israel possessed fields and vineyards, homes and household articles. What would they do when leaving the country, since the Egyptians would plunder their homes and possessions, leaving them empty handed? Hashem therefore informed them that they would not leave destitute.

Oznayim LaTorah explains similarly that "every woman should ask of her neighbor and boarder to take possession of her property."

The acquisition of the Egyptian gold and silver was thus a mutual exchange of possessions, although the Torah does not describe the details of the transaction between the two peoples. In any event, the arrangement was in keeping with normal ethical standards.

R' Tzvi Hirsch Chayes, in his commentary to *Sanhedrin* 81, quotes the *Targum*, regarding the verse in *Tehillim* (105:37), "Hashem took them out with silver and gold, and none among the tribes stumbled." They left with silver and gold, but did not enter into any misdeed with the Egyptians. In other words, they trespassed no moral bounds in taking gold and silver, for it was their natural right.

Some *acharonim* inject a humorous note. Hashem commanded the Jewish people to take the silver and gold as a loan. Since no one wishes to be seen by his creditor, it was thus assured that they would not return to Egypt.

Other commentaries, however, following the defense argument of Gaviah ben Pasisa in Tractate *Sanhedrin*, regard the silver and gold as uncollected wages for past labor. This explanation actually appears in *Midrash HaGadol*, quoted in *Torah Temimah:*

> Moshe said to Hashem, "Master of the World! The Egyptians gave them no straw. Will they give them silver and gold?" Hashem responded, "It belongs to Me, and because the Egyptians submitted the Jewish people to forced labor, their lives are forfeit and their property belongs to them as uncollected wages, as it is written (*Sh'mos* 12:36), "And they saved [their possessions from] the Egyptians."

Here we find two justifications for the taking of the Egyptians' wealth. The first is that of Ibn Ezra: The wealth belongs to Hashem and He gives it to whomever He wishes. The second is that of the other commentaries, for whom this wealth represents unpaid wages.

The latter point is the chief argument used by Kli Yakar, who writes:

> Although the Holy One, Blessed is He, could simply have given them great wealth, He wished them to receive it as wages for their labor, as Gaviah ben Pasisa said in the Talmud. That was the only way to placate that righteous one (Avraham) for whom the possessions had to be that of the Egyptians, in exchange for the work. That is why it is written (*Bereishis* 15:14), "Afterwards, they will go out with great wealth," i.e., after completing their labor.

Torah Temimah also quotes an ancient variant of *Midrash Tanchuma*, in which Avraham told Hashem, "You must pay them their wages."

Why, however, did this payment take the form of a loan? Answers are forthcoming from those commentaries more concerned with subtle interpretation than with literal meaning. *Shaarei Simchah* states that had they seized their wages by force, they would have had to return them. If one illegally seizes money that is owed to him, he must return it. But if he receives it as a loan, he may keep it even against the will of the one who owes it to him, since it came into his hands in a legal manner.

R' Yitzchak Diskin injects his own sharp comment. The commentaries note that if an individual commits an act incurring both a monetary penalty and capital punishment, only the capital punishment is administered. Why then should the Egyptians, sentenced to death, have had to pay wages as well? One response cites *Maharshal*, who states that while this individual who commits a capital offense may be exempt from paying back what he owes, if the victim forcefully takes back what is owed him, he cannot be compelled to give it up again.

Maharshal further explains that this exemption restricts only the court's right to punish (*Sh'mos* 22:8), "whomever the courts declare guilty." This teaches that a court can punish him for one "guilt" but not for two. Moshe represented the Jewish court, so he could not obligate the Egyptians for their second offense, i.e., the payment of back wages. Hence, Hashem used the word נָא in verse 11:2, implying that Moshe should ask the Jewish people to take the initiative into their own hands, and to appropriate their wages legitimately, as a loan.

◆§ The Placation of Avraham

Hashem's promise to Avraham, says the Dubno Magid, could have been fulfilled with the spoils taken after the Splitting of the Sea. Nonetheless, Hashem meticulously made sure that the Children of Israel would leave Egypt with great wealth, to fulfill the verse: "Afterwards they will go out with great wealth."

The Dubno Magid likens this to two kings who were about to lead their armies against one another. One said, "Why must we always engage in wars and bloodshed? Let us each appoint a single gladiator to do battle, and the results will determine who is supreme." The fight began. One seemed to overcome the other, carrying him to the pit to cast him in. On the edge of the pit, the second one recovered, disentangled himself, overcame his antagonist and threw him into the pit. After the victory his king approached the winning gladiator and asked, "Why did you leave me in suspense until the last moment, when you obviously could have beaten your challenger when the match first began?"

It is the same here. If Hashem had waited until the Splitting of the Sea to fulfill His promise, Avraham would have been disturbed over the fact that He had waited until the last moment. Hashem therefore commanded that the Jews request articles from the Egyptians, even before the Exodus. And since Hashem had promised Avraham that his descendants would go out with great wealth, He forced them to claim this wealth, despite their initial opposition and refusal. Thus the Torah testifies that the Jewish people requested silver and gold articles of their neighbors, not to satisfy their greed, but (*Sh'mos* 12:35) "to follow Moshe's word." They took spoils only because they wished to fulfill Moshe's command.

Or HaChaim states that Moshe intended to permit the Jews to commit fraud, by having them ask for something with the intention that they would not be returning it. *Rambam* (*Hilchos Yesodei HaTorah*, 9) determines that if an established prophet, speaking in Hashem's name, commands us to temporarily trespass a given Torah prohibition, we obey him. Moshe was accepted by the Jewish people as a prophet, hence they obeyed him, borrowing silver and gold articles. But they did so only because Moshe permitted it.

Interestingly, the Torah states (*Sh'mos* 11:2), "Let everyone ask of his neighbor." Prior to the Sinai Revelation, notes Rabbenu Bachya, a non-Jew was referred to by the term "neighbor" — *re'a*, whereas afterward, the term could apply only to a Jew. On the other hand, the Vilna Gaon and later commentaries say this verse is a command to the Jewish people themselves to borrow precious articles from each other, to make the non-Jews think that these were needed to serve Hashem. That way, the Egyptians would not be suspicious when approached with an identical request.

⊷§ You Shall Despoil Egypt

The word וְנִצַּלְתֶּם — "and you shall despoil" — is interpreted in many ways by the commentaries. As noted above, *Or HaChaim* holds that the term refers to the rescue (*hatzalah*) by the Jewish people of those objects that are legally theirs. From here may be deduced that one is permitted to rescue a stolen object from an oppressor in any way possible. *Malbim* too views וְנִצַּלְתֶּם as in *Bereishis* (31:9), where Yaakov tells his wives that God "rescued" their father's flocks and gave them to him. In the same sense, Hashem commands Israel to rescue their wealth from the Egyptians, and not to leave Egypt empty-handed.

HaKesav VeHaKabalah, however, defines וְנִצַּלְתֶּם in ethical terms, as a means of assisting the Egyptians to repay old debts. Just as a borrower is duty bound to save himself from the sin of retaining an object that does not belong to him, so too must the lender save his property from a borrower who willfully refuses to repay his debt. In the same way, we are told (*II* Shmuel 8:15), "David performed acts of justice and charity." To what do "justice and charity" refer? *Chazal* explain that King David would free the thief of sin by taking the stolen object from his possession. This is considered an act of "charity" towards the thief. Similarly, after the Egyptians had enslaved the Jewish people, the command "וְנִצַּלְתֶּם" was issued to "save" the Egyptians by having them relinquish what they had taken.

This could also be *Chazal's* intent in saying that Egypt was transformed into "a net holding no fish." The Egyptians spread a net to ensnare the Children of Israel as if they were fish. When the time came to raise the netting, it contained no fish. They then learned that all their efforts had been in vain, and that they had gained nothing by enslaving the Children of Israel. Instead, they ended up paying very heavily for the services that the Jewish people had rendered them.

II.

Milestones in Time

he Jewish people mark the passage of time in two ways. We count the days of the week beginning with the seven days of Creation. We count the months starting from the Exodus from Egypt, as it is written (*Sh'mos* 12:2), "[*Nissan* shall be] for you the first of all the months of the year." Had the months been counted from Creation, *Tishrei* would come first, for its inception coincides with the Jewish New Year that commemorates the first day of Creation.

Ibn Ezra enlists Biblical proofs that Rosh Hashanah takes place in *Tishrei*. The Torah refers to Sukkos as (v. 23:16) "the harvest festival, the end of the year." The harvest season is the conclusion of the outgoing year, and therefore also the beginning of the coming year. Furthermore, the beginning of the Jubilee year is sanctified in *Tishrei*. Regarding *Shemittah*, the Torah says first (*Vayikra* 25:11), "Do not plant" and then "Do not harvest." Planting takes place around *Tishrei*, and harvesting after *Nissan*. If the new year were to coincide with *Nissan*, then whoever had planted in the sixth year would be unable to harvest his crops, for the *Shemittah* year would be upon him.

We see from the above that *Tishrei* is the beginning of the year in terms of Creation. Our *parashah* says, however, "[*Nissan* shall be] for you the first of all the months of the year." Thus, the onset of the months was determined by a different occurrence, that being *yetzias Mitzraim* — the Exodus from Egypt. (This is "the beginning of the year" with regard to those purposes derived by *Chazal* and referred to as "for the festivals" and "for the reigns of kings.")

It follows that the phrase "for you" in *Sh'mos* 12:2 points out the uniquely Jewish nature of the calendar system that Hashem ordained. Hashem commanded the Jewish people, who left Egypt in *Nissan*, that they must establish a way of commemorating this event in their calendar, different from the rest of humanity. *Rashbam* and *Ramban* even see this as inherent in the literal intent of this verse. As Jews, we must commemorate Creation through the days of the week, and the Exodus through the months of the year.

Following the Babylonian exile, adds *Ramban*, the months were assigned Babylonian names to remind us also of the Babylonian exile and our redemption from it (*Yirmiyahu* 16:14,15), "No longer shall it be said, 'As Hashem lives, Who brought the Children of Israel out of Egypt,' but 'As Hashem lives, Who brought the Children of Israel out of the land of the north.' "

Only the names of the months changed, however. The landmark events retained their significance. The Exodus and Creation have an ancient place in the Jewish calendar, established by the Torah. From this *Chasam Sofer* concludes that we must use the Hebrew and not the secular calendar to mark dates in order to further our belief in the Exodus and Creation.

◆§ The Calendar: Determined by Beis Din

The calendrical memorial to Creation, namely the reckoning of the weekly Shabbos, remains constant, while the anniversary of the Exodus depends on the calculations of the Jewish lunar calendar. These calculations, according to *Chazal*, are a task for *beis din*, who follow the principles established by the Torah for this purpose. *Chazal* in *Rosh Hashanah* 22 learn this from (*Sh'mos* 12:2), ["*Nissan* shall be] for you the first of all the months of the year." The words "for you" refer to the great Torah scholars of Israel, first represented by Moshe and Aharon, to whom this was originally commanded.

The first *mitzvah* that the Jews as a people were commanded concerned the fixing of months and leap years by the Sanhedrin at Jerusalem. This *mitzvah* combines elements of both the Written and

Oral Law. In this most basic of institutions, the maintenance of an accurate calendar, the Sages of Israel play a vital role.

The role of *beis din* is vital not only because of the mathematical expertise required to calculate new months and leap years, but also in order to adjust the lunar calendar according to the solar one, thereby totally subjugating the dimension of time to Torah wisdom. The Torah hints at our duty to make this adjustment. The meaning of *chodesh* — month — is similar to the Hebrew word for "renewal," with the moon as that object which allows us to actually see the renewal of time. The Torah also links the Jewish holidays to the solar year (*Sh'mos* 34:22).

In order to adjust the lunar and solar calendars, *Chazal* were authorized to fix months according to the lunar cycle, and years according to the solar cycle. Between these two cycles is a discrepancy of ten days, twenty-one hours and 204 *chalakim* [since there are 1080 *chalakim* to an hour, 204 *chalakim* are the equivalent of eleven minutes and twenty seconds]. Seemingly, it might have been possible to add this amount of time at the end of each year, and then to fix all holidays according to the sun. Yet, *Chazal* in Tractate *Megillah* deduced from the Torah that "we must count whole months, not days." There is therefore no choice but to add an entire month to the cycle approximately once in three years, thereby correcting the discrepancy between the lunar and solar calendar.

The present system of calculating the months and years according to fixed formulae was established in the years following the destruction of the Second Temple, when there were no longer any ordained courts in *Eretz Yisrael*. When the Temple was standing, the Sanhedrin would divide the year into seasons so that *Pesach* would come out in the spring, *Shavuos* in the reaping season, and *Sukkos* in the harvest season. Other factors were taken into account as well, such as delayed arrival of Jews from the Diaspora to Jerusalem for Festival pilgrimages. This sometimes occurred when rain ruined roads, when bridges collapsed or when those making the pilgrimage from distant lands were detained. In such cases *Chazal* employed the authority granted them by the words "for you," fixing the leap year whenever necessary. They exercised this same authority when determining the beginnings of the months, whether by calculation or through the testimony of witnesses.

What is unique about this *mitzvah* is that time and the *mitzvos* bound by it are determined in accordance with the tradition of the Torah sages operating on authority given them by the Torah. Here is the foundation for the veracity of the Oral Law. In fact, *Kuzari* (3:35) demonstrates in this way the inseparable link between the Written and Oral Torah. He sees it as a cornerstone of our faith in the sanctity of the

Talmudic tradition. Of this *mitzvah*, the Torah says (*Devarim* 4:6), "It is your wisdom and understanding in the eyes of the nations;" for this *mitzvah* determines milestones in time, through careful, precise calculations of the movements of heavenly bodies.

⊷ Who May Decree Leap Years and Sanctify Months?

According to *Rambam*, in *Sefer HaMitzvos* (153), only Torah sages of *Eretz Yisrael* with the ancient *semichah* ordination going back in an unbroken chain to Moshe are eligible to determine leap years and the onset of new months. If there are no such sages in *Eretz Yisrael*, then those of the Diaspora may do so, if they have *semichah* from authorized courts in *Eretz Yisrael*. *Rambam* stresses: "This is a great tenet of our faith whose importance only profound thinkers can know and understand." These words, which apply even today, refer to the role of *Eretz Yisrael* in our Torah.

For *Rambam*, the only reason that we today rely upon the sages for fixing the Jewish calendar is that the Sanhedrin in Jerusalem once established the calendar for all future generations. Our current calculations serve only to convey what was previously determined.

Rambam's view is of great interest, considering his supposed attitude to *Eretz Yisrael* which seems to differ from that of *Ramban*, who regards settling the land as one of the 613 *mitzvos*. And yet *Rambam*, unlike *Ramban*, links the *mitzvah* of proclaiming the months in the Jewish calendar to *Eretz Yisrael* and its sages. By contrast, *Ramban* proves from the Talmud that proclaiming the new month cannot be linked to *Eretz Yisrael*, its sages or those ordained by them. Otherwise, he claims, today when such ordination does not exist, our holidays would be nullified.

We cannot, of course, establish from here *Rambam's* attitude to the settlement of *Eretz Yisrael*, but it is an indication of the significance of the Land in terms of the Torah and *mitzvos*.

Commentaries on *Rambam*, *rishonim* and *acharonim* alike, struggle to explain his views, according to their particular talents and leanings. *Meshech Chochmah* explains *Rambam's* view as follows: If the Jewish people today wished to ordain their sages with full judicial powers, these sages would have all the authority of a fully ordained *beis din*. If organized Diaspora Jewry possesses such a prerogative, it is by virtue of the authority originally granted their predecessors in *Eretz Yisrael*. This prerogative, therefore, allows us to function as if our local Torah sages were ordained.

In the same manner, *Meshech Chochmah* explains why Diaspora communities must keep a second day of *Yom Tov*, despite our expertise in fixing the calendar. *Chazal* (*Beitza* 4b) offered the reason that this maintenance of an additional day of *Yom Tov* is to prevent violation of the Torah due to possible errors in fixing the calendar. But *Meshech Chochmah*, quoting the Vilna Gaon, notes that there are other hidden reasons that *Chazal* do not reveal. One of these could be based on that which *Rambam* (*Perush HaMishnayos*, beginning of *Sanhedrin*) says, that before the *Mashiach*'s arrival, a fully ordained court will be established in *Eretz Yisrael*, which will once more inaugurate months through the witness system, as in the Temple period. At that point, if the moon should appear on the thirtieth day of the month, there would be the possibility that the Jews of the Diaspora would not be informed in time. *Chazal* therefore left the two days of *Yom Tov* intact, to cover all possibilities in the future.

According to *Rambam*, the Jewish lunar calendar is linked to *Eretz Yisrael*. That explains why Israel's enemies banned the Jews from abiding by their "calendar legislation, *Shabbos* and *milah*" during the Chashmonaim period. We might wonder why the enemies of Israel should have been angered by calendar legislation, and how it could belong together with the latter two, which make the Jewish people unique and distinct from other nations. Yet, *Rambam*'s associating calendar legislation with *Eretz Yisrael* makes this clear. Like the other two Jewish observances that were banned, calendar legislation is an exclusively national institution, distinguishing the Jewish people from the nations by exhibiting their connection to a special Land, and their subjugation to *Chazal*.

It is interesting to note *Rambam*'s outlook regarding the inauguration of leap years and its link to the Land of Israel:

> If we were to consider by way of illustration that all the inhabitants of *Eretz Yisrael* were to be absent from the Land (God forbid that should happen for He promised that our manifestation as a nation would never be eradicated), then without a *beis din* either in *Eretz Yisrael* or one ordained in *Eretz Yisrael* functioning abroad, our calculation [of the calendar] would be entirely worthless.

Two fundamental conclusions emerge. Coming from *Rambam*, who does not number settling *Eretz Yisrael* among the 613 *mitzvos*, they are highly surprising. First of all, if ever a single Jew were not to remain in *Eretz Yisrael*, the Jewish holidays would be discontinued, for we would have no sanctioned means of determining proper calendar dates. Second of all, the disappearance of all Jews from *Eretz Yisrael* would represent the destruction of our nation, which Hashem promised us would never happen.

Chasam Sofer in his responsa (*Yoreh Deah* 234) presents these conclusions explicitly:

> It seems from his words that if, Heaven forbid, there would ever not be a single Jew in *Eretz Yisrael*, even though there would be those residing in the Diaspora, this would be considered the "destruction of the Jewish people." That is so because there would be no courts authorized to determine the onset of months or to decree leap years. *Rambam* holds that the calculations of the earlier sages, establishing the calendar for all time, are of no avail if the Land is empty of Jews, unless there are [at least] farmers and vine growers in *Eretz Yisrael* who, when the need arises, can fix correct dates for the holidays based on what is written in the calendar. Otherwise, those early calculations are of no benefit, the entire Torah is nullified and the Jewish nation is, Heaven forbid, no more.

These are piercing words, particularly from *Rambam*, who does not number the settling and conquering of *Eretz Yisrael* as one of the 613 *mitzvos*. From here it seems clear that his failure to do so is not because of the inferred insignificance of *Eretz Yisrael*, but rather the Land's greatness which the *Rambam* views as a foundation of the Torah and the Jewish people. As *Avnei Nezer* says, *yishuv Eretz Yisrael* — the settlement of the land — is *more* than a *mitzvah*, for the *mitzvos* and the survival of the Jewish people depend upon it.

◄§ Decision in the Hands of Beis Din

Chazal investigate the unique phenomenon of *beis din* having jurisdiction over the calendar and the dates of holidays. Ibn Ezra and *Akeidas Yitzchak* hold that the Torah wished to dispel the false belief that the world is controlled by the constellations, as if they determine the calendar. The Torah hereby established a fundamental tenet of faith: Time is subject to Torah, and remains under the control of *Chazal*. In this context, no one can say that Jewish holidays merely "mark the passage of the zodiac."

Akeidah also points out that Israel, according to *Chazal*, are likened to the moon because they share a similar fate. The moon was at one time a great luminary, and it was diminished. So too Israel. The moon sometimes shines; at other times its light is hidden. So too Israel.

Moonlight reflects from the sun, Israel's light reflects from the Holy One, Blessed is He. In this way *Akeidah* goes on to enumerate twelve similarities between the Jewish people and the moon.

Rabbenu Bachya takes a similar path. Nowadays the sun is our major and the moon our minor source of light. In the same way, the nations are likened to the sun, and Israel to the moon. One day, however, the opposite will hold true, as in our prayer (*Bircas HaLevanah*): "May it be Your will to correct the deficiency of the moon".

Rama explains accordingly our declaration from that same prayer: "Long live David, king of Israel!" Our hope remains. The kingdom of Israel endures and shall live forever.

Likewise, the other accompanying prayers and the great importance attached to *Bircas HaLevanah*, the New Moon Blessing, focus on the redemption of the Jewish people and their Land. The *maskilim* of the Enlightenment ridiculed this sense of importance, and mocked our wish that Hashem "correct the moon's deficiency," misunderstanding its veiled meaning. *Chazal* concealed in these prayers our nation's aspirations, and thereby were able to proclaim them in public, under the very eyes of the gentiles. Even the dancing during *Bircas HaLevanah* is interpreted by the great Chassidic personalities as symbolizing a wedding dance, in accordance with *Midrash Sh'mos* which says that because the Jewish people in "this world" are only in a state of betrothal, Hashem makes the Jewish people like the moon. In the world-to-come, however, which is the world of marriage, He will give us the sun. Through our dancing, we therefore express our yearning for the Messianic era and the marriage which follows the period of engagement.

Chazal suggest yet another splendid simile. Just as the moon renews its cycle, so too the Jewish people are, in the words of *Bircas HaLevanah*, "destined to be renewed."

Kuzari (3:5) states that *Rosh Chodesh* is a day of atonement, for it is symbolic of renewal and change. Similarly, R' Samson Raphael Hirsch in a comment on (*Sh'mos* 12:2), "This month shall be for you a beginning of months," explains that "this month" [Nissan] is the head and beginning of all renewals. "Let us learn from the month to renew ourselves and increase our light and luster."

Elaborations on this theme are found in Chassidic literature. "חִידּוּשׁ — renewal," says *Chidushei HaRim*, "belongs only to Israel. The nations of the world are bound by unalterable laws of nature, while the Jewish people transcend nature. Therefore, 'הַחֹדֶשׁ הַזֶּה — this month shall be for you.' Only for you is renewal possible, but for no other nation."

In any event, time represents a philosophical and symbolic foundation of Judaism. According to *Chazal* in *Midrash Rabbah*, it plays a vital role in our improving the world. If we did not mark milestones in time, it would be impossible for us to conduct business transactions involving receipts and contracts, or to maintain social relations, both of which depend upon clear dates. The *Midrash* in *Sh'mos Rabbah* (15) states the following regarding the verse in *Tehillim* (147:19), "Hashem tells His words to Yaakov, His laws and judgments to Israel."

> Laws refer to calculations of the holidays upon which judgments depend. How are the judgments dependent? A man sells a field, house, or servant ... if he then attempts to cheat his comrade, the "laws and judgments to Israel" intervene. The judges check out the months, for they rule according to the accountability of time [whereby the contract is produced, the place, date and manner of writing are examined to investigate the validity of the transaction, and justice is ensured].

In light of this source, we can well understand the words (*Sh'mos* 12:2): "This month is for you" — i.e., for the benefit of your society.

Moshe had difficulty with the laws of the New Moon. He did not understand how and why to create milestones in time. Yet, Hashem told him, "When the moon looks so, usher in the new month." Law and order depend upon maintaining a calendar. Without it, society would collapse in anarchy.

III.

The Slaughter of the Pesach Sacrifice

efer HaChinuch, in contemplating the rationale of the *mitzvah* to partake of the *Pesach* sacrifice, explains that its general purpose is to commemorate the Exodus. Hence its specific details serve to highlight our freedom and our princely status:

> We were specifically commanded to eat it roasted, because when served that way it is a dish of kings, fine and delicious. Ordinary people cannot afford such savory meat, and must boil their meat so

as to better fill their stomachs. Since the *Pesach* is eaten to commemorate our departure from Egypt on our way to becoming a kingdom of priests and a holy nation, we should surely do so in a free and princely fashion.

Moreover, the *mitzvah* that prohibits leaving any part of the *Pesach* until the following morning (*Sh'mos* 12:10) is, according to *Chinuch*, a way of accentuating our freedom "like kings and princes, who never have to save their leftovers from one day to the next."

Or HaChaim extends the analogy to the *matzah* and the *marror* — "bitter herbs". Of *marror* he says, "Those who eat roast meat customarily add a sharp-tasting side dish to enhance its flavor and stimulate the appetite," and he considers *matzah* to improve the flavor of roast meat as well.

Chinuch applies the same principle to the law that forbids anyone outside the predesignated group of the particular *Pesach* sacrifice to eat from it, likening it to the practice of kings for whom everything is prepared beforehand in their palace and who dine with a large group of their subjects.

Aside from the basic rationale of "commemorating the Exodus," there is actually a broad mixture of explanations offered. Clearly, however, the fundamental principle of freedom stands out prominently in many of the *mitzvos* involved, and hence all the commentaries make analogies to the conduct of kings.

HaKesav VeHaKabalah explains the word *Pesach*, too, as meaning "deliverance," based on (*Yeshayahu* 31:5), "He will pass over it and deliver it." Thus, the festival of *Pesach* is the festival of our deliverance.

Some commentaries view the original *Pesach* sacrifice as intended to mock the Egyptian religion and its deity, represented by the sheep they worshiped. Yet, even these commentators agree that this sacrifice serves to accentuate the achievement of freedom on the spiritual and philosophical level. According to *Chizkuni*, the blood of the *Pesach* was smeared upon the doors to demonstrate our new-found spiritual freedom, showing the Egyptians that we had slaughtered their god and were proud to have done so. Various details of the *Pesach* sacrifice are explained similarly by others as well.

In summary, the purpose of the original *Pesach* performed in Egypt was to imbue the Jewish people with a feeling of both spiritual and physical freedom, whereas the *Pesach* of subsequent generations is obviously meant to commemorate the Exodus.

✑§ Symbols of Spiritual Freedom

The objective of delivering the Jewish people from alien and idolatrous views is obvious. But, at the same time, the blood of the *Pesach*, designated to be (*Sh'mos* 12:13) "a sign on the houses," occupies all of the commentaries on account of its sorcery-like feature.

Also, the Torah says (v. 12:23), "And He will not allow the *mashchis* to plague your houses." The nature of this *mashchis*, or "destroying angel," must be clarified as well, since Hashem had said that He Himself would pass through Egypt, He and no other. Quoting *Sh'mos* 12:12, *Chazal* explicitly stress this: "'I will pass through the land of Egypt' — I and not an angel; 'I will smite every firstborn' — I and not a *seraph*; 'I will punish all the gods of Egypt' — I am He, there is no other."

In light of this source, what need was there to ward off the *mashchis* by marking the houses with blood? What purpose did the "sign" serve? Who was this *mashchis*?

The Torah said (v. 12:13), "The blood shall be for you as a sign." *Chazal* (*Mechilta*, quoted by *Rashi*) focus on the nature of this sign: "By virtue of the *mitzvah* that you are performing, I will reveal Myself to you and take pity upon you." Thus the blood served to announce that the Jewish people had sacrificed the *Pesach* in accordance with Hashem's command, and therefore deserved to be saved.

A similar but slightly more elaborate explanation is that of Rabbenu Bachya:

> It was not the blood that prevented the plague. Instead, as the Torah tells us, those who placed their faith and trust in God, publicly slaughtering the Egyptian deity and smearing its blood on the doorpost and the lintel without fear of Pharaoh or his decrees, were righteous and deserved Hashem's protection.

This explanation gives the act of smearing the blood profound meaning. Anyone who performed this act not only fulfilled Hashem's word but endangered himself. Placing this sign involved a prominent display of faith and self-sacrifice. Such a person announced he was unafraid of Pharaoh, and by virtue of that announcement he was worthy of Hashem's shelter.

Or HaChaim explains in somewhat similar fashion. He pays no attention to what the blood demonstrated to the Egyptians. Rather, he views the act of smearing the blood as a Divine seal proclaiming, "This individual has done his Master's bidding." When the *mashchis* has been given opportunity to destroy, he does so without discretion. But when he sees Hashem's seal, i.e., the *mitzvah*, he recoils and is afraid to attack.

Others, however, regard the blood differently. *Akeidas Yitzchak* views it as a covenant between Israel and their Father in Heaven:

> Heaven forbid that this blood should have the same status for the Blessed One as the scarlet thread in the house of Rachav (*Yehoshua* 2:1-19). The Torah says (*Sh'mos* 12:13), "The blood shall be for you as a sign," and *Chazal* comment, "for you, and no one else." [Hashem says,] "This blood shall represent a covenant between us, lodged in your hearts. I will see it in these habitation places of yours as I go by and I will pass over you."

Thus, *Akeidah* holds to the view that the sign of the blood was indoors and not outside so that its purpose was to cause the Jewish people to reflect upon the covenant of blood they have with their Father in Heaven.

Alshech, as well, symbolically explains the nature of the blood as an interior sign. Yet, he speaks not of a covenant, but of *korban* — "sacrifice". When an animal is slaughtered for a *korban*, it takes the place of the one who offers it. Like the Egyptians, the Children of Israel were worthy of destruction since they had been influenced by the lamb worship of their neighbors. The *korban* therefore was their atonement. They needed to know their guilt, and the blood was that "sign."

Ibn Ezra mentions that many commentaries view the blood as a public renouncement of the Egyptians and their faith, and as a sign that the Israelites did not fear them. Yet, he rejects this view. Were it so, he counters, the blood should have been put at the outer-courtyard gates where it could be easily seen, not merely at the front door. The Children of Israel closed their front gates, and slaughtered the *korban* at dusk when no one was outside. They were required to remain at home and perform the sacrifice in secret. The Egyptians, in fact, did not even know that they planned to leave Egypt for more than three days. Therefore, says Ibn Ezra, the blood must be viewed as a redemption for everyone partaking of the roast lamb, a mark to be viewed by the *mashchis*, as in (*Yechezkel* 9:4), "Set a mark upon their foreheads."

HaKesav VeHaKabalah views the blood as a sign that the Jewish people in Egypt had repented:

> According to *Chazal*, the Jewish people in Egypt had worshiped idols, and this prevented their redemption. Hashem, wishing to purge them of sin, commanded that they bring the *Korban Pesach*. By slaughtering the alien gods they had worshiped, they could demonstrate their full repentance.

Now, when one is to show his unequivocal love for someone, he does not allow fear to prevent him from fulfilling the wishes of that person, even if danger is involved. Hashem therefore commanded that the slaughtering of the idol should include three actions performed in the open streets and markets of Egypt, before the eyes of the inhabitants with no regard for the tremendous danger that the Egyptians might become enraged. The Egyptians, seeing their gods degraded, were quite liable to rise up to massacre the Jewish people, as Moshe had [told Pharaoh] (Sh'mos 8:22), "Could we sacrifice the sacred animal of the Egyptians before their very eyes without their stoning us?" Nonetheless, the Jewish people were to ignore such risks. With ostentatious and brazen contempt for the Egyptians they were to bring the animals home.

Moreover, the slaughter was to be carried out by large family groups, with great fanfare showing no fear of the enemy. As if these first two conditions were not burden enough, the lamb was to be consumed with great publicity as well. This was to consist of smearing its blood upon the doors and lintels of their homes, to the great despair of the Egyptians. That way, all Egyptian passersby would be able to see that their deity was being consumed. Would they not be driven to distraction by their desire to avenge the Children of Israel with sword and spear? Despite these risks, Hashem's will would be performed without fear. This sign was a wondrous mark of their full repentance and devotion to Hashem, and their absolute rejection of idolatry. It was a "sign" of their good intentions and sincerity towards Hashem. His pity was thus aroused not to destroy them as they deserved for having become idolatrous like the Egyptians.

Indeed, in Mechilta R' Yitzchak states, "The blood was not placed inside but outside their homes, so that the Egyptians, on seeing it, would be made heartsick." This proves that the blood was meant to demonstrate courage.

HaKesav VeHaKabalah explains that the root of the word וְרָאִיתִי — "and I will see" — can mean "to choose," as in (Bereishis 41:33), "יֵרֶא פַרְעֹה — "Now let Pharaoh choose a discreet, wise man." Hence, the statement (Sh'mos 12:13), "and I will see the blood," connotes Hashem's choosing the Jewish people by virtue of the sign of true repentance which they exhibited outside their homes. This explanation is parallel to Rabbenu Bachya's, quoted briefly above. Yet, it affords deeper meaning to the blood, attributing to it not just a show of faith, but of repentance motivated by love, and severance from the idolatry with which the Jewish people were stained. This is an outward sign, unlike Akeidah and others who say that it was inwardly directed to influence the Children of Israel themselves. It may very well be that the debate alluded to in the *Mechilta*, whether the blood was placed in or outside the home, hinges on the various opinions among *Chazal* pertaining to the essence of the sign, as pondered by subsequent commentators.

৺§ Severance from Idolatry

Chazal in several places view *Korban Pesach* as serving to break the ties to idolatry. This is no innovation of the later commentaries. Consider *Sh'mos Rabbah* 16:

> We find that when the Jewish people were in Egypt they worshiped idols, as it is written (*Yechezkel* 20:8), "They did not cast away the abominations of their eyes." Hashem told Moshe, "As long as the Jewish people worship the gods of Egypt they shall not be redeemed. Go, tell them to abandon their evil deeds and atone for their idolatry." That is what is written (*Sh'mos* 12:21): "Draw and take for yourselves" — Draw your hands from idolatry and take for yourselves lambs, and slaughter the Egyptian gods and perform the *Pesach*.

Mechilta as well mentions several times that when their redemption began, the Children of Israel were commanded to renounce their idolatry. To allow time for this to occur, the lambs were only slaughtered four days after they were taken.

"Draw and take for yourselves" is likewise interpreted by *Mechilta*, "Draw away from idolatry and cling to *mitzvos*." Furthermore, the refusal of the Children of Israel to heed Moshe's tidings due to "impatience and harsh labor" is explained there in terms of "their difficulty in separating themselves from idolatry."

Ramban suggests that the purpose in sacrificing the *Pesach* lamb was to convince the Children of Israel that the horoscope had nothing to do with their departure from Egypt since they went out in the sign of Aries, representing the maximum strength of the lamb, the Egyptians' god. But even he ultimately prefers *Chazal's* view that this *mitzvah* served to sever them from idolatry and to degrade the Egyptian deity.

Akeidah elaborates, providing a basis for the commentary of *HaKesav VeHaKabalah* quoted above:

> It was publicly well known that harming even the smallest part of the lambs or sheep was tantamount to abusing their god, leading

to capital punishment. Now, in an instant the tables were turned. The miserable Jews plundered the choice flocks of their masters which were worshiped as Divine. A pathetic and wretched people who were enslaved lifted their hands against the herd of animals that were embraced as gods by their masters. Each took a lamb and bound it to his bedpost, in full view of the Egyptians (*Mishnah, Keilim* 19:2). No one could stop them as they watched over the lambs for three days or as they slaughtered them in the afternoon of the fourth. The lamb's blood cried out from the doorpost, but none could do anything to prevent it. So that all would recognize the outline of a lamb, it was not boiled in water but roasted, including the head, legs and internal organs. With casual contempt, the Children of Israel consumed all its flesh down to the bone, and what remained at dawn was burnt. Wild dogs could not bark. Likewise, the Egyptian masses, accustomed to the reverent treatment of sheep, seethed with frustrated anger at this affront.

Akeidah's source is *Zohar Devarim* which explains the roasting of the lambs in accordance with the command (*Devarim* 7:25), "And burn their idols in fire." Likewise, the preparation according to which the lamb was to be consumed complete with head, legs and internal organs was to make clear to the Egyptians that their deities had been burnt.

The idea of the *Pesach* as severing the Jewish people from idolatry is made explicit in *Yechezkel* 20:6-7.

On that day I raised My hand to take them out of Egypt, to the land I spied out for them, flowing with milk and honey, the most beautiful of all lands. Then I said to them, "Cast away every man the abominations of his eyes. Do not defile yourselves with the idols of Egypt. I am Hashem your God."

From this it is clear that the Children of Israel were submerged in idolatry, and were commanded to turn away from it before leaving Egypt. As *Chazal* relate, when they stood with their backs to the sea, the prosecuting angel complained, "Are they any less idolatrous than the Egyptians?" The slaughter of the *Pesach* is therefore tied to Hashem's promise (*Sh'mos* 12:12), "I shall punish the gods of Egypt." These punishments were meant to teach the Jewish people that the Egyptian gods were worthless, and certainly no match against the strength and might of the Creator. The same purpose was served by the fearless destruction of idolatry by the Children of Israel themselves, which found expression in the slaughter of the Egyptians' flocks before the Egyptians' eyes.

Ma'asei Hashem states that all the gods of Egypt destined for punishment were believed by the Egyptians to draw their power from the lamb, the chief Egyptian deity. They considered holy, and treated as godlike, any person born under the sign of Aries, the Lamb. Hashem punished those human-gods together with the firstborn. This, in fact, is why the Torah states (*Bamidbar* 33:4), "And the Egyptians were still burying all their firstborn whom Hashem had smitten, and He destroyed their gods." In other words, they were burying the human-gods who were killed together with all of the firstborn.

Thus, Hashem commanded the Children of Israel to slaughter the lamb, the chief Egyptian deity, while He Himself destroyed all those Egyptians born under the sign of Aries and whom the Egyptians considered godlike. These, the Children of Israel lacked the power to destroy. (Several commentaries, among them *Ramban* and *S'forno*, follow the *Zohar* in interpreting any reference to "the gods of Egypt" as the angelic princes appointed over Egypt. *Ma'asei Hashem*, however, questions this, wondering why Hashem would smite the heavenly hosts.)

◆§ Warding off the Mashchis from Entering Your Homes

The blood above the door is a sign of the cessation of idolatry. It therefore distinguishes between the Jewish people and the Egyptians, and justifies exempting the former from suffering the last plague. Yet, the nature of this *mashchis* — "destroying angel" — remains unclear. Who is he? What role does he play when Hashem, Himself, is smiting Egypt? Why also must the Children of Israel remain indoors?

Rashi explains that once the *mashchis* is given freedom to destroy, it does not distinguish between righteous and wicked, and nighttime is when the demons have a free hand, as it is written (*Tehillim* 104:20), "[At night] all the beasts of the forest creep forth." It seems as though *Rashi* struggled over the meaning of *mashchis*, and finally identified it as the demonic force that does damage at night.

Ramban explains why *Rashi* preferred to view *mashchis* as forces existing every night rather than on this night alone: Because Hashem smote the Egyptians Himself, there was no need for Him to employ any additional force at this time. Nonetheless, having explained *Rashi's* view, he then challenges it. If the *mashchis* was not unique to that night, why then were they forbidden to leave their homes until daybreak?

In light of this question, *Ramban* offers his own view that Hashem's appearance in Egypt drew with it the appearance of a Heavenly retinue, as in (*Zechariah* 14:5), "Hashem my God shall come, and all the holy ones with You." As is normal with a king's appearance, certain emissaries were charged with clearing the way, and these emissaries are apt to strike down anything in their path.

Rabbenu Bachya and *Rivash* define *mashchis* as embodying *midas hadin* — the strict and harsh hand that accompanies the Heavenly retinue, with serious consequences for those encountered in the process.

Surprisingly, *Abudraham* identifies *mashchis* as the Holy One, Blessed is He, Himself, for Hashem was at that moment destroying the Egyptian firstborn. But *Ma'asei Hashem* expresses wonder at this explanation.

Abarbanel explains *mashchis* logically as referring to the Egyptians. Hashem promises that the Egyptians will not break into Jewish homes, rioting over the death of their firstborn. *Ma'asei Hashem* also offers a natural explanation. The tenth plague was a contagious blight that descended upon the world, striking all, but killing only the firstborn. This infectious disease affected all, Jew and Egyptian alike, but it led only to the death of the Egyptian firstborn.

Several commentaries explain Hashem's command (*Sh'mos* 12:22), "Let no one leave his home," in a similar way. *Shaar Bas Rabbim* contends that the prohibition was meant to prevent the recently circumcised Children of Israel from being exposed to the harmful air outdoors. On the other hand, *Tzror HaMor* maintains that the Children of Israel were commanded that if Pharaoh ordered them to leave in the middle of the night, they were to ignore him and remain home. Otherwise, they would have seemed to be taking advantage of the night to run away.

Some, however, quoting the Vilna Gaon and others, say that *mashchis* refers to the angel of death, whose appointed role is to take lives. The night that Hashem struck the firstborn none of the Children of Israel died, even of natural causes, so that the Egyptians would not be able to insist that Jews were harmed as well.

I heard a fine exposition regarding "Let no one leave his home." *Chazal* declare that a person saved from disaster by his own merits is permitted to watch as disaster befalls others. Yet, one saved through the merit of others is forbidden to watch as his neighbors fall. Thus, Hashem told Lot (*Bereishis* 19:17), "Do not look back." Since the Children of Israel were tainted with the sin of idolatry, they were forbidden to watch as catastrophe struck Egypt. They had to confine themselves to their homes.

IV.

Educating Children in the Paths of Torah and Belief

We are taught in *Mechilta*, relative to our *parashah*, that "the Torah speaks of four sons: one wise, one wicked, one simple and one unable to ask questions."

This *drash* is based on the four occurrences of the word "son" in the Torah associated with *yetzias Mitzraim* — the Exodus from Egypt. The first three are from our *parashah*, the fourth is from *Devarim* (6:20):

(a) "And when it happens that your sons ask, 'What is this service to you?' "

(b) "And when it happens that your son asks you tomorrow, 'What is this?' "

(c) "And you shall tell your son on that day."

(d) "And when it happens that your son shall ask you tomorrow, as follows, 'What are these testimonies, statutes and judgments which Hashem our God commanded you?' "

The same *drash* appears in the Jerusalem Talmud, *Pesachim* 10, with some variation. Instead of "a simple son", we find one who is "foolish." Regarding the wise son, we find, "Tell him 'With a strong hand Hashem took us out of Egypt.' " And regarding the foolish son, we find the same advice the *Mechilta* offers regarding the wise son: "Teach him the laws of the [*korban*] *Pesach*: 'We do not proceed to any dessert after eating the *Pesach*.' "

The commentators of the Jerusalem Talmud provide explanations and reasons for the variations that differ with the *Mechilta*. I shall deal with one particularly puzzling difference. This is the manner in which the verse quoted by the Jerusalem Talmud, in reference to the wise son, differs from the source in the Torah. There, and in the *Mechilta*, the son asks (*Devarim* 6:20), "What are these testimonies . . . which Hashem our God commanded אֶתְכֶם — you?" In the Jerusalem Talmud, the verse reads "which Hashem our God commanded אוֹתָנוּ — us."

The Vilna Gaon maintains that "you" and not "us" is, in fact, the proper version in both texts. Yet, the *acharonim* still strive to explain our version in the Jerusalem Talmud.

R' Menachem Kasher quotes R' David Hoffman who says that the intelligent question of the wise son can only be expressed in the form of "us" and not "you", since a good Jew perceives himself as included among the faithful by saying "which Hashem our God commanded." Such a son surely identifies with the laws of *Pesach*. As to the Torah's use of the word "you," this is not the wise son speaking, but Moshe. Moshe tells Israel, "You are going to enter the Land, not I, therefore the questions will be addressed to you. The son will be asking you and not me."

R' Hoffman shows how his perception of the text is correct: The verse in *Devarim* begins in the singular, "And when your son will ask you." As such, the end of the verse should also be in the singular form: ". . . which Hashem your God commanded אוֹתְךָ — you [singular]." Instead, the words appear in the plural form: "Which Hashem our God commanded אֶתְכֶם — you [plural]." This is not the response of a father to his son. It is, rather, Moshe addressing the Jewish people.

Ateres Zekeinim offers another explanation. The Jerusalem Talmud, as the *Mechilta*, recognizes that the son's question is addressed to the plural "you," as related by the Torah. But the use of the word "us" is intended to show that this son includes himself in the Exodus from Egypt.

If so, when the evil son uses the plural form "you," why do we not give him the benefit of the doubt and assume that he too means "us?"

The answer is to be found in the manner in which the wise and wicked sons pattern their speech. The wise son asks (*Devarim* 6:20), "What are these testimonies, statutes and judgments which Hashem our God commanded you?" Without "you" at the conclusion of his sentence, we might infer that his question pertains to all "the testimonies, statutes and judgments" in the entire Torah. His addition of "you" limits his context to what he sees before him, i.e., the *Pesach* holiday. On the other hand, the wicked son whose question is, "What is this service?" obviously relates to *Pesach*. He has no cause to conclude with the word "you." Necessarily, then, his addition of "you" emphasizes his reservations. It is as if he wishes to say: "Your service, not mine!"

The first *mitzvah* of the Exodus is explicitly tied to Jewish education. *Avnei Ezel* observes that the Jewish people had for the first time reached a state of holiness, and become an *am segulah* — "a chosen people". This then was the appropriate time for them to be taught that Jewish education is the foundation of our faith. That is why when the *tannaim* were engrossed in telling about the Exodus from Egypt on the night of *Pesach*, their students came and announced, "It is time to recite the *Shema*." The *Shema*, synonymous with our accepting the yoke of

Heaven, includes the command (*Devarim* 6:7), "And you shall teach them to your children." The students thus made clear their understanding that our Exodus from Egypt and acceptance of the yoke of Heaven are impossible without providing our children with Jewish education.

We can now more easily understand the wording used by the wise son. By saying, "which Hashem our God commanded," he accepts the yoke of Heaven, and at the same time reminds parents of their special obligation to educate and guide their children in Torah. This is the *mitzvah* "which Hashem our God commanded you" — the parents.

ᴥ§ The Wise and Wicked Sons

Both the *rishonim* and *acharonim* dwell on the reason why our *parashah* is said to feature the wicked son, whereas in *Devarim* the reference is to the wise son. *Ritva* holds that the use of the phrase "testimonies, statutes and judgments" in *Devarim* indicates the wisdom of the questioner, as does his very interest in the *korban Pesach*.

Yet, how do we know that *korban Pesach* is what interests him? *Shibbolei HaLeket* says this can be proven from the Torah's answer (*Devarim* 6:21,24), "Tell your son, 'We were slaves ... And Hashem commanded us to perform all these statutes,' " whereby the use of the word "statutes" implies the reference to the *korban Pesach*, as in (*Sh'mos* 12:43), "These are the statutes of the *Pesach*."

The wise son's use of "you" seems also to imply his deliberate exclusion from the Jewish people. Yet, *Rashi*, *Rashbam* and *Rokeach* explain that this is not the case, for the wise son emphasizes (*Devarim* 6:20), "which Hashem *our* God commanded." For these commentaries, the word אֶתְכֶם — you, as used by the wise son, is read as if it were vowelized אִתְּכֶם — with you, i.e., "which Hashem commanded you and me together."

Shibbolei HaLeket holds that the wise son necessarily uses the pronoun "you" in accordance with the *mishnah* (*Pesachim* 8:7), which makes clear that one may not slaughter a *korban Pesach* if no one over age thirteen will partake of it. The wise son, who is presumably a minor, expresses himself as he does because the law excludes him from this *mitzvah*.

By contrast, the son in our *parashah* asks (*Sh'mos* 12:26), "What is this service לָכֶם — to you?" He thereby excludes himself from the Jewish people. According to *Rashi*, this must be the wicked son speaking.

Shibbolei HaLeket finds the first hint of wickedness in this son's emphatic use of the expression, הָעֲבֹדָה הַזֹּאת — this service. The word in

Hebrew — עֲבוֹדָה — can imply drudgery and inconvenience.

The author of *Chukas HaPesach* knows that this is the wicked son speaking, based on the fact that the verse reads (ibid.), "When your sons will *tell* you," and not, "when your sons will *ask* you." The wicked son does not ask his father anything. He tells him bluntly, in an attempt to raise doubts regarding matters of faith and belief.

The *drash* authorities focus on the way the wise son's question is introduced (*Devarim* 6:20), "And when it comes to pass that he may ask you tomorrow . . ." The wise son first fulfills the *mitzvah*. Only on the morrow does he ask questions so he can understand. The wicked son, however, asks even before he has fulfilled the *mitzvah*, in order to avoid its performance.

R' Samson Raphael Hirsch deftly applies a fine point of grammar, albeit one previously noticed by the Vilna Gaon. The response to the wicked son does not begin, "Say to him," but simply (*Sh'mos* 12:27), "Say." The wicked son asks no question. He wishes only to infuse us with his own doubt. Therefore, we owe him no response. Instead we should confront his doubts with our own holy faith. Therefore he is to be told (ibid.), "It is the *korban Pesach* for Hashem," You are to emphasize the stability and consistency of your faith. This will influence him more than anything.

Chazal knew that the verse does not represent a direct answer to his words. They therefore said that our response must be emphatic: "This is on account of what Hashem did for me." We say "for me," and not "for him." Had he been there, he would not have been redeemed. The statement, "It is the *korban Pesach* for Hashem" demonstrates the father's identification with faith, although he has offered the wicked son no direct answer. Sometimes, such a display works better than the most convincing arguments. The wicked son is more impressed by our religious fervor than by any logical reasoning.

R' Samson Raphael Hirsch, in *Nachalas HaSar*, makes another point as well. The son who is wise in Torah does not ask specifically about the rhyme and reason of the *korban Pesach*. Rather, he is interested in understanding the deeper meaning behind all the laws of the Torah.

Therefore, the *Haggadah* declares, "You too must tell him of the laws of the *Pesach*" — take him back to the very beginning, to the redemption from Egypt and the first *mitzvos* Hashem commanded at that time. Then he will grasp the whole of the Torah and *mitzvos*. If he personally experiences Hashem's unique revelation at the Exodus, he will understand everything.

The answer to the wise son's question offers a key to the entire Torah: "We do not proceed to the dessert after eating the *korban Pesach*," i.e., our senses must never be dulled to the great experience of the Exodus. Its taste must never leave our mouth. Then we will easily understand all the testimonies, statutes and judgments of the Torah.

Abarbanel, in his commentaries on the Torah and the *Haggadah*, enlarges on many of the ideas already mentioned regarding the wise and wicked sons, adding his own embellishment. The wicked son, he says, does not refer to a single person: The Torah says (*Sh'mos* 12:26), "And if it comes to pass that your sons may tell you." This emphasizes the great variety of arguments employed by the various wicked persons. Also, the wicked son's use of לָכֶם (i.e., the plural form of "*you*") alludes to different types of heresy.

The wicked son denies: (a) the Divine origin of Torah and *mitzvos*, attributing them to man; and (b) the connection between the *mitzvos* of this night and the events of the Exodus, viewing all that we do as only לָכֶם — for you, i.e., for personal gratification and to indulge one's appetite.

In face of these challenges, the Torah commands us to publicly proclaim the Divine, spiritual essence of the *mitzvos* of *Pesach* (*Sh'mos* 12:27), "And you shall say, 'It is the *korban Pesach* for Hashem.'" It is Divine, both in origin and purpose. Since it is eaten on a full stomach, after we are already physically satiated, one may not claim, as the wicked son tries to do, that it is an exercise in gluttony. By repeating the words of verse 27, we undermine the wicked son's entire world view, and emerge stronger in our faith.

Yet, the *Haggadah* goes on to say that we must not be satisfied with this goal alone. We must "set his teeth on edge" and shame him for daring to deny the uniqueness of our faith. "You must also tell him." You, who hear him, must not restrain yourself from responding to his heresy. Tell him, "This is on account of what Hashem did for me. By virtue of our faith, and our firmly rooted heritage, we were redeemed from the house of bondage. Had the wicked son been there, he would have assimilated among the gentiles, and no trace would have remained of him or his children."

◆§ Responses of the Torah and the Haggadah to the Wicked Son's Question

The Torah's response to the wicked son is not identical to that given by the *Haggadah*. *Akeidas Yitzchak* explains exquisitely how they differ. The Torah recommends that the father respond (*Sh'mos* 12:27), "It is the *korban Pesach* for Hashem, for He passed over the houses of the Children of Israel in Egypt. While he smote the Egyptians, he spared us." This verse states an explicit theme: Hashem separated the Jewish people from the Egyptians, to reward one and punish the other.

The *Haggadah*, as well, stresses the theme of separateness. However, whereas the Torah distinguishes between two nations, the *Haggadah* distinguishes between the guilty and innocent of a single nation, as it is stated: "This is on account of what Hashem did for me when I left Egypt — For me and not for him. Had he been there, he would not have been redeemed."

Ritva contrasts the responses of the Torah and the *Haggadah* differently. The Torah, by introducing the wicked son's question with (*Sh'mos* 12:26), "Your sons may tell you," includes various types of rebellious children, some of whom rebel out of ignorance, and others knowingly. The generation of the Exodus, for example, were not rebels. Judaism was something new to them, hence they must not be blamed for their question, even if it is posed in unacceptable fashion. The Torah commands us to appease such children, to draw them close, explaining the reasoning behind the *korban Pesach*. The *Haggadah*, on the other hand, is referring to rebellious children of later generations. These know their Maker, and intentionally rebel against Him. Such children must not be pampered. Rather, we must shame them and "set their teeth on edge."

Oznayim LaTorah explains similarly. The wicked son of the Torah is not a rebel but an *am ha'aretz* — an ignoramus. As *Chazal* say, "The generation of the desert received the evil tidings that the Jewish people are destined to forget the Torah." We must therefore teach and remind such children of the statutes of the *korban Pesach*. By contrast, the wicked son of the *Haggadah* is an intentional heretic. He requires stringent treatment.

Other commentaries see in the Torah's answer a direct response to the wicked son's complaint in the *Haggadah*. The Torah's answer emphasizes the idea of separation between the guilty and the innocent. The wicked son complains that the *mitzvos* involving the *korban Pesach* are *avodah*, i.e., a burdensome drudgery. The Torah therefore responds that for us, this *avodah* is the *zevach Pesach* (the *Pesach* sacrifice). The word *zevach* implies a willing act, as written (*Vayikra* 22:29), לִרְצֹנְכֶם תִּזְבָּחֻו — "Sacrifice it willingly." We observe the *mitzvos* out of love for Hashem. As *Chasam Sofer* says, all our lives we sacrifice ourselves, "like a *korban Pesach* for Hashem."

There is a great gap between the wicked son's view of *avodah* and our own idea of self-devotion. The two can never meet.

Kesav Sofer, however, decreases the gap between the two sons. The wicked son's query, he says, concerns only one *mitzvah*, the *korban*

Pesach. He sees his father struggling on his own to slaughter the lamb and to fulfill all the other *mitzvos* bound up in this. He sees that his father takes on no helpers, although he could if he wished. Puzzled, he therefore asks, "Why must this *mitzvah* be for you (i.e., carried out by yourselves) more than are the other *mitzvos*?"

The Torah responds, "It is the *korban Pesach* for Hashem, for He passed over the houses of the Children of Israel in Egypt." Hashem Himself performed the entire act of our rescue, He and no other. He Himself passed over the houses of the Children of Israel. Therefore, by right, we too must ourselves take the trouble to fulfill the *mitzvos* of the *korban Pesach*. We do not allow anyone else to take our place.

R' Meir Simchah of Dvinsk invests spiritual significance in the wicked son's question and the answer given. The wicked son's attitude is well known to us. He claims that during our presence in Exile there is no rhyme or reason to observing the *mitzvos* of *Pesach*, since they are symbols of freedom. He asks, "What is this service to you? — to you, Diaspora Jews! To you who dwell in the dark shadow of death!"

The Torah responds, "It is the *korban Pesach* for Hashem." The *mitzvos* of *Pesach* carry a freedom more exalted than anything physical. They symbolize the eternal struggle between holiness and impurity. Elsewhere the Torah says (*Vayikra* 23:41), "Celebrate it as a festival to Hashem." If you understand the Divine significance of the *mitzvah* of *Pesach*, then you will celebrate it forever, in every age and under all circumstances.

The expositors of the Torah have always sought to present the wicked son's question, and the answer given him, in terms relevant to their own age. *Chida* states that the wicked son's criticism is aimed against the necessity for practical *mitzvos*. Instead, the wicked son insists that having a Jewish heart is what really counts, in the pattern of the so-called "enlightened". The wicked son therefore asks, "What is this service to you?" What need have we of *mitzvos* that involve performance and activity?

In response, the *Haggadah* offers the following advice: "On account of this . . ." On account of such *mitzvos* as the blood of circumcision and of the *korban Pesach* were we redeemed. Had this "enlightened one" been there, he would not have been redeemed, for he scorns the *mitzvos* which require concrete performance.

Similar, but in a humorous vein, is the explanation of the Magid of Koznitz. The wicked son argues against observing *mitzvos* that involve eating and drinking. He mocks the connection between the physical and the spiritual. Therefore, we must "blunt his teeth." If he does not recognize the need to fulfill mitzvos involving eating, he does not need his teeth, and he has no right to eat. His disposition is that of a body without a soul, which cannot exist.

⊷§ Tidings of Children

Immediately following the wicked son's question and his father's response (Sh'mos 12:26-27), the Torah states, "The people bowed down and prostrated themselves." *Mechilta* comments that their behavior was a joyous response to Hashem's tidings regarding their children.

The commentaries are puzzled by the significance of these tidings. Inasmuch as the preceding verse concerns the wicked son, what joy could they feel in being informed that they would produce wicked children?

Chassidic literature answers that even the heretical son is joined to his Jewish roots. As *Bnei Yisaschar* notes, there is always hope that even the wicked son will improve in the future. This hope is implied by the Torah's prelude to the wicked son's question. The words, "and it will come to pass," imply happiness and hope. True, "had he been there, he would not have been redeemed." Yet, since he has in fact been redeemed, he is now here with us, hence we must not lose hope for him.

The *Haggadah* uses the word אֶחָד — one — alongside each of the four sons: one wise, one wicked . . . etc. This teaches that every one of the sons has a link to the Ultimate One — Hashem.

Shem MiShmuel explains the message of the tidings differently. On the *Seder* night, he says, we must also answer the questions of the wicked son, because it is a moment of repentance even for souls already residing in *Gehinnom*. The *Seder* night is an opportunity from Hashem to draw the wicked son to holiness. These are the tidings that the Jewish people received concerning their sons.

Furthermore, *Shem Mishmuel* declares, the very fact that a particular figure is personally dealt with by the Torah indicates that he has a share in *olam haba* — the world to come. For example, *Zohar* tells us that Moshe was uncertain whether Tzelafchad, who had died in the desert for some unnamed sin (*Rashi, Bamidbar* 27:3), had a share in the world to come. Yet, when Moshe heard Hashem dealing with the case of Tzelafchad's daughters, mentioning him by name in the verse (*Bamidbar* 27:7), "The daughters of Tzelafchad speak justly," Moshe knew then that he did have a share. Similarly, in our *parashah*, the Torah deals personally with the wicked son's questions. This bodes well for his fate, and signifies that he will not be lost to the Jewish people. Thus, it represents good tidings for the Jewish people.

The wicked son complains, "What is this service to you?" — Why are you suddenly celebrating events you yourselves neither saw nor felt? Were you at the Exodus? The wicked son sees only himself. His people's history and spiritual unity are unimportant to him. Had he been in Egypt, he would not have been redeemed. Rather, he would have died during the three days of darkness for denying the chief essence of our nation, which remains constant in every generation.

Interpreting the wicked son's question, the zealous and brilliant R' Shaul Brach offers an idea that is highly relevant to our day. The wicked son is not satisfied with his own wicked heresy, but must force his poison on others as well. It is not bad enough that he eats no *matzah* and performs no other *mitzvos*, but he incites and compels others to do as he does. He mocks the observant saying, "What is this service to you?"

Those who tried to force their own way on others, turning them against the Torah, were destroyed during the three days of darkness so they would do no harm later on. Had this evil son lived then, he too would have been destroyed. Such people, who impose their wicked ways on others, cannot be saved. Regarding them we pray (*Shemoneh Esrei*), "May all heretics and evildoers be destroyed in an instant."

Many other timeless ideas could have been compiled from our *parashah* as well. I cannot quote them all, as they are simply beyond measure.

V.

The Philosophical Foundation of Tefillin

wice in our *parashah* (*Sh'mos* 13:9 and 16) the Torah links the *mitzvah* of *tefillin* to *yetzias Mitzraim* — the Exodus from Egypt:

(a) "It shall be for you a sign upon your arm and a remembrance between your eyes ... that Hashem took you out of Egypt."

(b) "It shall be for you as a sign upon your arm, and as a frontlet between your eyes that with a strong hand did Hashem take you out of Egypt."

Rashbam explains these verses according to their plain meaning:

It should be for you a perpetual remembrance, as if [these events] were written on your hand, analogous to (*Shir HaShirim* 8:6), "Set me as a seal upon your heart," and adjacent to your eyes as gold ornaments that are intended to adorn the forehead.

Doubtless, *Rashbam* wishes to emphasize the purpose of *tefillin*, and to state that the external act of putting them on leads to the remembrance mentioned above.

All the commentaries view the religious deed embodied in the *mitzvah* of *tefillin* as a basic act for inculcating the fundamentals of faith. Nonetheless, Ibn Ezra reacts sharply against the idea of *tefillin* as a symbol, saying that we are forbidden to consider any part of the Torah as a metaphor.

Both *rishonim* and *acharonim* agree that the Torah here attributes special importance to the *mitzvah* act as vital for inculcating faith in Hashem and Divine Providence. The *korban Pesach* and the accompanying *mitzvos* bolster our faith once a year. On the other hand, *tefillin* is meant to be a constant, perpetual means towards this end, serving to protect our *yetzer tov* — "good impulse" — and to help us to overcome the evil within us. As *Rambam* states (*Hilchos Tefillin* and *Mezuzah* 4:25): "As long as an individual has *tefillin* upon his head and forearm, he will behave modestly and fear Heaven. Neither frivolity nor chatter will attract him, and he will think no evil thoughts, for his heart will be focused upon truth and justice." *Rambam's* words are based upon *Chazal* who said, "Whoever has *tefillin* upon his head . . . is certain to be protected from sin" (*Menachos* 43).

Nonetheless, the Chassidic literature states that it is not enough for us to place *tefillin* on our heads. Rather, we must grasp their meaning with our heads. Only then we will be assured of not sinning.

◆§ Perpetual Struggle Between Matter and Spirit

Sefer HaChinuch (*Mitzvah* 421) explains *tefillin* as an aid to man's spirit in his struggle with matter. By nature, man's physical self would seek beastly pleasure if not for his heavenly soul that prevents him from sinning. But the soul resides in man's body, far from its source, and is in danger of being overcome by matter. It therefore requires many safeguards to protect it from its evil neighbor, within whose reach it finds itself:

Hashem wished to make His holy nation meritorious, so He commanded us to appoint mighty guards to protect us. For this reason we were commanded to study Torah day and night; that we attach *tzitzis* to our four-cornered garments; *mezuzos* to our doors and *tefillin* to our head and arm. All such devices function as a reminder that we must not exploit our fellow man, and that we must follow neither our eyes nor the temptation of our hearts . . . And now, my children, consider how much stronger we are in body than in spirit, for we sometimes lose control of ourselves despite all these [safeguards]. May the merciful Hashem help and protect us.

This reasoning coincides with the words of *Chazal* and *Rambam* brought above. As R' Yehudah Halevi states in the *Kuzari* (3:1), "Through *tefillin* we sanctify the site of our minds, and the wellspring of our energies in serving the Creator."

Just how is this act carried out? Obviously, by delving into those *parshiyos* of the Torah contained inside the *tefillin*, "which involve the unity and uniqueness of Hashem," as well as the miracles He performed for us.

Ramban elaborates on the manner in which the Exodus and all other miracles have influenced the thinking of the Jewish people throughout the generations, if we hold their memory in our hearts. Such miracles strengthen our faith in Divine Providence, and in Hashem as Creator.

As Hashem does not reorder the existing scheme of things in every generation, we are commanded to refresh our memories of those events and to instill them in the hearts of our children. For this reason we were severely warned to keep the *mitzvos* that serve as reminders. We must inscribe these miracles upon the doorpost of our houses, upon our arms and between our eyes, and we must recall them by reciting the *Shema* several times a day. All these acts serve to silence the heretic, whoever would deny the truth of those miracles — witnessed by Jewish eyes alone — which testify to Hashem's uniqueness and Providence.

HaKesav VeHaKabalah describes with profundity the philosophical foundation of *tefillin*. They are a symbol of *splendor* — תִּפְאָרֶת, as the *Targum* translates to Aramaic the words of the Prophet Yechezkel (24:17), "Attach your splendid headdress." The word פְּאֵרְךָ — "your splendid" — is rendered טוֹטָפְתָךְ — "your *tefillin*".

The Torah uses the term "splendid" to refer to spiritual supremacy. The Temple garments worn by the *Kohen* are to be (*Sh'mos* 28:2) "for glory and splendor." Of the Temple and its vessels we find (*Yeshayahu* 60:7), "I will glorify the House of My splendor," and (*Tehillim* 78:61), "His splendor is in the enemy's hand."

Tefillin too are a garment of splendor for the Jewish people. They show that Hashem's treatment of the Jewish people is supernatural, not natural, as is the case for other nations. The gentiles are commanded only to perform logic-based and society-related *mitzvos*, being that they themselves are bound by the laws of nature. The Jewish people, however, transcend nature, as does, therefore, their conduct. It is this condition which *tefillin*, the garment of splendor, exhibits.

Pri Megadim is on target with his literal translation of *tefillin* in *Orach Chaim* 25. He holds that the word stems from the root *aflaiyah* — "segregation", and that *tefillin* serve to separate Israel from the nations. Hashem made this distinction especially prominent at the time of the Exodus, and we must guard over it lest it be diluted in the course of time. Through our observance of the *mitzvos*, we cause this separation to be actively and genuinely manifested.

◄§ Not by Might, Nor by Power

Subjugating the mind and senses to serving Hashem is only possible if we reflect upon His deeds. At the same time, the *mitzvah* of *tefillin* itself fills an educational role with regard to man's action. *Meiri* offers an interesting explanation of why there are four compartments in the *shel rosh* (the head *tefillin*) and only one in the *shel yad* (the arm *tefillin*). In *Tehillim* 119:10, King David says, "With all my heart have I sought you out," i.e., with all my five senses. The head is the seat of four senses — sight, hearing, taste and smell — which correspond to the four compartments of the *shel rosh*. The arm, however, possesses only one sense, that of touch, hence the *shel yad* has only one compartment.

Kli Yakar extends the above to the significance of the choice of the left arm, i.e., the "weak arm," over the right one in placing the *tefillin*. Doing so draws attention to the fact that in Egypt our "hand was weak," and only "the hand of Hashem" rescued and redeemed us. From this we can understand that we must not attribute any success we have to our own might or power. Rather (*Sh'mos* 13:14), "With a strong hand did Hashem take us out of Egypt." Because Hashem did so, we are commanded to subjugate human energy and activity to the service of Hashem. R' Samson Raphael Hirsch and others interpret the *mitzvah* of *tefillin* in much the same way as *Kli Yakar*.

Both *rishonim* and *acharonim* discuss the fact that the left arm is preferred over the right for the *mitzvah* of *tefillin*. Ibn Ezra quotes R' Moshe HaKohen, who said that in *Tanach*, the use of the word "hand" usually refers to the left hand as in (*Yeshayahu* 48:13), "My [left] hand (*yadi*) laid the foundation of the earth and My right one (*yemini*) spanned the heavens," or (*Shoftim* 5:26)," She put her [left] hand to the tent peg and her right one to the workman's hammer."

Ibn Ezra rejects R' Moshe HaKohen's inference with the surprising remark that "the Oral Tradition is strong and needs no reinforcement." Yet, *Chazal* themselves employ the same inference in *Menachos* 36 and in the *Mechilta*, although some *amoraim* employ different proofs.

Or HaChaim explains the symbolism behind the concept of the *left* hand. In the Torah, "a great hand" implies kindness (*chessed*) and "a strong hand" implies strict justice (*din*). (Sometimes, "a great hand" can be used when the attribute of mercy acquiesces to the execution of strict justice, but generally each attribute has its own term.) Now, the Torah says (*Sh'mos* 13:14), "With a strong hand did Hashem take us out," implying that He applied might and strict justice in carrying out the Exodus. As *tefillin* commemorate the Exodus, we put them on our left hand, for left (according to Kabbalah) corresponds to strict justice.

An interesting interpretation of "with a strong hand" is found in *Haamek Davar*, by *Netziv*. The Holy One, Blessed is He, gave the Jewish people Torah and *mitzvos* to educate and adapt them to serving Hashem. The Jewish people did not want to leave Egypt and assume the yoke of Heaven by themselves. They had to be forced to leave, as *Rashi* comments on the verse, "With a strong hand will Hashem drive them out of Pharaoh's land." This means that it was necessary for Hashem to force the Jewish people to leave Egypt against their will. We must understand, therefore, that at the time of the Exodus, the Jewish people had not yet struck their roots in the *mitzvos*, and *tefillin* was intended to do this. They, the *tefillin*, create a perpetual link between man and Hashem through the holiness emanating from the *mitzvah* and the eternal lesson it teaches. According to *Chizkuni*, the *shel rosh* serves to recall Hashem's signs and wonders, as written (*Devarim* 28:10), "All the peoples of the earth shall see." On the other hand, the *shel yad* recalls Hashem's strong hand.

According to *Meshech Chochmah*, *tefillin* also serve to encourage us in times of trouble. Even when our hand is weak, we will still emerge from darkness to light. Even when our heads are plagued by doubt and spiritual confusion, we will draw strength from Hashem Whose outstretched arm has reigned throughout history.

R' Avraham Yitzchak Kook states that the events in Egypt are not a one-time occurrence. Rather, the gates of Divine light remain revealed for all time. Hashem's outstretched arm is perpetually spread over the universe, purifying souls of their dross, thereby elevating them to their holy source. The holy spirit embodied in the *shel rosh* continues to hover in the world from the time of the Exodus and up to the present.

Since then, the heavenly fountain has been opened and its Divine light has spread throughout the world, whereby all creation has merited the abundant and ever-present light of Hashem.

~§ Two Separate Mitzvos

Our philosophic discussion of the purpose of *tefillin* is carried on in the halachic sphere. *Rambam* treats the *shel rosh* and *shel yad* as two separate *mitzvos*, so that the lack of one does not invalidate using the other. Abarbanel and others find this difficult to understand due to the significant unity of the *shel rosh* and *shel yad*. Even so, the commentaries do acknowledge that the two types of *tefillin* actually differ in significance.

Torah Shleimah quotes *Midrash HaGadol* and *Mechilta* of R' Shimon bar Yochai in agreement with *Rambam*: " 'It shall be for you as a sign upon your arm.' From this we deduce that the lack of either *tefillin shel rosh* or *shel yad* does not invalidate using the other."

Struggling to understand this, *Torah Shleimah* eventually focuses on the law that the *shel yad* is worn on יָדְכָה [an unusual form of the expression יָדְךְ — "your arm" — which, *Chazal* say, indicates that the *shel yad* is placed on the יַד כֵּהָה — "the weaker arm". This term confirms that the *shel yad* carries special significance. Therefore, it is distinguished legally as well and treated as a separate *mitzvah*.

Rambam, however, bases his ruling on *Menachos* 34 which states explicitly that the *shel yad* and *shel rosh* are distinct, separate *mitzvos*. The *mishnah* there states, "Having no *shel yad* does not preclude putting on the *shel rosh*, neither does having no *shel Rosh* preclude putting on the *shel Yad*." The Talmud comments:

> R' Chisda said, "Only regarding an individual who possesses both *shel Yad* and *shel Rosh* did the *tannaim* say that one does not detract from the other. Otherwise, it does." The rabbis asked him, ("Do you follow this ruling?") and he answered, "No! If someone does not have both *mitzvos* [i.e., a pair of *tefillin*], should he be unable to fulfill even one?"
>
> What is the basis of R' Chisda's original statement? It was a rabbinic decree lest a person become negligent [and not bother to buy both the *shel yad* and *shel Rosh* even when he can afford them].

From this source we see explicitly that the *shel Yad* and *shel Rosh* are considered two separate *mitzvos*.

Nonetheless, R' Avraham, *Rambam's* son, cites *Ma'asei Nissim* by R'

Daniel HaBavli, who challenges Rambam's ruling. *Chazal* say in Tractate *Sukkah* 36, "Why do we take the *esrog* in our left hand and the *lulav* in our right? Because the former comprises only one *mitzvah*, but the latter, three." Here we see that *Chazal* describe as a *mitzvah* even parts of a single *mitzvah*, although the components of *lulav* and *esrog*, which consist of the four species, are actually only one *mitzvah* among the total 613 *mitzvos*.

Without going into the defense which R' Avraham offers for the position of his father *Rambam*, we can assume one thing. The Talmud's calling *shel yad* and *shel rosh* "two *mitzvos*" in *Menachos* was probably not *Rambam's* sole source for considering them such, although this is the reason he quotes in *Sefer HaMitzvos*. More likely, his chief proof was the practical halachic ruling pronounced in that source: R' Chisda states, "If someone does not own both *mitzvos*, should he be unable to perform even one?"

In light of this reasoning, he determines practically that not having both types of *tefillin* does not deter one from putting on the type he has. From his conclusion we see prominently that there are two *mitzvos* before us, not just two parts of one *mitzvah*. This differs from the case of *lulav*, where although the four need not be bound together, the single *mitzvah* cannot be fulfilled unless all four types are present. Regarding *tefillin*, however, R' Chisda extends the phrase "two *mitzvos*" to the halachic realm, to teach that the absence of one type of *tefillin* does not invalidate the use of the second. This conclusion is the foundation of *Rambam's* legal determination, not the fact that *Chazal* called them "two *mitzvos*." After all, regarding *kriyas Shema* as well, *Chazal* refer to parts of the one *mitzvah* as separate *mitzvos*.

Legally determining the *shel yad* and *shel rosh* to comprise two *mitzvos* justifies philosophically attributing distinct meaning to each. The *shel yad* symbolizes Hashem's weakening the might of the wicked and destroying the power of idolatry, hence we must use our "weak arm." The *shel rosh*, on the other hand, symbolizes spiritual liberation from Egyptian defilement.

This distinction may be inherent in the text (*Sh'mos* 13:9), "It shall be for you a sign upon your arm and a remembrance between your eyes, so that Hashem's Torah will be on your lips, for with a strong hand did Hashem take you out of Egypt." Two elements surface here: (a) "So that Hashem's Torah will be on your lips" — this is the spiritual element; (b) "For with a strong hand" — this refers to the physical defeat of evil. These themes serve to explain the two *mitzvos* of *tefillin*.

Beshalach – בשלח

I.

The Desert Has Closed Them Off

Rishonim wonder why Hashem had to trick Pharaoh into thinking that the Children of Israel were trapped in the desert. After Pharaoh was shown Hashem's signs and wonders, he was afraid of pursuing the Jewish people unless he could be assured in some way that the situation had changed and that he would succeed in catching and once more enslaving them. Pharaoh was told that instead of bringing sacrifices in the desert as they said they would, the Children of Israel had fled. He took this as a sign that even Hashem Himself had not told him the whole truth, and that he apparently still had a chance of preventing their escape. Thus, despite the miracles of the ten plagues, he was not really convinced of Hashem's power. Hashem made the Jewish people seem entangled in the desert so Pharaoh would pursue them. Only thus could Hashem eventually remove Pharaoh's doubt and convince him that none can be saved from Hashem's exalted hand.

Ibn Ezra rejects any explanation of Hashem's act that caters to human logic. He states simply that Hashem's deep wisdom is incomprehensible to man, and that human wisdom is as nothing in comparison. Hashem could have compelled Pharaoh to pursue the Jewish people any way He wished, and it is beyond our intellectual means to understand why, with His profound logic, He chose to deceive him.

Or HaChaim, however, ventures an explanation. Hashem wished the Jewish people to sense that He was tricking Pharaoh into thinking they were entangled in the desert. Knowing this, they would have the strength not to grumble or scream. They would understand that all was being done for their own good, that for their own benefit Hashem wished to set a trap for Pharaoh. They were afraid, and they criticized Hashem. Out of fear they had started to blaspheme. For this reason

Hashem employed this conspicuous strategy, to prove to them that Hashem had a deliberate plan.

Abarbanel explains this in an entirely different manner. The only purpose of the deceit was to drown Pharaoh and his army in the sea, and thus to frighten those nations whose lands the Jewish people were going to conquer. Seemingly, drowning the Egyptians was unnecessary as they had already received their full measure of punishment through the ten plagues, and the Jews had received the Egyptians' property in return for their labor, after which the Egyptians expelled the Children of Israel from Egypt. Hashem, however, wanted to keep His promise to bring them into the bountiful Land of Israel. He knew that the people leaving Egypt were at a low point, powerless to conquer large, fortified cities, as Moshe was to tell them (*Devarim* 9:1): "Hear, O Israel! Today you are crossing the Jordan to dispossess nations both larger and stronger than yours, cities great and fortified, reaching up to heaven."

Because of the Jews' lowly condition which made this effort difficult for them, Hashem in His kindness struck the Egyptians a dreadful blow that was publicized throughout the world. Hence, the splitting of the sea paved the way for the conquest of the Land of Israel (*Sh'mos* 15:13-16): "With Your kindness, You led this people that You redeemed ... Nations heard and shuddered; terror gripped those who dwell in Philistia. Edom's chiefs then panicked; trembling gripped the powerful ones of Moav; all of Canaan's residents melted away ... Until Your people crosses through, Hashem."

Similar are the words of Rachav (*Yehoshua* 2:9,10): "I know that Hashem gave you the land and that your fear took hold of us. All the residents of the land trembled before you, for we heard how Hashem dried up the Sea of Reeds before you when you were leaving Egypt."

Thus, the drowning of the Egyptians on the sea was not only a punishment to them for throwing the Children of Israel into the river, but a way of frightening those nations that the Jewish people were now going to conquer. Hashem tricked Pharaoh to make him pursue the Children of Israel. This led to the drowning of his army. The nations of Canaan were frightened by this. They saw the Jewish people by the sea in their state of inner weakness. Hashem therefore had to stun them once more with an enormous demonstration of His willingness to champion Israel's cause against Egypt and all other antagonists.

The plan of deception was to bring the Children of Israel to a spot between Migdol Eisam and the sea, where Pharaoh would be certain they had nowhere to flee. The desert cut them off. They could not travel in it because of the wild animals there. Before them stood the impassable sea. Migdol Eisam was a high place from which it was easy to wage an attack. Thus, the Children of Israel had entered a strait with no exit.

Pharaoh thought he would succeed here as he had not before. S'forno states that Pharaoh believed the Jewish people were cut off by the huge idol, Baal Tzafon, which he believed to be stronger than Hashem. Therefore, Pharaoh resumed his evil planning regarding the nation he had banished from his land. He saw Baal Tzafon as able to bewilder them on their way through the desert.

The words (Sh'mos 14:3), וְאָמַר פַּרְעֹה לִבְנֵי יִשְׂרָאֵל — "and Pharaoh will say to the Children of Israel," should be read as if written, וְאָמַר פַּרְעֹה עַל בְּנֵי יִשְׂרָאֵל — "Pharaoh will say of the Children of Israel" that they are entangled in the desert. In other words, Pharaoh will think this in his heart regarding them. Yet *Targum Yonasan* explains that Pharaoh was actually addressing Dassan and Aviram who had not yet left Egypt. According to this explanation of *Targum Yonasan* one may wonder when it was that they left Egypt. Perhaps it was only after Pharaoh and his army drowned. Perhaps they joined the Egyptians in chasing down the Children of Israel.

Eidus Bihoseif questions *Targum Yonasan's* interpretation. If Dassan and Aviram did not wish to leave Egypt, why were they not killed during the three days of darkness, like all other wicked Jews? He answers that Moshe had not revealed to every one of his people the plans to leave Egypt, leaving some to believe, as did Pharaoh, that they were only going into the desert to bring sacrifices for three days. It was by virtue of this that the Egyptians lent them silver and gold articles. Moshe did not divulge his secret of the coming redemption to informers. Thus, regarding the borrowed silver and gold we read (v. 11:2) "Speak now in the ears of the people." Tell them discreetly the ultimate goal.

Dassan and Aviram did not know that the Jews were leaving Egypt for good, hence they were not punished for remaining. Their only sin was not wishing to take part in the sacrifices going on in the desert. We might consider them "secular nationalists." They took part in the exit to freedom, but not in the bringing of offerings.

◄§ The People Have Fled

All the commentaries strive, each after his fashion, to explain the report handed to Pharaoh saying "the people have fled." Had not he and his nation sent them away, and actually banished them from Egypt? How could they suddenly be considered to have fled?

Well known is *Rashi's* explanation, quoting *Chazal*, that Pharaoh sent Egyptian couriers with the Children of Israel. When after three days they saw that the people had not stopped to bring sacrifices, but were continuing on their way, the couriers returned to Egypt and informed Pharaoh that the people had fled.

Oznayim LaTorah asks a question. Did not the Egyptian couriers see that the Jews were heading back to Egypt? How did it occur to them that they were fleeing? He answers, quoting the *Mechilta*, that the people turned back only after the couriers had left them.

Ibn Ezra quotes others who say that the Egyptian magicians had, through sorcery, devised a roadblock of idols that could prevent any slave from escaping. Once the Jewish people had passed these roadblocks, Pharaoh realized they were no longer slaves, but free men heading on their way. Yet, Ibn Ezra, himself, explains simply that Pharaoh heard Moshe say (*Sh'mos* 8:23), "We shall walk a distance of three days into the desert." From this it appeared to Pharaoh that Moshe knew the way and had a specific destination in mind. When the couriers returned with reports that the Jewish people were backtracking, and had gotten lost, Pharaoh began to suspect that Moshe had tricked him in claiming they were going to bring sacrifices. Perhaps they were really going to flee, for only an escapee, with no clear destination in mind, loses his way.

Ramban explains similarly, but adds that the manner in which they left signified that they were fleeing (v. 14:8), " 'And the Children of Israel were leaving with a high hand.' They made themselves a flag and banner for display, and they left with joy, with singing, with drums and harps, like liberated men, not slaves destined to return to their labor."

Ibn Ezra as well explains that the "high hand" signifies that "they did not conjure up the image of escapees. Furthermore, they were armed." S'forno, however, interprets the "high hand" as a sign of naivete. They imagined they could defeat the Egyptians, whom they outnumbered, and they were certain that they were stronger than the Egyptians: "Thus does the Torah inform us that they were ignorant of war; for they had more to fear from the small but well-trained army pursuing them than from all the population of Egypt who followed."

Or HaChaim, however, links that portion of the verse, "and the Children of Israel were leaving with a high hand" to the opening, where it is written, "and Hashem hardened Pharaoh's heart." The Torah here stresses Pharaoh's foolishness. He saw the Jewish people leaving in triumph, and he should have understood that they had a basis for doing so. They were certain that the Egyptians would not be able to confront them. But Pharaoh failed to deduce this since Hashem had hardened his heart in order that he pursue them.

According to *Ramban*, Pharaoh's hardened heart made him too dull witted to think clearly. It was Pharaoh himself who had originally agreed that the Children of Israel could leave Egypt. He had even requested that they (v. 12:32) "bless me as well." Had Hashem not hardened his heart, he would not have pursued them, even had he realized they were fleeing. But Hashem did harden Pharaoh's heart to pursue them. And He again hardened his heart to follow them into the sea. Logically, Pharaoh should have flinched at pursuing the Jewish people when he saw the open miracle of the splitting of the sea, and how the people were walking through it on dry land. Logically so, but Hashem confused him so he set out in pursuit.

Another interpretation of Pharaoh's sudden awareness that (v. 14:4) "the people had fled" is offered by *Or HaChaim*. The expression עַם — "people" — always connotes the עֵרֶב רַב, or "mixed multitude." Pharaoh was informed that not only the Children of Israel had departed but that a mixed multitude of other peoples had fled with them. Then (ibid.), "Pharaoh and his servants changed their minds because of the people." They decided to pursue the Jewish people because of the mixed multitude that had departed with them. This explains his regret for allowing the Jews to leave.

Kli Yakar explains a similar point by different means. Pharaoh heard that a mixed multitude had left with the Jewish people, and that they were "entangled in the land." Then, "Pharaoh and his servants changed their minds because of the people." Pharaoh's mind was changed to look *favorably* upon the mixed multitude, and he decided to enlist their aid. He believed that when put to the test, they would rebel against the Children of Israel, and would thus comprise a fifth column from within who would complement the efforts of Pharaoh's army from without.

The Midrash comments that Pharaoh was aware that Avraham was told by Hashem (*Bereishis* 15:13), "Your descendants shall be strangers for four hundred years." Since they had only been slaves for 210 years (the numeric value of בָּרַח — "fled" — says *Torah Temimah*), Pharaoh believed he could still return them to their labor.

An original interpretation of כִּי בָרַח הָעָם — "the people have fled" — is provided by *HaKesav VeHaKabalah*. ברח — "to flee" — is cognate with בְּרִיחַ — the bolt on a door. Pharaoh was told that the Jewish people were totally boxed in at Pi HaChiros, where the Sea of Reeds empties into a long, wide inlet. They were encamped between Migdol Eisam and the sea. They were caught between falling into the sea or dying in a war waged by the Egyptians from Migdol Eisam and Baal Tzafon.

Intransitive verbs can have passive meanings (e.g., in *Tehillim* 105:25,

הָפַךְ לְבָם — "He turned their heart" — is interpreted by *Radak* as "their heart was turned." Similarly בָּרַח — "he locked in" — may be read "he was locked in." In other words, the people were locked in a strait with no exit, hence Pharaoh immediately decided to pursue them.

Paane'ach Raza holds that Pharaoh's change of heart stemmed from his failure to make their release conditional on their making themselves available in the future to do his bidding wherever they might be (*Sh'mos* 14:5): "What have we done? How could we have released the Children of Israel from *doing our work*?" Pharaoh regretted not that he had let the Jewish people go, but that he had freed them from all future servitude, wherever they would be.

Or HaChaim likewise emphasizes the last words of this verse: "What have we done? We have released the Children of Israel from doing our work," and they did not go just to sacrifice to their Hashem, as we thought. This explains Pharaoh's change of heart and pursuit.

Shaar Bas Rabim offers an interesting explanation. After Pharaoh decided to go to war against the Jewish people, he concluded that six hundred warriors would not suffice. Rather, he would need to enlist the entire Egyptian nation to pursue them. This is the meaning of the verse, "and Pharaoh's heart turned to the nation" — he turned to the nation of Egypt and demanded that they go to war. The nation accepted his demand "so they could recoup the property they had lent them," as *Rashi* explains, quoting *Chazal*.

◆§ Not a Time for Prayer

In their distress, the Jewish people prayed to their Father in Heaven, as it is written (v. 14:10), וַיִּצְעֲקוּ בְנֵי יִשְׂרָאֵל אֶל ה'. The Children of Israel "cried out to Hashem." Yet, not all commentaries translate וַיִּצְעֲקוּ — "they cried" — to mean "prayer." *Onkelos* renders וַיִּצְעֲקוּ as וּזְעִקוּ, implying complaint or anger, the exact opposite of prayer. *Ramban* brings proof of this explanation from (v. 5:15), "They cried out — וַיִּצְעֲקוּ — to Pharaoh, 'Why must you treat your servants this way?' " and (*Nechemiah* 5:1), "The cry — צַעֲקַת — of the people and their wives against their brethren, the Jews, was great." In both cases, צְעָקָה means anger.

Ramban quotes *Mechilta* as well, that actually the Jewish people first "took up the profession of their forefathers" and cried out to Hashem with all their heart to make Pharaoh relent and turn back. Yet, when their prayers proved fruitless they began to entertain suspicions regarding Moshe. As *Ramban* later explains, while they still believed and trusted in Hashem, they began to doubt the validity of Moshe's mission. They suspected him of taking them out solely to rule over them. Although they witnessed signs and wonders, they thought Moshe had employed his own genius to produce them, or that Hashem had smitten Egypt, not because Israel deserved to leave Egypt, but only because the Egyptians were themselves evil. They reasoned that if Hashem had wished them to leave Egypt, He would not have let Pharaoh pursue them.

Rambam further states that the Children of Israel split into different groups. One cried out to Hashem in prayer, while another cursed Moshe and his deeds. *Chazal*, indeed, count four groups among them (Jerusalem Talmud, *Taanis* 2). *Kesav Sofer* reads the division among the Jewish people into the verse (*Sh'mos* 14:10), "Egypt was traveling behind them." The Egyptians were united, hence they are described in the singular form. The Jewish people were divided, hence the use of the plural "them."

In any event, the Children of Israel severely criticized the Exodus. Regarding this, *Ramban* asks a highly justified question: How can individuals cry out in prayer to Hashem one moment, and at the next moment reject His salvation and announce that they would be happier to die in Egypt? The transition from prayer to extreme blasphemy is bizarre, and all the commentaries struggle to deal with it.

Equally puzzling is Hashem's reprimand to Moshe (v. 14:15), "Why are you crying to Me?" Was Moshe crying to Hashem? Was it not the Jewish people?

Ibn Ezra and *Ramban* answer that "Moshe" symbolizes and embodies the Jewish people. Hashem addressed His words to Moshe, but meant Israel.

Abarbanel, however, wonders why Hashem was angered by their crying out. Under the circumstances, was it not justified? To answer this, *Ramban* adopts *Chazal*'s view that although Moshe cried and prayed to Hashem, he did not know what to do now. Although Hashem had told him (v. 14:4), "I will triumph over Pharaoh," it was unknown just what Hashem would do, for the Jewish people were standing by the seashore with the enemy in pursuit. Therefore Hashem asked him, "Why are you moving heaven and earth with your cries instead of asking Me what to do?"

S'forno ventures the novel idea that Moshe's cry was not directed to Hashem, since he had just advised the Jewish people (v. 14:13), "Stand still and see the salvation of Hashem." Rather, his cry was addressed to the princes of Israel who had dared say (v. 14:11), "Are there no graves in Egypt that you have taken us to die in the desert?" Moshe yelled at them for fear that these leaders would not wish to enter the sea. Hashem then told Moshe he was harboring unjustified suspicions against righteous people (v. 14:15), "Speak to the Children of Israel" and they will move willingly forward. There is no need to argue with them. Just tell them to go. That will suffice.

Abarbanel explains simply that Hashem told Moshe, there is no need for you to defend My honor or debate their criticisms: "Stand still and see the salvation of Hashem." This entire argument is unnecessary. Tell them to move and they will.

Or HaChaim explains Hashem's response as an instruction in how to be saved. The Jewish people, standing by the sea, were at their low ebb of faith. This caused midas hadin — strict justice — to prosecute them saying, "How are the Jews any better than the Egyptians?" Hashem therefore commanded Moshe to rekindle the spark of faith. "Speak to the Children of Israel and they will move forward," and by virtue of their great faith they will be saved.

Meshech Chochmah elaborates on this idea. Until now the Jewish people had followed Moshe like sheep following their shepherd through the valley. By the sea, however, Hashem commanded Moshe to walk behind the people, so they would enter the sea on pure faith, by virtue of which the waters would split. That is why it is written (v. 14:19), "The angel of Hashem who walked before the camp now walked behind it." The word "angel" signifies a prophet, in this case Moshe, as we see from Chaggai 1:13: "And [the prophet] Chaggai, the angel of Hashem, said . . ."

Salvation came by virtue of the Jewish people having walked forward into the sea. As Chazal say, while they were still discussing what to do, Nachshon ben Aminadav proceeded to jump into the sea. Thus did he fulfill Hashem's command: "Speak to the Children of Israel and they will advance." Hashem meant that they should travel in front, with Moshe behind.

Most interesting is the comment of Rashi quoting the Midrash. Moshe was engaged in a long prayer. Hashem admonished him saying, "Now is not the time for lengthy prayers." The Jewish people are in trouble, and needed immediate help. Hence Hashem said, "Speak to the Children of Israel and they will advance."

II.

The Prophetic Vision
of Moshe's Shiras HaYam

Abarbanel and others speak at length on the structure and composition of *shiras hayam* — the song that Moshe and the Children of Israel sang upon crossing the Sea of Reeds. Its content may be tersely summarized as follows: It praises almighty Hashem as the unique deliverer, God of the *Avos* and master warrior, Whose right hand is awesome in power, and Whose wrath destroys His enemies like straw. At the same time, the *shirah* reviews the miraculous drowning of the Egyptians: their plot to give chase and divide up the spoils, their bitter end, when Hashem — putting forth His right hand — caused them to be swallowed by mighty waters.

The second half of the *shirah* deals with what will occur after the drowning, when all the nations hear what happened and tremble, and Hashem leads His nation to His holy sanctuary. It ends with several verses of prayer which we shall explain later on, quoting the commentaries, and a declaration — or call — (*Sh'mos* 15:18) that "Hashem will reign forever and ever."

This, in short, is the *shirah*, a work of unified content and style from beginning to end. Nonetheless, a few exceptional matters are singled out by the commentators as requiring examination: (a) Verses 1-5 praise Hashem for His miraculous punishment of the Egyptians who were drowned in the sea. Verse 8 then goes back to an earlier event, telling of the waters that piled up, standing upright like a wall, and of the enemy's plot to pursue Israel and divide up spoils. Why this repetition? (b) To what time period do the prayer verses, such as "Hashem will reign for ever and ever," refer? (c) What place has verse 19, "For the horse of Pharaoh, with his horsemen and chariots, went into the sea ..."? Is it connected to the *shirah* or to the section about to begin?

Before quoting the commentaries on these questions, we shall further clarify the division of the *shirah*. *Tosefos Yom Tov* (*Sotah* 5:4) states that the *shirah* divides into topical sections. Moshe would recite a section and the Jewish people would repeat it, in keeping with the view of *Chazal* in *Sotah* 30. *Maharsha* too, on the same *Gemara*, quotes *Chazal* in *Rosh HaShanah* 31, "At Sabbath afternoon *minchah*, the Levites would recite

אָז יָשִׁיר and מִי כָמוֹךְ." This implies that both commentators view the *shirah* as composed of sections.

Avnei Shoham divides the *shirah* into three parts. Part one (vs. 1-8) praises Hashem, enumerating His mighty acts and especially emphasizing the attribute of majestic might (v. 6) — "Your right hand is awesome in power (majesty), Your right hand crushes the foe (might)"; reference to revenge against the enemy (v. 7) — "You broke Your opponents;" and (v. 8) — "The depths congealed in the heart of the sea."

Part two begins with renewed excitement (v.9): "The enemy said, 'I will pursue, overtake, and divide the spoils.' " It continues with the cry of awe (v. 11): "Who is like You among the gods, Hashem?" Followed by (v. 12): "You put forth Your right hand. The earth swallowed them," and (v. 13): "Mercifully You led forth the people You redeemed." The section concludes with faith and trust: "With might, You led them to Your holy habitation," and (v. 14): "Nations heard and shuddered."

Section three begins (v. 15): "Edom's chiefs then panicked," and continues with a supplication (v. 16): "Let fear and dread befall them." The Jewish people are certain that (v. 17) Hashem will bring them in and plant them on the mountain of His inheritance.

Finally there is acknowledgment (v. 18) of God's kingdom on earth: "Hashem will reign forever and ever."

The commentaries, each in his own way, also analyze the first word of the *shirah*: אָז — "Then." *Haamek Davar* explains that only then, at the end of the rescue, did the Jewish people thank Hashem, not when they first entered the sea. The same point appears in the Jerusalem Talmud (*Pesachim* 10:6), regarding the verse (*Shoftim* 5:2): "When Hashem takes revenge for Israel, when His people volunteer, praise Hashem."

> This verse means that when Hashem performs miracles for us we should say *shirah*. What of the Exodus from Egypt (where no *shirah* was sung)? That is different, for it represents the beginning of a redemption (and praises are sung only at the end). As it is written here (*Sh'mos* 14:30), "And Israel saw the Egyptians dead upon the sea shore," (v. 15:1), "Then Moshe sang."

❦ The Enemy Said, "I Will Chase"

This verse seems odd, as we have already read (ibid.), "Horse and rider He threw in the sea." *Ramban* quotes *Midrash Chazis*, in the name of a *tanna* from the *beis midrash* of R' Yishmael, who states that, in terms of the sequence of events, the verse should appear at the beginning of the *shirah*, but that the Torah is not chronologically ordered. But, *Ramban*, himself, maintains that the verse is chronologically in the right place. The *shirah* first states simply that the Egyptians drowned, then goes on to elaborate how this occurred. First the waters piled up, standing upright like a wall. Then the Egyptians plotted to pursue and overtake the Jewish people. Ultimately it became clear that Hashem had laid a trap to destroy the enemy, hence the *shirah* concludes (v. 11): "Who is like You among the gods, Hashem?"

Likewise, *Rashbam* and *S'forno* both maintain that the Egyptians pursued only after the sea became dry land, and they became convinced that they could now more easily execute their plan. According to *Or HaChaim*, they were actually tricked into entering the sea. Likewise, *Malbim* interprets the words נֶעֶרְמוּ מַיִם in verse 8, where it is said that the "the waters piled up," as derived from the word עָרְמָה, which implies trickery, i.e., "the waters tricked them." The waters that had stood like a wall turned to liquid without the Egyptians noticing it. This is actually the way Onkelos had already interpreted נֶעֶרְמוּ מַיִם. He translates the latter to חַכִּימוּ מַיָּא, which implies that the waters behaved craftily.

Avnei Shoham, however, suggests the novel interpretation that the Egyptians never even entered the water. They stood upon the shore, planning their pursuit, but Hashem blew with His wind upon the water, and it rose and swept away all in its path.

Abarbanel states that verse 9, in which the Egyptians plot to "give chase, overtake and divide the spoils," serves to justify their drowning. After the Children of Israel had left Egypt, the Egyptians chased them. Yet, their goal was not to recapture them as slaves, but to kill them and take their booty. Fittingly, they themselves were killed.

After the description of the action, comes praise to Hashem for the wonders He performed (v. 12): "You put forth Your right hand. The earth swallowed them," and for His (v. 13) leading the Jewish people to His "holy habitation," which Ibn Ezra holds is a reference to Mount Sinai, "where Hashem's glory resided."

Similarly, *S'forno* explains that the purpose of leading the Jewish people is to bring them to Hashem's holy habitation, and there to consecrate them to serve Him. Yet, *Rashbam* sees this verse as referring to *Eretz Yisrael*, their ultimate goal and final destination: "Hashem now leads the Jewish people in order to bring them to the Land of Canaan, which is the site of His holy habitation, so that they can acquire it."

For *Ramban*, the reference to "holy habitation," where they are being conveyed, is the *Beis HaMikdash* in Jerusalem, in accordance with Yeshayahu 2:2, "and all nations will flow unto it," and as *Mechilta* notes, "'habitation' means the *Beis HaMikdash*," as it is written

(*Yeshayahu* 33:20), "Look upon Zion, our festival city, our tranquil habitation." But in contrast to *Ramban*, for whom reaching the *Beis HaMikdash* is the goal of the Exodus from Egypt, *Mechilta* views the rescue as taking place through the merit of the *Beis HaMikdash*.

◆§ Let Fear and Dread Befall Them

Until verse 15, the *shirah* consists of a narrative of the splitting of the sea, and praise for the miracles and wonders Hashem performed for His nation at the time of the Exodus. From here on, prayers are also added, the first being (v. 16) that Hashem instill fear and dread upon the nations "until Your people crosses through, Hashem."

Why must they still cross? Have they not already crossed the sea? The answer is that verse 16 is not a song of praise, but a prayer about the future. According to the Targumic literature, the content and essence of verse 16 is a supplication that Hashem will instill fear in those nations dwelling between Egypt and *Eretz Yisrael*, so that Jewish people will be able to cross the Jordan and Arnon rivers without impediment, as they did the Sea of Reeds.

What connection with the Exodus have the Philistines (v. 14), and the Edomites and Moavites (v. 15) who bordered the Land of Israel? According to *Rashi*, their fear of the Jewish people was bound up with the Exodus. The Philistines had killed members of the tribe of Efraim who left Egypt prematurely, and now they feared revenge. As for Edom and Moav, they were simply jealous of Israel's glory. They had no reason to fear, for the Jewish people were not headed towards their lands. Alternately, as *Mechilta* comments, they did fear, for now the day of reckoning had arrived regarding the quarrel between the shepherds of Avraham and Lot, father of Moav, and between Yaakov and Esav, father of Edom.

Ibn Ezra holds that starting with verse 14, the words of the *shirah* concern only the future. The nations cited were not directly affected by the Exodus, yet when they heard of it, they trembled and shuddered all the same. Moshe prayed that such fear would continue, and in the case of Edom and Moav, it did. When the Children of Israel passed near them in their entrance into the Land, they did not allow them to pass through their land, yet they did not deter their entrance into Canaan.

As explained by Ibn Ezra, Moshe's prayer that the nations continue to fear Israel was aimed at Edom and Moav, and not at the Canaanites, since it was Mount Seir that the Jewish people avoided as they entered the Land. Yet, it is likely, states *Ramban*, that the Canaanites were frightened by Israel as well, and did not do battle with them until confronted. As for the Canaanites of Arad who fought Israel, they were not true Canaanites. *Rashbam*, however, maintains that the prayers pertained to when the Jewish people would be at the entrance to *Eretz Yisrael*. Philistia, Edom and Moav are neighbors of *Eretz Yisrael*, and Moshe prayed that they would not be aroused to battle before the Jewish people would cross the Jordan.

Or HaChaim relates the prayer to our future redemption, when all the nations will fear and tremble. *Chazal* in *Sotah* say that the repetition of the expression (v. 16) "until Your people crosses over" corresponds to the two redemptions at the time of Yehoshua and Ezra. During Ezra's times, the Jewish people would have been redeemed with miracles such as were performed in the days of Yehoshua, but their sins deprived them of these. Moshe prayed that the redemption led by Ezra would be carried out proudly, and that the nations would tremble with fear. Unfortunately Israel sinned, and this caused the redemption to occur by non-miraculous means.

Starting with verse 17, Moshe prays that the redemption will be eternal, that Israel will take root in their land, and that they will never again be exiled. Thus, Ibn Ezra and S'forno interpret (v. 17), "O bring them and plant them on the mountain of Your inheritance," as referring to Mount Moriah or Mount Zion, where Hashem's Temple will stand, established by His own Hand (*Sh'mos* 25:8-9): "They shall make Me a sanctuary . . . following the plan that I am showing you." Moshe prayed that the redemption from Egypt would be just the beginning of a complete and everlasting redemption, never again followed by exile.

At the end of the prayer, it becomes clear that the true purpose of the miracles performed is to influence the world so that (v. 15:18), "Hashem will reign forever and ever." For *Ramban*, this prayer is a natural sequel to the Exodus. Hashem has just shown that He is King and Master of the universe, rescuing those who serve Him and destroying those who rebel. Therefore, according to *Ramban*, Moshe prays: "So may it be in every generation. May Hashem never ignore the good deeds of the righteous or the sins of the wicked."

Nonetheless, *Rashbam* and Ibn Ezra hold verse 18 to be a separate prayer and a proclamation. Moshe tells the Jewish people that once they settle in *Eretz Yisrael*, Hashem's kingdom will become known to all humanity, and Hashem will become King over all the universe. In this sense, the verse parallels (*Yeshayahu* 2:3), "For from Zion shall go forth the Torah."

Mechilta rebukes the Jewish people for saying "Hashem *will* reign forever and ever" — a prayer for the future. Had they said, "Hashem is an everlasting King," no nation would have been able to threaten them.

Chasam Sofer states that when the Jewish people uttered, "Hashem will reign," instead of "Hashem is King," they sensed that the redemption from Egypt would not endure forever, that the Temple would be destroyed, and only later would Hashem reign eternal. This idea, which he attributes simply to "*Chazal*," must come from the *Mechilta*, for it appears nowhere else.

In conclusion, as we have seen, the last verse of the *shirah* is viewed by some as relating to the future, yet by others, notably Onkelos, as a declaration regarding the present.

III.

There Hashem Made for Them a Statute and an Ordinance

Rashi, based on *Chazal* in *Sanhedrin* 56b and *Mechilta*, states that "At Marah, Hashem gave the Jewish people a few Torah *parshiyos* to study: the Sabbath, the Red Cow, and court law." The commentaries are puzzled by *Rashi's* inclusion of the Red Cow when this does not appear in either source. They explain that *Rashi* was interpreting "statute and ordinance" from verse 25. The word חֹק, or statute, means a law whose rationale is unknown, such as the *mitzvah* of the Red Cow. Even so *Rashi's* words are puzzling. There are other "statutes" in the Torah as well, such as *shaatnez* (cloth combining wool and linen) and *kilayim* (the mingling of diverse species). How does *Rashi* know that חֹק here refers specifically to the Red Cow, when there is no source for this in *Chazal*?

Torah Temimah states with certainty that there is a printing error in *Rashi*. פָּרָה אֲדֻמָּה — Red Cow — should read כִּבּוּד אָב — honoring parents, as in *Sanhedrin* 56. He ventures a novel guess at the way the mistake occurred. כִּבּוּד אָב may have been abbreviated כ"א. A later editor may have transformed the כ into a פ and printed פ"א which was then written out as פָּרָה אֲדֻמָּה. This explanation is hard to accept, although *Torah Temimah* was not the first to suggest it.

In the *piyut* (liturgy) regarding the Red Cow, which we read during the week of *Parashas Parah*, we find, "it is a statute decreed at Marah." Clearly the *piyut* accepted *Rashi's* version. Furthermore, in *Seder Olam*

Zuta we find, "At Marah, in the second month, Israel was given a few *parashiyos* of the Torah: the Sabbath, the Red Cow and court law." It seems likely, therefore, that there existed a source in *Chazal* for placing the Red Cow on the list of *mitzvos* taught at *Marah*, but we have lost that source.

Paane'ach Raza, quoting the Tosafist, Rabbenu Yaakov of Orleans, poses a few questions concerning these words of *Rashi*. *Chazal* said that the Red Cow atoned for the sin of the Golden Calf: "Let the mother come and make amends for her child's excrement." Yet, at Marah, the Golden Calf had not yet been fashioned! He answers that this matter is linked to the familiar question of how man can be said to have free choice if Hashem knows the future. The Jewish people were commanded regarding the Red Cow before they fashioned the Golden Calf, but the reasoning for this *mitzvah* remained open, pending events to follow. Even if they had not sinned with the Golden Calf, they would still have received the *mitzvah* of the Red Cow. Having sinned, which Hashem knew they would do, the Red Cow served as atonement.

Puzzling as well are *Ramban's* comments on *Rashi's* explanation. According to *Ramban*, when *Rashi* says that Hashem gave the Jewish people "a few Torah *parashiyos* to occupy them," the *mitzvos* this referred to were not compulsory but optional. Hashem had not yet made the *mitzvos* mandatory. He had only taught and informed the Jewish people about *mitzvos*, as He had done with Avraham. Hashem did this in order "to accustom them to the *mitzvos*." This explanation seems difficult to accept, for *Chazal* in *Sanhedrin* 56b and in *Horios* 8 say, "There were ten *mitzvos* at Marah: the seven Noachide laws, and the Sabbath, honoring one's parents, and court law." This implies that the three applying to the Jewish people were compulsory, for the descendants of Noach were surely obligated to uphold theirs. This problem requires further study.

◆§ Lack of Faith

Ramban offers an interesting explanation of the statutes and ordinances given Moshe at Marah. In his opinion, they do not refer to Torah decrees, but to the proper societal regulations by which the Jewish people were to abide until reaching settled land. These are referred to as חֹק, as in (*Mishlei* 30:8), הַטְרִיפֵנִי לֶחֶם חֻקִּי — "Feed me my proper portion." מִשְׁפָּט means the planning necessary to complete any enterprise, as in (*I Shmuel* 27:11): כֹּה עָשָׂה דָוִד וְכֹה מִשְׁפָּטוֹ כָּל הַיָּמִים — "Thus did David, and this was his practice all the days." Hashem most likely taught the Children of Israel that they were obliged, under desert conditions, to love one another, to follow the teaching of the elders, and to behave modestly in their tents with their wives and children. They were also duty bound to treat peacefully those foreigners who came to conduct business in the camp, and not to exhibit vulgar or destructive behavior. When we read (*Yehoshua* 24:25) that Yehoshua established חֹק וּמִשְׁפָּט for the people of Shechem, this too does not refer to Torah law, but to the customs and ordinances necessary for government to function, such as the "ordinances of Yehoshua" outlined by *Chazal* in *Bava Kamma* 80.

On the other hand, the phrase (*Sh'mos* 15:25), "And there He tested them," does not refer to the "statutes and ordinances," but to the fact that the Jewish people had been brought to a place where the water was bitter. It is in harmony with that which is written in *Devarim* (8:16), "And He afflicted you and tested you, for your ultimate benefit."

Ramban holds that the tree Moshe cast into the bitter waters had natural qualities that made them drinkable. Therefore, the Torah says (*Sh'mos* 15:25), וַיּוֹרֵהוּ ... עֵץ — "And He *taught* (versus "showed") him a tree." Hashem taught Moshe which tree could make the water drinkable by natural means.

According to *Chazal*, however, that tree was itself bitter, and its use comprised a double miracle: Bitter sweetened bitter. For *Chazal*, therefore, the verse means that Hashem "taught" Moshe where the tree could be found, or created it miraculously, for there were no other trees around.

Rabbenu Bachya agrees with *Ramban* that *chukim* and *mishpatim* in 15:25 refer to laws of good conduct for desert living. He adds that according to some, Hashem taught Moshe the science of herbs. Some herbs are like *chukim*, in that they possess medicinal qualities that defy reason. Others are like *mishpatim*, for their effect can be explained scientifically. Therefore, the next verse reads (v. 15:26), "If you listen to the voice of Hashem your God ... I will not subject you to any of the diseases I brought upon Egypt, for I am Hashem your healer." That is to say, although I have revealed to you the secret of medicinal herbs, do not pin your hopes upon them, for it is I, Hashem, who is your healer.

Hashem showed them the double miracle of one bitter thing making another bitter thing sweet to strengthen their faith and trust. Elisha the Prophet performed a similar act, making the water at Yericho drinkable (*II Melachim* 2:20): "Bring me a new flask and put salt in it." Salt normally makes water undrinkable. Yet, by adding salt to bad water, Elisha did the opposite. With this double miracle, he showed that Hashem is Master of nature.

Chafetz Chaim's comment on the verse that follows is in harmony with the preceding ideas (*Sh'mos* 15:27): "They came to Elim, where there were twelve springs of water and seventy date palms." He explains that the Torah wished to show man how short sighted are his complaints, which result from a lack of faith and trust in Hashem. Not far from Marah, and unbeknown to those complaining, were springs of water standing ready to refresh. From this they were to learn that what they lacked was not water, but faith. They did not know what was ahead of them or behind them, yet they dared to complain about their lot. Were they blessed with a bit more faith, they would have had water without complaining.

◄§ The Lesson to be Learned from Nature

Akeidas Yitzchak sees the incident of the bitter waters as serving an educational purpose, to teach the Jewish people the essence of Torah and *mitzvos*. Rooted in the impurity of Egypt, it was hard for them to wean themselves away from Egyptian practices and behavior, and to adapt themselves to a pure and holy Torah life. They were always looking back upon Egypt with nostalgia, so that Hashem had to urge them (*Vayikra* 18:3-4): "Do not act like the Egyptians among whom you dwelled. Do not follow their practices. Keep My laws."

Towards this educational goal, Hashem brought them to Marah. For three days they walked without water, and what they at last found was undrinkable. This brought them unbearable grief. Yet, in a single moment they were miraculously rescued from their terrible suffering. Moshe, with instructions from Hashem, made the water drinkable, proving to them that the world does not operate the way they thought it did. By Hashem's command, what seemed bitter became sweet.

The Torah tells us (*Sh'mos* 15:25), "There Hashem gave them decrees and laws and there He tested them." As a result, at Marah their spiritual and philosophical outlook changed. They realized that what they consider *chok*, defying human logic, is actually *mishpat*, highly logical. Hashem then took them to Elim, to prove that He could give them as much water as He wanted them to have. At Marah He had only been testing them, to instill in them a truth they could not grasp as long as they remained mentally in Egypt.

Chasam Sofer develops this idea more deeply. Not all natural phenomena can be explained in natural terms. Regarding some, we can only acknowledge their existence. It is a fact that magnets attract iron, but that they should do so is not logically necessary. Regarding the rewards the Torah promises in return for *mitzvah* fulfillment, *Ramban* says that the connection is a spiritual one (*segulah*), rather than one based on natural law. We cannot explain why the rains fall when we keep the Torah, and cease to fall when we do not.

In actual fact, all such revealed connections are natural phenomena dictated by reality, but we are ignorant of this, for we do not know how nature operates. We cannot understand why a magnet should attract iron any more than we know why Divine excommunication (*kares*) is the punishment for eating non-kosher fat. We do not understand the laws of the Red Cow, or of *shaatnez*. If. we understood nature, we would know all, including what seems incomprehensible.

At Marah, Hashem showed how bitter wood can make bitter water drinkable. The matter could not be explained logically, but it was a fact. From this the Jewish people learned not to question Hashem's *mitzvos*. They concluded that even what seems illogical, in the realm of "statute", is really dictated by reality, even if they did not understand its rationale. Their lack of understanding was due to ignorance. The logic they were familiar with did not answer their questions. To know how bitter wood made bitter water drinkable, or any other unnatural phenomena, they would have had to understand how *mishpat* is embodied in *chok*.

The author of *HaDrash VeHalyun* makes this very point, without knowing that *Chasam Sofer* had preceded him. The same idea can also be seen in the following words of *Rashbam*: "Hashem made the Israelites thirsty at Marah, and then made the bitter water drinkable. Having done so, He admonished them to keep the statutes and laws they were destined to receive, and He would supply their needs."

Abarbanel, however, explains this differently. Marah was a trial by which Hashem intended to instill simple faith in the Jewish people, so that they would beseech Him and direct their hearts to receive the Torah out of faith. Still moved by their experience at the Exodus, they engaged in no outbursts when trouble struck. Rather, they correctly inquired, "What shall we drink?" After the water was made drinkable, Hashem gave them "statutes and ordinances." He made them understand that He saves them in times of trouble, and that nature — the "ordinances" — belong to Hashem to alter as He wishes. "And there He tested them"; at Marah, Hashem performed open miracles whose purpose was not only to punish the wicked, but to show them that nature is in Hashem's hands to bend to His will.

Interestingly, *Rambam* in *Moreh Nevuchim* (3:32) views the decrees and laws of Marah as the main principles of our faith, embodying its most quintessential values. After Marah it became clear that the Jewish people could not adapt to pure service of Hashem based exclusively on intellect and belief, and only then were they commanded regarding Temple offerings. The prophet, quoting Hashem in reference to Marah, said (*Yirmiyahu* 7:22), "When I took them out of Egypt, I did not command them regarding burnt offerings and sacrifices." At Marah, the Jewish people were commanded only about the Sabbath, the mark of Hashem's having created the world, and about those laws instituted to cleanse man of evil. They were still not commanded about the means to achieving these things.

Thus, *Rambam* views the Marah legislation as the pinnacle of spiritual perfection. For other commentaries, however, it represents only a first stage in the Jewish people's understanding Torah and *mitzvos*, when they had so recently left the decadence of Egypt. The greatest gap, however, is between *Rambam* and *Ramban*. For the latter, these *chukim* are only rules of correct social conduct to be applied among the Jewish people and between them and foreigners.

In line with the preceding, the Chassidic literature offers a fine explanation of the verse (*Sh'mos* 15:26) "I will not subject you to any of the diseases I brought upon Egypt." The "disease" of Egypt was stubborn denial of Hashem's existence, with no chance of repentance. Whatever the state of the Jewish people will be, they will never suffer from this "disease." The wisdom acquired at Marah and at the Exodus were sufficient to remove this disease from their hearts forever.

Hashem said (ibid.), "I am Hashem your healer". God's miraculous revelations and His identifying Himself as Hashem were what provided the everlasting cure. Even if the Jewish people sinned, they would still return to Hashem and rectify their misdeeds. They would never stubbornly refuse repentance the way Pharaoh did. Hashem cured them of this disease, now and forever. The Torah says, "Hashem gave them statutes and ordinances." This cure is an everlasting statute.

This Chassidic interpretation is a priceless gem, containing an idea of immense importance, as well as an answer to a question *Chazal* and all the commentaries struggle to answer: If Hashem has removed sickness from us, why does He need to be our healer?

According to the great Chassidic leaders, the principle "I am Hashem" is itself the eternal cure for the Egyptian disease.

◄§ Never Despair, Whatever Life Brings

In accordance with the episode at Marah, involving the bitter water made sweet (15:22-26), many of the commentators have expounded on the theme that we must study Torah under all conditions and circumstances. After analyzing the surface meaning of this episode,

Haamek Davar concludes with a relevant lesson on a more contemplative level.

At Marah, the Children of Israel were not thirsty as they were at Refidim. Their primary concern was the future, wondering how they would attain water when they needed it. Yet, as with any element of nature that is lacking in one place and found elsewhere, here too there was a tree standing ready to make the bitter water drinkable. Hashem showed Moshe the location of this tree. The chief reason Hashem brought them to Marah was to test them (*Devarim* 8:16): "In order to afflict and test you for your ultimate benefit."

This generation of the desert personally witnessed Divine Providence at every turn, yet Hashem wished them to learn not to despair, under even the most trying conditions. Hashem was showing them that the way to Torah may be one of affliction and toil. The Children of Israel walked three days without water, to adapt themselves to the principle (*Avos* 6): "Salted bread shall you eat, little water shall you drink." The Torah way is the path of restraint.

True, Hashem said (*Sh'mos* 23:25), "I shall remove sickness from your midst," but an absence of sickness is far from a state of luxury. Only after the Jewish people had risen spiritually in Torah did they merit the comforts of Elim, with its twelve springs and seventy date palms. Until that moment, their path was strewn with thorns, and they tasted bitterness. "Such is the way of Torah" (*Avos* 6).

Kli Yakar explains similarly. *Chazal* say that the tree which made the water drinkable was an olive tree. Elsewhere they say, "Why is Torah likened to an olive tree? Just as olives are at first bitter and then sweet, so too Torah." Hashem here teaches that *mitzvos* are not given to us that we may derive pleasure from them.

Hashem ordered Moshe (v. 19:3), "So must you tell the Children of Israel," and, according to *Chazal*, he was ordered to rebuke them with words "as tough as sinew." Furthermore, King Shlomo said (*Mishlei* 2:7), Hashem stores up תּוּשִׁיָּה — "sound wisdom" — for the righteous, and *Chazal* ask, "Why is Torah called תּוּשִׁיָּה? Because it drains (מַתֶּשֶׁת) man's strength."

The cure for spiritual sickness is a hard, demanding life of toil in Torah. This is a severe trial for individuals who wish a life of convenience. Yet, Hashem showed His people the example of the waters of Marah, where what is bitter ultimately becomes sweet. "At Marah, Hashem gave them statutes and ordinances, and there did He test them." A Jew undergoes a similar test when he is studying the decrees and laws of the Torah. At first he tastes bitterness, but in the end it is as sweet as honey. The main lessons he must learn are to endure his situation and to know that bitterness leads to sweetness.

Mechilta states that the "tree" Hashem showed Moshe to sweeten the bitter waters is the Torah, which is (*Mishlei* 3:18) "a tree of life for those who support it." *Chasam Sofer* explains what *Chazal* mean by this: Those who wish to support Torah study are obliged to sweeten the bitterness in the lives of Torah scholars. This is the lesson *Chazal* learn from the bitter wood sweetening bitter water. The Torah scholar lives under bitter physical conditions. The individual, duty bound to support him, suffers spiritual bitterness. Only full cooperation between them can sweeten their bitterness so they both benefit.

Obviously, these ideas are only interpretations, but they have their source in *Chazal*. The latter deduced from the three-day walk without water the lesson that one must not go three days without Torah. This, in fact, became the basis for Ezra's instituting three Torah readings per week.

IV.

Hashem Tests Israel with the Manna

hazal are divided over which test is greater, wealth or poverty. Wealth leads one to the arrogant view that all his success is the result of his own efforts, while poverty has a dulling influence, destroying a person's individuality. In the *parashah* of the manna, the text seems to describe a trial of wealth (*Sh'mos* 16:4): "The people should go out and gather [the manna] . . . so I can test them to see if they follow My Torah or not." We shall dwell on the way the commentaries have understood this trial.

Abarbanel first asks, "In what way was Hashem testing them by giving them a daily portion of food? . . . This was no test, but an act of kindness." At first glance, this does not seem such a difficult question. Sometimes kindness can be a trial as well, when it tests whether the recipient knows how to use kindness offered him for the proper purpose. Some people, given the good life, rebel against Hashem. Others pass their life in idle boredom, dining on luxuries acquired without toil or effort.

So, in fact, does S'forno view this trial. Hashem wished to see if the Jewish people would follow His Torah when they were being supported without suffering. *Or HaChaim* explains similarly: "Food from Heaven needs no improvement. They were free of all worry. Hashem wished to see if they would then follow the Torah."

According to this interpretation, the trial of wealth makes one's life not harder but easier. Until this point, the Children of Israel had an excuse for not turning to Hashem — their impatience and hard labors in searching for food in the arid desert. Now they were being supplied all their needs without effort on their part, to see if they would actually be more emotionally free to direct their hearts towards Heaven and to keep the *mitzvos* Hashem commanded them.

Rashi states that in 16:4, when Hashem wonders if the Jewish people will "follow His Torah or not," He is referring to the *mitzvos* involving the manna itself. Hashem commanded them that they must leave nothing over to the morning, and must not go out on the Sabbath morning to collect. Now, He waited to see if they would understand that the manna afforded them not only privileges but responsibilities. According to *Rashi*, therefore, the test did not involve the wealth itself, but the *mitzvos* attached to it. Hashem gave the Jewish people manna. In addition, He commanded them regarding how they must eat it. It was a test to see if they could restrain themselves and remain within their assigned framework.

Ramban labels *Rashi*'s interpretation "incorrect," without elaborating. His disapproval seems to stem from the unexpected wording of Hashem's answer in verse 4. In verse 3, the Children of Israel complained about the hunger that had plagued them since the Exodus. Hashem's answer should therefore have been that He was giving them food from Heaven to satisfy them. The test should have been secondary. We would expect Hashem to say, "I shall also test them." The use, instead, of "so I can test them," shows that the entire purpose in giving the manna was in order to test them.

Ramban therefore explains that Hashem's test involved placing the Jewish people in a situation of severe dependency. The manna was food with which neither they nor their ancestors were familiar. It was given to them in the uninhabited desert, a place of snakes, serpents and scorpions. They received it one day at a time, in such a way as to leave them worried about tomorrow, lest it not fall. Such a trial was severe, yet Hashem wished to refine and strengthen them, to find out whether they were loyal to Him even under such crushing and difficult circumstances, for if so, they were worthy of reward (*Devarim* 8:2), "Remember the whole way that Hashem took you for forty years, afflicting and testing you to see if you would keep his *mitzvos* or not."

According to *Chazal*, being refined in this way was supposed to bring them to pure belief and complete trust. As we read in Tractate *Yoma* 76:

> R' Shimon bar Yochai's students asked him, "Why did the manna not fall for Israel once a year?" He answered, "It was so they would all worry that perhaps tomorrow it would not fall and their children would die of famine. That way, everyone would direct their hearts toward their Father in Heaven."

According to this answer, the test was the very fact of being provided with a type of food they knew not, in a place they were unfamiliar with, the desert, and through unfamiliar means of distribution (*Sh'mos* 16:4), "They shall gather it one day at a time."

In line with this, *HaKesav VeHaKabalah* explains that a trial forces one to make active use of inner strengths that have lain dormant, in order to overcome one's weaknesses. Through the manna, the Jewish people strengthened the enormous inner resolve they would need during their lives. If they could be satisfied with such a life, it was a sign that they were prepared for any test that would come their way, and that their attachment to the Torah was in no way dependent upon physical circumstances.

Abarbanel, even if he expresses himself differently, has identical intent. He does not link the educational message with difficult conditions, but with Israel's becoming accustomed to thanking God for His kindness. If by eating manna, they are constantly dependent upon Hashem's mercy, having their needs fulfilled without toil or effort, they will become accustomed to constantly thanking Him for His kindness, and their faith will thereby be strengthened. The trial in verse 16:4 refers to their making active use of inner strengths and adapting themselves to a life of faith and trust. After such a trial, it will be easy for them to choose good over evil.

Rashbam and Ibn Ezra apparently have a similar idea in mind as well, both adding to "so I can test them," the words, "for they will need Me every day." Hashem tested them to see what effect the constancy of that need would have upon them. If none, then they would never follow Hashem's Torah in the future. There would be no hope for them. This, then, was the question to be answered here: ". . . if they will follow My Torah or not."

◦§ Assuming the Yoke of Torah

Rambam in *Moreh Nevuchim* (3:24) elucidates the nature and purpose of the trials in the Torah. He quotes a view that such trials serve to reward those who withstand them. Nonetheless, he rejects this view. Hashem does not torment individuals so He can reward them for unnecessary suffering. *Rambam* also rejects the opinion that Hashem tests people to closely examine their character. Hashem knows man's thoughts and has no need of tests.

For *Rambam*, the tests recorded in the Torah serve only to publicize Hashem's righteousness and that of the individual tested, to teach the world a lesson. Through the trial of the manna, Hashem wished to let all know that He sustains those who turn aside from worldly pursuits to serve Him, who wholeheartedly cling to Him. This explanation appears in the *Mechilta* of R' Shimon bar Yochai (quoted in *Torah Sheleimah*). The Holy One, Blessed is He, demonstrates to the entire world that whoever resolves to serve Hashem with all his heart shall have his needs fully provided for, come what may.

Rambam's view is identical with *Chazal*'s statement that "The Torah was given only to those who ate manna," i.e., individuals who dedicate themselves to full-time Torah study must be freed of the burdens of earning a living. Then they will be able to devote themselves totally to serving Hashem.

Rambam expands on this at the end of *Hilchos Shemittah VeYovel* (13:12-13), explaining why the tribe of Levi received no portion in the Land of Israel:

> Levi was separated to serve Hashem, to teach His straight ways and righteous laws to the masses, as it is written (*Devarim* 33:10), "They shall teach Your laws to Yaakov, Your Torah to Israel"...
>
> These words do not apply solely to the tribe of Levi, but to any man in the entire population whose intellect understands and whose spirit prompts him to stand aside in worship and devotion to Hashem, seeking to know Him. Whoever follows this path, walking straight as Hashem made him, throwing off the yoke of the many calculations that mankind pursues, is consecrated as holy of holies. Hashem shall be his lot and portion forever and ever. Here on earth Hashem supplies his needs as He did for the *Kohanim* and *Leviim*.

These words seem to contradict *Rambam*'s statements in *Hilchos Talmud Torah* 3:1 and *Pirush HaMishnayos* (*Avos* 4:5) that a Torah scholar is forbidden to burden the community by living off charity. *Kesef Mishnah* differs with *Rambam* in *Hilchos Talmud Torah*, holding that if we do not support Torah scholars, Torah runs the risk of ceasing, God forbid, from the Jewish people.

I believe, however, that there is no contradiction. While a Torah scholar is forbidden to burden the community for his support, the community is commanded to enable such people to fulfill their purpose without having to work and toil for a livelihood — and this in fact is how *Shulchan Aruch* rules in *Yoreh Deah* 246.

Chazal, however, hold three different views on the matter. R' Eliezer HaModai deduces from (*Sh'mos* 16:4), "They shall gather it one day at a time," that we are forbidden to worry about tomorrow. He states, "Whoever has food for today and worries about tomorrow is considered to lack faith, as it is written (ibid.), "so I can test whether they will follow My Torah or not." According to this, a man must strive to support himself on a day-by-day basis. Worrying about tomorrow is forbidden. Rather, he should trust in Hashem to support him tomorrow as well.

An extreme view is voiced by R' Shimon bar Yochai in *Mechilta*, totally rejecting worry about one's livelihood: "'The Torah was given only to those who eat manna.' How does one fulfill this? He should sit and study Torah without knowing how he will eat, drink, or clothe himself." This parallels R' Shimon bar Yochai's well-known statement that "as long as the Jewish people fulfill Hashem's will, their work is performed by others."

In contrast with these two views is that cited by *Mechilta* in the name of R' Yehoshua, who states that an individual must work unceasingly to support himself. Furthermore, just as the Children of Israel would gather manna on the sixth day for the Sabbath, not relying on miracles, we too must worry about tomorrow: "If someone studies two laws in the morning and two in the evening, performing his work all day long, he is considered as if he had fulfilled the entire Torah." This view parallels that of R' Yishmael son of R' Yossi, who finds support for his view in the verse (*Devarim* 14:29), "So that Hashem your God blesses you in all that you do."

Today, as in Talmudic times, opinions differ on this matter, and all draw their inspiration from ancient sources. R' Dushinsky interprets "They shall gather it one day at a time" as referring to philosophical and ideological "gathering." In other words, from the manna episode each individual can extract his own philosophy on the problem of a livelihood. Furthermore, the *Shulchan Aruch, Orach Chaim* 15 rules that one must recite the section on manna every morning after *shacharis*, since "it contains a fine lesson in trusting Hashem." As stated, the verses dealing with the manna include the sources of all the views on this matter.

The Barshov Gaon explains that because all who ate the manna tasted whatever flavor they wished, Hashem could naturally see a person's character by whether he desired permitted or forbidden foods.

⋖§ Work: A Blessing or a Curse?

Maglei Tzedek explains that the manna was supposed to test the Children of Israel by presenting the opportunity for indolence and idleness, the prime causes of sin. In his opinion, there is a positive and a negative side to work. On the one hand, a person's preoccupation with earning a living deprives him of the chance to study Torah deeply, as he would wish to do. On the other hand, this preoccupation prevents indolence and boredom.

Chovos HaLevavos as well stresses man's duty to work as a means of avoiding sin. The generation of the desert, unoccupied with earning a living, eating food from Heaven, faced a challenge: Would they use their free time for Torah study or would they become indolent and waste their time on frivolities? That is what the Torah meant by (*Sh'mos* 16:4), "I shall test them to see if they follow My Torah or not." In other words, Hashem said that he would wait and see how they made use of their free time, now that they did not need to work for a living.

Chovos HaLevavos is teaching a profound lesson. Man was created by Divine plan. It was Hashem Who made man's drive to be productive a part of his physical and psychological makeup. Doctors speak highly of physical exercise from a medical standpoint, yet it is just as important for a healthy mind, for it leads to mental balance and sound decision-making capacity. Without it, man is as free as a bird, with a penchant for foolishness and sin.

The Chassidic literature finds in the manna episode a great opportunity to criticize greed. According to *Tiferes Shlomo*, the purpose of the manna was to liberate the Jewish people from their lust for money. Previously we read (v. 15:22), "And Moshe led the Children of Israel away from the sea," and *Chazal* explain that he had to pull them away forcibly from plundering the booty remaining after the Egyptians were drowned. *Chazal* refer to monetary greed as *bizah*, for the root of the word *bizah* means "contemptible," and greed is a contemptible trait. Similarly, Avraham gave all the money he had ever received from non-Jewish kings to the children of his concubines. He did not wish to benefit from it, because it was contemptible.

✑§ Who Is Rich? He Who Is Happy with His Lot

Some commentaries view the manna episode as teaching that Jews must totally reject their working lives in favor of Torah study. The majority, however, take a position more in tune with everyday life. A few see the manna as serving to strengthen the faith and trust of the Jewish people. *Kli Yakar* states that Hashem wished to achieve this point with His command regarding the manna (v. 16:19): "Let no man leave of it until the morning." As mentioned, this command served to teach the Jewish people to believe in Hashem and to trust that His salvation would surely come. *Kli Yakar* further states that the manna was a trial to see if the Jewish people could withstand the temptation of wealth.

Other commentaries view the manna as Hashem's show of love for His people, for it brought them into daily contact with Him. As the Chassidic *tzaddik* R' Yaivi relates: The *Baal Shem Tov* said that there is great good fortune in poverty, for everyday the poor man merits to approach Hashem to ask Him for sustenance.

Nonetheless, some commentaries view the manna as teaching us to be satisfied with what we have. *Ma'asei Hashem* states that Hashem's intent was to imbue the Jewish people with the attribute of contentment, so they would be satisfied with their lot and would learn Torah in a calm state of mind. *Chazal* say, "The Torah was given only to those who eat manna." This does not mean that whoever does not have all his needs readily satisfied is exempt from Torah study. Rather, the Torah was given only to those who are satisfied with what they have, as were the Israelites who lived on manna.

Akeidas Yitzchak here develops his view that the righteous should accustom themselves to making do with natural foods such as vegetables, while avoiding meat and luxuries. So was the manna. It satisfied only one's most essential physical and psychological needs.

All the commentaries agree that the manna was a means of teaching us a proper outlook on earning a living. It also served as a test of discerning man's nature, as indicated by the Torah (v. 16:4), "So that I may test them." *Imrei Yosef* explains this in accordance with *Chazal*'s words in Tractate *Yoma* 75, that manna would fall at the doors of the righteous, those bordering between sin and merit would have to go out and collect it, while the wicked would have to wander far from their tents to find theirs. Thus, the manna announced publicly the spiritual level of all.

Concerning the integration of Torah study and work, *Chazal* say, "Toil drives sin away." In innumerable places, *Chazal* sing the high praises of labor. Some heretics charge that the Torah has a negative regard for a life of hard work, based on its having cursed Adam (*Bereishis* 3:19), saying, "By the sweat of your brow shall you eat bread." Yet, there is no truth to such a charge, for it is based on misreading a verse. Even before his first sin, Adam was commanded (ibid. 2:15) "to till and maintain" the Garden of Eden. From this, *Avos DeRabbi Nassan* concludes, "Great is work, for even Adam tasted nothing until he had toiled."

After the Sin, Adam was cursed, but only that his labor would now be backbreaking. The earth was cursed with thorns and thistles, and Adam would have to use his strength to remove the obstacles, and bring forth his food by the sweat of his brow. Yet, work per se is part of man's essence, and makes him superior to all other creatures. Livelihood gained by hard backbreaking labor — that is Adam's curse. Other creatures support themselves without hard toil.

It is impossible to say that the manna liberated the Children of Israel only from the results of Adam's curse, i.e., "working by the sweat of their brow." It did not liberate them from work itself, which is part of man's essence. They still had to collect the manna (*Sh'mos* 16:4), and this activity afforded them physical rejuvenation and mental balance. Only on the Sabbath were they freed from collecting manna, as from all other work (v. 34:21), "Six days shall you work, and on the seventh shall you rest." True, the *mitzvah* here is not to work during the week, but to rest on Shabbos. Nonetheless, although there is no *mitzvah* to eat, it is still vital to man's survival, and the same may be said of work.

The forty years of manna represented a return to Eden. In Eden, as in the desert, Adam was obligated to "till and maintain," but he could eat from all the trees of the garden. He was not compelled to earn his living by the sweat of his brow. Moshe said (v. 16:15), "This is the bread which Hashem has given you to eat." This is food as Hashem originally meant it to be, free of Adam's curse. Even so, He commanded them (v. 16), "Gather of it every man according to his need." The gathering is the work, vital to man's physical and mental well-being.

V.
Miraculous
Versus Non-miraculous Warfare

ur entire *parashah* deals with Hashem's miraculously altering nature. Included however, is the war against Amalek, waged by natural means. If the Jewish people had the capacity to successfully wage war, why did Hashem have to alter nature on their behalf? It is all the more surprising, for at the beginning of the *parashah* (v. 13:17), Hashem's decision to take an indirect desert route is explained as due to the danger that "if they see war, they will return to Egypt." How then were they able to wage war with Amalek without the risk that they would return to Egypt?

Another puzzle is *Rashi*'s first reading of (v. 13:18) "וַחֲמֻשִׁים — Armed — the Children of Israel ascended from Egypt." If they were armed, what risk was there that on facing war they would return to Egypt? Why, after all, did they need weapons if not for battle?

Old *Rashi* texts, appearing in parentheses, state that the Torah mentions their being armed to explain the source of their weapons in their wars later on with Amalek, Sichon and Og. Yet, we must still wonder why they used weapons to fight those nations, and not against Egypt.

◆§ Slavery Fosters Feelings of Inferiority

Ibn Ezra deals with the aforementioned questions in terms of Israel's fear when they stood at the sea. He puts forth a psychological theory regarding freedom and slavery, and their respective effects upon fighting spirit. The generation just freed from Egypt was unfit, in his opinion, to fight its masters.

> They had been trained from youth to bear the Egyptian yoke, and suffered feelings of inferiority. How then could they fight their masters? They were indolent and untrained in warfare. The proof is that Amalek despite their small numbers would have done serious damage if not for Moshe's prayer. Hashem alone is responsible for great events, and history unfolds according to His plan. He caused all of the males who had been in Egypt to circle

about until they died out, for they were incapable of fighting the Canaanites. A new generation that had not known exile arose and, as I mentioned regarding the words of Moshe in *parashas Sh'mos*, they had a high spirit.

Ibn Ezra in the concluding sentence refers to his explanation in *Sh'mos* of Moshe's growing up in Pharaoh's palace. It was so "he would be of a high caliber regarding learning and behavior, and he would not be degraded and accustomed to slavery."

A parallel to the above commentary is provided by S'forno on the verse (13:18), "Armed — the Children of Israel ascended from Egypt". Although they were armed, they lacked courage, and were liable to return to Egypt for fear of war.

Rambam in *Moreh Nevuchim* (3:24) takes a course similar to Ibn Ezra:

> If not for their toil and struggle in the desert, they would have been unable to fight or conquer the inhabitants of Canaan. The Torah tells us so (*Sh'mos* 13:17-18), "For God had said, 'Lest on facing war they will have regrets and return to Egypt. And God led the people through the desert towards the Sea of Reeds, and armed, the Children of Israel ascended from Egypt ...'" This is because rest decreases courage, whereas the challenge of self-support and labor increase courage.

Thus, *Rambam* associates their weakness with their habits acquired in Egypt of not opposing impediments and not fighting harsh reality. These habits differ from those Ibn Ezra mentions, and result, according to *Rambam*, not from crushed spirit, but from dull inactivity. Ultimately, however, both *Rambam* and Ibn Ezra blame slavery for the lack of fighting spirit which the Jewish people acquired in Egypt. In *Rambam's* view, the desert spirit leads to courage as a result of the suffering the nomadic life entails. In 3:32, he reiterates this:

Hashem wisely led them around the desert until they had learned courage. As is known, the austere life of the desert, without human comforts and conveniences, such as bathing and the like, make one brave, while a luxurious existence fosters cowardliness. There in the desert, a generation was born, unaccustomed to degradation and slavery.

According to *Rambam*, a fighting spirit and love of freedom develop from toil and hardship, a lack of every pleasure and convenience of life. This is why Hashem led His nation through the desert before bringing them into the Land.

This explains the verse, "And God led them through the desert." Psychologically, the Jewish people were still not ready to face their enemies, and could not have beaten even a small nation like the Philistines.

◆§ Justifications for Fear

Other commentaries take a less extreme view of the psychological condition of the newly freed slaves, asserting that, under the circumstances, even normally courageous men would have had cause for fear. According to *Ramban*, they were not ready for an offensive war. As the Philistines would not have allowed them to pass through in peace, they would have had to attack. It was this they feared. On the other hand, they were unafraid of defending themselves against Amalek, who in his hatred had attacked them. Only when they had distanced themselves from Egypt, and had also realized that Hashem would not let them turn back, did they dare attack Sichon and Og offensively.

Chizkuni explains similarly, defending their fear as rational. The Children of Israel were afraid of being attacked from both front and rear. While the Egyptians pursued from behind, the Philistines would meet them head on to prevent them from seizing Canaan. He also offers yet another theory based on *I Divrei HaYamim* (Ch. 7). Members of the tribe of Ephraim had left Egypt prematurely, before the Exodus, and were killed by Philistines from Gass. There was now the risk that the Philistines, thinking that the Children of Israel were coming to take revenge, would themselves attack.

This explanation has its source in the Midrash, although the idea is expressed there differently: Had Hashem taken the Children of Israel through Philistine territory, they would have seen the bones of their dead brethren, and chosen slavery to avoid a similar fate. The Torah says that Hashem avoided Philistine territory (*Sh'mos* 13:17-18), "lest on facing war" the Children of Israel would reconsider and return to Egypt. In other words, they would see the bones of their dead brethren as a reminder of what happens when war is waged for the sake of freedom. They would not distinguish between themselves and their brethren who had left Egypt prematurely. Rather, they would conclude that they were forbidden to strike out for freedom, and would return to Egypt.

Kesav Sofer offers a highly novel thought. The Philistine culture was highly advanced. The Children of Israel, passing through such a country, would adopt its practices, learning advanced military tactics.

They would then return to Egypt to conquer it and settle there instead of going to *Eretz Yisrael*.

Despite the risks of what might happen in the event of war, the Children of Israel were well armed, for in the final analysis, the desert route had its own dangerous enemies. As we saw from the old *Rashi* texts cited above, they used these weapons to defeat Amalek.

Abarbanel views the arming of the Children of Israel as a directive not to rely on miracles, but to prepare to defend one's life by non-miraculous means: "Although they had faith in Hashem, they went armed, in accordance with the idea of, 'Have a steed ready for war — but salvation is Hashem's.' "

Rabbenu Bachya expands on this: "It is the way of the Torah to require man to act naturally and in a conventional manner. Only then will miracles happen. Thus, Yehoshua was told (*Yehoshua* 8:2), 'Set up an ambush for the city of Ai.' " Why should a nation so familiar with miracles need to employ an ambush? But as Rabbenu Bachya explains, "The Torah wishes man to do his utmost with the natural means at his disposal, and to leave the rest to Heaven."

According to this view, verse 13:18 of our *parashah*, stating that the Children of Israel emerged from Egypt armed, teaches a timeless lesson about the nature of faith. While Hashem leads the Jewish people with miracles, they themselves must prepare through non-miraculous means, and must realize that salvation will come from Hashem.

Not in vain do *Chazal* comment that when they were trapped at the Sea of Reeds, one group wished to go to war against the Egyptians. They had the means, for they were armed. Nonetheless, Hashem was satisfied that the Children of Israel had done their part, and at the last moment saved them miraculously. Why did Hashem do so? Because they were not really fit for battle, despite the weapons they possessed. They were ignorant of military strategy, and did not understand the principle that in battle, not quantity but quality is decisive. As S'forno states:

> "And Bnei Israel went out with a high hand" — Due to their numbers, they were certain they would be victorious. Yet, the Torah thereby informs us that they were unaware of military strategy. For their enemies, though few in number, were highly trained, and this should have struck fear in their hearts.

Chasam Sofer explains why Hashem preferred to employ miracles against the Egyptians rather than having the Children of Israel do battle with them. The saying goes, "Do not throw stones in the well from which you have drunk." Elsewhere the Torah states (*Devarim* 23:8),

"Do not abhor the Egyptian, for you were a stranger in his land." It would have been unethical for the Children of Israel to kill the Egyptians themselves. The Torah here teaches proper behavior and conduct. Although armed, the Children of Israel did not fight the Egyptians face to face, because of the haven they had found in Egypt throughout the hundreds of years they had dwelled in that land.

Besides what *Chasam Sofer* says, there is yet another ethical lesson to be learned: We must not wield an avenging sword when we are on land that is not ours. The Torah says, "And the Children of Israel ascended armed out of the Land of Egypt." Yet, they did not fight until they were at the borders of *Eretz Yisrael*. We cannot liberate ourselves from exile through the sword. For that we depend upon Heavenly mercy. True, *Chazal* stated that there are three means of self-defense against an enemy: appeasement, prayer and warfare, yet in exile, only two apply. The third may only be used in *Eretz Yisrael*.

◂§ Go and Fight Amalek

In the battle against Amalek, Moshe, for the first time, commands Yehoshua to respond militarily to an enemy attack, while he himself assists through prayer and raising his hands to Heaven. The waging of war by non-miraculous means, when until now all of Israel's battles have been won supernaturally, is explained in the Midrash as serving to educate Yehoshua in military strategy. He is the one who will bring the Jewish people into *Eretz Yisrael*.

In the *Mechilta*, R' Yehoshua and R' Eliezer argue over the meaning of Moshe's orders to Yehoshua (*Sh'mos* 17:9), "Choose men for us." According to the former, Yehoshua was commanded to pick brave warriors, and according to the latter, God-fearing men. This debate, while essentially a matter of ideology, also indicates the differing opinions regarding the extent to which Hashem intervened supernaturally in the war against Amalek. Abarbanel states that the Children of Israel deserved no miracles, having just asked (v. 7), "Is Hashem among us or not?" Moshe was afraid that their expression of doubt about Divine Providence would deprive them of miraculous salvation. Therefore, he commanded Yehoshua to wage a non-miraculous war, while he himself prayed for their success in battle. Why did he not lead the battle himself? Possibly, states Abarbanel, to humiliate Amalek. He did not wish them to have the honor of fighting him personally, and he sent Yehoshua, his young servant, in his place.

The other commentaries agree to Abarbanel's view of a non-miraculous battle. *Ma'asei Hashem* interprets Moshe's command to

Yehoshua, as related by *Chazal*, "Go out of the clouds [of glory]," as an indication that the time had come for him to leave the comfort of Divine shelter and enter into the non-miraculous world. Moshe's raising his arms was meant only to encourage Yehoshua, to improve morale, and to remind the Jewish people to keep their thoughts on Hashem.

Ramban has a similar explanation of Moshe's climbing the hill and raising his arms to Heaven. Moshe wished to observe the soldiers in battle, and he also wished them to see him with arms raised, to bolster their courage.

Interestingly, several well-known commentaries even explain the staff Moshe held as a non-miraculous battle implement. For *Rashbam*, it was a battle flag: "Soldiers in battle generally take strength in seeing their flag raised high. When they see it fall to the earth, they flee, assuming defeat." Abarbanel, too, interprets in this way Moshe's lifting up his staff, comparing it to the way kings raise their scepter in battle.

Abarbanel views the war against Amalek as non-miraculous, accomplished with the weapons *Bnei Yisrael* brought out with them from Egypt. This is what is meant by verse 13: "And Yehoshua weakened Amalek and his people with the sword." Through this we can understand *Rashi's* comment at the beginning of *Beshalach*, that the weapons carried by the Children of Israel when they emerged from Egypt were in preparation for the future battle with Amalek.

At the beginning of *parashas Yisro*, *Chasam Sofer* offers a fine comment on the forms of war Hashem chooses for Israel. When the Jewish people left Egypt armed, Pharaoh assumed Moshe's spiritual powers had becomes so weak that he no longer had recourse to miracles. Pharaoh, thinking he could emerge the victor in non-miraculous battle, pursued Israel with six hundred elite charioteers, boasting (v. 15:9), "I shall unsheath my sword." Hashem could have shown him that physical force is meaningless, by having Pharaoh lose in battle to the Children of Israel, who were weaker. Instead (v. 10) Hashem "blew with the wind and the sea covered them." He destroyed them supernaturally.

Later, when Amalek approached with arrow and sword, Hashem could have crushed them with stones from the heavens. Instead, He allowed the Jewish people to vanquish them non-miraculously in battle. Why? To demonstrate to Israel that He could save them as "*Elokim*," employing nature, or as "*Hashem*," employing supernatural means. (The Chassidic works point out that the *gematria*, or numerical value, of הַטֶּבַע — "the nature" — is eighty-six, the same as that of אֱלֹהִים — "*Elokim*.") Thus, at the beginning of Chapter 18, the Torah tells (v. 1) how Yisro had heard about "all that *Elokim* had done," referring to

Israel's non-miraculous battle against Amalek, and about (ibid.), "Hashem taking Israel out of Egypt," supernaturally.

Following the battle with Amalek, the Torah states (v. 17:15), "And Moshe built an altar and called it 'Hashem is my banner.' " *Rashi* comments, "Here, Hashem performed a great miracle for us." Since this was a battle fought by non-miraculous means, whereby Israel vanquished Amalek with the sword, there remained the possibility that they might entertain the mistaken idea that the victory was through their own power. Therefore, Moshe publicly announced that Hashem had performed the miracle for them.

The *parashah* concludes (v. 16): "Hashem will be at war with Amalek forever." *Kesav Sofer* comments, "Know this rule forever: When the Jewish people gain victory over their enemies by the sword, it is not through their own power. Rather, 'Hashem is their banner.' It is He who brings us victory."

Yisro – יתרו

I.

Yisro Arrives in the Desert

Our *parashah* tells of Yisro's coming to rejoice with Moshe and Israel in the good fortune Hashem had granted them, and to thank Hashem for the miracles and wonders He had performed. Some of *Chazal* question Yisro's sincerity. Accordingly, they read וַיִּחַדְּ יִתְרוֹ (*Sh'mos* 18:9) (literally, "Yisro felt joy") as בְּשָׂרוֹ נַעֲשָׂה חִידוּדִין חִידוּדִין — "His flesh was filled with goose pimples" — over the destruction of Egypt (*Rashi* based on *Sanhedrin* 94a).

We can understand this explanation by *Chazal* based on Yisro's behavior. When Moshe suggested that Yisro join the Jewish people, who were going to inherit their land, Yisro responded negatively: "Rather than go with you, I will return to my own land and birthplace" (*Bamidbar* 10:30). Such a man, who had heard and seen all that had befallen the Jewish people, yet was unwilling to join them, must have had mixed feelings about their success.

In *Beha'alosecha*, we see how Moshe attempted to persuade Yisro to remain with the Jewish people. The commentaries interpret the debate between Moshe and "Chovav," as Yisro is referred to there, along the lines of *Chazal*. Yisro argued that as a convert he would inherit no portion in the Land of Israel. Moshe rebuffed this claim, promising him a portion: "That same good which Hashem will bestow upon us He will be bestow upon you" (ibid. v. 32). Sifri, in fact, states that Yisro's sons inherited Doshna at Jericho.

Ramban is almost the only commentator who says that after receiving Moshe's promise of an inheritance, Yisro actually joined the Jewish people. He quotes the Jerusalem Talmud which declares that the descendants of Yisro can bring *bikkurim* and read the declarations involved (which refer to the entire saga of the Jewish people), based on the verse, "Go with us and we shall be good to you" (ibid. v. 29).

S'forno, however, holds that Moshe only succeeded in convincing Yisro to leave his sons with the Jewish people. Yisro himself returned to his native land, and, according to S'forno, the reasons he gave are the same ones we hear even today: "My old age cannot bear the climate or food of a new country."

Yet these were not the only arguments Yisro employed to justify his remaining among the gentiles. According to *Sifri*, he used other well-known arguments as well: "I have a family. I have a country. I have property."

Rashi, quoting *Chazal*, likewise comments: "I will return to my own land and birthplace — both for the sake of my property and for the sake of my family."

According to R' Eliezer HaModa'i, Yisro employed a religious argument as well. He wished to remain in the diaspora to convert the gentiles: "A candle is of no benefit except in the dark. What good can I do before the sun and moon? I will go back to my land to convert my countrymen, then they will come to learn."

Seemingly, Yisro had a point, but Moshe did not accept it. *Or HaChaim* explains: Moshe responded, "By going back, you will profane Hashem's name. The Midianites will say that you studied our faith, valued it highly, yet abandoned us anyway."

One of the *rishonim*, R' Yosef Bechor Shor (*Rivash*), states another reason for Yisro's refusal to join the Jewish people. Yisro was afraid of the fighting bound up in the conquest of the Land of Israel. According to *Rivash*, Moshe tried to persuade Yisro to accompany them, saying, "Do not fear the wars that will take place, for Hashem has spoken well of the Israelites, and the natives will not be able to withstand our attack." Nonetheless, Yisro was unconvinced by these words, which were based on faith and trust in Hashem. Therefore, according to *Rivash*, he responded: "I shall return to my land and my birthplace. I shall not abandon certainty for doubt."

A well-known figure from *Tanach* with an entirely different personality is the proselyte Rus, mother of the Davidic dynasty. What great difficulties her mother-in-law placed in her path so she would remain in Moav! What great efforts Naomi made to convince Rus to part ways and return to her land and birthplace! Yet, Rus did not wish to be convinced: "Naomi saw that she was steadfast" (*Rus* 1:18). Rus accepted upon herself the yoke of Torah and *mitzvos*, as well as the challenge of *Eretz Yisrael*. She did not wish to remain a Jewess in Moav. Rather, she understood that she had to join the Jewish people in their ancestral land. Because she grasped the connection between the Torah and *Eretz Yisrael*, she merited to have the Kingdom of Israel built and established through her. Upon her lap, the future King David was born, the same king who later declared, when forced to leave *Eretz Yisrael*: "For they have driven me out this day from being joined with the heritage of Hashem, saying, 'Go serve other gods' " (*I Shmuel* 26:19). This confirms *Chazal*'s statement that "If someone lives outside *Eretz Yisrael*, it is as if he has no God." King David carried on the tradition of Rus who, through her love of Hashem, understood both empirically and intuitively the significance of *Eretz Yisrael*.

I heard an important explanation from R' Akiva Glassner, the Rav of Klausenberg, of how Rus was greater than Yisro. Boaz told Rus, "May you receive a full reward from Hashem, the God of Israel, under whose wings you have come to take refuge" (*Rus* 2:12). R' Chasa comments in the Midrash, "The expression 'you have come' is used." All the commentaries wonder what R' Chasa's point is. What does he add to what the verse already states? According to the Klausenberger Rav, R' Chasa seems to be explaining why Rus, of all the converts we have had over the centuries, received such a great reward as having the Kingdom of David established through her descendants. Surely, many converts have joined the Jewish people, among them Yisro. Why, among them all, did Rus merit to receive *maskores sheleimah* — a "full reward" — which *Chazal* take as an allusion to Shlomo, King David's son? R' Chasa's stressing the phrase "you have come" teaches that the great reward Rus received resulted not only from her conversion, but from her originally grasping that becoming a Jew requires her to come to *Eretz Yisrael*, to join the Jewish people in its Land. This is how Rus surpassed Yisro in greatness.

❧ When Did Yisro Arrive in the Desert?

Chazal in *Zevachim* 116 and the *Mechilta*, as well as the *rishonim*, are divided over whether Yisro came to visit Moshe in the desert before or after the Sinai Revelation. Ibn Ezra holds that he arrived afterwards, based on the following proofs: (a) The Torah states that Yisro offered burnt offerings to Hashem (*Sh'mos* 18:12), but does not say that he built the altar for them; this indicates that he brought his offerings on Israelite altars built following the erection of the *Mishkan*; (b) Moshe told his father-in-law, "I make known Hashem's decrees and laws" (v. 16) — a sign that the Torah had already been handed down at that point; (c) Moshe states in *Devarim* (vs. 1:6-7), "Hashem, our God, spoke to us at Chorev saying, 'You have been at this mountain long enough. Turn and travel onward.' " Clearly, these words were spoken just before the Israelites left the Sinai Desert. In that same section Moshe mentions the increased burden he faces due to Israel's rising population (v. 12), and he describes the appointing of judges in charge "of thousands and of hundreds." This was Yisro's advice on the second day of his stay in the desert. We see that Yisro arrived just before the Israelites left the Sinai desert.

Thus, in *Beha'alosecha*, Moshe told Yisro, "We are traveling to the place Hashem told us He would give us. Come with us" (*Bamidbar* 10:29). Yet Yisro refused. This corresponds exactly to our own *parashah*: "Moshe let his father-in-law depart, and he returned to his land" (*Sh'mos* 18:27). Now if Yisro arrived in the desert after the Sinai Revelation, why did our *parashah* precede it in the Torah? Ibn Ezra answers that the Torah intentionally placed our *parashah* immediately after the battle with Amalek, to contrast the very best and worst of the non-Jewish world. Amalek attacked us, hence we must remember its wickedness, while Yisro treated the Jewish people with kindness, so he deserved reward.

Before King Shaul attacked Amalek, he warned the *Keini*, Yisro's descendants, who lived near by: "Go! Depart! Go down from among the Amalekite, lest I destroy you with them, for you showed kindness to all of Israel when they came up from Egypt" (*I Shmuel* 15:6). Regarding Amalek, however, we find, "Blot out the remembrance of Amalek" (*Devarim* 25:19). *Ramban* quotes Ibn Ezra, and a verse from our *parashah* which seems to support the latter's view: "Yisro, Moshe's father-in-law, came with his wife and sons to Moshe, who was encamped in the desert at the mount of Hashem" (*Sh'mos* 18:5). This should indicate that Yisro arrived at Sinai during the year the Israelites remained there following the giving of the Torah, before they traveled on. Yet *Ramban* wonders why Yisro, who did mention *yetzias Mitzrayim*, never mentioned the giving of the Torah, which involved greater miracles: "Has any nation ever heard Hashem speaking out of fire, as you have, and survived?" (*Devarim* 4:33). Furthermore, Moshe told his father-in-law of all that Hashem did to the Egyptians (*Sh'mos* 18:8), and Yisro replied, "Now I know that Hashem is greater than any other" (v. 11). Why didn't Moshe tell him about the giving of the Torah? That surely would have verified for Yisro that Hashem and His Torah represented truth.

Possibly, states *Ramban*, Yisro left Midian when he heard about *yetzias Mitzrayim*, but reached the desert only after the giving of the Torah. At that moment, the giving of the Torah was so well known that Moshe did not have to mention it. Ultimately, however, *Ramban* accepts the view of R' Yehoshua, that Yisro arrived after the war with Amalek, but before the giving of the Torah took place. At that time, the Israelites were encamped at Refidim, in the Tzin Desert. Yisro set out to visit Moshe, arriving at Mount Sinai, where Hashem had first revealed Himself to Moshe. Then he heard that the Israelites had left Egypt to worship Hashem on that same mountain. He sent a messenger to Moshe announcing his arrival, and Moshe set out to meet him half-way. After meeting with Moshe, rejoicing with the Israelites and thanking Hashem, their Redeemer, Yisro returned to his land and birthplace.

As for *Parashas Beha'alosecha*, in which Moshe asked Yisro to convert, that occurred during a second visit. Midian was nearby, and Yisro could come and go with ease. At first Yisro refused Moshe's urgings, but after much persuasion he did convert.

Why then do we find descendants of Yisro among Amalek's neighbors during the time of King Shaul? It is possible that one of Yisro's sons returned to Midian. Alternately, the Keini mentioned in *I Shmuel* were not Yisro's descendants but his relatives.

Ramban opposes Ibn Ezra's view, without attempting to refute the proofs upon which he based himself. This he leaves to Abarbanel, who holds, like *Ramban*, that Yisro's visit preceded the giving of the Torah. Unlike *Ramban*, however, Abarbanel holds that Yisro visited the Jewish people only once, remaining with them until they left the Sinai Desert. As to Ibn Ezra's bringing proof from the fact that the Torah stated that Yisro came on his visit when Moshe was "camped at the mount of Hashem" (*Sh'mos* 18:5), Moshe was there only because he had just drawn water from the rock, situated at that mountain (v. 17:6). Furthermore, this location was called "the mount of Hashem" only because the Torah was destined to be given there.

HaDrash VeHaIyun brings several proofs that the Torah sometimes names things based on their future purpose. We read of Moshe in Midian, "He came to Chorev, the mount of Hashem" (v. 3:1), and *Rashi* comments that it was called this on account of its future purpose. Moreover, the Torah, describing the rivers of Eden, says, "The name of the third river is the Tigris which flows to the east of Assyria" (*Bereishis* 2:14). The Talmud asks (*Kesubos* 10b), "Did Assyria exist at that time?" and answers, "The Torah was referring to the future." With similar logic, the Torah calls Moshe's father-in-law יִתְרוֹ — "Yisro", even before his conversion, when the ו was added (before that time he was known as יֶתֶר — Yeser). Similarly, *Maharsha* on *Sotah* 34 notes that Joshua's name is spelled יְהוֹשֻׁעַ with a י during the battle against Amalek (*Sh'mos* 17), even though he was not destined to have that letter added until after the spy incident.

Midian was near Egypt, as we know from Moshe's having fled there. Therefore, as soon as the Israelites left Egypt, Yisro heard about it, as he heard about Israel's war against Amalek. It was then, during the second month following *yetzias Mitzrayim* that he left his land, one month before the giving of the Torah at Sinai.

Ibn Ezra argued that Yisro brought burnt offerings, and must have used an Israelite altar built following the giving of the Torah. Abarbanel counters that Moshe built an altar following the war against Amalek, calling it "Hashem is my banner" (*Sh'mos* 17:15). It was upon this altar that Yisro brought his offerings.

As for Moshe's telling Yisro that he "made known to Israel Hashem's decrees and laws" (v. 18:16), Abarbanel and Rabbenu Bachya hold that this is a reference to what Israel learned, not at Sinai, but at Marah (v. 15:25). This includes the laws of *Shabbos* and the courts, and the rules of proper conduct for desert living, as given by Moshe.

Ibn Ezra argues that in *Parashas Beha'alosecha*, when Moshe begged Yisro to join them, the Children of Israel were about to leave the Sinai desert to go into the Land, and that this had to be a year after the Sinai giving of the Torah. Abarbanel responds that Ibn Ezra has not necessarily identified the journey properly. Starting with *yetzias Mitzrayim*, the Israelites were constantly on the move. At the very start of Moshe's mission, he stated: "I shall go down to save them from Egypt, to bring them up out of that land" . . . into Canaan (v. 3:8).

Ibn Ezra claimed that the appointment of the judges, according to *Devarim*, Ch. 1, took place before the exit from the Sinai desert, a year after the giving of the Torah. To this, Abarbanel answers that Moshe may have waited until then to implement Yisro's advice, but the advice itself was given before the giving of the Torah.

In *Parashas Yisro*, the appointment of the judges seems to have taken place immediately, just as Yisro seemed to return to Midian immediately as well. Nonetheless, all of these events actually happened separately. Yisro arrived and counseled Moshe before the giving of the Torah, but the judges were appointed and Yisro returned to Midian afterwards. Yisro remained in the desert with Moshe for two years before returning. There is no reason to be puzzled over the Torah's reporting events that happened only later, for the same occurred regarding the manna: "Moshe said to Aaron, 'Take a jar and put an omer full of manna in it' . . . Aaron laid it before the Ark of Testimony to be kept" (*Sh'mos* 16:33-34). Yet at that point in *Sh'mos*, when the Israelites were at Elim, the Ark was as yet unbuilt. How could Aaron have laid manna before it? Similarly, the next verse reads, "The Israelites ate manna for forty years until they came to an inhabited land." Did forty years pass with that one verse? Rather, the Torah completes its narrative of an event that ends much later. Here as well, in *Parashas Yisro*, the Torah briefly relates what happened two years hence. Then, in *Beha'alosecha* and *Devarim*, the Torah presents the details once more.

◄§ Rashi's View on Yisro's Arrival

Rashi's view on when Yisro arrived in the desert is unclear. While he mentions that Yisro had heard about the splitting of the sea and the war with Amalek, he does not mention the giving of the Torah, as if it had not yet happened. Later on, however, we read, "Yisro felt joy for all the good that Hashem had done for Israel" (*Sh'mos* 18:9). *Rashi* comments that this refers to 'the well, the manna and the giving of the Torah," implying that the giving of the Torah had already occurred. Furthermore, we know that there is a debate in *Zevachim* and *Mechilta* over what event brought Yisro to the desert. R' Yehoshua says it was Israel's victory over Amalek, while R' Eliezer says it was the splitting of the sea. As later commentaries ask, how could *Rashi* combine these two views to include both?

R' Eliyahu Mizrachi holds that *Rashi* responded to the sense of the text. The previous section concluded with the battle against Amalek, while this section commences, "Yisro heard . . . that Hashem had taken Israel out of Egypt" (v. 18:1). *Rashi* therefore included both in his comment.

Maharal holds that *Rashi* is actually quoting R' Yehoshua (victory over Amalek), but that R' Yehoshua only meant to add on to the reason already mentioned in 18:1, the splitting of the sea. According to *Maharal*, R' Yehoshua could not logically ignore a reason that the Torah mentioned explicitly. In any event, *Rashi* does not mention the giving of the Torah here. According to *Levush HaOrah*, its inclusion in *Rashi's* comments on verse 9 was due to the use of a common expression [which includes the manna, the well, and the Torah]. Alternatively, *Rashi* may have mentioned the Torah in verse 9 so that *Chazal's* comment, בָּשָׂרוּ נַעֲשָׂה חִידוּדִין חִידוּדִין — "His flesh became full of goose pimples" — would apply to it. However, *Rashi* did not mean that the giving of the Torah was a reason for Yisro's visiting Moshe.

Ma'asei Hashem offers a novel interpretation of 18:1. The Torah states that Yisro heard אֵת כָּל אֲשֶׁר עָשָׂה אֱלֹהִים לְמֹשֶׁה וּלְיִשְׂרָאֵל עַמּוֹ — which is usually translated: "all that God did for Moshe and for Israel, His people." But עָשָׂה may also mean "He made." Thus Yisro heard that Hashem had made the Jewish people His nation, choosing them and giving them the Torah. This is in accord with the verse: "On this day you have become a nation of Hashem your God" (*Devarim* 27:9). Verse 18:1 thus implies that Yisro arrived after the giving of the Torah.

Interestingly, this debate is also reflected in the Targumic renderings of הַר הָאֱלֹהִים (Sh'mos 18:5). *Targum Onkelos* has, "Yisro came ... to the desert, to the mountain where Hashem's glory appeared to them," while *Targum Yehonasan ben Uziel* reads, "Yisro came to the desert where Moshe was staying, near the mountain where Hashem's glory was to appear to him." According to *Onkelos*, Moshe had already camped at Mount Sinai, whereas according to *Yehonasan ben Uziel*, Moshe camped *near* the mountain, at a place identified by *Ramban* as Refidim.

II.

Yisro's Legislative System

hrough the legislative system he suggested to Moshe, Yisro added an entire section to the Torah. Even though some say that the giving of the Torah occurred first, the Torah still places the section of Yisro before it, thus hinting that proper behavior takes precedence over Torah study. Hashem wished to give Torah and *mitzvos* to a disciplined society capable of the orderly adoption of new law, and not to a wild, lawless people.

Tzror HaMor comments that the Torah accentuated Yisro's wisdom to show that Moshe knew how to choose a wife. He did not choose Tzipporah casually or at random. Yet, whoever examines this chapter will find that it contains more than a description of Yisro's personality. The Torah states that Moshe listened to Yisro and accepted his advice: "Moshe listened to his father-in-law and did all that he said" (Sh'mos 18:24). Not only was Yisro wise, but he was capable of giving Moshe the practical advice he needed. Without a doubt, this section of the Torah serves to teach a special lesson. Hashem gave His people righteous laws and judgments, "our wisdom and understanding in the eyes of the nations" (Devarim 4:6). Could Hashem possibly have needed Yisro's advice to establish court protocol? What did the Torah mean to emphasize in this section, which preceded the giving of the Torah?

Or HaChaim holds that by means of this *parashah*, Hashem wished to express openly His special love of the Jewish people, and the reason He chose them. It was their spiritual superiority which prepared them to be a kingdom of priests and a holy nation, for in terms of wisdom and culture, they were no better than any other people. Yisro came to the desert to teach the Israelites procedures for maintaining law and order.

In this way, Hashem demonstrated that the nations of the world were more cultured than they, for they could not manage for themselves even something so simple as these procedural arrangements. Even so, because Israel was spiritually superior, Hashem chose them and not the Midianites to receive the Torah: Hashem wished to show the Jewish people of the desert, and all future generations as well, that some nations possess much more inborn wisdom than the Jewish people. In fact, we can learn this from Yisro himself, and from the organizational system he devised. Yisro's brilliance is proof that the Jewish people were not chosen because they were more intelligent than anyone else, but because they were more kind, and because Hashem loved the Patriarchs.

This explanation views our *parashah* as confirmation of Israel's spiritual superiority over the nations. Hashem chose the Jewish people despite their being inferior in culture and deed to others. Other peoples were more socially and technologically advanced, but that is not what determines a people's worth, or at least not that of the Jewish people. Yet, our *parashah* not only highlights Yisro's wisdom, but states that Moshe accepted and followed his advice.

We might ask why Moshe was willing to do so. Did he need it? Did Yisro really suggest some new wisdom not included in the Torah? This last question is especially relevant according to the view that Yisro arrived after the giving of the Torah (*Zevachim* 116).

✑§ Yisro Suggested Nothing New

Abarbanel sees nothing novel in Yisro's recommendations. Yet, because he had good intentions, as he wished to help the Jewish people with their new efforts to maintain a legal system, the Torah honored him by mentioning his suggestions. The Torah deprives no living being of the reward due him; it therefore devotes an entire section to Yisro's words. Yisro's advice added nothing to what Moshe already knew. Even so, because Moshe respected Yisro and saw him as a friend offering the Jewish people guidance, he accepted his advice graciously.

A man like Yisro coming to help desert nomads surely involved a lovely gesture worthy of gratitude. (This idea is expressed clearly in *Sifri, Beha'alosecha*: "Was Moshe, himself, unaware of the system Yisro described? Why did he forget about it when he needed it? To provide a source of merit for Yisro.") R' Eliezer HaModa'i in the *Mechilta* expresses this idea even more clearly, separating with a period the two phrases, וַיִּשְׁמַע מֹשֶׁה לְקוֹל חֹתְנוֹ — "Moshe listened to his father-in-law," and, וַיַּעַשׂ כֹּל אֲשֶׁר אָמָר — "Moshe did all that He said." Moshe did listen to his father-in-law, but "all that He said" refers to what Hashem, and not Yisro, had told him. Moshe did only what Hashem had told him, not all that Yisro had advised.

According to Abarbanel, Moshe knew very well that a nation needs leadership, and that it cannot be provided by a single individual lest he wear himself out (v. 18:18). Yet, because the Torah was soon to be revealed, Moshe preferred waiting for Hashem to institute His system rather than doing so himself based on mere human understanding, and he was willing to face a short period of overwork. Moshe carried out only Hashem's plan. Although it was similar to Yisro's, differences existed: (a) Yisro recommended that Moshe pick judges himself, whereas, following Hashem's plan, Moshe handed over this authority to the Jewish people: "Choose for yourselves wise men" (Devarim 1:13). (b) Yisro called for the judges to have certain specific virtues, but "wisdom," in the sense of knowing a body of law, was not among them. Mankind did not yet possess written legal codes, and judges did not make use of spiritual or cultural knowledge in judging cases. Moshe, however, demanded first and foremost that the judges of Israel know the Torah and be "wise," i.e., that they judge according to Torah law. (c) Yisro recommended that Israel's judges come from the highest economic strata (Rashi on אַנְשֵׁי חַיִל: Sh'mos 18:21), while Moshe viewed all Jews as eligible, judging solely on merit. (d) Yisro recommended that the judges be appointed immediately to help Moshe with jurisdiction, while Moshe waited until the Jewish people had left the Sinai desert. (e) Yisro recommended that those appointed serve exclusively as judges, whereas Moshe eventually appointed them to head the army, and to take charge of conquering the Land of Israel. All this proves that Moshe executed Hashem's command, not just his father-in-law's advice.

Even if he ostensibly seemed to accept his advice and thank him for it, it was only in recognition of Yisro's effort, and the Torah added this section for the same reason. In establishing a legal structure, Hashem and his servant Moshe surely had no need of Yisro's plans. In Devarim, Ch. 1, when Moshe describes his establishing the legal system, he does not even mention Yisro. Although Moshe showed Yisro respect for his good intentions by sending him off to Midian with honors, the legal system eventually adopted came not from Yisro but from Hashem.

Yisro naively intended to teach non-Jewish wisdom and justice to the Jewish people, who were about to receive the Torah at Sinai. Thus, on the eve of his return to Midian, he demonstrated that he still had not grasped the significance of the Exodus, and had not applied its conclusions to his personal life. Although he now acknowledged Hashem and His wonders, Yisro remained what he was before he arrived. Returning to his land and birthplace, he did not merit to share in the one-time experience of the giving of the Torah at Sinai.

Chazal, who grasped the deeper meaning of what happened, explained its cause: A man who had not suffered together with Israel in Egypt, who had not shed his impurity through seeing Hashem's signs and wonders, was not fit to share in the religious experience of the giving of the Torah. Following are *Chazal's* words in *Tanchuma*: "Hashem said, 'While My children were slaves, working with bricks and mortar, Yisro was sitting in the quiet of his home. Shall he now share in their joy on receiving the Torah?' We therefore read: 'Moshe sent his father-in-law home' (*Sh'mos* 18:27)." According to this interpretation, Yisro was absent at the giving of the Torah, not because he did not wish to be present, but because he did not merit to be there. Among *Chazal*, some hold that Yisro eventually did convert to Judaism, accepting Torah and *mitzvos* upon himself. Nonetheless, he did not accept them as wholeheartedly as he would have, had he personally experienced the giving of the Torah at Sinai.

Yisro knew how close to Hashem Moshe was, and he knew that Moshe had taken the Israelites out of Egypt with signs and wonders. Even so, he naively tried to advise Moshe in laws of conduct. Thus, Yisro was far from understanding the essence of the Jewish people, or the reason for their selection. Moshe asked him to remain with the Jewish people and be their guide: "You are familiar with the places we are going to camp in the desert" (*Bamidbar* 10:31). Yet, he refuses: "I shall return to my home and birthplace" (ibid. v. 30). Yisro had a "birthplace" more important to him than Israel's birthplace. Moreover, he had his own "land," and he was unwilling to accept the land chosen by Hashem. Small wonder that *Chazal* responded with suspicion and criticism, despite their high praise for his having come to stay in the first place.

Chazal say that Yisro was psychologically torn, and that "his flesh was filled with goose pimples" when he heard that the Egyptians had drowned (*Rashi* on *Sh'mos* 18:9). Moreover, in *Yalkut Reuveni*, quoting *Galya Raza*, the opinion is expressed that Yisro, in advising Moshe about the legal system, wished to harm Israel, not help them. In suggesting judges for the hundreds and thousands, etc., and in stipulating that they be from among the wealthy, he wished to create rifts in the Jewish people, whose unity depends upon the Torah. He wished to cause their division into different sects and castes, thus preventing the equality demanded by the Torah.

The Kotzker Rebbe addresses the same point, saying that Yisro's call for "men of truth" was meant to rectify the harm done by his call for wealthy men. A "man of truth" is unimpressed by social or economic standing. According to the Kotzker Rebbe, Yisro, himself, advised ways of bridging the gap created by his social divisions. According to *Yalkut Reuveni*, on the other hand, Yisro wished to create an irrevocable caste system.

Thus, according to Abarbanel, Yisro added no wisdom to the Torah, only a section. He gave Moshe no new wisdom, and his advice did not compensate for anything lacking. Moshe heard all on Mount Sinai, including procedures for organizing a legal system. Yisro's only reward for his good will was the very fact that his advice was immortalized in a section of the Torah, even though the Jewish people did not need his advice.

~§ Qualities Necessary for a Judge

Yisro recommended four qualities that all judges should possess: "Capable [according to *Rashi* cited above this term means "wealthy," according to *Ramban* cited below it means "capable"], God-fearing and truthful men, who hate unjust gain" (*Sh'mos* 18:21). Yet, Moshe sought only *anshei chayil*, "capable" men (v. 25).

According to *Ramban*, *anshei chayil* is a virtue that includes all the others. Yisro spelled out the full meaning of the term, enumerating all the qualities it included, and Moshe chose men who had those qualities. Rabbenu Bachya and others explain similarly.

Or HaChaim holds that Yisro's four qualities correspond to the four ranks of judges he recommended. "Judges of thousands" must be *anshei chayil*. This is the highest quality, and includes all others. "Judges of hundreds" must possess the second quality, fear of Hashem, and the two qualities below it. "Judges of fifties" must at least be willing to establish truth. Yet, even the lowest ranked judges, the "judges of tens," must at least hate injustice. Anyone lacking this basic trait is unfit to be a judge of any kind.

Ibn Ezra holds that *anshei chayil* refers to those possessing the immense spiritual strength necessary to bear the burden of the nation. Parallel to this, Moshe says in *Devarim* 1:13, הָבוּ לָכֶם אֲנָשִׁים, literally, "Give men for yourselves," i.e., choose men who will be fit to bear the severe burden you yourselves will present. Yisro recommends "God-fearing men," while Moshe, instead, recommends "wise, understanding men, known to the tribes." Fear of Hashem is impossible without true wisdom.

By contrast, some explain *anshei chayil* literally in its military sense, as "brave soldiers of Torah and good deeds" (*Tanchuma, Shoftim* 3).

S'forno holds the unusual view that Moshe was unable to find individuals who epitomized all the desired traits, but found some who were outstanding in one of the traits and others who were outstanding in different traits. He then had to decide what was preferable: *anshei chayil* who were not exemplary in their fear of Hashem, or vice versa. On consideration he concluded that he had better choose the *anshei chayil*, competent and industrious men with the expertise needed to investigate and clarify legal cases, bringing them to a successful conclusion. This was preferable to incompetent men whose only virtue was fear of Hashem.

No less interesting is a second comment of Ibn Ezra. In *Devarim* when Moshe mentions *anshei chayil*, he means men whose nature can be judged at a glance. "He did not mention 'God-fearing' men," says Ibn Ezra, "for only Hashem knows what is in a man's heart."

In *Parashas Devarim* we find yet another trait mentioned. Moshe asked the Israelites to choose wise men for their judges, for wisdom can be objectively measured. Yet some wise men do not fear Hashem. Moshe therefore asked for "wise men known to the tribes." The candidate's acquaintances would be able to confirm that he was not only intelligent, but spiritually wise as well. As *Rashi* comments, "When a stranger approaches wrapped in a *tallis*, I have no indication of whether or not he is reputable." Moshe picked traits he could ascertain — competence and wisdom. For all other traits, he relied upon the members of the candidate's tribe who knew him. (The letters of the word חַיִל — *chayil*, Yisro's criterion in *Sh'mos* 18:25, are a mnemonic for חֲכָמִים יְדֻעִים לְשִׁבְטֵיכֶם — "wise men, known to your tribes," Moshe's criterion in *Devarim* 1:13.)

Yisro was the first person to suggest a system whereby laws would be created by one body and carried out by another. He told Moshe, "You be the link between the people and Hashem" (*Devarim* 18:19). Moshe was to bring down the laws from the Supreme Lawgiver, while the courts were to be a separate institution.

According to the Vilna Gaon (quoted in *HaKesav VeHaKabalah*), Yisro recommended both a court system and an educational system. The judges of thousands and hundreds were to judge cases, whereas the judges of fifties and tens were to teach and guide the people. Furthermore, the judges of tens were to act as policemen.

As we have seen above, the steps Moshe took later on were under Hashem's direction. Nonetheless, Yisro was not deprived of the reward due him for his suggestions. The Jewish people are willing to hear advice from anyone as long as he then goes away and does not interfere:

"Moshe let his father-in-law depart and he went his way to his own land" (*Sh'mos* 18:27).

We find a particularly interesting idea in S'forno, who states that Yisro also recommended a court of appeals, enabling defendants to challenge legal decisions. The system was to work on a hierarchy going all the way up to Moshe.

III.

Is "I Am Hashem Your God" One of the 613 Mitzvos?

A re the words, אָנֹכִי ה׳ אֱלֹהֶיךָ — "I am Hashem your God" (v. 20:2), which form the foundation of all *mitzvos*, counted among the 613? By this we are not asking whether a particular belief involving no physical action can be called a *mitzvah*. That question was already decided by the *rishonim* and *acharonim*, who counted many states of mind among both the positive and negative commandments.

Ibn Ezra asks how "You shall not covet" (v. 20:14) can be considered a *mitzvah*, for he wonders how it is possible to command a person not to covet. Yet, even he, in his comment on the first commandment of the *Aseres HaDibros* — the Ten Commandments — states that the *mitzvos* of the Torah include many Divine commands which require us to adopt a specific state of mind. We are positively commanded to love Hashem, to cling to Him and to fear Him, as well as to love our neighbor as ourself. In addition, there are Biblical prohibitions of this sort, such as "Do not hate your brother in your heart" (*Vayikra* 19:17), and "Do not take revenge nor bear a grudge" (ibid. v. 18).

Ibn Ezra continues:

> Many have believed that except for idolatry, the very worst sin, no human thought can be considered good or evil in and of itself. Yet, do we not have many verses that contradict this belief? "There are six things which Hashem hates ... a heart that devises wicked thoughts" (*Mishlei* 6:16,18); "You did well, for it was in your heart" (*I Melachim* 8:18); "Do good, Hashem, to those who are

good, and to those who are upright in their hearts" (*Tehillim* 125:4); "Let your heart be perfect with Hashem, our God" (*I Melachim* 8:61); "I am Hashem who searches the heart" (*Yirmiyahu* 17:10); "Hashem looks upon the heart" (*I Shmuel* 16:7). Thus, there is no argument over whether or not our thoughts are subject to Hashem's commands.

All the *rishonim*, agreeing that commands involving state of mind are considered to be commandments, counted them among the 613 *mitzvos*. The only debate involved whether belief in Hashem, so fundamental to all the other *mitzvos*, is to be included among the 613, or whether it is not a *mitzvah* at all, but a conclusion reached naturally through observance.

In the second view, the observant Jew will say, "How can there be *mitzvos* if there was no one to command them?" In this matter there are three opinions. *Rambam* and his followers hold that belief in Hashem, fundamental as it is, still represents one *mitzvah* among many. *Bahag* holds that this is not included among the *mitzvos*, but is a foundation of them all.

The third opinion, held by *Semag*, *Semak* and *Ikarim*, is a compromise between the first two. The verse, "I am Hashem your God who took you out of the land of Egypt," (v. 20:2) counts among the 613 *mitzvos*. Yet, in accordance with the reference to Egypt, it is not a command to believe in Hashem's existence, but to believe that Hashem watches over the whole world in general, and over each of its beings individually, or, as *Semag* states, it is a command to believe in Torah from Sinai.

⊷§ Faith in Hashem as the First Commandment: Rambam's View

Rambam counts faith in Hashem as the first of the 248 positive commandments, just as he counts denial of Hashem's existence as the first of the 365 prohibitions. The underlying principle of this *mitzvah* is "to believe in a Prime Cause Who brings all beings into existence." *Rambam* bases his view on *Makos* 23, quoting from there in his *Sefer HaMitzvos*: "613 *mitzvos* were handed down to Moshe at Sinai. Which verse in the Torah proves this? The verse (*Devarim* 33:4), 'Moshe issued us the Torah'; for the numerical value of the word תּוֹרָה is 611." Yet, since the word תּוֹרָה equals 611 rather than 613, what happened to the remaining two *mitzvos*? These are the first two commandments of the *Aseres HaDibros*, which the Jewish people heard not through

Moshe, but מִפִּי הַגְּבוּרָה — "from the lips of Hashem," so to speak. *Rambam* concludes there: "This makes it clear that the first commandment of the *Aseres HaDibros*, beginning, 'I am Hashem' (*Sh'mos* 20:2), is part of the 613 *mitzvos*, and represents a commandment to believe in Hashem, as I have explained."

Similarly, *Rambam* begins *Sefer HaMada* by saying: "The most central principle of our faith is the knowledge that there is a Prime Cause. He creates everything, and nothing in Heaven or Earth could exist without Him."

Rambam (ibid. 1:6) continues: "It is a *mitzvah* for us to know this, as the Torah states, 'I am Hashem, your God.' Whoever entertains the idea that there is any other god violates a Biblical prohibition: 'You shall have no other gods before Me' (v. 20:3). Such a person denies the essence of our faith, upon which all else rests."

It is interesting to note that in *Sefer HaMada*, *Rambam* places the accent not on our faith in Hashem, but on our knowing that He exists. In *Moreh Nevuchim*, *Rambam* interprets *Chazal's* statement that the first two commandments of the *Aseres HaDibros* were heard מִפִּי הַגְּבוּרָה as meaning that the Israelites observed גְּבוּרָת הַמּוֹפֵת — "Hashem's supernatural phenomena" — and this led them to rationally know that He existed. Yet, he concludes that in addition to such rational deduction, the Israelites also heard those first two commandments from Hashem's lips, affording them simple belief, which is stronger than rational knowledge.

We can thus understand that in *Sefer HaMada* as well, when *Rambam* speaks of "knowing" Hashem, he is doubtless referring to developing simple faith.

R' Eliezer HaLevi Landau explains this similarly in his *Yad HaMelech*. Having examined *Rambam's* writings, he concludes that *Rambam's* "knowing" refers not to rational deduction, but to simple and absolute awareness. When *Rambam* states that the angels in Heaven are living beings who "know" their Creator, that "knowledge" is not the result of rational deduction. Rather, it stems from their own will. The angels love Hashem's righteous and upright conduct and take joy in serving Him.

As *Chazal* established in the Blessing on Seeing the New Moon, the angels "rejoice in doing Hashem's will." Such knowledge involves an absolute awareness that is on a higher level even than faith, for faith exists only where there is room for doubt, yet the angels above have no doubt. Man, by nature, has a cruel, fearful streak. Yet, Hashem commanded us to love and cling to Him, so we would take joy in knowing Him and serving Him. King David had the same wish when he commanded Shlomo, "Know the God of your father and serve Him" (*I Divrei HaYamim* 28:9).

That knowledge is the future destiny of all Hashem's creatures. When the wolf dwells with the lamb, when love abides among Hashem's creatures, and between them and Hashem, then "the world will be filled with the knowledge of Hashem" (*Yeshayahu* 11:9). Such knowledge will be greater than faith. Yeshayahu did not mention "wisdom and understanding," but rather "knowledge," for knowledge based on simple faith is the greatest kind of knowledge there is.

Using a similar approach, R' Samson Raphael Hirsch interprets the obligation to know Hashem. The *mussar* works elaborate on this, stating that arriving at a belief in Hashem through reason is a self-centered act. The Torah tells us, "Moshe did as Hashem commanded" (*Vayikra* 8:4). Only a command from Hashem can create genuine knowledge and desire that will lead us to serve Him.

Without a doubt, when *Rambam* declared faith in Hashem to be the first *mitzvah*, he was referring to faith born of Divine command. From such a command stems clear, simple knowledge of Hashem which elevates faith to a higher plane. We shall later quote *Rambam* in *Moreh Nevuchim* to better understand his underlying philosophy in this matter.

R' Eliezer HaLevi Landau enlists support from *Chazal* for *Rambam's* view that the first commandment of the *Aseres HaDibros* counts among the 613 *mitzvos*. Hashem said to Israel, " 'I am Hashem, your God. You shall have no other gods before Me.' It was for My sake that you accepted upon yourselves the yoke of Heaven when you were in Egypt." When the Israelites had confirmed their acceptance of these words, Hashem continued, "Just as you have accepted the yoke of Heaven, so too must you accept My decrees" (*Mechilta* on *Yisro*). From this, R' Landau deduces that accepting the yoke of Heaven is part of the positive commandment of "I am Hashem, your God."

Yet, according to those who do not list faith in Hashem as one of the 613 *mitzvos* (see view of *Bahag* below), this *Mechilta* seems to prove just the opposite. Accepting the yoke of Heaven is not one of the 613 *mitzvos*, but the root and source of them all. Although *Bahag's* supporters accept *Mechilta* as proof that belief in Hashem is not part of the 613 *mitzvos*, they have no basis for doing so. As *Megillas Esther* states, the Israelites accepted the yoke of Heaven upon themselves willingly, and it cannot be labeled a "decree." Nonetheless, once the Israelites accepted it, belief in Hashem became one of the *mitzvos*, although it remained a foundation of them all. It is a *mitzvah* to accept this foundation, and it is a *mitzvah* to observe the *mitzvos* that branch out from it. Furthermore, *Ramban*, too, in his comments on the beginning of *Rambam's* list of the 365 prohibitions explains *Mechilta* according to *Rambam*.

◄§ Bahag: Faith is Not Among the 613 Mitzvos

Bahag holds that faith in Hashem is not among the 613 *mitzvos*. The very existence of *mitzvos* stems from there being a God who commanded them. Abarbanel, too, agrees with *Bahag*, finding support in the *Mechilta* quoted above for the idea that belief in Hashem is not included among the *mitzvos*. Several other sources support this view as well:

Chazal (*Horios* 8) say:

> "If you err and do not observe all of these *mitzvos*" (*Bamidbar* 15:22) — Which commandment is as weighty as all the other commandments? (i.e., because the verse states "*all* the other commandments"). That must be (violating the prohibition against) idolatry. The School of R' Yishmael quotes, "From the day that Hashem gave *mitzvos* and thereafter throughout the generations" (ibid. v. 23). What *mitzvah* was commanded first? Idolatry.

Here *Chazal* establish that the prohibition against idolatry, and not the command to believe in Hashem, was the first *mitzvah*. This source thus proves that the 613 *mitzvos* begin with the second commandment of the Decalogue, not the first.

Lev Same'ach has a simple rebuttal of this proof: The first *mitzvah* of the Decalogue, "I am Hashem," is as much a decree against idolatry as the second is. Despite this rebuttal, the second commandment of the Decalogue, forbidding idolatry, is a separate *mitzvah*, a reaction to the first commandment, but independent of it. Thus, *Chazal* were right in saying that the first *mitzvah* was the prohibition against idolatry.

Abarbanel enlists yet another proof, from *Mechilta*, that belief in Hashem is not counted among the 613 *mitzvos*:

> What do we learn from the words "You shall not have any other gods beside Me?" The next verse reads, "Do not make for yourself any carved idols" (*Sh'mos* 20:4), and that tells us we must not make new ones. How do we know we must not keep ones that are already made? "You shall have no other gods beside Me."

From here we see that, according to Abarbanel, "You shall have no other gods" encompasses two *mitzvos*. Now, in *Makos* 23, *Chazal* state that the Israelites heard 611 *mitzvos* from Moshe, and that they heard "the first two commandments of the Decalogue" directly from Hashem's lips. Thus, the two *mitzvos* involved must have been the two regarding idolatry, and these are what complete the number 613. Hence, we see that "I am Hashem" is not one of the 613 *mitzvos*. It is true that *Mechilta* mentions "I am Hashem," but when it refers to "two *mitzvos*," it has in mind "You shall have no other gods."

This second proof of Abarbanel meets with much opposition, as well, from the authors of *Megillas Esther* and *Lev Same'ach*, who comment on *Rambam's Sefer HaMitzvos*. In their opinion, when *Chazal* in the *Mechilta* say "the first two commandments of the Decalogue," they do not mean the two prohibitions involving idolatry. Otherwise, they would have to mention either two phrases from within the second commandment, such as "You shall have no other gods" (v. 20:3), and "Do not bow down to them" (v. 5), or just the first commandment, "I am Hashem" (v. 2). The fact that *Chazal* mentioned both the first and second commandments shows that they refer specifically to the *mitzvah* of belief and its converse, the prohibition against idolatry.

Further proof is that *Rambam* derives not two but four prohibitions from the second commandment: (a) You shall have no other gods; (b) do not make any carved idols; (c) do not bow down to them; (d) do not worship them.

Ramban notices this in his commentary on *Sefer HaMitzvos*, and asks: If the first two commandments which the Israelites heard directly from Hashem account for five *mitzvos*, then the Israelites did not hear 611 *mitzvos* from Moshe, but rather 608! However, according to other commentaries on *Sefer HaMitzvos*, it does not matter how many *mitzvos* emerge from the basic prohibition of idolatry. In any case, Hashem gave the Israelites two oral commandments: "I am Hashem" and "You shall have no other gods." The rest were uttered by Moshe, although they, too, include *mitzvos* associated with the ban on idolatry.

Ramban, in explaining the first positive commandment of *Rambam's Sefer HaMitzvos*, quotes at length the view of *Bahag*, that belief in Hashem is not one of the *mitzvos*. He brings so many proofs in support of *Bahag's* view that he seems to favor it. In this way he provokes the ire of the other commentaries on *Sefer HaMitzvos*, and they argue against his proofs, bringing their own support for the other view, that of *Rambam*.

Lev Same'ach enlists proof from *Pesikta Rabasi*: "Each of the Ten Commandments corresponds to one of the commands by which Hashem created the world. 'I am Hashem' corresponds to 'Let there be light;' 'You shall have no other gods' to 'Let there be a firmament.' " This source demonstrates that "I am Hashem" is considered the first *mitzvah*, and "You shall have no other gods" is considered the second. Yet, all the trouble that these commentaries go to, proving *Bahag* wrong, is unnecessary. In his remarks on *Rambam's* list of prohibitions, *Ramban* himself offers *Rambam* full support, bringing numerous proofs that "I am Hashem" should be counted among the 613 *mitzvos*. This is a fundamental ruling, for it establishes that we must observe the *mitzvos* because Hashem commanded them, and not because we rationally understand their importance. No *mitzvah* demands as much rational understanding as belief in Hashem. Since we are obligated to observe the *mitzvos*, we are surely bound to believe in He who commanded them. Even so, Hashem still treats our belief in Him as a distinct *mitzvah*, to teach us that believing in Him involves more than rationally understanding that He exists, and we must not rely upon our own ability to reason.

Interestingly, of all the commentaries, *Rambam*, the rationalist, views belief in Hashem as the fulfillment of a Divine decree, and establishes one positive and one negative commandment involving our thoughts about Hashem.

Semag, as well, stresses that we must not entertain the thought that there is any other god.

Maharshal, in his remarks on *Semag's* list of the *mitzvos*, expresses puzzlement over this view. He quotes *Mechilta* which states that the commandment of "You shall have no other gods" is a prohibition not against heretical thoughts, but against the act of worshiping idols and keeping them in one's house. He concludes, however, by declaring that a Torah verse cannot be divorced from its surface meaning. The chief purpose of "You shall have no other gods" is therefore to prohibit heretical thought. Even if the verse prohibits heretical acts as well, the foundation of our religion will still be to believe in Hashem and to reject belief in any other deity.

◄§ The Nature of the First Two Commandments of the Decalogue

The distinction between the first two commandments and those that follow is reflected in their very style. In the first two, Hashem makes His Presence felt by referring to Himself, while in the rest He does not. *Chazal* stated that the Israelites heard the first two directly from Hashem, and the rest from Moshe, and the commentaries interpreted the Decalogue in accordance with this. Yet, *Rambam* in *Moreh Nevuchim* 2:32 expresses a unique view. There he proves that the Israelites did not hear Hashem's words, but only the sound of "His voice" (*Devarim* 5:20); "When you heard the sound of His words" (ibid. 4:12). The Israelites heard not Hashem's words, but only "the sound of His words." Moshe alone heard the words themselves, and he explained to the Israelites what the voice meant. In this there is no difference between the first two commandments of the Decalogue, and those which follow. How then would *Rambam* explain *Chazal's* distinguishing the first two from the rest?

Rambam answers as follows:

> "I am Hashem" and "You shall have no other gods before Me" are the foundations of our faith. These two commandments teach that Hashem exists, and that He is one. Human reflection and the supernatural wonders man observes (מוֹפֵת) can bring him to as great a belief in Hashem's existence as any prophet can. In fact, the prophet has no advantage in understanding these principles, for they are not in his realm. The Torah states, "You were shown that Hashem is God, there is none beside Him" (*Devarim* 4:35). Other *mitzvos*, however, are not attainable through reason, but are decrees announced by Hashem.

Rambam's view aroused the opposition of those who negate the rational approach to *mitzvos*. *Ikarim* (*Sh'mos* 17:3) poses the following question: If the principles of faith can truly be attained through reason, why did Hashem give them to Moshe as a prophet? Furthermore, why did *Rambam* count them among the 613 *mitzvos*? As a result of these questions, *Ikarim* states that the first *mitzvah*, originating with the words "I am Hashem," does not teach faith in Hashem, but belief that the Torah is Divine, and that Hashem watches over the world. These principles cannot be attained through rational processes. However, faith that Hashem exists can be attained by these means.

Various commentaries on *Rambam* have offered many explanations of his words. *Ephodi* affirms that the Israelites heard the voice but not the words of all the Ten Commandments. Yet, regarding the first two, unlike the remainder, they were able to figure out the meaning of Hashem's voice without Moshe explaining it to them.

Abarbanel interprets *Rambam's* view differently: *Rambam*, he says, was only explaining why *Chazal* said that the first two commandments were uttered by Hashem. The Israelites had been previously prepared intellectually to understand the first two commandments. Thus, they grasped both that Hashem was addressing them and in addition they actually understood what He said. By contrast, for the remaining eight commandments, the Israelites could do no more than discern that Hashem was talking to them. Thus, *Rambam* does not radically change the meaning of *Chazal's* words in order to explain them. Rather, he strengthens them with a highly reasonable explanation.

Kinas Sofrim expands on this idea in his commentary on *Sefer HaMitzvos*. When *Rambam* mentions מוֹפֵת, he does not refer to man's ability to reason, but to miraculous wonders that the Israelites saw and heard. The Israelites witnessed great and awesome signs and wonders in Heaven and Earth. This showed them that Hashem has the might and power to do anything, and that He mercifully watches over the Jewish people. After these miraculous preludes, the Israelites delved into Hashem's nature on a high level, eventually reaching prophecy. They merited Divine revelation with the first two commandments, receiving prophecy and enlightenment from Heaven.

Even with all of these explanations, it is difficult to fully understand what *Rambam* meant by the words גְּבוּרַת הַמּוֹפְתִים.

IV.

The Prohibition Against "Other Gods"

he Torah states, "You shall have no other gods beside Me." According to *Rambam*, this even forbids idolatrous thought: "Whoever entertains the thought that there are gods beside Hashem violates a prohibition: 'You shall have no other gods beside Me'" (*Hil. Yesodei HaTorah*, Ch. 1).

Chinuch, too, states, " 'You shall have no other gods' forbids us to believe in any other god beside Hashem." Thus, for *Rambam*, the two *mitzvos* of "I am Hashem, your God" (*Sh'mos* 20:2) and "You shall have no other gods" both address the same matter. The first is a command to believe in Hashem, while the second is a command not to believe in idolatry.

Ramban states that "other gods" can only exist in one's mind. Hence, while "You shall have no other gods" forbids idolatrous belief, it does not apply to action. It would have made no sense for the Torah to say "Make no other gods but Me." The prohibition against "other gods" applies specifically to forbidden belief, as we find explicitly proven by the many sources quoted in the *Torah Sheleimah*.

Mechilta says that the prohibition of "You shall have no other gods" is against holding idols in your possession, even those made by others:

The Torah says, "Do not make for yourself any carved idol or likeness" (v. 4). This forbids the fashioning of new ones. How do we know that one may not hold an existing one in his possession? This is deduced from "You shall have no other gods beside Me" (v. 3).

Bahag, Semak and other *rishonim* follow the *Mechilta*. Furthermore, R' Ovadiah Bartenura declares that the prohibitions of the second commandment increase in severity. First we find "You shall have no other gods" (v. 3), forbidding us to keep existing idols in our possession, a sin involving no physical act. Then we read "Do not make for yourselves any carved idol" (v. 4), which does involve a physical act, but which still does not incur the death penalty. Then we come to "Do not bow down to them" (v. 5). This does incur death, although bowing down to an idol does not constitute full-fledged idol worship. Finally, the Torah says, "Do not worship them" (ibid.), which involves both full-fledged idol worship and a death sentence.

Ramban, however, holds that *Mechilta's* comments here are the opinion of a single *Tanna*. In *Sifra* at the beginning of *Kedoshim*, R' Yossi says that whoever makes an idol for himself violates three prohibitions: (a) "Do not make;" (b) "for yourselves;" and (c) "you shall have no other gods." In other words, this verse refers to a person who makes an idol and keeps it in his possession. Yet, the *Tanna Kama* quoted there differs on the nature of the prohibitions involved, and in this case the law is in accordance with the *Tanna Kama*. *Ramban* therefore holds like *Rambam* that "You shall have no other gods" prohibits idolatrous thoughts.

In his remarks on *Rambam's Sefer HaMitzvos*, *Ramban* quotes the debate on the nature of לֹא יִהְיֶה לְךָ אֱלֹהִים אֲחֵרִים — "You shall have no other gods." R' Yose argues that just as in וְנַחֲלָה לֹא יִהְיֶה לוֹ — "He shall have no inheritance" (*Devarim* 18:2), לֹא יִהְיֶה means owning and maintaining something in your possession, the same is true here. For the *Tanna Kama*, however, לֹא יִהְיֶה means refusal to recognize the existence of any other god, in harmony with Yaakov's וְהָיָה ה' לִי לֵאלֹהִים — "Hashem shall be my God" (*Bereishis* 28:21).

These two views are not necessarily so divergent. It is logical to assume that the prohibition against keeping idols in one's possession originates from a prohibition against believing in them. Whoever keeps them demonstrates his belief in them. Why else would one hold on to them and not destroy them?

Abarbanel's opinion seems identical to *Ramban's*. Abarbanel says that the prohibition of "You shall not have any other gods" is a warning to us not to profane Hashem's glory by accepting other gods upon ourselves. As profaning Hashem's glory is what the prohibition seeks to prevent, it also includes a prohibition on denying Hashem's existence.

ৰ্ই Accepting Any Other Deity Is Forbidden

R' Yitzchak Arama, in his *Akeidas Yitzchak*, expands the prohibition of "Do not have any other gods" to include recognizing any power in the world beside Hashem as Divine. According to *Akeidah*, this prohibition is not intended to limit man, but to liberate him. If a person is blessed with true faith, he will not acknowledge any other mastery over the world. The Torah says, "The tablets were the work of Hashem, and the writing was the writing of Hashem, engraved upon the tablets" (*Sh'mos* 32:16). *Chazal* comment, "Read not חָרוּת — 'engraved,' but rather חֵרוּת — 'freedom': freedom from the angel of death, freedom from monarchs, freedom from suffering." Thus, according to *Akeidah*, it is not only forbidden to believe in idolatry in its conventional sense, but to see wealth and possession as the most important thing.

It would be worthwhile here to quote *Akeidas Yitzchak* directly:

> Idolatry as it exists today is quite strong. Many people invest all their thought and effort in achieving wealth and success. These are their mighty gods and upon them do they rely. As for Hashem's glory, they deny that He exists and abandon His Torah to a lonely corner. This is the very essence of idolatry: "If I have made gold my hope, or have called fine gold my shelter; if I rejoiced because my wealth was great and because my hand has gotten much . . . this, too, is a criminal offense, betraying Hashem above" (*Iyov* 31:24-25,28).

The prohibition against idolatry, according to *Akeidah*, does not correspond to any specific form. Rather, it forbids acknowledging any physical entity as having mastery over the world, and relying upon it in place of Hashem. *Akeidah* expresses sorrow that the Jews of his day live in countries where the population worships money, and he adds: "We yearn hopelessly for wealth and are never satisfied with what we have. Thus, we violate, 'Do not make a statue of anything associated with Me. Do not make silver or gold gods for yourselves' (*Sh'mos* 20:20)."

The accent is not on what form the idolatry takes, but on ascribing powers of mastery to the object that one worships, as in this case, where society worships money. In accordance with *Akeidah's* explanation, "idolatry" takes on a much broader meaning. *Akeidah* happened to pick the particular entity that the people of his generation worshiped, but the crutch they choose can change in every generation according to circumstances. Whatever its form, the prohibition of "You shall have no other gods" still applies.

S'forno holds that even if a person who believes in Hashem worships one of His servants to show that servant honor, that too is idolatry. Regarding those non-Jews who settled in *Eretz Yisrael* after the First Temple was destroyed, we read, "They feared Hashem and served their own gods" (*II Melachim* 17:33). The second commandment states, "You shall not have any other gods before Me" (*Sh'mos* 20:3). For S'forno, the words "before Me" remind us that Hashem is everywhere. As this is so, it is inappropriate to give honor to His servants.

Similar to this is the view among the *rishonim* that the second commandment forbids the belief in שִׁיתּוּף — "shituf," the idea that Hashem created and/or rules the world in cooperation with other powers, albeit subordinate to him. It is forbidden to believe in *shituf*, even if one also believes in the Living God.

S'forno's understanding of the verse differs in one regard. For him, even one who believes in one God and just worships one of His servants to bring Hashem honor is violating this prohibition. Since Hashem is omnipresent, worshiping His servants constitutes *shituf*.

Similarly, *Torah Sheleimah* quotes *Midrash Aseres HaDibros* of R' Moshe HaDarshan:

> One might say, "Hashem has commanded me to direct my heart towards Him. I will therefore make a graven image of Him, such as people erect to help them remember the past." The Torah responds, "You shall have no other gods עַל פָּנַי — to help you concentrate on My visage."

According to this interpretation, the next verse, "Do not make yourself any carved idol" (v. 20:3), is an explanation of "You shall have no other gods." Either they are identical, or verse 3 is more general, including the making of all graven images, even those not representing Hashem, but other deities.

Here it would be worthwhile to quote Rabbenu Bachya on verse 3, similar to S'forno quoted above:

> After Hashem forbade believing in "other gods" (v. 2), He forbade making images of them (v. 3). Now, many *mitzvos* in the Torah, such as *Sukkah*, *Pesach* and *Matzah*, serve to remind us of Hashem's deeds. A person may therefore wish to make an idol or likeness commemorating one of those *mitzvos* which testify to Hashem's greatness or a likeness glorifying the physical means by which Hashem achieved miracles and wonders. Yet, let no such person think he is performing Hashem's will. Such idols are

entirely against the will of Hashem. The command against idolatry includes even making physical representations of Hashem, and applies even to those individuals intent on serving Hashem sincerely.

This explanation helps to answer the *rishonim's* question about why the Torah included making statues to represent Hashem in the category of "other gods." Any physical representation of any deity, even of Hashem, is foreign to us, and idolatrous.

Mechilta attempts to explain the phrase "other gods." We note that one of those interpretations is quoted in *Rashi*: " 'Other gods' means whatever we accept upon ourselves as a deity, even a splinter or potsherd." According to this, "other gods" has the meaning attributed to it by *Akeidas Yitzchak*: attributing mastery over the world to an entity other than Hashem, whether or not one subjugates oneself to it.

Ramban explains this this way as well, but he interprets "other gods" as accepting an alien deity with intent to worship it. He thus confines the concept to three types of idolatry that existed during three periods of history.

Or HaChaim, on the other hand, holds that the Torah's use of the expression "other gods" teaches us that if we budge even a hair's-breadth from our belief in monotheism, we will eventually be led to polytheism. Then, we will have not one but many foreign gods. It really does not matter whether we worship one or many foreign deities. The Torah only describes, for its shock value and to instill in us the importance of monotheism, the developments that will take place if we swerve from monotheism to the slightest degree.

⋖ You Shall Not Have Any Other Gods Beside Me

The expression עַל פָּנָי — "beside me" — engages the attention of all the commentaries. The surface level meaning is expressed by "You shall have no other god beside me." The word עַל occurs elsewhere in the Torah with this meaning. The *Shabbos* burnt-offering is brought עַל עוֹלַת הַתָּמִיד — "beside" or "in addition to," the regular daily burnt-offering (*Bamidbar* 28:10). Yet, *Mechilta* interprets עַל פָּנָי as "for ever and ever." It therefore renders to v. 2 the following significance: Hashem's use of the phrase עַל פָּנָי deprives the Jewish people of the excuse that idolatry was forbidden only to those Israelites who participated in the Exodus. Hashem says, "Just as I live and endure forever, so too are you, your children and grandchildren forbidden to worship idols until the end of time."

Markeves HaMishnah questions this view. Why should Hashem have stressed the eternity of this *mitzvah* and no other? *Torah Temimah* answers, quoting *Tzeidah LaDerech*: It is because the preceding commandment begins, "I am Hashem, your God, who took you out of the Land of Egypt" (*Sh'mos* 20:2). The Torah here is telling us that future generations are as much bound to accept Hashem on faith, as did the first generation which actually saw His Revelation. Faith must replace empirical proof. Those generations that did not see or hear are as much obligated as those that did. Hashem says, "The generations pass, but I endure. I am He who appeared to your ancestors at Sinai."

Ibn Ezra explains that the prohibition applies wherever Hashem lives and endures, i.e., throughout the world (or even the planets, if man reaches them). עַל פָּנַי is thus read in the sense of וַיָּמָת הָרָן עַל פְּנֵי תֶּרַח אָבִיו — "Haran died while his father Terach was yet alive to see it" (*Bereishis* 11:28). Hashem is everywhere and His eyes roam throughout the world. He sees what we do, even in the darkest corner.

Ramban, as well, states that when an event occurs in someone's presence, we call that "עַל פָּנָיו." The prohibition thus warns against idolatrous acts performed openly or secretly.

By contrast, Abarbanel holds that the verse means, "You shall have no other gods from among those who stand constantly before Hashem," i.e., the heavenly bodies and the angels.

Chizkuni and *Kli Yakar* interpret עַל פָּנַי to mean anger. Hashem says, "If you accept other deities, you will incur My wrath." Yechezkel gave the Israelites a similar warning: "What comes into your mind shall never come about ... With a mighty hand, and with an outstretched arm, and with anger poured out will I rule over you" (*Yechezkel* 20:32,33). Hashem's anger is not just something abstract. It can be turned into a concrete threat. Those who seek to throw off Hashem's yoke shall ultimately be compelled to accept it.

Netziv offers a novel interpretation of עַל פָּנַי. We are forbidden to crown other authorities over ourselves, but this prohibition only applies to those that will be "in place of Me," i.e., that will replace Hashem. By contrast, accepting the spiritual authority of holy men — referred to in Tanach as *Elohim* — is not only permissible, but advisable. Hashem forbids us only to recognize other gods as masters of the world, and to substitute them "in His place."

In another novel approach, *HaKesav VeHaKabalah* says that עַל פָּנַי means "Because of Me." עַל means "because of," as when Hashem tells Avraham אַל יֵרַע בְּעֵינֶיךָ עַל הַנַּעַר — "Do not grieve because of the lad" (*Bereishis* 21:12). פָּנַי can indicate importance, as in the Mishnaic expression, פְּנֵי הַדּוֹר — the important men of the generation; and לֶחֶם

הַפָּנִים — the showbread (Sh'mos 35:13). Also, we read כָּל פְּנֵי הָאָרֶץ (Bereishis 41:56), which Rashi explains to mean, "all the wealthy people of the land." The idolaters at first said, "Since Hashem is so exalted and supreme, we should worship Him through a middleman." Through this evolved the worship of stars and constellations. Those who took part in such devotions did not deny Hashem as Master over all, but thought He was too removed to be worshiped directly. The Torah therefore warned, "Do not have any other gods עַל פָּנָי — because of Me," i.e., due to My supremacy.

V.

A Command to Control Our Thoughts

Do not covet" (Sh'mos 20:14) commands us to restrict our thoughts and suppress our desires. Not only our actions but our thoughts and will are subject to spiritual and ethical authority. Many have expressed puzzlement over whether man is able to control his own lusts and desires, directing them as the Torah wishes. Yet if Hashem issued such a command, man must be able to comply with it. The Torah testifies that the power to control himself is embedded in man. Following are Chinuch's words on Mitzvah 416:

> Do not ask, "When a person sees that his neighbor owns a house full of luxuries that he himself lacks, how will he possibly be able to avoid desiring them? How can the Torah impose a restriction that we cannot endure?" Such a question is fallacious, and only wicked, sinful fools would ask it. Man is fully capable of quelling his desires, and it is up to him to decide what to seek out and what to reject. His will is his own. He directs it wherever he wishes.

Thus, Chinuch holds simply that man is psychologically strong enough to overcome his desires, as the Torah bids him to do.

In commenting on this verse, R' Samson Raphael Hirsch takes the opportunity to prove to those who have strayed that Torah Law is Divine. Mortal kings and lawmakers can control only the deeds of their subjects. They cannot uproot any evil in their souls. By contrast, Hashem, the Supreme King, reads our mind like an open book, and is just as aware of our thoughts as He is of our deeds. Hashem knows man can control his desires.

Ibn Ezra attempts to explain Hashem's command that we remove covetousness from our hearts. He holds that the purpose of the verse is to make us fear Hashem so much that it will never even enter our minds to covet what we lack. Man has no natural desire for things he cannot possibly attain. Such objects do not interest him. He knows he has no wings, so he does not long to fly. The Torah forbids man to covet his neighbor's wealth. If a person has been imbued with the fear of Hashem, this will make him even less interested in his neighbor's wealth than a peasant is in the king's daughter. He will see it as unattainable.

S'forno explains the nature of this prohibition similarly: "It makes your neighbor's wealth absolutely unattainable, and by nature, man does not covet what he cannot attain. It is like, 'No man shall covet your land' (Sh'mos 34:24)." This is a puzzling analogy. In the quoted verse, Hashem promises those who go up to Yerushalayim for the pilgrimage festivals that none will covet their fields while they are away from home. What link does this have with our verse, in which Hashem commands man not to covet? Even so, S'forno's principle is identical to Ibn Ezra's. "Do not covet" is a command taking advantage of a man's faith and reverence for Hashem to make what belongs to others seem unattainable.

HaKesav VeHaKabalah explains this slightly differently. If a man's heart is brimming with love of Hashem, it has no room for covetousness, like an overflowing cup to which nothing can be added. Such a person will naturally comply with "Do not covet."

R' Yosef Dov Ber Soloveitchik in Beis HaLevi focuses not on love, but on fear of Hashem: A man who feels fear cannot feel desire or longing. We are commanded to fear Hashem: "What does Hashem, your God, ask of you but to fear Him?" (Devarim 10:12). With such fear, covetousness automatically goes away.

The Chassidic literature deepens this idea. We must elevate covetousness to the level of lofty yearning for Hashem. Then, its negative side will be nullified like a tiny flame before a great fire.

Sefas Emes defines this simply: "Even if we desire worldly luxury, we must also yearn to fulfill Hashem's word. This yearning will overcome all other desires. Of this Chazal said, 'Nullify your own will before His.'"

Just as the first commandment of the Decalogue, belief in Hashem, involves our thoughts, so too the last, "Do not covet." This teaches that "action" is not the sole domain of the Torah, nor is "thought." The Torah rules over our heart and mind, just as it rules over our actions.

✑ Do Not Covet: One or Two Mitzvos?

Rambam counts the prohibition of "Do not covet" as two *mitzvos*. The first is, "Do not covet your neighbor's house" (*Sh'mos* 20:14), and the second, "Do not desire your neighbor's house" (*Devarim* 5:18). While *Bahag* and *Chinuch* also count them as two *mitzvos*, R' Sa'adiah Gaon and *Semag* consider them as one.

According to *Rambam's* definition (*Mishneh Torah, Hil. Gezeilah V'Aveidah*), covetousness is defined as follows: "When you desire a neighbor's object and pressure him heavily until he gives it to you, even if your pressure was friendly, and even if you pay handsomely for it, you have violated the prohibition." This prohibition is thus linked to an act, although it involves none itself: The person does not violate the prohibition until he takes the object he coveted: "Do not covet their silver and gold, taking it for yourself" (*Devarim* 7:25). By contrast, "Do not desire" is unlinked to any act. Whoever desires the house, wife, clothing or any salable item his neighbor owns, violates the prohibition as soon as he starts to wonder how he might acquire it. The Torah says "Do not desire," and "desire" belongs to the heart.

In *Sefer HaMitzvos*, as well, *Rambam* repeats his definition, stating that the two *mitzvos* serve different purposes. The first refers to desire that leads to sinful action, and the second to desire that remains in the heart. Yet, *Rambam* adds: "If a person puts heavy pressure on his neighbor, tricking him into giving up one of his possessions, that person violates both prohibitions, 'Do not covet' and 'Do not desire.'"

Semag questions *Rambam's* view, according to which it seems less of an offense to desire one's neighbor's wife than his servant. The former is covered by "Do not covet" (*Devarim* 5:18), and "coveting" is only a sin when an act accompanies it, whereas the latter is forbidden by "Do not desire" (ibid. v. 19), meaning even desires of the heart.

The commentaries on *Rambam*, though, state that *Semag* seems to have overlooked some of *Rambam's* remarks in *Mishneh Torah*. There, *Rambam* explicitly forbids heartfelt desire for one's neighbor's manservant, maidservant or his wife. Why? Because he learns from the words "and all that belongs to your neighbor" (*Devarim* 5:18) that "Do not desire" includes everything to which "Do not covet" refers.

Ra'avad, however, differs with *Rambam*. He holds that even if someone forces his neighbor to sell him something, once the neighbor expresses his acceptance of the transaction it is valid, and the prohibition of "Do not covet" does not apply. *Ra'avad's* view is based on *Bava Basra*, Ch. 3, which states that if someone is forced to sell something, as when the buyer tortures him until he consents and does so, the sale is valid.

Magid Mishneh explains the basis of *Rambam* and *Ra'avad's* argument. *Rambam* holds that although the sale is valid, the buyer still violates "Do not covet." Seemingly the law should not be so, for the *halachah* is in accordance with *Rava* in *Temurah* 3 who states, "We do not allow a person to benefit from any act that violates a Torah prohibition." Even so, in this case, as the buyer has paid for the object, it becomes his, in the same way that a thief who makes an alteration in an object he stole gains possession of it.

The *acharonim* are puzzled by how, if the sale is valid, the buyer still violates "Do not covet," when *Chazal* state explicitly that a valid sale proves no violation has occurred (*Bava Kama* 62a): "R' Ada asked, 'What is the difference between a *gazlan* and a *chamsan* (two types of thieves)? The *chamsan* pays for what he grabs but the *gazlan* does not'." The Talmud then asks, "If a man pays for what he takes, can he be called a *chamsan*? Did R' Huna not say, 'If a man tortures someone until he agrees to sell him an object, is the sale valid?' " This question proves that no violation can be said to occur if a sale is considered valid, otherwise, the Talmud could surely have answered that despite the valid sale, the buyer is still a *chamsan*.

The *acharonim* further ask how *Magid Mishneh* can compare the coveter to the *gazlan*. It is true that, despite the principle that we do not allow a person to benefit from any act that violates a Torah prohibition, a *gazlan* takes possession of objects he steals if he alters them. Yet, is this not learned from a special exposition in *Maseches Temurah*, applying to that case alone? How can *Magid Mishneh* deduce from the rule of the *gazlan* that a person can violate "Do not covet" even while his purchase is valid?

Various *acharonim* work to clarify the various views. Yet, whoever delves deeply into *Rambam* will see that his position is clear and simple. According to *Rambam*, "coveting" is a sin we commit with our mind, and as long as the sin remains one of thought, we violate only one prohibition: "Do not desire." If a covetous thought finds expression in action, a second prohibition is added: "Do not covet." This is so even if the coveter pays for the object, and the seller agrees to the transaction. In any event, desire has led to a sinful act. The fact that the sale is valid does not change what happened. This is the actual difference between theft and coveting. If an object is stolen but then paid for and the owner concedes the sale, no theft is said to have occurred, for the occurrence of a lawful sale redefines the unlawful act that led to it. With the prohibition of "Do not covet," however, the owner's thoughts have no bearing on the coveter's act. Even if the owner concedes the sale, the coveter still violates "Do not desire" from the first moment he desires the object and "Do not covet" from the moment the transaction takes place.

If the owner does not concede the sale, the buyer violates a third prohibition against *chamas*, forceful acquisition, when he pays for the item. Otherwise, the third prohibition is removed, but two remain.

Magid Mishneh is thus correct in stating that while the sale is valid, the prohibition of "Do not covet" remains.

Migdal Oz concisely summarizes *Rambam's* view: "The owner's acceptance of a sale forced upon him only establishes that the sale was valid, but not that the buyer who forced the sale is innocent of 'Do not covet.' "

We may even be able to develop *Rambam's* logic even more thoroughly, although what follows has no basis in the *poskim*. "Do not covet" is a prohibition involving no physical act, but only thought. The Torah did not place this under the jurisdiction of the courts, as no court can read a man's thoughts. The Torah simply addressed man and commanded him not to covet.

Earlier, we said *Chazal* do not allow individuals who have violated Torah prohibitions to benefit from their act. Yet, this applies only to sins involving concrete action. Hence it does not nullify a sale forced by the covetous individual. Were we to say that the prohibition of "Do not covet" should nullify such sales, no transaction would ever be valid, lest the buyer coveted the object he was about to buy. This prohibition is addressed to the conscience of the individual. He is forbidden to covet, and if he covets, he is forbidden to acquire the object, for then he violates two prohibitions.

ৰ৾ড় From Bad to Worse

Of all *rishonim*, *Rambam* is the most strict regarding the sin of coveting, saying that one violates "Do not desire" even if he only "thought about how to take hold of it." In his comments on *Devarim* 13:9, *Ramban*, as well, states that according to *Rambam's* definitions, this sin accounts for two prohibitions. Yet, in *Devarim* 5:18, *Ramban* interprets "Do not desire" as dealing with "someone who desires to steal something from his neighbor, yet is unable to do so because his neighbor is stronger than he." We must examine if *Rambam* would agree on this point. *Rambam's* source is *Mechilta* on *Parashas Yisro*, which distinguishes between "coveting" (חֶמְדָּה), and "desire" (תַּאֲוָה), stating that the Torah seeks to make them separate sins.

Interestingly, *Malbim*, in his *HaTorah VeHaMitzvah*, distinguishes between תַּאֲוָה and חֶמְדָּה based on their linguistic differences alone. He holds that חֶמְדָּה focuses on the way the coveted object is perceived, as in נֶחְמָד לְמַרְאֶה — "lovely to see" (Bereishis 2:9). On the other hand, תַּאֲוָה focuses on the mind of the coveter, without regard for the object's desirability. This is why in Parashas Va'eschanan the Torah says, לֹא תַחְמֹד — "Do not covet" (Devarim 5:18), regarding one's neighbor's wife, and לֹא תִתְאַוֶּה — "Do not desire" (ibid.), regarding his property. Likewise, Parashas Yisro employs "Do not desire," regarding all property.

Few commentaries deal with the fact that "one's neighbor's house" is mentioned before "one's neighbor's wife" in Sh'mos 20:14. Haamek Davar explains that one's neighbor's house requires special emphasis. Houses, being stationary, seem invulnerable to theft. Surely, someone who trespasses in his neighbor's house cannot be said to have stolen it. Even so, he violates "Do not covet your neighbor's house." By contrast, "Do not covet your neighbor's wife" deals with tempting her to leave her husband (any misuse of a married woman is covered by Sh'mos 20:13 — "Do not commit adultery"). The same logic can be applied to explain why in verse 14 "one's neighbor's wife" precedes "and all that belongs to your neighbor." It is to make clear that covetousness is defined as that state of mind that begins with desire in the heart and ends with the active pursuit of one's neighbor's possession.

Rashbam offers an interesting interpretation of the verses in Parashas Va'eschanan. He links "Do not bear false witness" (Devarim 5:17), with "Do not covet your neighbor's wife" (ibid. v. 18), explaining the former as involving someone falsely testifying about a dead man in order to have the courts recognize his eligibility to marry the man's wife.

Mishpatim – מִשְׁפָּטִים

I.

Mount Sinai: Source of the Oral Law

Chazal's tradition that "an eye for an eye" means monetary restitution has occupied the commentaries throughout the generations. Today as in former times, there are heretics who view this not as Hashem's word, but as if, Heaven forbid, *halachah* is constantly changing. In recent times, after a well-known secular writer expressed such a view in writing, the free-thinking secularists in the Israeli government, including Ben-Gurion and his camp, became even more entrenched in this view, and they often quoted that writer's ideas.

For anyone not deeply imbued with faith, *Chazal's* interpretation of these words, seemingly different from the text, are impossible to understand. *Chazal* dedicated a number of Talmudic utterances to proving how much we must respect the Rabbinic tradition that the Torah meant not physical, but monetary retribution (*Bava Kama* 83). Yet, most of these passages are intended for those whose believe so strongly that Rabbinic tradition stems from Sinai that they need no proof. Anyone without this will not be swayed by the logic of those utterances, for a refutation follows almost every proof they offer. Most likely, the source of the law is not these Talmudic proofs, but Rabbinic tradition itself.

Chazal commonly sought textual support for known Rabbinic traditions. Whichever proofs *Chazal* considered unconvincing or out of line with Talmudic convention, they themselves would refute. These disproofs do not, however, challenge Rabbinic tradition, God forbid. Rather, they serve to inform us that we cannot rely upon this or that line of reasoning. Whoever wishes to find a logical basis must seek different support.

Chazal's proofs run as follows:

(a) The Torah states, "Whoever kills a beast shall pay for it, a soul for a soul" (*Vayikra* 24:18). The next verse reads, "If a man maims his neighbor, as he did, so shall be done to him" (ibid. v. 19). The Talmud reasons, "Just as when a person kills a beast, although the Torah states 'a soul for a soul,' his restitution is still monetary, so too with maiming one's fellow man."

(b) *Chazal* present yet another argument. The Torah says, "Take no ransom for the life of a murderer" (*Bamidbar* 35:31). *Chazal* comment, "No ransom is to be taken for murder, but it is to be taken for the maiming of limbs." The Talmud does not refute this.

(c) The school of R' Chizkiyah reasons: The Torah states עַיִן תַּחַת עָיִן — "an eye for an eye" (*Sh'mos* 21:25) and not "an eye and a life for an eye." Removing an eye can sometimes be fatal, hence if עָיִן meant a real eye, the punishment would not always fit the crime.

Yet, *Chazal* disprove this: "Perhaps the court must estimate if the guilty party could survive having his eye removed. If he were judged so and then died after punishment, the court would be absolved of guilt."

(d) The school of R' Chiya deduces proof from the case of the false witness, where the phrase "a hand for a hand" (*Devarim* 19:21) refers to money — "that which is passed from hand to hand." *Chazal* disprove this as well.

(e) The school of R' Yishmael points out a seeming repetition. *Vayikra* 24:19 states, "If a man maims his neighbor, as he has done, so shall be done to him." Why then must the Torah add, "as he has maimed a man, so shall it be done to him" (ibid. v. 20)? They conclude that יִנָּתֶן (translated in the second verse as "shall be done"), which normally means "shall be given," must refer to money. (Note *Malbim's* comments on R' Yishmael, which will be quoted later.)

(f) R' Zevid, quoting Rava, notes that in addition to "an eye for an eye," the guilty party must pay for pain he caused. If the "eye for an eye" were literal, that would mean that the person must both compensate the victim's pain and suffer it himself. Nonetheless, the Talmud refutes this reasoning.

(g) R' Papa, quoting Rava, asks the same question about the fact that the guilty party must pay the victim's medical bills: "He shall pay for time lost from work, and shall see that he is healed" (*Sh'mos* 21:19). If "an eye for an eye" is to be taken literally, why should the guilty party have to pay anything? *Chazal* refute this as well.

(h) R' Ashi, redactor of the Talmud, deduces a *gezeirah shavah* from the section regarding rape: "He must pay ... fifty shekels ... because he afflicted her" (*Devarim* 22:29). Just as the word תַּחַת (translated above as "because") refers to monetary compensation, so too does עַיִן תַּחַת עָיִן refer to monetary compensation. R' Ashi's argument is not refuted. The arguments that preceded it were not absolutely refuted either.

Chazal did not, God forbid, question the *halachah* as a result of the refutations, but only the legitimacy of these proofs as support for that *halachah*. Beside the arguments mentioned, *Chazal* offer two more proofs:

(a) R' Dustai notes that the victim may be a midget with small eyes, and the guilty party a giant with large ones. In that case it will be impossible for the punishment to fit the crime if "an eye for an eye" is taken literally. The Talmud refutes this as well, asking what difference there is between the two as far as the result. In both cases, eyesight in one eye is destroyed. After all, in murder cases, the murderer is killed, even if his victim is smaller than he.

(b) R' Shimon bar Yochai presents the same argument, employing a different example: If "an eye for an eye" were taken literally, it would be impossible to punish a blind man who had blinded someone. Yet, the Talmud refutes this argument as well: "Perhaps where possible the law is applied, and otherwise it is not."

✑ Rabbinic Tradition: The Foundation of Jewish Law

The preceding were all the arguments *Chazal* employ to deduce that "an eye for an eye" means monetary compensation. They surely are not the source of this principle, but only a support of it. *Nimukei Yosef*, in his comments on *Rif* in *Bava Kama*, questions R' Ashi's undisputed argument. How, he asks, can R' Ashi initiate a *gezeirah shavah* by himself, thereby nullifying the literal meaning of an explicit Torah verse? He answers that the monetary nature of "an eye for an eye" was well known beforehand, hence the *gezeirah shavah* was nothing but a support for it. It did not serve to create a new law, but only to support an old one, so it was legitimate. *Nimukei Yosef's* words seem to apply to all the arguments *Chazal* offered in this matter. The true nature of "an eye for an eye" was always known to the Jewish people. *Chazal* only sought to find textual proof for it. Possibly, these arguments were meant to support the Pharisees against the Sadducees who differed with them on this point. (See *Megillas Taanis* for R' Sa'adiah Gaon's polemic against the Karaites in this matter, quoted by Ibn Ezra in our *parashah*.)

It is an axiom of faith that the foundation of the Torah is the Oral Law handed down from Sinai. After quoting R' Sa'adiah Gaon's proofs, Ibn Ezra adds his own apt remark: "If we do not trust *Chazal's* interpretation, we will be unable to fully understand the *mitzvos*. Just as we received the Written Torah from our ancestors, so did we receive its oral interpretation. The two are inseparable." Thus, Ibn Ezra concludes that there is no proof as telling as faith in oral tradition. Surprisingly, however, he quotes R' Sa'adiah Gaon, who brings the proof in *Chazal* of the case of a blind man who blinds his neighbor, where one cannot possibly say "an eye for an eye." Didn't *Chazal* refute this, saying, "Perhaps where possible the law is carried out, and otherwise it is not?" Despite the refutation, R' Sa'adiah Gaon evidently employed this proof as a means to counter the Karaites, who read "an eye for an eye" literally. What R' Sa'adiah Gaon proves, from the distinction between "where possible" and "where not possible," is that the literal reading of "an eye for an eye" cannot be applied in every case. Having shown this, it becomes more logical to establish a monetary understanding of the phrase, for this makes possible uniform execution of justice across the board.

The Karaite Ben Zuta questions this: If the guilty party is too poor to compensate the loss of an eye, what will his punishment be? R' Sa'adiah Gaon answers: If the poor man later becomes rich, Hashem will punish him monetarily for his previous act. Yet, what could possibly happen to a blind man to make him capable of being blinded under the Karaite ruling?

In any event, according to our faith, the final proof of this law is Rabbinic tradition. *Rambam* in his introduction to his commentary on the Mishnah states: "There was never any rabbi, from the time of Moshe until R' Ashi, who ruled, based on 'an eye for an eye,' that he who blinds another should himself be blinded." Similarly, he states (*Hilchos Chovel U'Mazik* 1:6), "Our ancestors witnessed monetary execution of 'an eye for an eye' in the courts of Yehoshua, the Prophet Shmuel, and every other court system from the time of Moshe until the present." *Rambam's* proof is established tradition, which no rabbi has ever challenged.

Rambam (ibid.) reviews at length scriptural sources for this law, in contrast to his normal terse style. In 1:3 we find: "The Torah states, 'As he has maimed a man, so shall be done to him' (*Vayikra* 24:20). By this, the Torah does not mean that one should be maimed or wounded as he has maimed others, but that he deserves to have this done. Instead, he must pay damages." *Rambam* also quotes *Chazal's* exposition: "No ransom is taken for murder, but ransom is taken for the maiming of limbs."

In *halachah* 1:1 *Rambam* ignores *Chazal's* other arguments from *Bava Kama*, producing his own:

> How do we know that "an eye for an eye" means monetary compensation? The Torah declares, "bruise for a bruise" (*Sh'mos*

21:25), and we find explicitly, "If one smites another with a stone or with his fist ... he shall pay for time lost from work, and shall see that he is healed" (vs. 18,19). From here we learn that the word תַּחַת, used regarding bruises, relates to monetary compensation. The same holds for תַּחַת mentioned regarding loss of an eye or other organs.

Lechem Mishneh wonders why *Rambam* ignores R' Ashi's unrefuted *gezeirah shavah*, quoted above. In his attempts to answer this question, he suggests that *Rambam* had a different version of R' Ashi before him, or perhaps found his own argument from a different source. At least in his second point *Lechem Mishneh* is correct. *Rambam's* argument appears in *Mechilta* of R' Shimon bar Yochai, in the name of Ben Ezra. *Rambam* seems to have used the most convincing argument he could find. Once we learn that "a bruise for a bruise" means monetary compensation, we can easily deduce the same for other cases. (Some hold that *Rambam's* argument is identical to that of R' Papa quoted above.)

In 1:6, *Rambam* once more takes up the theme of "an eye for an eye," and the other equations, and he says, "Although these words seem to have a straightforward literal meaning, each was Divinely interpreted for Moshe on Mount Sinai. All are *halachah leMoshe* — they go back to Moshe." (In the Padua edition of *Rambam*, instead of *halachah leMoshe*, we find *halachah lema'aseh* — practical law. This is compatible with *Rambam's* previously quoted introduction to his commentary to the Mishnah. There *Rambam* said that the monetary understanding of "an eye for an eye" is "from the Torah," since there is no debate over it. This is a higher level than *halachah leMoshe*.)

◆§ Rambam's View in Moreh Nevuchim

The great length to which *Rambam* goes to prove that "an eye for an eye" refers to monetary compensation demonstrates that he was engaged in a polemic with those who in his day opposed this view. *Rambam's* lengthy arguments against the non-believing Karaites are well known. For example, in *Hil. Ma'achalos Asuros* he offers a long explanation of *tereifah* — non-kosher — meat, concerning which the Karaites differed. Similarly, in *Hil. Shabbos*, Ch. 24, *Rambam* elaborates on *muktzah*, the Rabbinic ban on moving certain objects on *Shabbos*. In *Hil. Chametz U'Matzah*, Ch. 2 and 4, he deals with *bitul balev*, the ability to mentally renounce ownership of an object, which the Karaites deny. As in these and many other examples, it appears that *Rambam* offers numerous explanations and proofs that the Karaites are wrong regarding "an eye for an eye" (see *Kuzari* 2:46 on this matter, and see as well R' Yehudah Muscato and *Otzar Nechmad*, which comment on this).

Remarkably, however, in *Moreh Nevuchim* 3:41, *Rambam* interprets "an eye for an eye" literally: "Do not be disturbed by my interpreting 'an eye for an eye' literally rather than monetarily, for my purpose here is to explain the Biblical text, not its Talmudic commentary. As for the Talmudic commentary, I possess an oral tradition."

This pronouncement disturbed the commentaries. R' Shem Tov states sharply: "Has not *Rambam* taught us that if the Messiah rejected Rabbinic tradition to interpret a Biblical verse literally he would deserve death?" and he concludes, "Where has our teacher and luminary gone wrong? May the benevolent God forgive us all!"

Yet, although *Akeidah* and other commentaries wonder greatly at *Rambam's* words, one may venture to say that this question can be answered. In *Moreh Nevuchim*, *Rambam* offers the literal meaning of the verse, explaining that in the Torah the punishment always fits the crime. Whatever one does will be done to him in return. This is exactly what *Rambam* means in *Hilchos Chovel U'Mazik*, 1:3, when he states that "Whoever bruises or maims someone deserves to be bruised or maimed in the same fashion." Yet, in accordance with Rabbinic tradition, such a person is not physically punished as he might "deserve." The rationale for this is given by *Rambam* not in *Moreh Nevuchim*, but in *Hilchos Chovel U'Mazik*, where he alludes to the oral explanation he received of how essential are *Chazal's* words: The Rabbinic Sinai tradition is Torah. Because no rabbi has challenged or questioned it since the time of Moshe, it determines Jewish law.

◆§ Other Proofs for Figurative Interpretation

Rishonim such as *Akeidah*, S'forno, *Ramban* and Ibn Ezra explain the Torah's use of the expression "an eye for an eye" like *Rambam*: The Torah wished to inform us that in terms of absolute justice, whoever bruises his neighbor deserves an identical physical punishment in return. Yet, where one man blinds another, absolute justice is not always possible. Sometimes the perpetrator is blind himself. If the victim is a *Kohen*, blindness invalidates him for the priesthood. If, in such a case, the perpetrator is not a *Kohen*, no equal punishment can be carried out.

Malbim reads this idea into the words of R' Yishmael in *Bava Kama* 83, where he resolves a seeming redundancy. In *Vayikra* 24:19 we are told, "If a man maims his neighbor, as he has done, so shall be done to him," whereas the very next verse reads, "as he has maimed a man, so shall be done to him" (ibid. v. 20). *Malbim* understands R' Yishmael's solution to this seeming redundancy to mean that the two phrases (both of which are translated above as "shall be done to him" but which are different in Hebrew) are references to two different things. כֵּן יֵעָשֶׂה לּוֹ refers to what ought to be, while כֵּן יִנָּתֶן בּוֹ, which *Chazal* interpreted as monetary compensation, refers to the punishment actually carried out.

Let us conclude with two beautiful expositions from the *acharonim*, demonstrating that "an eye for an eye" (*Sh'mos* 21:25) refers to monetary compensation. First, Vilna Gaon suggests that the verse עַיִן תַּחַת עַיִן is to be interpreted by taking the letters which follow each letter of the word עַיִן (as if the word תַּחַת meant "following"). Now the letter of the Hebrew alphabet following ע is פ; the letter following י is כ; and the letter following נ is ס. Together, these three replacement letters spell כֶּסֶף — money.

Second, R' Shimon Sofer of Erlau (quoted in *HaKesav VeHaKabalah* on *Parashas Emor*) explains that the Torah always mentions the damages caused first, and then the punishment of the person who inflicted the damage. For example, "Whoever kills a beast shall pay for it" (*Vayikra* 24:18). The same is true here. The first "eye" refers to the act, i.e., "If someone hurt's his fellow man's eye." The remaining words, "for an eye," are the punishment: payment in exchange for the victim's eye.

II.

Five Oxen for an Ox, Four Sheep for a Sheep

f a man steals an ox or a sheep, and kills it or sells it, he shall restore five oxen for an ox and four sheep for a sheep" (*Sh'mos* 21:37). The commentaries struggle to resolve several matters involving the theft, slaughter and sale of sheep and oxen. Why should the punishment for slaughter or sale be greater than that for theft alone? Why is there a fourfold penalty for sheep and a fivefold penalty for oxen? Why do the laws of slaughter and sale (v. 21:37) precede the more basic law of twofold payment for unconfessed theft? (v. 22:3).

R' Menachem Kasher (*Torah Sheleimah*), quoting *Mechilta*, states that these laws represent "a decree of the King," i.e., they are beyond human comprehension. To the extent that the difficulties posed defy human logic, this definition seems in place. Nonetheless, starting with *Mechilta*, we shall trace the path of our Sages, who applied their superb intellects to understanding what motivated these laws: The Torah states, "If the thief be found, he must pay double" (v. 22:6). This seems to include one who slaughters or sells what he steals. Why then does the Torah need to tell us, "If a man steals an ox or a sheep" (v. 21:37)? This is to teach that whoever slaughters or sells the animal he stole must pay four or five times its value. *Malbim* struggles to explain what this *Mechilta* tells us that we do not know already, concluding that it answers the following question: Should not the Torah have taught the law of simple theft (v. 22:6) before that of sale and slaughter (v. 21:37)? Rather, the Torah here teaches that one must pay the larger penalty even if he did not steal the cow or sheep originally, but only found it (according to the opinion of R' Chiya bar Abba, *Bava Kama* 63). Verse 21:37 thus serves to stress that in all theft cases, one pays at least a penalty of double value, and in slaughter and sale cases, four and five times the value, even if the person did not steal the animal but only found it, as explained in verse 22:6. Nonetheless, this explanation is quite problematic. First of all, *Mechilta* does not even allude to it. Second of all, even if *Mechilta* did wish to allude to this law, there would have been no reason for putting the law of the four- and fivefold penalty before the twofold one. The twofold penalty could have been brought first as a general law, applying to all cases, and the four- and fivefold law could have been brought afterward.

R' Menachem Kasher explains this differently, in response to *Moreh Nevuchim*. There *Rambam* states that the Torah placed the law governing a person who sold or slaughtered an animal before that of one who simply stole it, because those who steal sheep and cows normally slaughter them so their owners do not recognize and claim them. The Torah mentioned the ordinary action first, and then the out-of-the-ordinary. *Rambam's* answer in essence eliminates the need to explain *Mechilta* as *Malbim* does, for we no longer need to ask why the four- and fivefold penalty precedes the twofold one.

R' Kasher, after quoting *Rambam*, offers his own simple explanation: *Mechilta* is telling us that if the Torah had placed the twofold penalty first, it would apply where the thief sells or slaughters the animal as well. The Torah therefore taught the four- and fivefold penalty first, informing us that it was a decree of the Torah. This automatically tells us that the twofold penalty which follows does not include cases of sale and slaughter.

Yet, even this explanation seems somewhat lacking, for what does it matter if the Torah singles out cases of slaughter and sale for a special law, before or after the twofold law?

∿§ Respect for the Servant and for His Master

Chazal offer a psychological explanation of why the Torah more heavily penalized one who steals by stealth (*ganav*) than with one who steals openly (*gazlan*). The latter, despite his brazen nerve, shows no more fear of man than he does of Hashem. He sins with open and conspicuous boldness. The former, on the other hand, fears only man, shown by the fact that he comes stealthily, but does not fear Hashem.

As R' Yochanan ben Zakkai told his students (*Bava Kama* 27a):

The *gazlan* pays equal respect to servant and King. The *ganav* pays more respect to servant than to King, treating Hashem as blind and deaf: "Woe is to them that seek deep to hide their counsel from Hashem. Their works are in the dark and they say, 'Who sees us? Who knows us?' " (*Yeshayahu* 29:15).

R' Meir adds the following parable: Imagine that two people have made a feast in the city. One invited the townspeople but not the king. The other invited neither the king nor the townspeople. Won't the first receive greater punishment?

Meiri develops this explanation: "If a man sins secretly, it is as though he casts aside the Divine Presence, intellectually denying that Hashem watches over the world." Such a person sins not only against man, like the *ganav*, but against Hashem as well. More precisely, the *gazlan* does not infringe upon the realm of faith, but does his act out of love of money. The *ganav*, on the other hand, chooses to carry out his plot in such a way that man cannot harm him. He does not fear Hashem. This explanation overturns the accepted values of society, transforming the *ganav* into not only a coward, but a heretic. He deserves even worse punishment than the *gazlan*, who steals openly. The *gazlan* commits a crime against society that is neither more nor less serious than his crime against Hashem.

In this context, it would be worthwhile to quote the interesting and unique explanation of R' Samson Raphael Hirsch. Like *Chazal*, he attempts to understand why stealing sheep and cattle incurs a stricter penalty than stealing other articles, by explaining the essence of theft.

Nonetheless, his direction is slightly different. One cannot hide live-stock in one's home. Rather, one must keep them in the fields, hence their welfare depends upon the community. Whoever steals livestock is therefore violating the trust of all society. In effect, he harms all of humanity, hence his punishment is great. Whoever steals from a private home is different, for he violates the individual's trust, not society's. An individual is better at guarding his home than society is at guarding livestock in an unprotected marsh. Therefore, one who steals from an individual receives a lesser punishment.

At this point it is worth quoting a perplexing Midrash (Sh'mos Rabbah 30):

> The Torah states, "If a man steals an ox or a sheep and kills it or sells it, he shall restore five oxen for an ox and four sheep for a sheep" (21:37). The Jewish people said to Hashem, "This verse is full of meaning. Because we stole an ox and made the Golden Calf, we had to replace it with five oxen, i.e., the death of our ancestors in the desert. The four sheep for a sheep are the four kingdoms that ruled over us: Babylonia, Persia, Greece and Rome. When we stole Joseph, we became slaves in Egypt for four hundred years."

This is a puzzling Midrash. What is this "ox that our ancestors stole?" What connection is there between the punishment our ancestors in the desert received, and the fivefold penalty for stealing cattle?

Rabbenu Bachya answers only the last question. The fivefold penalty refers to: (a) death by sword, carried out by the Levites (Sh'mos 32:28); (b) Hashem's plague (v. 32:35); (c) the pulverizing of the Golden Calf by Moshe and his pouring it into the water supply to test the Israelites, similar to the law of the sotah, the adulterous woman (Midrash); (d) the destruction of the Temple (this is based on a similar phraseology used regarding the Golden Calf in Sh'mos 32:34 and the destruction in Yechezkel 9:6); and (e) Hashem's eternal memory of what they did.

R' Menachem Kasher found another version of this Midrash in one of the rishonim:

> The Jewish people said to Hashem, "Because we stole an ox from the celestial chariot and made a Golden Calf, we therefore had to pay fivefold compensation. We lost five of our ancestors in the desert: Moshe, Aaron, Miriam and Aaron's two sons.

Although this version establishes a connection between the Golden Calf and the fivefold punishment, the version in Midrash Rabbah remains difficult to understand.

✦ The Great Importance of Physical Labor

Why must one who steals an ox and sells it pay five times its value, while one who steals a sheep and sells it pays only four? *Mechilta* offers two views on this. According to R' Yochanan ben Zakkai, the Torah takes human dignity into account. One who steals a sheep must carry it on his shoulders. This indignity is treated as part of the punishment, hence the thief pays only fourfold. When, however, an individual steals a cow, he does not carry it but merely leads it; hence he must pay the fivefold penalty.

R' Meir sees the discrepancy between oxen and sheep as pointing to our positive view of physical labor. Stealing an ox, a beast of burden, incurs greater punishment than stealing a sheep, which is not a beast of burden. R' Meir states, "How precious is physical labor to the One Who created the world!" *Sefer HaZikaron* on *Rashi* comments:

> Physical labor is essential to society. If someone works with his hands, let him always work diligently and never view himself with scorn, for the Torah itself insisted upon the importance of physical labor. When a man steals another's ox, the Torah requires him to compensate its owner for time lost due to the ox's absence. This teaches that work is considered as important as money.

R' Shabsai HaKohen (*Sifsei Kohen*) emphasizes that the work a man does to remain free of debt is more important to Hashem than his prayers. He cites the following halachos [some of which are not applicable today]: When workers are on the job and it comes time to recite the *Shema*, they may continue working as they recite the second and third paragraphs. When it comes time for the *Shemoneh Esrei*, and if they are working in olive or fig tree tops, they do not descend. When workers eat bread, they say the *Hamotzi* blessing beforehand, but they recite only an abridged version of *Bircas HaMazon* — Grace after Meals — when they have finished. All these laws stem from the gravity with which the Torah treats private property and wealth. Why then, asks R' Shabsai HaKohen, does R' Yochanan ben Zakkai give a different reason from that given by R' Meir for the discrepancy between cows and sheep? The answer that he gives is that R' Meir's reason applies only to a thief's slaughtering the animal he stole, for in that case, the animal's work ceases. If he sells it, however, the animal goes on working for his new owner. That is why R' Yochanan ben Zakkai introduced the element of human dignity. It follows from this explanation that there is no disagreement between R' Meir and R' Yochanan ben Zakkai, except that the latter adds to the former's words, to explain the penalty for sale by a thief.

Targum Yehonasan quotes both R' Meir's and R' Yochanan ben Zakkai's explanations for the penalty, and several *acharonim* ask how he can imply they are both right. It would appear, though, that *Sifsei Kohen's* explanation answers this. The two reasons the two *tanna'im* give complement one another. In truth, R' Yochanan ben Zakkai's reason would suffice, but *Chazal* found this a suitable opportunity to stress the value of physical labor.

The Lutzker Gaon (*Oznayim LaTorah*) states that in Talmudic times, the chief function of livestock was the cultivation of fields. Hence, one who stole an ox caused its owner's fields to lie uncultivated. Likewise, in *Shabbos* 118, R' Yochanan states, "I have never called my cow 'my cow,' but rather 'my field'." The punishment for sale and slaughter is so great because when a thief slaughters a cow intended to work a field, he ruins his neighbor's field in the process. One who steals an ox and slaughters it is punished for making it impossible for his neighbor to work.

The concept of the preciousness of labor proves that not only a matter of monetary loss is involved here, as some explain, but the endangering of a spiritual value, beloved by Him Who created the world.

R' Simcha Zisl of Kelm also emphasizes the moral value which emerges from R' Yochanan ben Zakkai's reason. The Torah takes into account the dignity of the thief who has broken a Biblical commandment, lowering his penalty to account for the trouble to which he has gone. If this is how the Torah treats sinners, how great must be the reward to those who struggle to fulfill *mitzvos* of the Torah, and surely to those who suffer to avoid sin.

In contrast to R' Yochanan ben Zakkai's reason of human dignity stands the view of *Midrash Rabbah* on *Sh'mos* 30. There the Midrash explains the fivefold penalty for theft of oxen in terms of the public nature of the crime: Two persons arrived in court for judgment. One had kidnapped a nobleman's son and sold him as a slave, while the other had merely thrown a rock at a public statue of the nobleman. The former had to pay four hundred pieces of silver to the prince's father, but the latter was punished with five life-threatening lashes. The relative severity of a punishment depends not on how much effort the sinner invests, but on the level of his audacity. One who steals an ox deceives through his audacity, hence he pays fivefold its value.

Ibn Ezra, quoting Rabbenu Yehoshua, and Chizkuni explain this similarly. To steal an ox, one must be a seasoned thief. Otherwise, he would be unable to carry out such a large, conspicuous undertaking. However, one who steals a sheep might be a novice. His punishment is therefore smaller.

✎§ A Sin That Includes Many Other Sins

Rambam in *Moreh Nevuchim*, 3:41, explains that the relative severity of selling and slaughtering stolen livestock is because thieves customarily do so to make their act untraceable. In just the same way he explains the severity of stealing sheep and cattle over stealing other items. The more susceptible something is to being stolen, the more severe its punishment. Livestock are normally kept in the fields and cannot be guarded as one would guard a household object. Their theft is therefore more severe.

In quoting this explanation of *Rambam*, *Ralbag* concludes, "This does not apply to non-kosher animals." This remark seems puzzling. Would *Ralbag* say that the law does apply to other kosher animals beside ox and sheep?

A text-oriented interpretation, not in harmony with *halachah*, is cited by Abarbanel:

> The Torah does not say "five male oxen per male ox and four male sheep per male sheep." Rather, it speaks more generally: "five cattle per ox and four sheep per sheep" (*Sh'mos* 21:37). The general penalty for unconfessed theft is double-value payment. Regarding sheep and cattle, once the animal is stolen or slaughtered, correct assessment becomes impossible, because the thief can claim that the animal was worth less. Bearing in mind that male sheep and cattle are worth more than females, the Torah therefore reassessed the double-value payment in such cases. For stealing one male, the thief must pay five oxen of either gender, each of which may be worth less than the original stolen ox. Likewise, for stealing one sheep, he must pay the value of four female sheep.

Abarbanel adds, "If this is the Rabbinic tradition regarding these laws, we must accept it happily." Yet, we know that this is not Rabbinic tradition. We have no tradition as strong as that which we quoted originally — that these laws are simply Hashem's decree.

III.

Separating Meat and Milk:
Logic-based or Divine Decree?

hazal (Nazir 37 and Pesachim 44) state that the command to separate meat from milk is a chiddush, i.e., something which human logic would not have deduced on its own. The commentaries attempt to produce an understandable explanation of this chiddush, and to explain that it follows the same lines as the law of first fruits: "The very first fruits of your land must be brought to the house of Hashem your God. Do not cook a kid in its mother's milk" (Sh'mos 23:19). They also strive to understand how "a kid in its mother's milk" can refer to all milk and all meat, and how "do not cook" can prohibit eating or deriving benefit. Countless arguments have been offered. We shall present some of the most original and fundamental, particularly those of the rishonim.

Ramban holds that the most fitting place for this prohibition is Parashas Re'eh. There it appears in the context of other forbidden foods, making clear that it prohibits not just cooking, "as the ignorant and non-believing might think," but eating as well. Yet, since it was customary to bring up to Jerusalem, together with the first fruits, the firstborn lambs and kids, and sometimes the mother was brought along if the lamb or kid was nursing, the Torah therefore attached this prohibition to the law of first fruits mentioned in our parashah. According to Ramban, the reason for the prohibition is unclear. He suggests both that it is because we are a holy nation, and that it is to prevent cruelty, although the prohibition includes much more than "cooking a kid in its mother's milk."

Interestingly, just those commentaries who customarily seek out reasons for the mitzvos, such as Ibn Ezra and Ramban, tend to view this one as a chok, unfathomable by human logic, although they look for logical explanations anyway. Of even more interest, although the link between the text of this verse and the halachah that emerges from it is tenuous, the Karaites never questioned it. These laws correspond to a Rabbinic tradition which has never been challenged throughout the generations.

As is his normal practice, R' Yaakov Tzvi Meklenburg (HaKesav

VeHaKabalah) attempts to find linguistic support for the prohibition within the verse. He proves that the root בשל — "to cook," has many meanings, including not only cooking, but eating and benefiting. גְּדִי — "kid" — is related to מֶגֶד — "delicacy," and corresponds to every type of meat. חֲלֵב אִמּו — "its mother's milk" — reads as חֲלֵב אֻמּו — milk of the same nation, i.e., milk from a kosher species of animal. It is difficult to view this explanation as a substitute for our Rabbinic tradition.

◆§ The Harmful Effects of Mixing Meat with Milk

Chinuch, *Mitzvah* 92, takes the path of those commentaries who view the combination of meat with milk as physically or spiritually harmful. The cause of this harm is known only to Hashem. Hashem, who created nature, knows the elements upon which Creation was based, and knows what combination of elements will harm man. According to *Chinuch*, one who benefits from the combination of meat and milk is like the sorcerer who mixes together elements that ought not to be mixed, causing harm to emerge from those elements Hashem created for our good. According to *Chazal*, sorcerers deny Hashem's power. As with mixing meat with milk, similar harm is introduced through *kilayim* (crossbreeding plants or animals) and *shaatnez* (mixing wool and linen).

R' Samson Raphael Hirsch's explanation in *Chorev* is similar: Hashem created every species "after its own kind" (*Bereishis* 1:12), and He forbade the mixing of certain species, including interbreeding different species of livestock; interspersing grapevines and fruit trees in one field; *shaatnez*; letting an ox and a donkey pull a plow together; and mixing meat and milk. Unlike *Chinuch*, Hirsch does not see such laws as being aimed at preventing spiritual harm to the species involved, but as a means of asserting the independence and distinctiveness of each. Yet, he adds that these theories are just a means of showing that we respect and value Hashem's decrees: "It matters little whether these ideas carry weight, for the laws they explain were commanded by Hashem." This addition strengthens what we said previously: Even those who attempt to explain the reason behind the *mitzvos* know that the prohibition against mixing meat with milk is a *chok*. They are only trying to link this *mitzvah* to the prevalent thoughts of their day, and to derive educational lessons from it.

R' Isaac Breuer, in his *Nachliel*, fuses together reason and Divine decree, categorizing this prohibition and those similar to it as belonging to a "Torah of nature." In his opinion, just as man must be sanctified through the *mitzvos*, so must nature. All such *mitzvos* serve to impress

Hashem's stamp upon nature, and His absolute mastery over Creation. Hashem made man master over His handiwork, but did not leave all to man's whim, limiting his authority in various realms. These limits, according to R' Breuer, are the key to the various prohibitions that effect man's mastery over nature, and they include the prohibition against mixing meat and milk.

Rabbenu Bachya refutes *Ramban's* logic-based explanations for this law. He defines it instead as a *chok*, whose rationale, according to *Chazal*, Hashem will reveal to us in the future, along with the reason for the Red Cow and for the scapegoat of Yom Kippur. Even so, early in his comments on our *parashah*, Rabbenu Bachya does suggest that meat and milk may be harmful when consumed together. He makes this prohibition compatible with human understanding by explaining that milk, when combined with meat, reassumes the properties of blood, which *Chazal* believe to be its bodily source. When blood first turns to milk, its harmful influence fades away, yet is aroused once more when milk is mixed with meat. When a person consumes this combination, he ingests many evil traits such as coarseness and cruelty. The same explanation appears in *Kli Yakar*.

There is a common Talmudic principle that, "When like substances combine, they awaken." R' Aharon Levin of Raisha (*HaDrash VeHalyun*) likens Rabbenu Bachya's explanation to *Rashi's* second interpretation of this principle in *Avodah Zarah* 73: "When like substances combine, the original properties of each are aroused and reinforced." R' Levin finds textual support for Rabbenu Bachya's view as well. The Torah states: "Only be sure that you do not eat the blood, for the blood is the life. You may not eat the life with the meat" (*Devarim* 12:23). Since the Torah says, "the blood is the life," is not the final clause superfluous? In fact, this last clause hints that we must not consume the "life with the meat" under any circumstances, even in the form of meat and milk. Rabbenu Bachya further explains the juxtaposition of this prohibition to the law of first fruits. Our going to Jerusalem with the first fruits serves to sanctify us, preparing us to attain knowledge of Hashem. The Torah therefore warns us not to dull our hearts with the sort of food that would defile us or detract from our efforts to sanctify and elevate ourselves.

᳗ The Torah Uses the Common Case

Ibn Ezra, quoting *Chazal*, states that the Torah forbids us to cook, consume or benefit in any way from meat and milk combined. The *gedi*, or kid, is mentioned only because that was a common animal at the time. Other parts of the Torah exhibit this use of everyday language as well. Among the non-kosher birds, the Torah mentions the *bas haya'anah*, the young female ostrich. Surely, the adult male ostrich is itself non-kosher. Yet, because its flesh is as dry as wood, it was not commonly consumed. The young female, on the other hand, was commonly consumed for its fine flavor. So too with meat and milk. Although meat takes a while to cook, milk scorches quickly, so they are not generally cooked together. Likewise, in the Middle East, milk and lamb are not usually consumed together, because both are very watery. The male kid, however, being soft but dry, is customarily cooked with milk, so that is why the Torah mentioned it specifically.

Do not be puzzled, said Ibn Ezra, that in our region we do not eat the meat of young goats. Medically speaking, there is no better meat. It is widely consumed throughout the Middle East and the Orient, and our ancestors consumed it as well, as we see from Rivkah's having prepared two kids for Yitzchak before he blessed Yaakov (*Bereishis* 27:9). Later on we shall see that Ibn Ezra does not make do with these reasons for the Torah's specifically mentioning a kid, but elaborates further. At the same time, he refutes every explanation that does not concur with the Rabbinic tradition regarding meat and milk. He concludes, "We need not seek an explanation of the prohibition, for it eludes even the wise."

At the end of his comments on this verse, Ibn Ezra blesses *Chazal*, who, to remove all possibility of sin, issued many related decrees strengthening these laws: "May Hashem, Who granted them wisdom, reward them in full."

Rashbam, as well, strives to interpret the wording of the verse as the Torah's employing everyday language. In his words, goats generally bear two kids at once, and it was customary to slaughter one of them immediately. Now, because in ancient times, goats provided the most common source of milk, "and you shall have goats' milk enough for your food" (*Mishlei* 27:27) — the newborn goat was normally cooked in its mother's milk, "and this was a disgraceful, greedy and gluttonous act." *Rashbam* likens this law to our not slaughtering a cow and its calf on the same day (*Vayikra* 22:28), and to our sending away a mother bird before removing its eggs from the nest (*Devarim* 26:6). Such laws "teach us that the Torah meant to civilize us." Finally, because it was customary during the pilgrimages to consume much meat, this prohibition appears in the section on pilgrimages.

Other commentaries attempt to explain the rationale for this prohibition similarly. The above-mentioned laws from *Devarim* and *Vayikra* are widely invoked. Following the path of several *rishonim*, the Lutzker Gaon (*Oznayim LaTorah*) concludes that there is twofold cruelty in cooking a kid in its mother's milk. Only because of the world's moral weakness following the flood was Noach permitted to consume meat. Milk, coming from a live animal, might logically be forbidden as well, yet the Torah revealed that it is permitted. Milk was chiefly meant to sustain newborns, but when the Torah allowed even newborns to be slaughtered, milk became permissible as well. Be that as it may, to cook a newborn animal in milk counts as a twofold evil, involving great cruelty, and it is forbidden just as is slaughtering a calf and its mother on the same day.

R' David Zvi Hoffman develops this idea in his comments on *Devarim*, viewing the mixing of milk and meat like any other limitation placed upon meat consumption. When the Israelites were in the desert, only meat from sacrifices was permitted them. Even later, when other meat was allowed (*Bamidbar* 11), several limits still remained in force, accentuating the holiness of the Jewish people. One of these was the prohibition against mixing meat and milk. The use of a common case to describe a law is an accepted phenomenon in the Torah. The Torah states, "Do not eat flesh torn off in a field" (*Sh'mos* 22:30), although it doesn't matter whether the animal was attacked in the field or in one's home. Only because animals are normally attacked in fields does the Torah speak that way. By the same token, when the Torah speaks of a kid in its mother's milk, it is because that is a common phenomenon, but the *halachah* is not limited only to that case.

◦§ Meat and Milk in Pagan Rites

Rambam in *Moreh Nevuchim*, 3:48, surmises that the combination of meat and milk may play a part in some pagan rite, although he can find no such rite in the literature of the Babylonian Sabean cult. *Rambam's* grounds for this are the Torah's placing this prohibition in the section on pilgrimages.

S'forno, however, believes that the members of the Sabean cult combined meat and milk to improve agricultural productivity. The Torah commanded us to bring our first fruits to the House of Hashem, teaching that this, and not the vain steps taken by the idolaters, would bring a blessing upon the earth.

Abarbanel expands on this idea. Through research and investigation he found that in his own times, Spanish shepherds would convene twice a year to take counsel and deal with problems in shepherding. At those gatherings, meat and milk would be consumed together. When he investigated England, where there are many shepherds, Abarbanel ascertained that they also had the same custom. On the basis of his research, Abarbanel concluded:

> I truly believe that the prohibition regarding meat and milk appears in the section on pilgrimages as a warning to us not to cook them together like the non-Jews when we are gathered at *Sukkos*. Hashem forbade the combining of any type of meat and milk to keep us as far removed as possible from idolatrous practices, so the wicked would be unable to say, "What difference is there between Jew and pagan?"

Acharonim such as *Malbim* and *Netziv* employ this reasoning as well. On the other hand, R' David Tzvi Hoffman declares that idolatrous practices have no bearing here. He associates the prohibition exclusively with the Jewish concept of abstaining from permitted foods to raise one's spiritual level. Furthermore, R' Hoffman finds a convincing way to interpret the text according to the Rabbinic tradition, such that "Do not cook a kid in its mother's milk" will primarily forbid eating meat and milk together: In *Sefer Devarim*, these words appear immediately following the verse prohibiting us to eat meat improperly slaughtered. The Torah does not have to explicitly state the prohibition against eating meat and milk together. In the context of what precedes it, we should understand it ourselves. R' Hoffman also says that the word גְּדִי does not refer specifically to a young male goat, for in the Torah we find several places where the expression גְּדָיֵי עִזִּים is used with other meanings. In ancient times, it was more common to roast meat than to cook it, except in the case of tender newborns. As for the expression "its mother's milk," the only reason the mother is mentioned is to make clear that חלב, which, depending on its vowels, can mean either milk or fat, here means the former. Moreover, the Torah thus indicates that only the milk of a kosher animal is forbidden to be cooked with meat.

The reason for bringing so many of the commentaries' ideas here was to show how powerful and full of significance is our Oral Tradition. There is no absolute logic to the separation of meat and milk. It belongs among those laws that we cannot comprehend with our logic. From this prohibition we derive a lesson regarding those laws whose reason we supposedly know. Without the Sinai Tradition and our observance of the Torah in keeping with it, the Jewish people could not remain a nation. The Talmud states, "Whatever the Torah forbade has a permissible parallel" (*Chulin* 109), and *Maharsha* offered a nice interpretation of this: The *mitzvos* are not dependent upon logical explanations, for all are Divine decrees.

If everything Hashem forbade has a permissible parallel, it shows that neither the one's being forbidden nor the other's being permissible can be logically defended. Hashem forbade us to consume blood. If we try to explain that blood is repulsive, we must confront the fact that liver, which is very nearly just a mass of blood, is permissible. Countless other examples exist of prohibited pleasures with permissible parallels. This clearly proves that the positive and negative commandments are all Hashem's decrees. We are not allowed to question them, but only to practice them as we were commanded, whether or not our intellect can fathom them. The prohibition against mixing meat and milk is decisive proof of this principle.

IV.

The Mitzvah of Free Loans

ur duty to show kindness by making loans to the needy is a positive commandment of our *parashah*. From the wording, it seems not to be a command but an option, "If you lend money to any of My people among you who are poor" (*Sh'mos* 22:24). Nonetheless, *Mechilta*, quoting R' Yishmael, rules that "every appearance of אם in the Torah refers to an option, i.e., the word means 'if,' except for this and two other cases." On the basis of this *Mechilta*, the *poskim* count free loans to the poor among the 613 *mitzvos*, although *Semak* deduces this *mitzvah* not from here but from, "You shall surely lend him sufficiently for his needs" (*Devarim* 15:8).

Rambam (*Hil. Loveh U'Malveh*, Ch. 1) concludes that the source of free loans is our *parashah*. From the verse in *Devarim*, "You shall surely lend him," he proves that the word אם here refers not to an option but to a duty. Later commentaries expressed puzzlement at *Rambam's* needing two verses to produce but one positive commandment. Why should not the verse from *Devarim* suffice? Also puzzling is *Rambam's* having deleted from his discussion of free loans, the laws of precedence mentioned in *Mechilta*. In deciding who most deserves a loan, Jews precede non-Jews, the poor precede the rich, the local needy precede those from elsewhere and poor members of one's own family precede all other people. While *Rambam* does apply this law to *ma'aser ani* — the tithe given to the poor as a gift — he totally ignores it regarding loans. *Rambam* stresses his omission even more by stating, "It is a positive commandment to make loans to the poor," when according to the law of precedence, lending to the rich is a *mitzvah*, too, if no poor people are thereby deprived.

Chinuch, Mitzvah 66, speaks at length on the importance of free loans, calling them even greater than outright charity:

> Hashem wished humanity to accustom itself to showing kindness. This is a laudable trait, the practice of which prepares one to receive Hashem's goodness. As I have written previously, Hashem always showers His goodness on the benevolent, never on the wicked. By showing benevolence to the benevolent, Hashem's will is fulfilled, for it is His wish to be benevolent to the world. If not for this, He would not need us to help the poor, for He could surely provide the poor with all they needed without us. He only made us his emissaries to bring us merit.

In contrast to *Mechilta* and the *poskim* quoted above, Abarbanel holds that "If you lend money to My people" is not a command but an option. At the end of *Parashas Yisro* he states, "With all due respect to R' Yishmael and his learning, the three cases of אם that he mentions are not commands but options." In harmony with this, in our *parashah* Abarbanel repeats that the true *mitzvah* is to give outright charity. If a poor man does not want to accept a gift, we must lend him money, but even then, the constraints the Torah places on collection repayment transform it into a virtual gift. We are forbidden to press for repayment, to sue for it in court or to collect interest for delayed payment. Obviously, collecting interest is always forbidden, even from the rich. Yet, where the borrower is poor, a second prohibition applies. If the lender suggests that in lieu of interest he be allowed collateral, the Torah states, "If you take your neighbor's garment for a pledge, you must return it to him until sundown" (*Sh'mos* 22:25). Finally, because this *mitzvah* seems to break with common practice and accepted norms of justice, the Torah warns, "If he cries out to Me, I shall hear, for I am compassionate" (v. 26).

Akeidah interprets our *parashah* similarly. He, too, sees our basic duty as involving not loans but outright gifts, "When your brother becomes poor and can no longer support himself in the community, you must support him" (*Vayikra* 25:35). Yet, when a man makes a loan to the poor, he is forbidden by the Torah to "oppress" the borrower (*Devarim* 15:2), and *Chazal* said he must even avoid coming into the borrower's presence lest he appear oppressive. Thus the loan, in effect, becomes a gift.

R' Samson Raphael Hirsch distinguishes quite succinctly between Jewish and non-Jewish justice and mercy. In every other society, borrowers hide from creditors, while according to the Torah the creditor must hide from the borrower. As *Chazal* state in *Bava Metzia* 75b: "R' Dimi asked, 'How do we know that if someone has lent his neighbor money and knows that the borrower cannot return it, he must avoid the borrower's presence? The Torah states, "Do not act to him like a creditor" (*Sh'mos* 22:24).' "

◆§ A Duty Expressed as an Option

Many commentaries wonder why, if free loans are a *mitzvah*, the Torah makes them seem optional by saying, "*If* you lend money to My people" (*Sh'mos* 22:24). S'forno notes that the Torah states, "There shall be no poor among you" (*Devarim* 15:4), but it also states, "The poor shall never cease in the land" (ibid. v. 11). In using the word אִם — if, ("if you lend money . . .") the Torah meant the following: If only the latter verse, rather than the former, comes true, there will surely be poor people in need of free loans, and we will be duty bound to assist them.

Alternatively, *Da'as Zekeinim MiBa'alei HaTosafos* quotes R' Yehudah HeChassid who explains that sometimes, as when a potential borrower has a reputation for not paying back loans, we are not duty bound to lend to him, so that in such a case the loan is indeed voluntary rather than obligatory.

Chidushei HaRim sees the verse as referring to an individual whose help is requested, but who is himself in need of money. There we say, "One's own life takes precedence over that of one's neighbor." Yet, even in such a case, where the loan will involve one's sacrificing the capital he needs to support himself, he must not imagine that he may lend at interest. Even regarding optional loans, the Torah commands, "Do not take interest from him" (*Sh'mos* 22:24). Thus, *Chidushei HaRim* suggests that the optional tone of the verse refers to a case in which the lender himself needs the money for necessities.

Employing this idea, R' Y. Perla, in his commentary on R' Sa'adiah Gaon's *Sefer HaMitzvos*, answers a question of *Penei Yehoshua: Chazal* state (*Bava Metzia*) that as potential recipients of loans, Jews take precedence over non-Jews. The Talmud establishes this as referring to a choice between giving a free loan to a Jew, and a loan with interest to a non-Jew. *Penei Yehoshua* asks why this is so. Do we not say that one's own needs take precedence over the needs of others, based on "There shall be no poor among you" (*Devarim* 15:4)? R' Perla answers that the Talmud in *Bava Metzia* is referring specifically to a lender with spare capital. In such a case, a free loan to a Jew precedes an interest-bearing loan to a non-Jew. If, however, the lender needs all his money for necessities, or to maintain a business, his own needs precede those of others. The Talmud could not be referring to a lender who needs all his money for necessities when it states that "Jews take precedence over non-Jews," because that is obvious. Such a person is even allowed to keep all his money to himself. It is the lender with spare capital regarding whom we need the Talmud's statement of precedent. For him, a free loan to a Jew precedes an interest-bearing loan to a non-Jew.

R' Eliyahu Mizrachi poses a question regarding *Rambam*. The Torah states, "If you lend money to any of My people among you who are poor" (*Sh'mos* 22:24), and *Rambam* deduces from the words "among you" that a free loan to a Jew precedes an interest loan to a non-Jew. Yet, asks Mizrachi, can this not be learned from elsewhere? Regarding animal carcasses we read, "Give it to the resident non-Jew in your gates so he may eat it, or sell it to a foreigner" (*Devarim* 14:21). *Chazal* comment, "This tells us that giving it to the resident non-Jew is preferable to selling it to the foreigner." This being the case, it is surely preferable to make a free loan to a Jew than to lend to a non-Jew at interest. Why else should we need the words "among you?" With all due respect, it is difficult to fathom why Mizrachi addresses his question to *Rambam* when the verse from *Sh'mos* is used explicitly this way in *Bava Metzia* 75. Quite the contrary, *Rambam* deletes this exposition entirely from his laws of lending.

As for the question itself, countless answers have been offered. We shall cite two compelling answers, one from *Taz* and one from *Nachalas Yehoshua*. *Taz* answers that a Jew has no duty to give animal carcasses to resident non-Jews. According to the Talmud, although we must sustain them, that is only if they need our help: "When your brother becomes poor and can no longer support himself in the community, you must support him, helping him to live with you, whether he be Jew or resident non-Jew" (*Vayikra* 25:35). If they do not need our help, we are allowed to throw the carcass of the dead animal to the field, neither giving it away nor selling it. Only when a Jew wishes not to throw it away, and wonders what is better, giving it to a resident non-Jew or selling it to a foreigner, do we say that the resident non-Jew takes precedence, since it is our duty to support him if he needs it. Free loans are different, however. If we have spare money, we are not allowed to leave it idle, for we must make loans to needy Jews. One might then think that one's having an opportunity to lend at interest to a non-Jew would remove his obligation to make free loans to Jews, as loss is involved. The Torah therefore states that we must use our money to make free loans to the poor even when it entails a loss.

Nachalas Yehoshua answers differently: We are obligated to support the resident non-Jew. If there is no non-kosher meat to give him, we will have to buy him kosher meat anyway. The Torah, wishing to spare us expense, therefore commanded us to give the needy resident non-Jew animal carcasses. Otherwise, i.e., if we sell it to a foreign non-Jew and feed the resident non-Jew kosher food, our expense will be greater than our profit. This is why the Torah commanded that the resident non-Jew take precedence over the foreigner. We can now understand why the Torah required a special verse to deal with loans.

৵§ All Wealth is Hashem's

The *mitzvah* of free loans to the needy, with all its limitations on reclaiming the sum, is one of those *mitzvos* based on the Divine belief that not man, but Hashem and Torah, control wealth and possessions. In the secular liberal tradition, loans without security to ensure repayment do not exist. Nonetheless, that is just what the Torah requires.

In his introduction to the *mitzvos* of securing an animal's pack, loans, interest and security, R' Samson Raphael Hirsch says:

> Always remember that no part of your wealth, large or small, is absolutely your own. Everything you own belongs to whoever urgently needs it. Suppose you observe your neighbor's business suffering in some way, and he lacks the means to correct matters. If you, yourself, have the wealth and ability to assist him, you must not stand by, ignoring his plight. Rush to his aid with all the means at your disposal. Remember your Creator, for it is He Who grants wealth and success.

This idea, that our fellow man is partner to our wealth and that Hashem gave us more than him so we would supply his needs, is embodied in the Torah, according to the commentaries. *Or HaChaim* finds this lofty truth in the verse, "If you lend money to My people" (*Sh'mos* 22:24). Some people wonder why one individual has more than another. Yet, some people do not merit to receive their livelihood straight from Heaven. For these, Hashem gathers together much wealth into one person's hands so that all those in need can be supported by him. Thus, a rich man must support the poor, not out of mercy, but by law. If a poor man's money is in your pocket, you are only giving him what is his own. The Torah states, "If you lend money to My people." If we have more than we need and are able to make free loans to the poor, then we must realize that the poor man's portion is in our hands. If we are lending him what is rightly his, then we must not act as if we are better than he is, for we are being supported by his wealth.

The *acharonim* delve into this more deeply, particularly in the sermonic literature. *Ma'asei Rokeach* quotes *Rambam* (*Hil. Zechiyah U'Matanah* 6:2) as a source of this idea. There it says that if someone writes a deed transferring all he owns to one of his sons, that son is only a guardian of the wealth. It remains on deposit with him and he must support the rest of the family.

R' Yosef Tzvi Dushinsky (*Toras Moharitz*) quotes an additional *Chazal* in harmony with this lofty idea: A poor man once approached Rava for alms. Rava asked him what kind of diet he was used to, and he replied, "Plump hen and old wine." Rava then asked him, "Are you not afraid of being a burden on the public?" and he replied, "My support does not come from the community but from Hashem." Meanwhile, Rava's sister, whom he had not seen in thirteen years, arrived with a plump hen and old wine. Here Hashem provided the poor man with his needs by means of Rava, as the poor man said, "My support does not come from the community but from Hashem." Our duty to give is surely all the greater if we possess more than we need. The Torah alludes to this with the word אֶת הֶעָנִי עִמָּךְ — "the poor man's portion is with you." It is not ours. Hashem sends the poor man his portion through us. If we do not give alms or make free loans, we are stealing from the poor.

R' Shabsai HaKohen (*Sifsei Kohen*) dismisses the very concept of accumulating wealth. Asking why the Torah commanded us to make free loans with the conditional, "If you lend money to My people," he states that it would have been better were there no money in the world. Nonetheless, if there is money, we must use it for the sake of Heaven, helping people with free loans and alms.

Regarding the words אֶת הֶעָנִי עִמָּךְ, *Rashi*, our most important commentary, states, "See yourself as if you were poor." We must put ourselves in the poor man's place, and picture ourselves with nothing. Then we will understand the importance of free loans.

Once, while collecting for the poor on a very cold day, *Chasam Sofer* approached a miser. The miser, who had come to the door without a jacket, stepped out onto his unheated porch where his visitor was standing, and there *Chasam Sofer* chose to make his appeal. *Chasam Sofer* spoke for so long that his host began to shiver with cold. At last the miser begged his visitor to come inside to his heated room, but he replied, "I planned to speak to you outside so you would understand the plight of our local poor who lack wood to heat their homes." This illustrates *Rashi's* words: "See yourself as if you were poor."

⮞§ The Rich Are Only Guardians of the Wealth of the Poor

The Talmud states, "Whoever gives charity in the hope that its merit will keep someone alive is thoroughly righteous." According to R' Mordechai Bennet, this refers to a rich man, fallen on hard times, who does not wish to accept charity. We may trick him into accepting the sum he needs by telling him we are paying him to pray to Hashem to save one of our children from death or some other misfortune. As such charity causes no shame, one who gives it in this manner is considered thoroughly righteous. Quoting R' Bennet's words, *Chasam Sofer* interprets the verse, "If you lend money to the poor man among you" (*Sh'mos* 22:44). We must give charity and free loans in such a way that the recipient thinks he is doing us a favor, and not vice versa. This is the highest form of charity.

Our great Sages have invested their choicest thoughts in the themes of charity and free loans to the poor, laws of social justice highly lauded throughout the Talmud. The common thread of every interpretation is that man is not free to do with his money as he wishes. He is only entrusted as its guardian to pay out the debts of Hashem, its owner.

V.

The Covenant Between Hashem and Israel

According to Abarbanel, the *rishonim* of France and Spain differ over where to place the events of Chapter 24, in which Moshe goes up to Hashem. The former say this occurred before the Sinai Revelation, and the latter say after. *Rashi* holds that it occurred three days beforehand, on the fourth of *Sivan*. At that time, Moshe was told to warn the people to cease marital relations and stay away from Mount Sinai until the Revelation, and this warning comprised the words of Hashem (v. 3) which Moshe told the people in our *parashah*. Besides this, Moshe handed down to them the seven Noachide laws, as well as the laws of *Shabbos*, honoring one's parents and court law which they had received at Marah. Then, Moshe wrote down all of Hashem's words (v. 4) from *Bereishis* until the Revelation, including those *mitzvos* given them at Marah. The morning of the fifth of *Sivan*, he erected the altar (ibid.). As this was still before the Revelation, he chose the young men (i.e., the firstborn) of Israel (v. 5), for until the sin of the Golden Calf, the Divine service was their responsibility. It was the firstborn who brought burnt offerings and peace offerings (ibid.). Moshe took the blood, placing half of it in two basins and sprinkling the other half upon the altar (v. 6); then he made a covenant with the Jewish people (v. 8).

In accordance with these verses, *Chazal* deduce that when the covenant was forged, in addition to circumcision and the sprinkling of blood upon the altar, the Israelites underwent *mikveh* immersion, for blood can be sprinkled on the altar only by one who has immersed. As for the "Book of the Covenant" which Moshe read before the people (v. 7), that refers to the Torah from *Bereishis* until the Revelation, including those *mitzvos* given at Marah. All this is *Rashi's* view, advocated by other commentaries as well.

Mizrachi agrees, but questions whether, as *Rashi* says, the Israelites were commanded on the fourth day both to cease marital relations and to stay away from the mountain. Did not *Chazal* declare in *Maseches Shabbos*, Ch. 9, that all agree that "on the fourth of *Sivan*, Hashem commanded that they stay away from the mountain, and on the fifth they separated from their wives"?

Maharal, in *Gur Aryeh*, sees no grounds for such a question. True, the Israelites separated from their wives on the fifth, but both commands were issued on the fourth. The command regarding the mountain, which applied to the fourth, was issued first, and then the other, which applied only to the fifth. *Maharal* proves logically that the command regarding marital relations was issued on the fourth. For the Israelites to separate from their wives on the fifth of *Sivan*, they needed to be told a day in advance. Otherwise, the morning of the fifth, before hearing the command, they might have had relations with their wives. *Gur Aryeh* also questions *Rashi's* statement that Moshe wrote out the entire Torah from *Bereishis* until the Revelation. Is there not an opinion in the Talmud that the Torah was given to the Jewish people all at once?

Mizrachi holds that while Moshe did write out the Book of *Bereishis* for them at this point, for the sake of the covenant being forged, the Torah was later handed down in its complete form, from the start of *Bereishis* until the end of *Devarim*. *Rashi's* source is *Mechilta* on *Parashas Yisro*:

> A verse states, "Hashem said to Moshe, 'Go to the people and sanctify them today and tomorrow.' " (*Sh'mos* 19:10). "Today"

refers to the fourth of *Sivan*, and "tomorrow" to the fifth. What did Moshe do on the fifth? He rose early in the morning and built an altar at the foot of the mountain (*Sh'mos* 24:4). Moshe built an altar, bringing burnt offerings and peace offerings (v. 5) ... The Torah continues, "He took the Book of the Covenant and read before the people" (v. 7).

What section did he read? R' Yehoshua ben Eliezer said, "From the beginning of *Bereishis* until that point."

R' Yehudah HaNasi said, "He read those *mitzvos* commanded to Adam, those commanded to Noach, the *mitzvos* the Israelites received in Egypt and at Marah, and all the other *mitzvos* as well."

R' Yishmael said, "How does this begin? 'The land shall rest before Hashem. Six years shall you sow your fields' (*Vayikra* 25:2-3), i.e., he told them of the *Shemitah*, of the seventh year, of the blessings and curses. How does this conclude? 'These are the statutes, judgments and teachings which Hashem established between Himself and the Jewish people' (ibid. 26:46). The people responded, 'We accept these laws upon ourselves.' Seeing that they had accepted them, Moshe took the blood from the offerings and sprinkled it upon the people, as we read, 'Moshe took the blood and sprinkled it upon the people' (*Sh'mos* 24:8). Moshe then said to them, 'You are now linked, tied and caught!' The following day, they accepted all the *mitzvos* upon themselves."

R' Yose ben R' Yehudah said, "Everything happened on the same day."

This *Mechilta* was a key source for *Rashi* in interpreting Ch. 24. All the *tanna'im* of *Mechilta* hold that the chapter took place before the Revelation. Of them all, R' Yose ben R' Yehudah is least explicit, saying that everything happened "on that same day," and *Ramban* on our *parashah* understands him to mean after the Revelation. Even so, R' Yaakov Tzvi Meklenburg (*HaKesav VeHaKabalah*) interprets R' Yose ben R' Yehudah as agreeing with *Rashi* that the chapter was said beforehand. For R' Meklenburg, R' Yose's chief point of disagreement concerns only whether the altar was erected on the fifth or sixth of *Sivan*. R' Yose ben R' Yehudah holds that Moshe "rose early in the morning and built an altar" (24:4) on the morning of the Revelation, regarding which we find, "The morning of the third day arrived" (19:16). As for all the other events, R' Meklenburg sees no disagreement between the *tanna'im*. All hold that the chapter occurred before the Revelation.

Another view derivable from *Mechilta* is that of *Rashbam*, who holds that the chapter occurred "on the day the Israelites heard the Ten Commandments." Uniquely, he believes these events took place later in the day, following the Revelation. No doubt, his source is R' Yose ben R' Yehudah, who said the events occurred "on that same day."

Ramban differs with *Rashi*, posing several questions regarding the view that the chapter occurred before the events of the Revelation:

(a) If Chapter 24 occurred before the Revelation, then the Torah is out of order, returning to the events of *Parashas Yisro* at the end of *Parashas Mishpatim*.

(b) In Chapter 24 we find, "Moshe came and reported to the people all of Hashem's words and laws" (v. 3). *Rashi* holds that this verse is referring to the laws handed down at Marah (v. 15:25). If so, however, the Torah should not have used the word וַיְסַפֵּר — "he reported"— for this implies new tidings rather than a review of what was previously said (Mizrachi, quoting *Radak*, states that according to the rules of grammar, only וַיַּגֵּד refers to new tidings, while וַיְסַפֵּר indicates review of the past).

In light of these arguments, *Ramban* explains that this chapter occurred after the Revelation. Hashem had already told Moshe, "So shall you say to the Israelites, 'You have seen that I spoke to you from Heaven ...' " (*Sh'mos* 20:19). He warned Moshe once more concerning idolatry (v. 20), taught him all the laws of *Parashas Mishpatim*, and concluded with a warning about the paganism and idolaters of *Eretz Yisrael* (v. 23:20-33). Chapter 24 begins with Hashem's command, "Go up to Hashem, you, Aharon ..." (v. 1). The Torah then describes how Moshe did as Hashem had previously commanded him. He approached the nation, relating Hashem's message from 20:19: "You have seen ...," and teaching them the laws of *Parashas Mishpatim*. The nation accepted it all joyfully. The next morning, Moshe rose early to forge a covenant binding them to all these laws. He built an altar, brought offerings and took the book he had written the previous night, reading it before them. The Israelites accepted the covenant, and Moshe sprinkled the blood upon them as a covenantal sign. After completing these tasks, Moshe set out to fulfill Hashem's command to "Go up to Hashem," ascending the mountain alone. Thus, the covenant was forged on the morning after the Revelation, and Moshe went up that very day.

Ibn Ezra, S'forno and the other Spanish *rishonim* comment similarly. This argument between the *rishonim* of France and Spain cannot be decided in favor of either, for the text can be read both ways. The major advantage of the latter view, saying that Chapter 24 occurred after the Revelation, is that it places the chapters in their chronological sequence.

◆§ A Blood Covenant Between Hashem and Israel

The covenant between Hashem and Israel in our *parashah* was carried out by means of the blood from the burnt offerings and peace offerings brought by Moshe. Half of it was sprinkled upon the altar, and half upon the nation.

Rabbenu Chananel views the covenant as a symbolic act. If the Jewish people fulfill the Torah, all will be well. Otherwise, their blood will be forfeit. In Rabbenu Chananel's view, the blood sprinkled "upon the nation" was actually sprinkled upon the Israelites' clothing, and not, as Abarbanel had said, upon the twelve stones of the altar. It is hard to understand how there could have been enough blood to sprinkle upon the clothing of every Jew. Yet, this is the view Rabbenu Chananel advocates. In fact, he holds that when the Torah uses the expression עֶדְיָם — "their ornaments" (*Sh'mos* 33:6) — it refers to the covenantal blood spots sprinkled upon the Israelites' clothing. These blood spots were witness to the link and covenant between Israel and their Father in Heaven. After the sin of the Golden Calf, Hashem commanded the Israelites to remove the ornaments, "The people took off their ornaments they had from Mount Chorev" (ibid.). This was a sign that the covenant would not be in effect until they were forgiven for their sin.

Rashi, as well, holds that the blood was actually sprinkled upon their clothing. He comments that the covenant was inaugurated with "circumcision, *mikveh* immersion, and the sprinkling of blood," in accordance with *Tractate Kereisos* 9a. We know that the covenant was inaugurated with circumcision, "All the people who came out of Egypt were circumcised" (*Yehoshua* 5:5); "I saw you wallowing in your blood" (*Yechezkel* 16:6); and with the sprinkling of blood: "And he sent the young men of Israel, and they brought burnt offerings and peace offerings of bulls to Hashem" (*Sh'mos* 24:5). Yet, how do we know the Israelites underwent *mikveh* immersion? The Torah states, "Moshe took half of the blood and put it in basins . . . He sprinkled it upon the people and said, 'Behold the blood of the covenant' " (v. 6,8). But no one may be sprinkled with the ashes of the Red Cow [which the Talmud obviously equates with the sprinkling of blood at Sinai] without first undergoing immersion. This source implies that the blood was sprinkled upon each individual Jew, and that it involved the rite of *haza'ah* — sprinkling — which is always preceded by immersion.

Targum Onkelos, through his translation of וַיִּזְרֹק עַל הָעָם (v. 8), expresses a view different from that of Abarbanel: "He sprinkled it on the altar to atone for the people." Thus, he translates עַל הָעָם not as "upon the people," but as "on their behalf." In terms of surface meaning, Onkelos' treatment is more logical than that of Abarbanel, for the words בְּעַד — "on behalf" — and עַל — "on" — are interchanged in many places throughout *Tanach*. These include וַתְּצַוֵּהוּ עַל מָרְדְּכָי — "She commanded him on behalf of Mordechai" (*Esther* 4:5); and נִלְחַם אָבִי עֲלֵיכֶם — "My father fought on your behalf" (*Shoftim* 9:17). Even so, we must still wonder why Onkelos changed the meaning of the verse וַיִּזְרֹק עַל הָעָם, especially when his view contradicts that of *Chazal* quoted earlier from *Kereisos*. There it states, "One cannot be sprinkled without first undergoing immersion."

Pardes Yosef, quoting *Toldos Adam*, resolves the contradiction by quoting the *Tosafos* on *Yevamos* 46b. According to the second answer there, R' Eliezer disagrees with R' Yehoshua, suggesting that it is possible for a person to undergo the rite of sprinkling even without *mikveh* immersion. One might wonder how R' Eliezer can differ in this matter when, as we showed previously, the text supports R' Yehoshua. The answer, however, is that R' Eliezer really agrees with R' Yehoshua that the rite of sprinkling cannot occur without immersion. Yet, he holds that the words וַיִּזְרֹק עַל הָעָם do not mean that he actually sprinkled the blood upon the people, but that he sprinkled it upon the altar on behalf of the people. There was really no sprinkling upon the people at all, hence no immersion was necessary.

Chazal in *Megillah* 3 state that Onkelos' translation of the Torah was based on what he learned from R' Eliezer and R' Yehoshua. The *rishonim* comment that Onkelos sometimes renders the Torah according to the former's understanding, and other times according to the latter's. Here, most likely, Onkelos is translating according to R' Eliezer, who held that the blood was not sprinkled upon the people themselves, but on the altar, as stated above.

R' Eliezer's and R' Yehoshua's debate is reflected in the *rishonim*. Some hold the blood was sprinkled upon the altar, and others hold it was sprinkled upon the people, or, according to *HaKesav VeHaKabalah*, in the air before them. In any event, through this sprinkling, a covenant was forged. In fact, the Torah calls this "blood of the covenant" (*Sh'mos* 24:8). Likewise, the book Moshe read before the people is referred to as "the Book of the Covenant" (v. 7). For *Rashi*, who says all this occurred before the Revelation, this refers to *Bereishis*. *HaKesav VeHaKabalah* holds that *Bereishis* was called "the Book of the Covenant" because of all the covenants mentioned therein: that of Noach after the flood, the thirteen times the word בְּרִית — covenant — is mentioned regarding circumcision and the covenant forged with Avraham, Yitzchak and Yaakov. He furthermore suggests the novel possibility that "the Book of the Covenant" really means the

Creation story, and that this thus refers to the Book of *Bereishis*. In Hebrew, the root בָּרָא — "creation" — can sometimes appear without the א, as in בְּרִיָּה and בְּרִיּוֹת, the singular and plural of "being" and בְּרִיּוֹתָיו, "His beings." Likewise, the Torah says: "He declared to you His covenant" (*Devarim* 4:13), and *Midrash Chazis* comments, "This refers to the Book of *Bereishis*, the beginning of Hashem's creation of the world."

✦§ They Beheld Hashem

According to Rashbam, seeing Hashem is part of a covenant. Wherever a covenant is forged, Hashem appears in all His glory. When Avraham made the *bris bein habesorim* — "Covenant Between the Pieces," Hashem "passed" between the pieces. Regarding the covenant of *Parashas Ki Sisa* we read, "Hashem 'passed' before him" (v. 34:6). So too here, Hashem appeared to them in all His glory. The Torah relates that seeing Hashem this way did not harm them: "Upon the nobles of Israel He did not lay His hand" (v. 24:11). Now, regarding the priestly family of Kehas we later read, "They shall not go in to see the sacred articles being covered, lest they die" (*Bamidbar* 4:20). Moreover, the people of Beis Shemesh were smitten, "because they had looked into the Ark of Hashem" (*I Shmuel* 6:19). Even so, when the elders were involved in the forging of a covenant, and Hashem honored them by allowing them to see His glory, they were not smitten.

Ibn Ezra, who states that the appearance of Hashem involved prophetic vision, explains similarly. Hashem did not harm them. Therefore, "they ate and drank" (*Sh'mos* 24:11) with great joy. Ibn Ezra quotes R' Yehudah HaLevi who states that the eating and drinking of the elders highlights their great inferiority to Moshe. Moshe camped on the mountain for forty days without eating, while the elders, although they had seen Hashem's Presence revealed, had to eat and drink to survive. This serves to mark how different they were from Moshe, despite their great achievements.

Ramban, as well, understands the Torah to be stressing the spiritual loftiness of Israel's nobles. Like Moshe, they too were fit to see a great vision, hence "Hashem did not lay His hand" upon them (v. 24:11) to smite them. At the end of their vision, they ate from peace offerings in Hashem's presence, before returning to their tents because we are restricted in where we can offer and consume peace offerings (later, when the *Beis HaMikdash* was built, one would only be allowed to consume peace offerings within the walls of Jerusalem). In this case, they were consumed before the altar.

Rabbenu Bachya explains that the elders held a celebration in honor of their having survived seeing Hashem, in the same way that, following *Yom Kippur*, the *Kohen Gadol* used to celebrate for having survived his entering the Holy of Holies.

According to S'forno, the elders achieved the highest level of prophecy without either losing their senses or entering a state of trance. As we see regarding King Saul, these were both prior conditions for the other prophets: "He stripped off his clothes and he too prophesied" (*I Shmuel* 19:24). We read that Hashem "did not lay His hand" upon the elders. As with the "hand," referred to in *Yechezkel* (2:9), the "laying of Hashem's hand" can refer to a prophetic experience in which one loses one's senses. The elders remained as they were, "eating and drinking," without any concrete physical change taking place. This is the high level of prophecy the Torah wishes to stress.

Da'as Zekeinim MiBa'alei HaTosafos attribute to the elders an even higher prophetic level. Unlike the vision of Hashem's glory which Moshe experienced in *Parashas Ki Sisa* (*Sh'mos* 33:22), the elders did not even need to have Hashem's countenance shielded from them. The revelation they experienced was in no way veiled. It was because they attained such great revelation that they felt such great joy.

Rashi, however, understands the verse negatively. Hashem did not discipline the elders despite their improper attitude. They ate and drank in a vulgar manner, showing scorn for the lofty status they had achieved. Having insulted Hashem's glory, they deserved death. Yet Hashem did not wish to disturb the joy of the covenant, so He waited until the day the *Mishkan* was dedicated to punish Nadav and Avihu, and until the episode of the complaints (*Bamidbar* 11:1) to punish the elders: "When the people complained ... the fire of Hashem burned among them and consumed those who were in the edge of the camp" (ibid.). The word קָצֵה, literally "the edge," is interpreted as קָצִינִים — the princes, i.e., the elders.

Rambam, in *Moreh Nevuchim* 1:5, explains similarly that the elders sinned through their fallacious outlook and their flawed vision: They perceived Hashem in a way that was corporeal: "There was under His feet a kind of paved work of sapphire stone" (*Sh'mos* 24:10), as if, God forbid, Hashem had a physical form. Through this concrete vision, they themselves became sunken in the physical, and "ate and drank" (v. 11). Hence they incurred the death penalty, yet Hashem waited until later to inflict their punishment.

Terumah – תרומה

I.

Building the Mikdash
— a Mitzvah for All Time?

"They shall make Me a מִקְדָּשׁ — Sanctuary — and I will dwell among them" (Sh'mos 25:8). The Torah calls the structure earmarked to house Hashem's Presence a *Mikdash* because of its future mission, the sanctification of the Jewish people. *Rashi* interprets the word *Mikdash* as a "house of holiness" — i.e., a structure from which holiness will emanate to the nation. Alternatively, Rabbenu Bachya and Ibn Ezra explain it as "a structure wherein Hashem's holiness will reside."

Rashbam and Chizkuni understand *Mikdash* as a "house of appointment," as in הִתְקַדְּשׁוּ לְמָחָר — "Prepare yourselves for tomorrow" (*Bamidbar* 11:18). The *Mikdash* is thus a place set aside for meetings between Hashem and man: "There I will meet with the Israelites" (*Sh'mos* 29:43).

Or HaChaim deduces from verse 25:8 that the sanctity of a *Mikdash* takes hold immediately after it is erected. Even before any worship takes place, before the Divine Presence resides in it, it is already holy.

The Chassidic literature notes the use of "And I will dwell among them," instead of "and I will dwell in it," which would logically follow the first clause. The *Mikdash* brings man so close to Hashem that all feel Him within them.

The *rishonim* deal at length with the *mitzvah* of building the *Beis HaMikdash*, which seems, Heaven forbid, to assign physical form to Hashem. King Shlomo wondered about this when he asked: "Behold, the heavens, even the highest heavens cannot contain You, how much less this house which I have built?" (*I Melachim* 8:27). Moreover, Yeshayahu quotes Hashem saying: "The Heavens are My throne and the earth is My footstool. Where is the house you would build for Me? Where is My place of rest?" (*Yeshayahu* 66:1).

It is odd that immediately after the Revelation, in which the Torah forbids us to assign physical attributes to Hashem, it issues this command which seems to confine Hashem to a concrete area.

Chazal explained this in various ways. The easiest explanation for us to understand is that of *Midrash Rabbah* (*Sh'mos* 34): "When Hashem gave Israel the Torah, they would not have survived His approaching them in His full might: 'If we hear the voice of Hashem, our God, any more we shall die'" (*Devarim* 5:22). Instead, He approached them according to what they could endure. The Torah says: "The voice of Hashem is power" (*Tehillim* 29:4). The verse does not say כחו — "His power" — but כּח — "power." Hashem approaches each being according to the power it is capable of enduring. The meaning of this is simple. The Torah takes into account man's limited ability to grasp abstract concepts. While we were commanded not to associate any picture with Hashem, we must absorb that command according to our own ability to understand. Man is limited by his five senses, with which he perceives the world. He is no more able to transcend those senses than to shed his own skin. When Hashem speaks to us, He employs our own language and concepts. He adapts the celestial concepts we must absorb to our intellectual faculties.

Chinuch goes to great length to explain rationally, as he does with other *mitzvos*, why we must build a physical Sanctuary for Hashem. After justifying Hashem's very right to do so in this case, *Chinuch* continues:

> Righteous acts perfect the heart spiritually. The greater the number and frequency of our good deeds, the more pure our thoughts. By assigning such acts, Hashem seeks to ensure man's welfare. Erecting a *Mikdash* and serving Hashem in it represent concrete and sustained acts through which we can be imbued with knowledge of Hashem.

Chinuch demonstrates our need for a *Mikdash* by alluding to prophecy among the Jewish people: "Just as Hashem wished to send the Jewish people prophets to teach them the path they should follow, He also wished to establish a place on earth which would benefit man and increase his merit. All this He did out of kindness to us."

Chinuch goes on to explain the effect of concrete action upon the human psyche:

> Our hearts cannot be purified by mere lip service, by our crying out to the four walls, "I have sinned." Rather, we must undertake a considerable burden, removing goats from their pen, and

bringing them to the Temple, seat of the priesthood. Through such acts we will grasp the wickedness of sin and avoid it in the future.

Man is limited by nature. As part of the human experience, he must learn about the abstract through the concrete means his intellect is capable of absorbing.

Chazal (Tanchuma 8) offer yet another rationale for the erection of a Mikdash. This command, while written following the Revelation, was given to the Jewish people only after the sin of the Golden Calf. Its purpose was to show the nations of the world that the Jewish people had been forgiven for the sin of the Golden Calf. Hashem says, "I will dwell among them," to demonstrate loudly before the world His love for the Jewish people. According to this explanation, the building of the Mikdash is not an educational act for the Jewish people, but a demonstration for the other nations.

S'forno takes this a step further: Not only does the Sanctuary place the Jewish people on display before the rest of the world, but it represents Hashem's descending to the Jewish people following the sin of the Calf. Previously, Hashem had shunned any act that represented Him concretely, commanding the people only: "Make for Me an altar of earth" (Sh'mos 20:21). After that sin, however, the Israelites needed Kohanim. Having shown that they were not on a high spiritual level, Hashem would now descend to them through intermediaries.

Rambam in Moreh Nevuchim offers an extreme version of this view, according to which the Mikdash and Kohanim serve a similar function to Hashem's taking the Israelites on a detour when they left Egypt (Sh'mos 13:18). In both cases, Hashem reckoned with the psychological state of the people. When the Jews left Egypt, they had just been freed from slavery, and were slowly adapting to a life of freedom and independence. Likewise, Hashem's command to serve Him through physical intermediaries took into account the concrete view of Hashem the Israelites had until then, and their belief, then common to the world, that direct contact between Hashem and man was impossible.

Rambam agrees with Chinuch that the Mikdash served an educational role. Even so, it was only a first step in fully weaning the Jewish people of their idolatrous views. It was enough at first for the Israelites to worship Hashem in concrete form. Yet, the long-range goal was for them to arrive at a refined understanding that serving Hashem is different from serving any other deity. Its purpose is to become spiritually close to Him, without intermediaries.

Rambam's explanation is similar to that quoted above from *Midrash Rabbah*, only it stresses even more the Sanctuary's educational role of removing the Jewish people far from those beliefs commonly held by the pagan world of those times.

Ramban, in his introduction to *Sh'mos*, views the building of the *Mikdash* as bringing the Jewish people closer to Hashem and restoring them to the level of the Patriarchs. These, he states, were the goals of the Exodus: The exile cannot end until the Jewish people return to the spiritual level of their ancestors. When the Israelites left Egypt, they were no longer slaves. Even so, entangled in the desert, in a land not theirs, they could not have been considered redeemed. Then they arrived at Mount Sinai and erected the Sanctuary. Hashem once more caused His Presence to reside among them, and they were restored to the spiritual level of their ancestors.

According to *Ramban*, the purpose of the Sanctuary was to turn the clock back to where the Israelites stood before entering Egypt. At that time, there was direct contact between Hashem and man. Hashem spoke directly with Avraham, Yitzchak and Yaakov. This spiritual state was achieved again with the erection of the Sanctuary.

Abarbanel, by contrast, views the erection of the *Mikdash* as a symbolic act. Its purpose was to instill Israel with the knowledge that Hashem resides not only in Heaven, as some mistakenly believe, but even on earth. Hashem wishes the Israelites to know that He dwells among them and constantly watches over them, seeing all they do. The Holy One, Blessed is He, commanded Israel to construct a *Mikdash*. Through it Israel would be taught that Hashem dwells in their midst. His Providence accompanies us at all times and He carefully observes our deeds. Such was the symbolism of the *Mikdash*, causing these principles to take deep root in the Jewish people.

Kuzari (3:23) offers a novel explanation of the *Mikdash's* function: Nature, as we know it, is composed of various elements which combine together to produce the world before us. As natural as the world seems to us, only Hashem knows the quantity and quality of elements needed to create it. Only Hashem knows why one combination of elements creates "vines" and another "living beings." So too with the *Mikdash*. Hashem commanded certain dimensions and specific materials for the construction of the *Mikdash*. These, coupled with the Israelites' donation of the necessary materials, combined to breed a new spiritual force which led Hashem to dwell among the Jewish people.

Kuzari states further:

We can only become close to Hashem through His *mitzvos*, for He alone knows their measure, weight, time and place, and all the other details by which we achieve Hashem's will and merit to cling to Him. Thus, regarding the erection of the Ark (*Sh'mos* 37:1), its covering (v. 6), the curtains (v. 36:14) and every other part of the Sanctuary, the Torah states that they were carried out "as Hashem commanded Moshe" (v. 39:1). In other words, without addition or deletion. If Hashem had not willed it, human logic would not require that these articles be fashioned. At the end of the section on the Sanctuary, the Torah states, "Moshe saw all the work, and behold, they had performed it just as Hashem had commanded, and Moshe blessed them" (v. 39:43).

What resulted was inevitable. Hashem's presence came to rest in the Sanctuary: "I will dwell among them" (v. 25:8).

This summary follows what *Kuzari* says regarding those elements, invisible to the naked eye, that compose matter. We recognize their function and purpose only from their end product.

In his *sefer Or Rashaz*, R' Simcha Zisl of Kelm, one of the great lights of the Mussar movement, offers another explanation of the *Mikdash's* function. He quotes Ibn Ezra, who likens the idea of holiness being concentrated and confined to a set "place" to man's sense of smell, which is confined to his nose. While one's entire being enjoys the smell of spices, it is absorbed through a small part of the body. Likewise, Hashem is everywhere, but He communicates through the *Mikdash*. R' Simcha Zisl then adds a metaphor of his own. Since the discovery of electricity, we know there is potential light everywhere, even in darkness. Nonetheless, to see this light, man must take action. The *Mikdash* is the light of creation which is revealed through actions taken by man. Like electricity, it proves conclusively that there is a spiritual force throughout the universe, which need only be activated.

This may well be the meaning of "They shall make Me a *Mikdash* and I will dwell among them." Our discovering the Divine Presence in the *Mikdash* attests and proclaims that "Hashem dwells among us." The Divine Presence is everywhere. Man, through thought and action, can make it shine forth, as was done in the *Mikdash*. This is like the metaphor of electricity.

❧ Transcending the Limits of Space

In one of his discussions of the weekly *sidrah*, the Lubavitcher Rebbe deals with the interesting fact that Hashem, who transcends spatial limits, designated a special place for His worship. According to the Rebbe, while Hashem is not bound by spatial dimensions, one still cannot say that He transcends them entirely, for even to say that is to describe and define Him, and any definition of Hashem limits Him. Only if we say that Hashem is bound by spatial dimensions and at the same time transcends them, thus joining opposites together in a manner incomprehensible to the human mind, do we touch upon an accurate description of Hashem, who is beyond our understanding. Within Hashem, polar opposites join together.

This unfathomable equation applies in the *Mikdash* as well. On the one hand, the *Mikdash* is bound by spatial dimensions, being composed of materials whose size and weight can be measured. On the other hand, it clearly exhibits the polar opposite of this as well. One of ten miraculous conditions that applied there was that "the Ark took up no space." Although the Ark measured two and a half cubits, and the width of the *Mikdash* was twenty cubits, there were ten cubits on either side of the Ark. Thus, through the Ark, which was both bound by spatial dimensions and transcended them, Hashem's great power and might were revealed.

The Rebbe transfers this remarkable idea, embodied in the *Mikdash*, to the Sanctuary of man's heart. The Torah says, "They shall make Me a *Mikdash* and I will dwell among them" (*Sh'mos* 25:8), and this verse can be read "I will dwell inside them." Man's purpose is not only to serve as a receptacle for holiness, but to make his material pursuits holy as well, as happened to the material substances from which the *Mikdash* was erected.

Other Chassidic luminaries, as well, interpret verse 9 as teaching that even man's natural and mundane activities can be holy. The Torah states, "So shall you do" (v. 9). *Sefas Emes* comments that man must perfect even his simple pursuits: "Hashem sent man down into the physical world so that through man, holiness could pervade the entire universe: "He has empowered His nation to carry on His works" (*Tehillim* 111:6). Man's main purpose on this earth is more important than the very creation of the world, for man has been sent to perfect what Hashem created. This verse from *Tehillim* was fulfilled in the *Mikdash*, for as *Chazal* state, "Betzalel understood the creation of the world well enough to engage in creation himself."

Hashem allowed the Jewish people to have Divine light, so that they could perfect the physical world. These thoughts are reflected in "They shall make Me a *Mikdash*," and "so shall you do." Thus, according to the great figures of Chassidus, the *Mikdash* was meant to illuminate the physical world so that even man's mundane activities could be made holy to Hashem.

◆§ A Mitzvah for All Time

Rambam (*Hil. Beis HaBechirah* 1:1) states that, "They shall make for Me a *Mikdash*" (*Sh'mos* 25:8), establishes an eternal *mitzvah* to build the *Beis HaMikdash*, and he repeats this in *Sefer HaMitzvos* 20 (see *Biur HaChaim*, who concurs). *Semag*, though, derives this *mitzvah* from, "Then there shall be a place which Hashem your God shall choose to cause His name to dwell there" (*Devarim* 12:11). *Chazal* in *Sanhedrin* quote this latter verse as well when they say, "The Jewish people were given three *mitzvos* prior to entering *Eretz Yisrael*." *Chazal*'s statement, though, serves only to place the three *mitzvos* in order, not to establish their Torah source.

For *Rambam* and *Chinuch*, the source of this *mitzvah* is the verse, "They shall make Me a *Mikdash*." *Kesef Mishneh* explains the basis of the argument between *Rambam* and *Semag*. According to *Semag*, the verse, "They shall make Me a *Mikdash*," deals only with the desert *Mishkan*, the Tabernacle. *Rambam*, however, holds that the use of the word *Mikdash* in the verse teaches us that it alludes even to the *Beis HaMikdash* of later generations. As proof, *Chazal*, as well (*Sanhedrin* 16, *Shavuos* 14), derive other laws involving the *Beis HaMikdash* from, "so shall you do" (*Sh'mos* 25:9), the very next verse.

(In his *Torah Temimah*, R' Baruch Epstein asks why *Kesef Mishneh* is troubled by *Rambam*'s deducing the *mitzvah* of building the Temple from 25:8, which concerns the Tabernacle, when *Chazal* themselves learn several laws from 25:9 — "so shall you do" — in the same section. R' Epstein's question seems puzzling, for *Kesef Mishneh* himself raises this point against *Semag*.)

Ramban on our *parashah* does not regard 25:9 as referring to the *Beis HaMikdash*, for there are several differences between the desert Tabernacle and the *Batei HaMikdash* that followed. Even so, *Or Zarua* is puzzled by *Ramban*'s ignoring the words of *Chazal* who did interpret this verse in this manner. As for *Ramban*'s question regarding the differences between the desert Tabernacle and the later *Batei Mikdash*, *Or Zarua* answers that these differences were instituted by the prophets. Thus, King David said: "All this is put in writing by the hand of Hashem Who instructed me" (*I Divrei HaYamim* 28:19).

A beautiful answer to *Ramban*'s question is given by *Chasam Sofer* in his responsa on *Orach Chaim* 208 and *Yoreh Deah* 236: Regarding the desert Tabernacle we have an explicit verse permitting the prophets to make halachic changes following Divine instruction: "According to all that I show you — the pattern of the *Mikdash* and the pattern of all its vessels — so shall you do" (*Sh'mos* 25:9). This teaches that later on, the Temples, as well, were made following Hashem's instructions to His prophets.

We have seen that *Rambam* learns the *mitzvah* of building the *Mikdash* from *Sh'mos* 25:8. Why then, in *Hil. Melachim*, Ch. 1, does he invoke, "There at His dwelling shall you seek Him, and there shall you come" (*Devarim* 12:5)? *Lechem Mishneh* suggests that *Sh'mos* 25:8 refers only to the desert Tabernacle, yet we have shown that that is not so. The question remains unanswered.

According to *Chinuch*, the *mitzvah* of building the *Beis HaMikdash* is in force when the majority of the Jewish people are in *Eretz Yisrael*. It has been pointed out that in the times of Ezra, this condition was not fulfilled and even so the Second *Beis HaMikdash* was built. R' Yehoshua of Kutna, in his *Yeshuos Malko* on *Terumah*, answers that since all had the chance to go up to the Land, those who did not do so forfeited their "vote." Hence, it was as if there was a majority in the Land.

Rambam, in a similar fashion in *Hil. Sanhedrin*, Ch. 4, suggests that in seeking to ordain a particular candidate with the ancient *semichah*, the agreement of Sages outside *Eretz Yisrael* need not be sought. Rather, a majority of those in *Eretz Yisrael* is sufficient (although *Rambam* at first wrote that "all the Sages" are needed, the meaning of these words is debated by Mahari Bei Rav and *Ralbach* in their respective treatments of *semichah*). While *Rambam* offers no final ruling (concluding, "The matter requires a decision"), he only does this because of reasoning given previously: When the majority of the Sages outside *Eretz Yisrael* cannot go up to the Land, the Sages in *Eretz Yisrael* cannot act as a majority.

Interestingly, *Minchas Chinuch* (*mitzvah* 95) takes the view that even if the Jewish people are under foreign occupation, if the occupying power allows them to build the *Beis HaMikdash*, the obligation takes hold. Thus, R' Yehoshua ben Chananiah began to build the *Beis HaMikdash* with the permission of the Roman Emperor. This law requires the clarification of our greatest Sages.

By law, the building of the *Beis HaMikdash* is not bound up with the bringing of the offerings, i.e., it comprises a separate *mitzvah* in the 613 *mitzvos*. Nonetheless, there is still debate over whether the two are interdependent or not (see *Rambam*, *Sefer HaMitzvos*, *Mitzvah* 20 and *Mishpat Kohen* 94).

II.

Removing the Poles from the Ark

Rambam's *Sefer HaMitzvos* lists as Prohibition 86 the ban on removing the poles from the rings of the Ark. Whoever violates this incurs lashes (*Makos* 22). In *Hil. Klei HaMikdash* 2:13, *Rambam* states further:

> When the *Kohanim* carry the Ark, they face it, keeping the poles upon their shoulders. Also, they are careful not to let the poles slip off the rings lest they violate a prohibition and incur lashes: "The poles shall be in the rings of the Ark; they shall not be removed from it" (*Sh'mos* 25:15).

Later on we will review the halachic source for this, and investigate the Torah's strictness regarding removing the poles from the Ark as opposed to the poles of the other vessels.

As with all other aspects of the *Mishkan* and its vessels, the commentaries explain this prohibition with a philosophic and symbolic bent. Basing themselves on *Chazal* and the Midrashim, the commentators are more interested in teaching timeless moral lessons than in explaining the surface meaning of the text.

◆§ It Is a Tree of Life for Those Who Support It

Midrash Lekach Tov, quoted in *Torah Sheleimah*, explains that the poles of the Ark symbolize those people who financially support Torah study. *Torah Sheleimah* also quotes the explanation of R' Yosef ben R' Yosef Nechemias that whoever supports Torah study in this world will enjoy the same reward as those who learn it, sharing their reward in Heaven forever.

Tzror HaMor, as well, views the poles that supported the Ark as teaching that the Torah's endurance is as much due to those who offer financial support for its study as to those who themselves study it: "It is a tree of life for those who support it" (*Mishlei* 3:18).

This theme is first found in *Chazal*. The Torah says, "They shall make an Ark" (*Sh'mos* 25:10), rather than "You shall make an Ark," the form we find regarding the other articles. *Chazal* view this as stressing that the entire Jewish people have a portion in the Torah. The command that the poles not be removed from the rings of the Ark (v. 15) serves to drive home this point. The Ark represents Yissachar, who studies Torah, and the poles represent Zevulun, who supports its study. This teaches how important for its survival are those who support Torah financially.

The Torah states, "Cursed is he who does not uphold the words of this Torah" (*Devarim* 27:26). *Chazal* (*Yerushalmi, Sotah,* Ch. 7) understand this as referring to failure to support Torah scholars and they declare, "Even if someone neither learns nor teaches Torah, but supports it financially, he is considered to have upheld it." To their credit, it should be noted that the Jewish people have always applied *Chazal's* understanding of the prohibition against removing the poles from the rings, actively keeping the Torah alive in this fashion. The partnership between Torah scholar and donor has been the norm from time immemorial.

Chasam Sofer, quoting his mentor R' Nassan Adler, offers a beautiful explanation of our *parashah*: The Ark symbolizes the Torah. The cherubs facing each other represent the love that must abide between Torah scholars when they discuss Jewish law. The poles used to carry the Ark symbolize those who financially support Torah scholarship, for, as the Talmud tells us, Hashem stated, "All the world is sustained through the Torah study of My son Chanina, yet Chanina is satisfied with a small quantity of carob." The Ark took up no space, because the Torah transcends the limits of space and time. Although these ideas are all symbolic, their relevance, and the truth they contain make them, in Jewish terms, integral to the meaning of the text.

Chasam Sofer's second mentor, R' Pinchas Horowitz, deals with this theme at length in the introduction to his *Hafla'ah*. In *Berachos*, King David is quoted as having responded to his advisors' reports that his nation's needs were great by saying, "Let the Jewish people support one another." R' Horowitz treats this as a moral lesson to those who support Torah scholars, teaching that it is not they who support Torah scholars, but the Torah scholars who support them. As *Chazal* state, "The Ark carried those who carried it."

Chafetz Chaim, in his commentary on the Torah, states that the Torah is the property of the entire Jewish nation. Those who study it, and those who support its study, are equally rewarded: The Torah warned us not to remove the poles from the Ark. Since they are the means by which the Ark is carried, they become sanctified with the Ark's holiness. As a result, they are kept perpetually together, even when the poles are not needed. So too with those who support Torah study. When someone finances the study of others, he merits to be with them in Heaven forever.

Sifsei Kohen quotes an utterance from *Chazal* that makes this point explicitly: "Whoever fills the Torah scholar's pockets shall merit to study in the Heavenly Yeshivah."

The above are metaphoric explanations, yet they afford timeless relevance to the prohibition against removing the poles of the Ark from their rings. How fortunate we are to have interpretations of the Torah that ensure our eternal survival!

◄§ The Poles of the Ark: A Historic Metaphor

Sh'mos 25:15 forbids us to separate the poles used to carry the Ark from the Ark's rings. Chinuch, Mitzvah 96, explains this in terms of our duty to maintain the Ark's glory and majesty:

> Because the Ark houses the Torah, it is our chief glory, and we must do our utmost to treat it so. We were commanded never to remove its poles from its rings. If there was ever a sudden need to travel somewhere carrying the Ark, the danger existed that the Israelites would be too rushed to ensure that the poles were well attached, and God forbid, they might suffer the indignity of falling to the earth. As long as they were kept ready for travel and never removed from their rings, they could remain strong and accidents could be avoided.

This is the most straightforward explanation offered. Hashem's command was meant to prevent mishaps resulting from sudden travel in the desert. The Ark had to be constantly ready to be moved.

Chizkuni views this prohibition as defending the dignity of the Ark by preventing excess handling of it, even when it is stationary. The Ark is too holy for all to touch it. He explains, following the text, that the poles must be well attached to the Ark. Then, when the Ark is carried, whether its porters are climbing mountains or descending into valleys, the Ark will not fall off their shoulders. Later we shall discuss to what extent this explanation is in harmony with Chazal's view of the matter.

Chizkuni, by contrasting the poles of the copper Altar with those of the Ark, offers yet another clear-cut explanation. The copper altar was located in the Temple Courtyard, where there was constant traffic and crowding. Because poles in a crowded place can cause accidents, the Torah did not require that its poles be kept attached. The Ark, however, was located in the Holy of Holies, which was entered only once a year by the Kohen Gadol. Therefore, the Torah could require that the poles be permanently attached.

In contrast to this straightforward explanation of why the poles could not be removed, Meiri offers a philosophical metaphor. The Ark's poles symbolize our mundane affairs while the Ark represents the spiritual. Our everyday activities must have a spiritual aspect to them, as in: "Acknowledge Hashem in all you do" (*Mishlei* 3:6). In a similar fashion, *Meiri* interprets, "I sleep, but my heart wakes" (*Shir HaShirim* 5:2): One's heart must always be attuned to spirituality, even when one is involved in the most mundane affairs.

Kli Yakar, as well, views this prohibition as accentuating the eternal link of the Jewish people to Hashem and His Torah. The command not to remove the poles is in line with Hashem's command to Yehoshua, "This Torah shall not depart from your mouth" (*Yehoshua* 1:8); and, "It shall not depart from your mouth or the mouth of your children, or your children's children henceforth and forever" (*Yeshayahu* 59:21).

Or Sameach attributes deep significance to this *mitzvah*: Rambam rules in *Hil. Temidim* 3:12 that even when one lights the lamps of the *Beis HaMikdash* during the day, when there is natural light, a *mitzvah* is still being fulfilled. This is in accordance with *Chazal* in *Shabbos* 22 who ask rhetorically, "Did the *Kohanim* light the lamps because they needed their illumination?" Their lighting during the day proves that the lamps bore loftier significance: This makes clear that the lighting at night likewise had a higher purpose. So too with the Ark. The *Kohanim* thought that they were carrying the Ark, when in fact, it was carrying them. Hashem commanded that the poles never be removed from the Ark to teach that carrying it was not their chief function. Just as the poles were not needed when the Ark was stationary, so, too, were they unnecessary during travel. They were only a decree of Hashem.

It is *Chinuch* who referred to our need to keep the Ark constantly ready for travel. The *acharonim* take this idea and invest it with historical and philosophical meaning.

R' Samson Raphael Hirsch distinguishes between the Table, incense Altar and Menorah, none of which required poles that were constantly in place, and the Ark, which was required to have its poles in place at all times. The former, with their fixed location, symbolize the Jewish people leading the spiritual and secular lives of a free nation in its own land. The latter, on the other hand, reflect the essence of Torah, which is not bound by location. Wherever the Israelites reached during the exile, the Divine Presence went with them. The Torah transcends restrictions of space. Even when it is in its fixed location, the poles of the Ark must be ready to carry it anywhere.

Netziv develops the same idea in his *Haamek Davar*. Regarding the Ark, the Torah states, "Put the poles into the rings" (*Sh'mos* 25:14). Likewise, regarding the outer Altar we find, "The poles shall be put into the rings" (v. 27:7). By contrast, regarding the table and the inner Altar we read only of the fashioning of the poles, but not of their being attached to the rings. The Ark and the outer Altar symbolize Torah study and service to Hashem, while the Table and the inner Altar symbolize royalty and priesthood. Torah study and prayer are *mitzvos* throughout the world, but the laws of royalty and priesthood apply only in *Eretz Yisrael*. Legally, however, there is no difference between the poles of the outer Altar, the Table and the inner Altar. Only the poles of the Ark must never be removed from their rings.

⧉ Adjustable but Not Detachable

In *Yoma* 72, R' Yose ben R' Chanina poses the following question: One verse states, "The poles shall be in the rings of the Ark. They shall not be removed from it" (*Sh'mos* 25:15). Elsewhere the Torah says, "The poles shall be put into the rings" (v. 27:7), implying that the poles were taken out and put back at will. How can this be? *Rashi*'s version of *Yoma*, instead of quoting the above verse, quotes, "Place the poles into the rings on the sides of the Ark" (v. 25:14). *Rashi* understands the Talmud's question as follows: One verse implies that the poles could never be removed, whereas the other implies that they could be taken out and put back. The Talmud answers this seeming contradiction by stating, "The poles were movable, but not detachable." *Rashi* explains that the poles had thick ends and could only be inserted by force. Even so, the poles were thin at the center. Thus, once the poles were attached to the sides of the Ark they could move back and forth, but could not be removed entirely.

Tosafos struggle to understand *Chazal*'s words. First of all they are puzzled by the Talmud's use of "the poles shall be put into the rings" (v. 27:7), for that does not deal with the Ark, but with the copper Altar. Second of all, they are puzzled by a command to the sons of Levi that before setting out with the Ark, they must insert its poles (*Bamidbar* 4:8). Why should they have had to do this if the poles were permanently attached to the Ark and could not be removed from it? After considering this, *Tosafos* arrive at the same conclusion arrived at by Ibn Ezra, that the Ark had two types of poles and eight rings. While some poles were never removed from the rings, others were only inserted before travel. *Ramban*, however, refutes this theory.

Other commentaries wonder at *Rashi*'s replacing "the poles shall be put into the rings" (v. 27:7) with "place the poles in the rings on the sides of the Ark" (v. 25:14), a verse which seems to have dealt with the initial insertion of the poles in the sides of the Ark. Why should anyone interpret the verse as dealing with desert travel? This, most likely, is why the other version used "the poles shall be put into the rings" (v. 27:7). There, however, an even more difficult question automatically arises: Doesn't that verse refer to the copper Altar, which has different laws entirely? Surely the prohibition against removing the poles from the rings cannot apply there at all.

Ritva nonetheless interprets the Talmud's question regarding "place the poles in the rings on the sides of the Ark" (v. 25:14) as involving not a contradiction, but a redundancy. Verse 15 reads, "The poles shall be in the rings of the Ark." Why then do we need the first verse? In answer to this, *Ritva* explains that the first verse (v. 14) teaches us that while poles could not be detached, they could, however, move back and forth within the rings.

A novel explanation is offered by *Netziv* in *Haamek Davar*: The Talmud's question on verse 25:14 is based not on the phrase, "Place the poles," but on the end of the verse: "so that the Ark can be carried with them." The latter phrase implies that the poles were only for travel. The next verse, however, states, "They shall not be removed from it," implying that the poles had a special purpose quite apart from use in travel. The Talmud answers, "They were movable but not detachable," i.e., although they could not be removed, they could be shifted to one side to serve their independent function.

After examining the *rishonim*, it is possible to say that the Talmud is focusing on the end of 25:14: "So the Ark can be carried with them," but in a slightly different manner. Verse 14 reads, "Place the poles in the rings . . . so the Ark can be carried with them." Likewise, regarding the copper Altar we find, "The poles shall be put into the rings" (27:7). Both verses imply that before travel, the poles had to be adjusted in some way. The Talmud therefore asks, "Does the Torah not state, 'They shall not be removed from it,' implying that the poles were always ready for travel?" The Talmud answers that while the poles were fixed to the Ark, they were loose enough to shift back and forth. Therefore a special alteration was necessary before travel to make them immovable. This explains the verse quoted from *Bamidbar*: "They shall put the poles." Each time the Israelites traveled, the Levites had to alter the poles so that they would not shift back and forth.

Support for this explanation comes from R' Elazar Moshe Horowitz in his remarks on *Yoma*: "Regarding the Ark, the Torah says, וְשָׂמוּ בַּדָּיו — 'They shall insert the poles' (*Bamidbar* 4:6). However, regarding the other articles the Torah states, וְשָׂמוּ אֶת בַּדָּיו, including the extra word אֶת (ibid. vs. 8,11)." In accordance with this distinction, R' Horowitz states that the Levites inserted the poles in the other articles each time they traveled. However, the poles of the Ark were permanently attached, and only had to be adjusted.

From this we can understand why in *Hilchos Kelei HaMikdash*, *Rambam* joins together the prohibition against removing the poles of the Ark with his instructions for how the Ark must be carried. As the poles were adjustable but undetachable, one may logically assume the Israelites were commanded to prepare them each time they were going to travel. Obviously the matter requires further clarification.

Such an explanation is found in *Pa'aneach Raza*, and can be attributed to *Ritva* as well.

Malbim explains that when the Ark was stationary, its poles were attached to corner rings. When the Israelites traveled, these poles were removed and reattached to rings on the sides. According to *Malbim* there was a difference between travel and encampment. This is what the Torah meant in *Parashas Bamidbar* when it said, "They shall insert the poles." The poles were always to remain in rings, but sometimes they were transferred from one set of rings to another. Likewise, the Torah later says regarding Betzalel, "He took the tablets of Testimony and placed them in the Ark. He then attached the poles to the Ark" (*Sh'mos* 40:20). If the poles were undetachable, why should Betzalel have had to attach them? Rather, the verse refers to the period before the Ark was in its fixed location, so Betzalel placed the poles in the side rings. Later, when they wished to put the Ark in its proper place, Moshe removed the poles and placed them in the corner rings. Thus, for *Malbim*, *Chazal* mean the following in *Maseches Yoma*: While the poles were shifted to the side for travel, they were not detached totally from the Ark, even when it was stationary. This explanation is offered by *Tosafos* in *Yoma*, and they conclude that further clarification is needed.

III.

The Nature of the Cheruvim

One remarkable aspect of the Tabernacle was the *Cheruvim* standing on the Ark covering (*Sh'mos* 25:18). *Chazal* in *Chagigah* 14 state that the word כְּרוּבִים — *Cheruvim* (Cherubs) — comes from רַבְיָא — "infant" in Aramaic. Hence, coupled with the prepositional letter כ, meaning "like," the word כְּרוּב means "infant-like". R' Papa asks, "*Tanach* states, 'The first face was the face of a *Cheruv*, and the second that of a man' (*Yechezkel* 10:14). Yet, are not these the same?" The Talmud answers that Yechezkel saw a vision of an adult and of an infant.

In accordance with this, Abarbanel, in one of his explanations, states that the *Cheruvim* had the form of two small children, innocent and without blemish, one male and the other female. These *Cheruvim* allude to the fact that every man and woman is obligated from youth to cling to Torah and *mitzvos*.

R' Simcha Zisl of Kelm finds ethical content in the appearance of the *Cheruvim* as children. Torah scholars must always be aware that they are like children who have not learned as much Torah as they should. This is why Torah scholars are not called *chachamim* — "wise men," but *talmidei chachamim* — "students of the wise." They are constantly bound to study and educate themselves. R' Simcha Zisl quotes Socrates, who once said: "The wise all believe they must know the answers to whatever questions are posed to them. Yet, from my own wisdom I have learned how ignorant I am." *Chazal* offered high praise for our ability to remember what we studied as children. We must always remember that we have never learned enough. We must always view ourselves as children starting our studies.

R' Baruch Epstein (*Torah Temimah*), quoting *Ein Eliyahu*, offers another explanation of why the *Cheruvim* had the faces of infants. It was to arouse Hashem's pity upon the Jewish people. As *Yalkut* states regarding the verse, "When Israel was a child, I loved him" (*Hoshea* 11:1): Moshe said to Joshua, 'This nation which I am handing over to you still consists of young goats, mere infants. Do not be angry at them for what they do, for even Hashem did not become angry at them.' "

Nonetheless, R' Epstein does not find this explanation convincing, for even in Shlomo's *Beis HaMikdash* the *Cheruvim* were set up in the form of infants, and by then, the Israelites were no longer infants, having already conquered nations. He therefore explains the childlike countenance of the *Cheruvim* according to *Chazal* in *Yoma* 54:

> When the Israelites used to go on pilgrimage to Jerusalem, the *Kohanim* would withdraw the curtain and show them the *Cheruvim* attached to one another, and they would say, "Observe how beloved they are before Hashem. Hashem's love for them is like the love of a husband and a wife."

The *Cheruvim* served to accentuate the love between the Israelites and their Father in Heaven. They were fashioned with the countenance of infants to remind Hashem all the more of His love for the Jewish people. R' Shabsai Kohen (*Sifsei Kohen*) states, "By emphasizing how precious are children, the Torah wishes to instill in us the importance of Jewish education." King David said: "Out of the mouths of babes and nurselings have You founded strength" (*Tehillim* 8:3). The Torah taught this important axiom even before the Tabernacle was built. In the Tabernacle, while the *Cheruvim* were placed above the Ark covering, the tablets of the law were below it. Hence, teaching small children Torah is a loftier goal than any other.

In *II Divrei HaYamim* 3:10, *Rashi* and *Radak* explain, like *Chazal*, that the *Cheruvim* were made in the likeness of children. That verse states, "In the most holy place he made two *Cheruvim* of figured work." According to the aforementioned commentaries, the word צַעֲצֻעִים may be read as צֶאֱצָאִים, "children", or, as *Chazal* call them, רַבְיָא. Even so, this verse is no real proof that the *Cheruvim* had the faces of small children, for the *Cheruvim* referred to were in addition to those Moshe had made, and they stood not upon the Ark covering, but upon the floor.

◄§ Cheruvim: "Angels" or General "Forms"?

According to *Rambam* in *Moreh Nevuchim*, 3:45, the *Cheruvim* represent angels. Their purpose is to instill in Israel the belief that there are angels who place truth on the lips of the prophets:

> When the wise understood clearly and empirically that there is a Being who has no body and no physical form, namely, the true, one God; and that other beings exist without bodies as well, these being the angels who have been showered with Hashem's goodness and light, and that these beings are distinct from the firmament and its stars, it became clear that neither the pagan idols nor the *asherah* trees place truth on the lips of the prophets. Rather, it is the angels who do this.
>
> In accordance with this preface, belief in the angels is connected with belief in Hashem. Through belief in God and in the angels, one is led to belief in prophecy and the truth of the Torah. To strengthen belief in this, Hashem commanded the Israelites to fashion a likeness of two angels upon the Ark, so that the masses might believe in the existence of angels, a belief second in importance only to belief in Hashem Himself. This belief leads us to belief in prophecy and Torah Revelation, and through it, idolatry is banished. Had there been one *Cheruv*, the Israelites would have thought it represented Hashem and was to be worshiped the way idolaters worship. Or, they might have thought that the one angel, represented by the *Cheruv*, was also a

deity, and they would have worshiped two gods. Furthermore, they would have considered that angel Hashem's equal, seeing each as a separate unity, creator of many.

This view of *Rambam* is refuted by those who comment on his works. Rabbenu Shem Tov asks, "If this be so, why is one *Cheruv* male and the other female?" *Rambam* is basically correct, however, for the word "*Cheruvim*" is in keeping with the concept of angels. In numerous places in *Tanach*, the two are synonymous. We shall quote just a few examples: "He placed the *Cheruvim* east of Eden" (*Bereishis* 3:24); "He rode upon a *Cheruv* and did fly" (*II Shmuel* 22:11, *Tehillim* 18:11). Yechezkel, as well, saw the *Cheruvim* standing in the *Beis HaMikdash*: "The sound of the *Cheruvim*'s wings was heard" (*Yechezkel* 10:5); "I looked and behold, the four wheels by the *Cheruvim*" (ibid. v. 9). Clearly, the *Cheruvim* of these verses are Heavenly angels, whatever form they might have had. As for Rabbenu Shem Tov's question of why the *Cheruvim* in the Tabernacle had to be male and female, *Torah Temimah* challenges Rabbenu Bachya's statement to that effect, saying Rabbenu Bachya had no source in *Chazal* for this idea. *Chazal* state only that the *Cheruvim* "stood for a love such as that between husband and wife," not that they really took this form.

Another view is that of Ibn Ezra, who holds that the word *Cheruvim* means "forms," and refers to nothing more specific than that. He is supported by Yechezkel who, in his chariot vision, saw a beast with four faces. One of those faces, an ox, Yechezkel described elsewhere as *Cheruv*, because to have called it an ox would remind us of the Golden Calf. For Ibn Ezra, this proves that *Cheruv* is a neutral word that can refer to any form.

Mishneh LeMelech (Hil. Kelei HaMikdash 8:15) questions *Rashi's* explanation of *Cheruv*, in which he appears to contradict himself. In *Sh'mos* 25, *Rashi* explains, as do *Chazal*, that the *Cheruv's* face was that of a boy, while in 26:1, regarding the expression, "*Cheruvim* artistically fashioned," he states, "A lion on one side, and an eagle on the other." Furthermore, in 26:31 he says, "the word *Cheruvim* means forms."

Lechem Mishneh discusses Onkelos' treatment of the word. Everywhere else in the *Chumash*, Onkelos renders *Cheruvim* as *Cheruvic forms*, whereas in our *parashah* he writes simply, *Cheruvim*. Onkelos evidently seems to hold that everywhere else, the *Cheruvim* were only drawings, but here they are actual statues, as explained in several places by *Chazal*.

❧ The Cheruvim: Graven Images?

Abarbanel asks how the Torah could have commanded the fashioning of statues: Seemingly, when Hashem commanded the Israelites to make the *Cheruvim* with the Ark covering, He was asking them to violate the prohibition of, "Do not make for yourself any carved idol, or any likeness of anything that is in Heaven above or on Earth below" (*Sh'mos* 20:4). How could Hashem have made such a demand? In struggling to answer this difficult question, Abarbanel suggests that making graven images was only forbidden if there was intent to worship them, for verse 5 continues: "Do not bow down to them and do not worship them." By contrast, Abarbanel concludes, the Divine service in the Tabernacle was for the sake of Heaven. The *Cheruvim* were not made to be intermediaries between man and Hashem, but only as a reminder of His awesome deeds.

Abarbanel explains that the purpose of the *Cheruvim* was to symbolize the eternal link between Hashem, the Prime Mover, and those beings acted upon — between Israel and their Father in Heaven. In short, the *Cheruvim* were a reminder of Hashem's influence, hence they were not covered by the prohibition of *Sh'mos* 20:4.

Kuzari, as well (1:27), rests upon there having been a Divine command. Minimizing the sin of the Golden Calf, he states that the Israelites did not wish to deny Hashem's existence, but only to make their worship of Him more concrete in a manner that seemed fitting to them. There was no great sin in the making of such an image per se. After all, we see that the *Cheruvim* were permitted. Even so, the Israelites in the desert tried to pray to Hashem in a way forbidden them. As the image they fashioned was for this prohibited form of worship, they were punished.

Interestingly, *Midrash Leket Tov* (quoted in *Torah Sheleimah*) points out how Hashem issued two commands regarding graven images that seemed to contradict each other. Yet, this is reminiscent of the Talmudic dictum that "Whatever the Torah forbade, it made permissible by other means." Thus, at the same time that Hashem said, "Do not make for yourself any carved idol," He also said, "Make two *Cheruvim*" (*Sh'mos* 25:18). Likewise, one is prohibited to marry the wife of his deceased brother (*Vayikra* 18:16), but is commanded to do so if his brother died childless (*Devarim* 25:5). We were forbidden to wear any garment made of mixed wool and linen (ibid. 22:11), but the next verse states "Make yourself tassels on the four corners of your garment," and these may be of wool even if the corners are of linen. The Torah states, "Those who violate the *Shabbos* shall be killed" (*Sh'mos* 31:14); yet commands: "On the *Shabbos* day, two year-old lambs without blemish shall be brought." Such an offering involves acts that violate Shabbos law.

Chizkuni explains the text almost identically: *Chazal* emphasized that here carved images are permitted whereas elsewhere they are forbidden, and that they are permitted here only in the form the Torah stipulates. The slightest deviation from that form constitutes an attack on the foundations of faith, and we violate "Do not make for yourself any carved idol."

Following are the words of *Mechilta* on our *parashah*, quoted in *Rashi*:

> "Do not make any idols of gold or silver to be associated with Me. Make them not for yourselves" (*Sh'mos* 20:20). These words serve to warn us that the *Cheruvim* made to stand in the Holy of Holies must not be of silver. Otherwise, they are like silver and gold idols. Why does the verse conclude, "Make them not for yourselves?" To teach that we cannot set up *Cheruvim* in the synagogues and *Batei Midrash* as we did in the Temple.

Meshech Chochmah in *Parashas Ki Sisa* speaks at length of the connection between the Torah's permitting certain symbols and Israel's having erred with the Golden Calf. The Israelites mistakenly viewed Moshe as a middleman to Hashem, and in his absence they sought a concrete crutch to replace him. Moshe therefore cried out loudly, "Do you think that I am your key to talking with Hashem? Heaven forbid! I am only a man like you. The Torah does not depend upon me, and had I never appeared, the Torah would be just as it is now."

As proof of this, during the thirty-eight years that Hashem was incensed with Israel until the generation born in Egypt passed away, Hashem never spoke to Moshe in terms of endearment (*Rashi* on *Devarim* 2:17).

One must not imagine that the Tabernacle and the Temple are inherently holy. Their holiness derives only from Hashem's residing among His children, and if those children break their covenant, the holiness of the *Beis HaMikdash* and *Mishkan* will be removed. They will be like everyday items destroyed by vandals. Thus, when Titus entered the Temple with a harlot, he was not harmed, for its holiness had already been removed. Even the tablets, the work of Hashem, have no holiness in and of themselves. When Hashem's new bride, Israel, committed adultery during her wedding ceremony, those tablets reverted to being nothing more than potsherds. Their holiness had been derived from the Jewish people's watching over them, and they failed in this.

Ultimately, nothing in the world deserves our devotion and subjugation but Hashem, for only He is inherently holy, and only to Him are praise and service acceptable. The *Mishkan* and the *Beis HaMikdash* are holy only because Hashem commanded that they be built, and the offerings brought there belong to Hashem alone. The *Cheruvim* must not, God forbid, be the object of any worship in thought or deed. Their only purpose is this: Just as the captain of a ship can tell from the sails what direction the wind is blowing, so, too, Hashem had the *Cheruvim* for His own measurements.

As long as the *Cheruvim* faced one another, it indicated that the Israelites were performing Hashem's will. The *Cheruvim's* limited function is shown by the fact that only the tablets of the law were inside the Ark, while the *Cheruvim* remained outside. They did not represent Hashem. Rather, they only indicated the existence of the angels (*Moreh Nevuchim* 3:45).

⋖§ The Cheruvim: Sign of Hashem's Love for Israel

R' Katina in *Yoma* 54 explains the *Cheruvim* as a sign of the love between Israel and their Father in Heaven: When the Israelites used to go on pilgrimages to Jerusalem, the *Kohanim* would open the curtain and show them the *Cheruvim* attached to one another. Then they would announce, "Observe how beloved you are before Hashem. It is like the love of a husband and wife."

Rabbenu Bachya, in accordance with this source, explains that the *Cheruvim* symbolize and stress the direct link between Hashem and His people. In Yechezkel's vision, the two *Cheruvim* had the faces of an adult and a child, for they symbolize the love of a father for his son. Yet, in the Tabernacle, the level of Divine love was even greater, and the attachment between Hashem and Israel was unsurpassed. This found expression in the form the *Cheruvim* took, and in their relationship to each other.

Netziv, in his *Haamek Davar*, expresses this idea in greater depth:

Israel's love for Hashem is love between a bestower of goodness and the recipient of that goodness. In such a relationship, the recipient constantly gazes toward his benefactor. It is Hashem's desire to shower love and blessings upon the Jewish people. As *Chazal* state in *Midrash Rabbah*, Ch. 20, "Hashem's desire is all directed toward the Jewish people, as it is stated, 'Hashem's desire is for me' (*Shir HaShirim* 7:11), while the Jewish people's eyes are turned toward Hashem."

The two *Cheruvim* constantly cling to one another: "Their faces shall look one to the other, to the covering" (*Sh'mos* 25:20). The two *Cheruvim*, together, face the Ark covering, below which is the Torah. Hashem, Israel and the Torah are one.

Various other meanings are attributed to the *Cheruvim* by other commentaries. *Malbim* holds that the two *Cheruvim* parallel the two types of *mitzvos*, those between man and Hashem, and those between man and man. These two types of *mitzvos* are engraved in the two tablets, and they are represented by the *Cheruvim* as well. To instill in the Jewish people an appreciation of both types of *mitzvos*, there are two types of leaders, each of whom fulfills the task earmarked for him. The *Kohen Gadol* represents man's devotion to Hashem, while the king represents those laws that apply between human beings. The *Cheruvim's* faces, representing the two types of *mitzvos*, must be turned toward one another, in contrast to the Second Temple period, when a wicked leadership separated the royalty from the priesthood. The *Cheruvim* raise their wings upward and look at one another. This is a hint that Jewish leaders must perform all their acts for the sake of Heaven, instilling Torah knowledge and faith in their people.

Chazal in *Bava Basra* 99 confront the contradiction between the *Cheruvim* of Moshe, which faced one another, and those of Shlomo, which faced the *Beis HaMikdash*. They explain that in the former case, the Israelites performed Hashem's will, whereas in the latter case, they did not. The Chassidic literature suggests that the sign that the Jewish people are performing Hashem's will is when they turn toward one other. Once they turn away each facing his own private corner, concerned with his own selfish ego, they are no longer fulfilling Hashem's will.

The Chassidic literature also states that the last letters of וּפְנֵיהֶם אִישׁ אֶל אָחִיו (not in that order) spell out the word *shalom* — "peace." This alludes to the importance of brotherhood and peace. It is this that the *Cheruvim* serve to stress.

Tetzaveh – תצוה

I.

The Nature of the Urim VeTumim

Place the *Urim* and the *Tumim* in the breastplate of judgment" (*Sh'mos* 28:30). The greatest commentaries argue over the nature of the *Urim VeTumim*. For *Rashi*, this was writing contained in the folds of the breastplate, engraved with Hashem's Ineffable Name.

Ramban quotes, and then totally rejects, Ibn Ezra's view that they were silver or gold figurines such as astrologers use. He enlists several proofs for *Rashi*, showing that the *Urim VeTumim* were actually made by Hashem himself:

> Nowhere are they mentioned among the works of the skilled craftsmen. There is no command regarding them, and no allusion to their being completed. We find, "He made the *ephod*" (*Sh'mos* 39:2), and, "He made the breastplate" (v. 8), but never, "He made the *Urim VeTumim*." Had they been the work of a wise artisan, the Torah would have elaborated on them more than on other articles. Even if the Torah did not wish to elaborate, it would at least have said, "Make the *Urim VeTumim* as Hashem showed you on the mountain. Make them of pure gold or silver."
>
> Likewise, nowhere beside the *Urim VeTumim* do we find the use of the definite article. Regarding the Ark we find, "Make *an* Ark" (v. 25:10), and regarding the Table, "Make *a* Table" (v. 25:23), etc. Only regarding the *Urim VeTumim* do we find *"the Urim* and *the Tumim"*. . . Thus, fashioning the *Urim VeTumim* involved a secret Moshe received from Hashem.
>
> The verb לַעֲשׂות — "to make" — is never associated with the *Urim VeTumim*, for they were never made physically by man. As for the use of a definite article, this is reminiscent of *Bereishis* 3:24:

"He placed the *Cheruvim* to the east of the Garden of Eden." The *Cheruvim*, like the *Urim VeTumim*, are a well-known miracle of Hashem.

Ramban explains the operation of the *Urim VeTumim* according to *Yoma 77*. Hashem's Name illuminated certain letters from the names on the breastplate, and the *Kohen Gadol* would arrange them to compose words. For example, when the Israelites asked, "Who shall go up for us against the Canaanite?" (*Shoftim* 1:1), the letters of the word "Yehudah" lit up, along with the letters י of Levi, ע of Shimon, ל of Levi and ה of Avraham, spelling out the word יַעֲלֶה — "Yehudah will go up." (*Chazal* state that the names of the Patriarchs — אַבְרָהָם, יִצְחָק, יַעֲקֹב — were included on the breastplate, together with the words שִׁבְטֵי יְשֻׁרוּן — "the Tribes of Yeshurun," since the letters ח ט צ ק do not appear in the names of the twelve tribes.)

According to *Ramban*, interpreting the letters lit up on the *Urim VeTumim* involved *Ruach HaKodesh*. This is a level of Divine intuition one step below prophecy yet one step above *bas kol*, the Divine voice of the Second *Beis HaMikdash* period. *Ramban* continues:

> Most likely, Moshe handed down the secret of the *Urim VeTumim* to the greatest men of his generation, and it was passed on down until it reached King David. He too wore an *ephod* (*II Shmuel* 6:14), apparently like the one that Moshe was instructed to make, with a breastplate identical to the one mentioned in *Parashas Tetzaveh*. Possibly, however, King David's *ephod* was of linen: "David was girded with a linen *ephod*" (ibid.). Similarly, in the priestly city of Nov there were eighty-five *Kohanim* wearing the *ephod*. From among the disciples of the prophet living at a particular time, they would appoint a *Kohen* to wear the *ephod*, and Hashem would occasionally communicate with them through it.

The Vilna Gaon, following *Ramban*'s path, offers a remarkable interpretation of the argument between Channah and the *Kohen Gadol* Eli, when she came to pray to Hashem for children (*I Shmuel* 1). When Eli chided her for being intoxicated, she responded, "No, my lord, I am a woman of sorrowful spirit" (ibid. v. 15). According to *Chazal*, she meant "You do not have *Ruach HaKodesh*, for I am a reputable woman." Eli saw a woman weeping silently, so he asked the *Urim VeTumim* about her, and the letters שכרה lit up. The proper arrangement of these letters was כשרה, which can be read as either כְּשֵׁרָה — "reputable" — or כְּשָׂרָה — "like our mother Sarah." Eli, though, combined the letters differently and derived שִׁכּוֹרָה — "intoxicated." After this error, Channah tactfully informed Eli that he did not have *Ruach HaKodesh* right then, for he should have known how to combine the letters properly.

◆§ Rambam's View

In *Moreh Nevuchim*, 2:45, *Rambam* lists thirteen levels of prophecy, associating the *Urim VeTumim* with *Ruach HaKodesh*. On this level, a wakeful person feels a spiritual force compelling him to utter wisdom or to praise Hashem. Employing *Ruach HaKodesh*, David composed *Tehillim* and Shlomo composed *Mishlei*, *Koheles* and *Shir HaShirim*. The books of *Daniel*, *Iyov*, *Divrei HaYamim*, *Esther* and the rest of *Kesuvim* were composed the same way. The seventy elders of the desert experienced *Ruach HaKodesh*, as did all who posed questions to the *Urim VeTumim*.

Quite surprisingly, *Rambam*, in discussing the breastplate in *Hilchos Mikdash*, makes no mention of the *Urim VeTumim*. R' Yaakov Tzvi Meklenburg (*HaKesav VeHaKabalah*) explains the reason for this: The stones of the breastplate are themselves the *Urim VeTumim*. They are called *Urim* because they emanate light (*Or*), and *Tumim* because they were sliced into two perfect halves (*te'omim* means twins) by the *shamir*, a unique stone-cutting worm (Midrash). Thus, when the Torah says, "Place the *Urim* and the *Tumim* in the breastplate of judgment" (*Sh'mos* 28:30), it refers to the stones of the *Urim VeTumim* being attached to the breastplate. (*Ralbag* and Abarbanel also cite the view that the stones are the *Urim VeTumim*.) Because *Rambam* had already explained how the stones were set in the breastplate, he did not mention the *Urim VeTumim*.

HaKesav VeHaKabalah brings proof that this is *Rambam's* view: In Ch. 10 of *Hilchos Kelei HaMikdash*, *Rambam* states that during the Second Temple period a set of *Urim VeTumim* was fashioned to complete the eight priestly garments. Now, if the *Urim VeTumim* were simply Hashem's Ineffable Name, it could not have counted as a garment. Despite this argument, *HaKesav VeHaKabalah* is puzzled that those who comment on *Rambam* did not deal with why *Rambam* omitted the *Urim VeTumim* from his discussion of the breastplate. *Kesef Mishneh*, for example (*Hil. Kelei HaMikdash*, Ch. 9), identifies the *Urim VeTumim* with Hashem's Ineffable Name. We do not know how he would answer R' Meklenburg's question.

Abarbanel, too, mentions the view that the *Urim VeTumim* were the stones on the breastplate. Yet, he rejects this view because stones require work, and no work was associated with the *Urim VeTumim*. Hashem commanded Moshe: "Place the *Urim* and the *Tumim* in the breastplate of judgment." Later we read: "He put the breastplate upon him, placing in it the *Urim* and the *Tumim*" (*Vayikra* 8:8). It seems that Moshe placed something into the breastplate. Therefore, Abarbanel is certain that the *Urim VeTumim* are the Ineffable Name, and it is that which Moshe inserted into the folds of the breastplate.

During the First Temple period, the *Urim VeTumim* answered every question posed to it, with the following conditions: (a) the questioner had to be either a king, the Sanhedrin, or an important public figure; (b) questions had to concern the public good; (c) questions could be addressed only to the *Kohen Gadol*, assuming he had *Ruach HaKodesh*, so he could combine the letters properly and derive an answer. During the Second Temple period, there were no *Urim VeTumim*, for two reasons. First of all, only two tribes, Yehudah and Binyamin, had returned from the Exile. The others, exiled by the King of Assyria, were lost. To compensate for the absence of the *Urim VeTumim*, Hashem invested the *Kohen Gadol* with *Ruach HaKodesh*, which derived its power from the two tribes that had returned. Secondly, during the Second Temple Period, Hashem's Ineffable Name, which had made the *Urim VeTumim* operable, no longer graced the breastplate. It had appeared only on the breastplate made by Moshe, and this had been laid to rest. Hashem told Moshe, "Place the *Urim* and the *Tumim* in the breastplate." Hashem wished only Moshe to place them there. Once the breastplate he had fashioned was laid to rest, there were no longer any *Urim VeTumim*.

Abarbanel asks how *Rambam* can say in *Moreh Nevuchim* that the *Urim VeTumim* are one step below prophecy, and he supports his question several ways.

(a) We know that Yehoshua employed the *Urim VeTumim*. Yet, being a prophet, why should he have needed them?

(b) According to *Chazal*, Hashem sometimes cancels prophetic visions before they can occur, whereas this never happens with prophecies of the *Urim VeTumim*. Does that not place the *Urim VeTumim* on a higher level than prophecy?

(c) We know that, beside Moshe, no prophet could have a prophetic vision whenever he wished. By contrast, whenever the *Kohen Gadol* wished to pose a question to the *Urim VeTumim*, he could do so, implying again that the *Urim VeTumim* were greater.

Abarbanel offers beautiful answers to all his questions:

Because of its elevated status, one requires great preparation to merit prophetic vision. This is not the case with the *Urim VeTumim*.

Yehoshua employed the *Urim VeTumim* because they did not require him to prepare himself spiritually.

The only reason the predictions of the *Urim VeTumim* never were retracted is that they never really offered prophecies about the future, but only about matters of immediate concern. For example, when the Israelites asked whether to go out to war or not, they needed an immediate response for this highly pressing matter. Prophecy, on the other hand, deals with the future. If something happens, meanwhile, that has bearing on the prophecy, as when a sinful Israel repents, the prophecy can be retracted.

⋖§ The Uniqueness of the Breastplate Stones

Rabbenu Bachya and Abarbanel offer lengthy and detailed explanations of the unique qualities possessed by the breastplate stones, and the connection between each stone and its corresponding tribe. One unique quality that Rabbenu Bachya finds mentioned in the *Sefer HaAvanim* is that the breastplate stones may only be worn by someone who is *tahor* — "ritually pure." Carried by anyone *tameh* — "ritually impure" — they are powerless.

R' Aharon Levin in his *HaDrash VeHaIyun* finds Rabbenu Bachya's words puzzling. Does it not state explicitly in *Mishnayos Kelim*, 12:8, that precious gems and pearls cannot become impure? He answers that although this is true, the stones of the breastplate can only operate through a pure man. Whoever carries them when he is impure will remain unaffected by their operation, not because the stones have become impure, but because he is impure.

Mahari'a HaLevi notes in his response that precious gems and pearls are unsusceptible to impurity because of *Chazal's* principle that "everything from the sea remains pure" (quoted in *Pardes Yosef*, page 292). Yet, in the responsa of *Maharsham* we find exception taken to Mahari'a HaLevi's comment. It is true that pearls come from the sea, but precious gems come from quarries on dry land, as we find in *Shekalim*, 5:2, "Hashem created a quarry of precious stones in Moshe's tent, and through it, Moshe became rich."

HaDrash VeHaIyun poses yet another question regarding the words of Mahari'a HaLevi: The principle that "everything from the sea remains pure" applies to whatever is made from the body parts of aquatic animals, but not to plant life or inanimate objects. This distinction is apparent from *Maseches Shabbos* 59. There *Rashi* explains that the reason a ring made of *almog* [a substance that comes from the sea] cannot become impure is that it is a wooden object which does not have a receptacle. The fact that *Rashi* does not mention that it comes from the sea and everything from the sea is pure proves that the principle does not apply to either aquatic plant life or inanimate objects. R' Levin leaves the question standing.

⊷§ The Breastplate of Judgment

Placing the twelve stones in the breastplate makes it a *Choshen Mishpat* — a breastplate of judgment (*Sh'mos* 28:15). According to *Rashi*, it was called this because it atoned for injustice or because it offered clear, true judgment. *Rashi's* source is *Chazal* in *Arachin* 16 and *Zevachim* 80. Yet, *Haamek Davar* states that whoever examines those sources will find only indirect support for these ideas. "Judgment", in the text, primarily teaches that the breastplate demands justice for Israel before Hashem, when they are wronged by the nations.

The Targum several times interprets *mishpat* as "zealous defense of Israel against insult." Most likely, the word חוֹשֶׁן comes from the expression חָשׁ בָּז, (*Yeshayahu* 8:1) meaning that Hashem rushes to exact judgment against the enemies of His people. That was the purpose of the *Choshen*, and it was consulted whenever there was a need to wage a battle against the enemies of Hashem's people.

In *Maseches Yoma* it explicitly states that the *Kohen Gadol* only presented questions to the *Urim VeTumim* on behalf of the king, the Sanhedrin, and "one vital to the community." The commentaries interpret this phrase as referring to the *Kohen* anointed to encourage the people before a battle and to lead them into battle (כֹּהֵן מָשׁוּחַ מִלְחָמָה). Because of the purpose it serves and the benefits it provides the Jewish nation, the *Choshen* is known as the *Choshen Mishpat* — the "breastplate of judgment."

Based on the expression "breastplate of judgment," *Baal HaTurim* compares the protocol of the *Urim VeTumim* to that of the *batei din* — the Jewish courts of law. For example, *batei din* operate only by day, and the *Urim VeTumim* answered questions only by day.

HaDrash VeHalyun questions this comparison, according to which the *Urim VeTumim*, like *batei din*, do not operate on *Shabbos*. Do we not find that, according to one *tanna* in *Menachos* 95, David arrived in the priestly city of Nov on *Shabbos*, and immediately asked the *Urim VeTumim* a question? *HaDrash VeHalyun* answers that there is a difference between *Shabbos* and nighttime. At night, it is forbidden by the Torah to judge, hence it is forbidden then to employ the *Urim VeTumim* as well. On *Shabbos*, however, the prohibition against judgment is only a rabbinic decree lest judges write anything down (*Sema, Choshen Mishpat* 5).

Even if no parallel decree applies to the *Urim VeTumim*, there is still another problem: *HaDrash VeHalyun* proves from *Tanach* that the *Urim VeTumim* were asked questions even at night. We read in *I Shmuel* 14:37: "Shaul asked counsel of Hashem: 'Shall I go down after the Philistines? Will you deliver them into the hand of Israel?' " Yet, we know this was at night:

> All the people brought every man his ox with him that night . . .
> And Shaul said, "Let us go down after the Philistines by night and spoil them until the morning light . . . Then the *Kohen* said, "Let us draw near here to Hashem." Shaul asked the counsel of Hashem (ibid. v. 34, 36,37).

Here we see explicitly that the *Urim VeTumim* were questioned at night. *HaDrash VeHalyun* offers no answer.

Kli Yakar quotes *Akeidah*, who finds allusions in the form of the breastplate of judgment for how Jewish justice must operate. Each row had three stones, an allusion to *batei din* manned by three judges. Some of the stones were precious, and others not. This teaches us that rich and poor are equal in the sight of the law, and that cases involving a few pennies must be viewed as gravely as those involving large sums. The names of Yaakov's sons were engraved in the stones according to their birth sequence, to teach that both the older and the younger judges' opinions must be heard. The *Urim VeTumim* were set in the breastplate to teach that *dayanim* — "the judges in *batei din*" — bring light to the entire world. The *dayanim* are called "the eyes of the community," for they shed light on the issues that confound the litigants.

R' Aharon Levin draws a nice lesson from the words, "Aharon shall carry the judgment of the Israelites upon his heart" (*Sh'mos* 28:30). Two primary forces control man: emotion and intellect. The first is in his heart, the second in his mind. A presiding judge is forbidden to pervert justice out of emotional considerations. If a poor man is tried, the judge may not declare him innocent just out of pity. As the Torah says: "Do not favor a poor man in his cause" (*v.* 23:3). Likewise, a judge must remain unmoved by the defendant's beseeching. The Torah warns, "Aharon shall carry the judgment of the Israelites upon his heart," i.e., above his heart. The judge in deciding guilt or innocence must rise above all sentiment.

R' Zalman Sorotzkin derives a lesson from the seeming redundancy of certain words and the variation in others. One verse reads: "Aharon shall bear the names of the sons of Israel on the breastplate of judgment"

(v. 28:29). The next verse reads: "Aharon shall carry the judgment of the Israelites upon his heart" (v. 30). The Torah is telling us about two periods in Jewish history. During the First Temple period, Hashem's Ineffable Name lay in the folds of the breastplate and the *Kohen Gadol* bore the judgment of the Israelites upon his heart. During the Second Temple Period, however, the Ineffable Name no longer lay there. Then, the *Kohen Gadol* bore only the names of the sons of Israel upon his heart.

Meshech Chochmah makes a similar observation based on the absence of the word *tamid* — "perpetually" — from the *Urim VeTumim*, while it appeared on both the head plate (צִיץ) and turban (מִצְנֶפֶת). After the First Temple period, the Ineffable Name no longer appeared on the breastplate, hence the word *tamid* did not apply.

II.

Glory and Majesty are Part of Judaism

Make holy garments for your brother Aharon, for glory and majesty" (*Sh'mos* 28:2). The expression, "for glory and majesty," associated with the priestly garments, expresses strikingly that even external beauty is part and parcel of Judaism. This idea appears in many places, and we shall deal with it. As we shall explain, some view external beauty as only a tool, while others see it as an end in itself. In any event, there can be no mistaking the message conveyed by the text: In serving Hashem, external beauty can help us to achieve the proper state of mind.

Haamek Davar states simply:

> When Hashem commanded Aharon to consecrate himself and to behave with saintliness and abstinence, he became separate from the rest of Israel. For this to be successful, Aharon had to command the respect of his fellow Israelites, and they had to understand that he was on a higher spiritual level than they. Otherwise his separation would be considered pompous. For this reason, the priestly garments had to be glorious and majestic. By this means, the Israelites understood that Hashem wished to honor Aharon, and that he was worthy of being a chariot for the Divine Presence.

According to this view, aesthetics serve as a means to an end. By means of the priestly garments, the masses became aware of the supreme importance of spiritual institutions. This accords with R' Yochanan's referring to his garments as his "honorers" (*Shabbos* 113b).

Haamek Davar's explanation summarizes everything the *rishonim* said on this matter. *Rambam* (*Hilchos Kelei Mikdash*, 5) rules: "It is a *mitzvah* for the priestly garments to be beautiful, new and full length, like the clothing of prominent men, as the Torah states, 'for glory and majesty.'" Later, *Rambam* states that the *Kohen's* Divine service is invalid if he performs it in garments that are defaced, or too long or short on him. If they become dirty, the *Kohen* is forbidden to launder them, but must set them aside to be cut up for wicks, and he puts on new clothing. These rulings are traceable to one view in *Maseches Zevachim*, yet *Rambam* seems independently to derive from the words "glory and majesty," that any aesthetic flaw in the clothes of the *Kohen Gadol* is forbidden.

Kuzari, as well (1:99), declares that the Torah insisted there be no flaw or blemish on the body, clothing or ornaments of the *Kohen*.

Chinuch views this attitude as a natural means of ensuring that the *Kohen* has a proper state of mind during the Temple service: A man is influenced by his own deeds. His actions shape his thoughts and state of mind. The emissary who atones for the people must concentrate all his thoughts on the service. He should therefore wear special clothing for the occasion. Then, whatever part of his body he looks at will arouse him to remember before whom he stands.

The *Kohen's* special clothing influence those around him, but they primarily influence the *Kohen* himself. When the *Kohen* sees how fine his clothing are, he will remember before whom he stands, and become more enthusiastic in his service before Hashem. At the same time, *Chinuch* mentions the effect of the special clothing on those who see the *Kohen* in all his glory: "When the Temple is more magnificent and awe inspiring, the sinners' hearts are softened, and they return to Hashem." External beauty serves as a means of magnifying the glory of Hashem and His service. As it is a means of influencing mankind, the *Kohen* is forbidden to make light of it, for his main task is to educate and influence his fellow man positively.

Ramban, S'forno, Rabbenu Bachya and others view "glory and majesty" as a requirement that the *Kohen* maintain a majestic appearance. Among other things, *Ramban* points out that the priestly garments were what kings and princes wore in those days, and he supports this with examples from the Torah and from history. The checkered tunic was a garment of prestige in Yaakov's day when he gave a "coat of many colors" to Yosef. In *Ramban's* time, the turban was still commonly worn by kings and princes. The *ephod* and breastplate were royal garments too. The headplate parallels the king's crown, sky-blue *techeiles*, the blue of royalty: "Even today, only a king would dare dress in this color." These clothes, according to *Ramban*, are the majestic trappings of power and royalty.

Chinuch, following *Ramban's* path, adds that while the *Kohen Gadol* is a messenger of Hashem, engaged in supernatural devotions, in the people's eyes he is a king and leader, and he must dress accordingly.

Ibn Ezra states that the Torah insisted on the *Kohen Gadol's* clothing being distinct to set him apart, i.e., to show his spiritual superiority.

Many commentaries attach not only external, but spiritual significance to the priestly garb. According to *Akeidah*, each garment symbolizes some lofty idea, creating an inner, spiritual majesty. The physical beauty is there, but only as an external tool to arouse purity of heart. *Akeidah* explains the lofty idea evoked by each garment.

Ramban and Rabbenu Bachya quote the Kabbalists, for whom "glory and majesty" refer not to the appearance of the clothing, but to the glory of Hashem. The *Kohen* must direct his heart toward Hashem's glory, the majesty of Israel: "For You are their power and majesty" (*Tehillim* 89:18).

Malbim, as well, comments on the symbolic nature of the priestly apparel. "Glory" (כָּבוֹד) refers to the *Kohen's* superior spiritual level, whereas "majesty" (תִּפְאָרֶת) refers to the effect that the devotions of such a person can achieve. Both are fundamental aspects of the priesthood. In light of this, it was Moshe who had to prepare the priestly apparel: "Make holy garments for your brother Aharon, for glory and majesty" (*Sh'mos* 28:2). If the only function of the priestly garments had been external beauty, a professional tailor would have made them. The garments were meant to invest the *Kohanim* with outstanding spiritual qualities, and only through Moshe could this be achieved.

In my humble opinion, the verse can be understood differently. Perhaps the Torah is insisting that not only must the *Kohanim* be spiritually outstanding, but that their garments be glorious and majestic as well, i.e., Moshe had to ensure that not only the *Kohanim's* intentions, but their actions also had to be majestic. Once this was carried out, a special command was issued: "Speak to all who are wise hearted . . . that they make Aharon's garments to consecrate him" (v. 28:3), i.e., Aharon had to be wrapped in lofty qualities, his garments had to be imbued with spiritual content and significance, in accordance with their sanctity and majesty.

HaKesav VeHaKabalah explains "for glory and majesty" in a way that addresses both the material and the spiritual: "For the glory of Hashem, as they are holy garments for serving Him, and for majesty, to make the *Kohen Gadol* awesome in the sight of all, who are his students."

◈§ The Priestly Garments: A Means or an End?

Rashi interprets לְקַדְּשׁו — "to consecrate him" — (v. 28:3) as "to initiate him into the priesthood by means of the garments." From this it seems as though the garments are not themselves a *mitzvah*, but only a means towards performing a *mitzvah*, a prelude to serving in the Temple. Nevertheless, we cannot infer a halachic statement from *Rashi's* words.

Rambam, in *Sefer HaMitzvos*, *Mitzvah* 33, counts the priestly garments as a distinct *mitzvah*, and not as a means of preparing for other *mitzvos*. *Ramban* in his remarks on *Sefer HaMitzvos* disagrees with *Rambam* on the following grounds: Even *Rambam* would admit that during the Temple service there is no *mitzvah* to wear the garments, hence they are only a preparation for, or an integral part of, the Temple service. Now, *Rambam* never counts parts of *mitzvos* among the 613 *mitzvos*. If he did, he would have to count the fashioning of the Table as a separate *mitzvah*, which he does not do. How, then, can he count the priestly garments as a separate *mitzvah*?

Megillas Esther, however, demonstrates that *Rambam* does sometimes count parts of *mitzvos* as *mitzvos* themselves. Slaughtering the *korban Pesach* before Pesach begins is not a separate *mitzvah* but a preparation for eating the sacrifice that night. The same goes for burning the *parah adumah*, the Red Cow. Yet, *Rambam* counts these in his list of *mitzvos*. It is therefore likely that the priestly garments are included as a distinct *mitzvah* even though they only prepare for what follows.

Lev Sameach, by contrast, holds that for *Rambam*, the *Kohen's* appearance in majestic garb is itself a *mitzvah*, unconnected to what follows. The Torah defines the purpose of the garments as being "for glory and majesty" (*Sh'mos* 28:2), without adding "to serve." *Lev Sameach* brings support of this from *Hilchos Me'ilah*, Chapter 5. There *Rambam* rules that a *Kohen* who dresses in new priestly garments for secular purposes is not guilty of *me'ilah* — "misuse" — since the garments are meant for the benefit of the *Kohanim*. Were the garments part of the *mitzvah* of the Temple service, one would be committing a sin if he benefited from them.

Behag holds that the priestly garments must not be viewed as a separate *mitzvah* but as part of the Temple service. *Rambam*'s viewing it as separate may conceivably explain why *Rambam* omits mention of the law that the garments must be made *lishmah* — "with specific intent to be used in the Temple service" — whereas *lishmah* is a requirement in the making of the Temple furniture. Yet, this omission is not enough in itself to indicate this is *Rambam*'s ruling.

Other *poskim* and commentaries do mention an obligation of *lishmah*. *Ramban* in our *parashah* requires that the priestly garments be "fashioned *lishmah*, and it is possible that they must be worn with specific intent as well." *Ramban* adds that when the Torah says, "Speak to all who are wise hearted, whom I have filled with a spirit of wisdom" (*Sh'mos* 28:3), it means that the craftsmen making the garments must concentrate on the purpose of what they are doing, and Rabbenu Bachya and S'forno explain this in a like manner. Moreover, S'forno adds, "When they work with the gold, they must concentrate as much as when they fashion the garments."

Minchas Chinuch (*Mitzvah* 99) questions *Ramban* and says that nowhere do we find that the priestly garments must be made with specific intent. He does not understand why this *mitzvah* should differ from all others, regarding which there is a controversy over whether specific intent is required. *Ramban*'s source is in the Jerusalem Talmud, *Maseches Yoma* (3:6): "The weaving must be in sanctity, and in sanctity must it be woven." *Korban HaEidah* explains, "Not only must the garments be earmarked for a holy purpose, but the very weaving must have this intent as well." Despite their holiness, one who dresses in new priestly garments for his own benefit does not commit the sin of *me'ilah*. As *Rambam* said, the *mitzvos* were given with the understanding that we could benefit from them. Only after the priestly garments become old and tattered does one who wears them for his own benefit violate *me'ilah*. Such garments are no longer meant to provide beauty.

⧉§ Transfer of the Priesthood from Moshe to Aharon

"Bring your brother Aharon and his sons near to Me from among the Israelites to minister to Me as *Kohanim*: Aharon, Nadav, Avihu, Elazar and Isamar" (*Sh'mos* 28:1). The commentaries understand from this verse that the priesthood was transferred from Moshe to Aharon before Hashem directed Aharon regarding the priestly garments. We all know that Moshe served as *Kohen* during the seven days of installation of the *Mishkan*. Now, on Hashem's command, the priesthood was transferred to Aharon and his sons.

Chazal in *Zevachim* state that Moshe was being punished for having refused previously to go on Hashem's mission to Egypt: "Hashem's anger burned against Moshe and He said, 'Is not Aharon the Levite your brother? I know he can speak well' " (v. 4:13-14). R' Shimon ben Yochai says, "Now he is a Levite and you are a *Kohen*. Henceforth you will be a Levite and he a *Kohen*." The majority, however, hold that no transfer was involved. Rather, from the first, Moshe was only meant to serve as *Kohen* during the seven days of installation.

Some of *Chazal* state that Moshe served with Aharon until Aharon's death, and only then did the priesthood transfer to Aharon's line. In *Midrash Rabbah*, *Sh'mos*, Ch. 2, Moshe's comment at the Burning Bush, "Here I am" (*Sh'mos* 3:4), means "Here I am for the priesthood, here I am for the throne." In other words, Moshe expressed interest in being not only the leader, but the *Kohen Gadol*. Yet, Hashem responded: "Do not come near" (v. 5), i.e., the priesthood is not yours, but your brother Aharon's.

Regarding our *parashah* as well, the Midrashim say that Moshe was upset when Hashem told him to "bring Aharon near." Hashem then told Moshe, "The Torah was Mine and I gave it to you, and if not for the Torah I would have destroyed the world." The Torah was Moshe's compensation for losing the priesthood.

Moshe's jealousy of Aharon, as mentioned by *Chazal*, seems puzzling to the commentaries. At the same time, some struggle to understand why Hashem turned down Moshe's request for the priesthood. Ibn Ezra offers a straightforward answer. Moshe bore Israel's burden. It was his task to teach them Torah, leaving him no time for sacrificial worship. Moreover, Moshe's wife was Yisro's daughter, hence his children lacked pedigree. This, in fact, explains the Torah's mentioning Aharon's four sons in verse 28:1.

Other commentaries agree with Ibn Ezra. The Dubno Magid (*Ohel Yaakov*) offers a fine psychological explanation of why Moshe was not chosen for the priesthood. A *Kohen's* task is to educate and direct the nation by personal example. Moshe, on his lofty level, stood beyond what the masses could attain. One who educates the nation must come from within the nation and must be part of it. *Chazal* state, "Yiftach in his generation was like Shmuel in his." Had Shmuel lived in Yiftach's days, his exalted spiritual level would have made it impossible for him to influence his fellow man, for every leader must be suitable to those he leads. During the worship of the Golden Calf, Hashem told Moshe: "Go down, for your people have become corrupt" (*Sh'mos* 32:7). A leader must descend to his nation's level to prevent their decline. Therefore, when Hashem saw that Moshe was upset at Aharon's being chosen over him, He commented, "The Torah was

Mine and I gave it to you." Hashem did not give the Torah directly to the Jewish people, for they were unfit to absorb it from so lofty a source. Rather, Hashem made Moshe his agent. For this same reason Hashem chose Aharon over Moshe for the priesthood. Moshe's spiritual level was so far above the people that he was unfit to direct them in their normal lives.

We may well be able to interpret the expression "from among the Israelites" (28:1) in a similar fashion. Hashem commanded that a *Kohen* be taken from among the nation, a *Kohen* who was part of the nation's body and soul. Such a person could lead them on the path of righteousness.

Abarbanel sees this verse as a command to announce among the people that Aharon had been chosen for the priesthood. Such an announcement from Moshe's lips would be accepted by the nation. They would understand that it was Hashem's command for, given a choice, Moshe would have chosen a *Kohen* from among his own sons.

Another fine explanation appears in *Shaar Bas Rabbim*. Hashem wished to include the Jewish people in the great holiness of Aharon's line, by separating Aharon from among them. When *ma'aser* — "a tithe" — is taken of livestock, the law is that all the cattle are driven into a pen and then counted one by one. The same goes for *terumah*, in which the produce must be gathered together before the *terumah* can be separated. The point is that the sanctity of the *mitzvah* must encompass the physical. The physical must be sanctified and attached to the Torah.

By contrast, *Sifsei Kohen* offers a different interpretation of the verse, "And you (Moshe) bring near Aharon, your brother ... from among the Israelites" (*Sh'mos* 28:1). This verse involves the *Kohen*, Levi and Israelite. "Bring near" refers to Moshe, the Levite. "From among the Israelites" refers to Israel, and "Aharon, your brother," is of course a *Kohen*. Combining all parts of the nation in the founding of the priesthood invests the nation with added sanctity and makes it stronger.

III.

The Korban Tamid

The rationale behind the *korban tamid* — "the perpetual daily sacrifice" — is no different from that of other offerings, although few commentaries devote special attention to it. Abarbanel, for example, states that the Israelites were commanded regarding other offerings only after the Golden Calf episode, as atonement for their sin. Better they should not have sinned, and not needed atonement. The *korban tamid*, however, does not serve to atone, but to thank Hashem for His kindness. Hashem favors such an offering, and instituted it before the episode of the Golden Calf took place.

At the beginning of this section Abarbanel explains the thankfulness expressed by this offering. Hashem performed two basic acts of kindness for His nation, one spiritual, i.e., the Revelation, and one physical, the Exodus. The two daily *tamid* sacrifices parallel these. The morning *tamid* symbolizes the Revelation: "It came to pass on the third morning . . ." (*Sh'mos* 19:16). The afternoon one symbolizes the *korban Pesach*, slaughtered in the afternoon.

Quoting an unnamed contemporary, Abarbanel offers another explanation. The two sheep represent our gratitude for the gifts of life and livelihood. We show gratitude in the morning for waking up, and towards evening for our daily sustenance. This is our expression of outright submission before Hashem our Master.

R' Yitzchak Breuer, in his *Nachaliel*, follows a similar path: Every day, through regular devotions at sunrise and dusk, the Jewish people renews its promise to be Hashem's flock. The flour and oil, as well, express our recognition that the economic life of our nation depends upon Hashem's will.

This idea is elaborated upon by *Chinuch*, *Mitzvah* 401: People normally eat twice a day to have strength to fulfill the *mitzvah* of "clinging to Hashem" (*Devarim* 11:22). It is therefore a *mitzvah* at those times to express Hashem's mastery over our deeds.

R' Yehudah Halevi (*Kuzari*, 2:26) views Temple offerings as a means of creating a link between man and his Maker. In Hashem's world, body and spirit are intertwined. Physical exhaustion can produce weakness of spirit. Even a child will see that the spirit can be influenced by physical acts and, at Creation, that is actually how Hashem established the world to be. Hashem programmed man so that he could develop his intellect through specific physical acts, and the same applies at the national level. If the *Kohanim* perform a rite fixed in the Torah on behalf of the Jewish people, the nation accumulates sanctity and wisdom.

Akeidah differs. The nation's spiritual growth does not result from the mechanical act of bringing offerings, but from the intellectual effort involved in serving Hashem. When we engage in a *seudas mitzvah* — "a festive meal marking a religious occasion" — we rise spiritually. Likewise, *Chazal* state that if we dine with a Torah scholar, we ascend as much "as if we had basked in the Divine light." In much the same way, when the Jewish people bring Temple offerings with proper intent, the Divine Presence clings to them, not because of the act itself, but because of the spiritual elevation which accompanies it.

This explanation does not apply specifically to *korban tamid*. One that does, however, comes from *Malbim* on *Parashas Pinchas*, quoting *Chazal*:

> The purpose of the *tamid* is to uproot the practice of sun worship from the Jewish people. Sun worshipers would face the east in the morning, and the west towards evening. Hashem commanded that the *tamid* be slaughtered in the morning at the northwest corner of the altar, and toward evening at the northeast corner, just the opposite of the sun's path.

Invoking *tamid*'s relationship to idolatry, *Malbim* is able to explain why in *Parashas Pinchas* the section on *tamid* follows Yehoshua's replacing Moshe. According to *Chazal*, had Moshe gone into *Eretz Yisrael*, the Jewish people's hunger for idolatry would have disappeared.

◄§ The Eternal Meaning of the Korban Tamid

Why, if the *tamid* is described here, must it be redescribed in *Parashas Pinchas*? *Rashi* in *Parashas Pinchas* sees the second description as applying for all time, and ours as referring only to the seven days of installation of the *Mishkan*. Various commentaries find *Rashi* puzzling. We find here the expression, "throughout your generations" (*Sh'mos* 29:42). Does this not imply eternity? *Chizkuni* answers that the expression could conceivably mean only two generations, hence the second reading in *Pinchas* is needed. This answer can be countered. The expression "throughout your generations" means "forever" in many places, and no further command is needed.

Ramban and Ibn Ezra differ with *Rashi*, stating that the *tamid* is repeated in *Bamidbar* only so that all the communal offerings can appear there together. *Parashas Pinchas*, states *Ramban*, deals with the division of *Eretz Yisrael*. In *Eretz Yisrael*, *musaf* offerings and wine libations would be brought that had not been brought in the desert. Once these communal offerings were mentioned, *korban tamid* was mentioned there as well.

Ramban further addresses this theme in *Parashas Shelach*. The Israelites, about to enter the Land, were filled with despair over what would happen if they sinned. In *Bamidbar* 15, Hashem therefore comforted them with the knowledge that they would have a way to atone if they sinned. He commanded them about wine libations, something they had no contact with outside the context of the *tamid*. (In *Sifri*, there is a controversy among *tanna'im* over whether wine libations were required before the Israelites entered the Land.)

S'forno on *Parashas Beshalach* suggests the following temporal division: Prior to the Golden Calf, offerings functioned only to provide a "sweet smell," as with Hevel, Noach and Adam. Moreover, there were no wine libations. Following the Golden Calf, however, meal and wine offerings were added, as part of the *tamid* — communal offering. After the sin of the spies, meal and wine offerings were added as an option in offerings brought by individuals.

Ibn Ezra, however, believes that the *tamid* was brought only in *Eretz Yisrael*, based on "a continuous burnt offering throughout your generations" (*Sh'mos* 29:42). In his view, only at Mount Sinai were offerings brought, and on *Yom Kippur* of the second year: "Did you bring Me sacrifices and offerings for forty years in the desert, O house of Israel?" (*Amos* 5:25). The Israelites faced a desolate howling wasteland. A half *hin* of olive oil was not something they came across every day. How were they to carry fourteen-thousand *hins* of oil for the forty years, and where were they to find enough sheep for the twice-daily offering?

According to Ibn Ezra they acquired sheep and cattle at Kadesh, a settlement where it was possible to make purchases. Then they took spoils from Midian, Sichon and Og, acquiring many sheep. At that time they even spoke in terms of "we and our sheep" (*Bamidbar* 20:4). Prior to that, however, they had no sheep; hence they could not bring offerings.

According to Ibn Ezra, when the Torah says, "made on Mount Sinai" (ibid. 28:6), this can be taken literally: Only at Mount Sinai on *Yom Kippur* of the second year, did they offer the *korban tamid*.

Actually, what happened at Sinai is a controversy among *tanna'im*

(*Chagigah* 6). According to R' Akiva, the *tamid* was offered on Mount Sinai, and after that never ceased. What then does R' Akiva do with the verse from *Amos*? He answers that it was not the Israelites who brought these, but the tribe of Levi, which had not worshiped idols.

Yechahein Pe'er wonders over R' Akiva's answer that the Levites brought the *tamid*, as the *tamid* is supposed to come from the *tzibbur*, which in the context of offerings means the entire Jewish people. Now, *Chazal* in *Horayos* 6 state that the Levites are not even considered a *kahal*, a smaller unit than *tzibbur*, since they have no portion in *Eretz Yisrael*. How, then, could they have brought the *tamid*?

A fine answer appears in *Nachalas Yaakov Yehoshua*: The Levites were not considered a *kahal* when compared to the generation of Israelites who conquered the Land, and to the era of that conquest. *Rambam* (*Hil. Shemittah Veyovel*), however, states that in the future, even Levi will have a portion in the Land. Therefore, in the desert, as long as the Land remained undistributed, Levi could not be discounted as either a *kahal* or a *tzibbur*, and could thus bring the communal offerings.

Numerous *rishonim* and *acharonim* struggle to understand the phrase הָעֲשֻׂיָה בְּהַר סִינַי — "made on Mount Sinai" — (*Bamidbar* 28:6) in regard to the *tamid*. S'forno derives from it that the *tamid* had been brought on Mount Sinai without a wine libation, and Hashem was now commanding that a wine libation be added. This agrees with his view, brought above, that before the Golden Calf episode, a wine libation and meal offering did not accompany the *tamid*.

Sefas Emes explains this philosophically: At Sinai, the Jewish people became eternally close to Hashem. Every Torah insight destined to be uncovered by future Torah scholars was revealed there. Since then, every *mitzvah* performed by the Jewish people has been meant to rekindle that original flame. Hence the *korban tamid* was truly עֲשִׂיָה (translated above as "made") — in this sense, "initiated" — at Mount Sinai.

R' Avraham Yitzchak HaKohen Kook philosophically links the *tamid* to Sinai as well. Until Sinai, holiness existed in the world, but not on a constant basis. With the Revelation of the Torah to the Jewish people and their appearance in the world arena, perpetual holiness descended to the world, and is symbolized by the *korban tamid*, the "perpetual offering." The Jewish people inherited this spiritual state when they said נַעֲשֶׂה וְנִשְׁמָע — "We will do and obey" (*Sh'mos* 24:7).

With this approach we can understand the word לְדֹרֹתֵיכֶם — "throughout your generations" — (v. 29:42) even according to *Rashi*, who limited the *tamid* of our *parashah* to the week of installation. True, the command for all time appears only in *Parashas Pinchas*, yet, even our *parashah* can be referring to the *tamid's* eternal significance, inaugurated at Sinai.

◄§ Consecrating the Altar

Malbim takes literally the statement that the *tamid* was "made on Mount Sinai" (*Sh'mos* 28:6). It was an essential requirement for consecrating the new Altar mentioned in our *parashah*, because by law a new Altar cannot be dedicated unaccompanied by a morning *tamid*. Since the Altar was new, a *tamid* was required, and specifically the morning one. This requirement is explained in *Maseches Menachos* 3a: "The rabbis learned: 'You shall offer the other lamb toward evening' (*Sh'mos* 29:41) — the second, not the first, towards evening. If the first was not offered in the morning, the second must not be brought at all."

Thus, by Divine decree, for a new, unused altar to be dedicated, it must be accompanied by a morning *tamid*. Yet, once an altar is no longer new, the *tamid* can be brought toward evening even if none was brought in the morning.

Rashi explains: "We read in *Parashas Pinchas*: 'You shall offer the other lamb toward evening,' but that verse does not mention that the first lamb must be brought in the morning." *Rashi* is puzzling. Do we not read in *Parashas Pinchas*, as here in *Tetzaveh*: "You shall offer the first lamb in the morning, and the second lamb toward evening" (*Bamidbar* 28:4)?

A beautiful explanation appears in *Torah Temimah*, based on the remarkable words of *Maseches Megillah* 28a: "R' Akiva asked R' Nechuniah the Great, 'If the singular word for lamb, כֶּבֶשׂ, is used, why must the word אֶחָד — one — be added?' He responded, 'It refers to the special one in the flock.' "

These words seem unclear. What does R' Akiva mean by his question? What bothers him in the wording of the text? What compels R' Nechuniah to take a word out of its context? Further, in commenting on the word כֶּבֶשׂ, *Rashi* quotes: "Bring the first lamb in the morning." It is unclear why *Rashi* simply quotes the verse in full.

Yet, says *Torah Temimah*, there is deep meaning here. Whoever examines the descriptions of the *tamid* here and in Pinchas will note an interesting distinction. Here we read אֶת הַכֶּבֶשׂ הָאֶחָד — literally "the lamb the one," but also translatable as "the first lamb" (*Sh'mos* 29:39), whereas in Pinchas we read אֶת הַכֶּבֶשׂ אֶחָד — literally "the one lamb" (*Bamidbar* 28:4). This distinction points out a difference in meaning. הַכֶּבֶשׂ הָאֶחָד — "the first lamb" — implies a second is to follow, hence if the first was not brought, the second should not be brought either. However, הַכֶּבֶשׂ אֶחָד — "the one lamb" — implies that the first and second are independent of each other. In accordance with this, *Rashi* in *Menachos* does well in stating that *Parashas Pinchas* uses הַכֶּבֶשׂ אֶחָד, and not הַכֶּבֶשׂ הָאֶחָד to highlight the independence of the two. Even if the morning *tamid* was not brought, the afternoon one is.

R' Akiva's question, as well, concerning why the Torah uses the word אֶחָד, relates to this lack of the definite article. In this light, R' Nechuniah does well in answering that the word אֶחָד means מְיוּחָד, i.e., the special sheep of the flock.

⋅৪ Prayer and Burnt Offerings

Chazal in *Maseches Berachos* quote R' Yehoshua ben Levi: "The *shemoneh esrei* was established to correspond to the *korban tamid*." In the Jerusalem Talmud, *Berachos*, 4:1, the same source is quoted as the majority view. The morning *shemoneh esrei* parallels the morning *tamid*, the afternoon *shemoneh esrei* parallels the afternoon *tamid*, and the evening *shemoneh esrei* parallels the burning of the *tamid*'s limbs and intestinal membrane, which could be burned all night. Likewise, *Zohar* on *Parashas Pinchas* states that the *shemoneh esrei* was established to correspond to the *korban tamid*.

Torah Sheleimah quotes R' Eliezer of Worms who notes that the *gematria*, or numerical value, of הָאֶחָד is eighteen, corresponding to the eighteen blessings of the *shemoneh esrei*. Others find eighteen in וְזֶה — "and so" — in the verse וְזֶה אֲשֶׁר תַּעֲשֶׂה — "and so shall you do" (*Sh'mos* 29:38), the first verse of the section of *tamid*.

R' Y. Perla, in his treatise on R' Sa'adiah Gaon's 613 *mitzvos*, mentions the correspondence between *shemoneh esrei* and *tamid* to explain why *Behag* does not count *shemoneh esrei* in his list of 613 *mitzvos*, and why R' Shlomo Ibn Gabirol did not include the *korban tamid* among the 613. *Ramban* at the end of *Shoresh 1* to *Sefer HaMitzvos* says that *Behag* did not include all rabbinic enactments in his list of *mitzvos*, counting only those *mitzvos* commanded by the Great *Beis Din*. Now, as *Behag* (ruling according to R' Yehoshua Ben Levi in ch. 4 of *Maseches Berachos*) states that the *shemoneh esrei* is meant to correspond to the *tamid*, he makes do with the inclusion of *tamid* on his list. R' Sholomo Ibn Gabirol, on the other hand, found it more preferable to include *shemoneh esrei* than *tamid*. If the two are really synonymous, it is more logical that the rule that applies today should be counted.

Interestingly, *Ramban* counts the morning and afternoon *tamid* sacrifices as two separate *mitzvos*, because the absence of one does not invalidate the performance of the other and because they have separate times. R' Sa'adiah Gaon, however, counts them only as one, because he holds that the afternoon *tamid* represents a completion of something begun in the morning.

R' Perla supports R' Sa'adiah Gaon by quoting *Maseches Yoma*, which states that no new lottery was employed to choose a *Kohen* to offer the afternoon *tamid*. Rather, whichever *Kohen* had won the opportunity to bring the morning *tamid* would bring the afternoon one as well.

Ki Sisa – כי תשא

I.

Permitted and Prohibited Censuses

hen you take a census of the Israelites, each man shall give a ransom for himself to Hashem so the census does not lead to plague" (*Sh'mos* 30:12). Both *rishonim* and *acharonim* raise several questions regarding this *parashah*. What is meant by the plague referred to in the first verse? What is the main point of our *parashah* — the census or the half shekel that was to be collected? What connection is there between counting the nation and raising funds for the sanctuary? Was the census a one-time *mitzvah* or a perpetual one?

Regarding the first question, S'forno holds that when something is counted, it is a sign that it is undergoing change and requires constant inspection. The change we are speaking of is death, and this death is the result of sin. Therefore, the tallies must be accompanied by atonement. Yet, *Rashi*, following *Chazal* and other *rishonim*, sees the plague as resulting not from sin, but from the Evil Eye, thus it is the result of the tally itself.

Rabbenu Bachya offers an interesting explanation. The tally draws every individual out of the general mass, establishing him as a separate unit, independently watched over by Hashem, and judged independently of others. Therefore, plague strikes him more severely than if he were being watched as part of a community. In line with this, when Elisha asked the Shunamite woman whether he should put in a good word for her to the king, she responded: "I dwell among my people" (*II Melachim* 4:13), i.e., she considered it better to be included with all of the people together rather than to draw individual attention to herself.

Chinuch views the collection as signifying Hashem's will to establish equality in the nation:

> To ensure Israel's welfare and increase their merit, Hashem wished them all to have an equal share in the constant offerings brought

before Him over the year ... All were included in this one *mitzvah*, and all, rich and poor, had an equal share. Hence, by this means Hashem would remember the entire Jewish people positively.

Even with this, an explanation is still required of what this *mitzvah* has to do with counting the nation and what purpose such a tally has. A basic disagreement exists among the commentaries over these matters.

ᴇ§ King David's Census

Ramban and *Rashi* agree that the reason the Israelites were counted here in *Ki Sisa*, in addition to the tally of *Parashas Pekudei*, is to teach that for every census, a half shekel must be collected specifically as atonement. The command takes the form, "When you take a census," to teach that this is a command for the future as well. Such a sum must be collected for that purpose whenever a census is taken. King David [*II Shmuel* ch. 24; *I Divrei HaYamim* ch. 21] mistakenly thought the half shekel had only been a one-time command. He therefore counted the nation, taking no sum as atonement, and was punished.

Proof that the *mitzvah* is for all time comes from King Yoash's question to Yehoyada the *Kohen*: "Why have you not required the Levites to bring out of Yehudah and Jerusalem the tax of Moshe, servant of Hashem?" (*II Divrei HaYamim* 24:6). From this it appears that collecting "the tax of Moshe" for the Temple treasury is a *mitzvah* that applies in all time.

The half shekel of our *parashah* was earmarked for the sockets into which the beams of the *Mishkan* were placed. It was collected after Yom Kippur, when work began on the Tabernacle. A second contribution was collected when the Tabernacle was completed, and corresponded to a census taken on the first day of the second month in the second year (*Bamidbar* 1:1). Half shekels were collected once more, and were used to purchase animals for communal offerings.

Remarkably, the result of both tallies was 603,550, despite the passage of two years in between. If the minimum age for inclusion was twenty, should there not have been some group who were nineteen years old during the first tally, and at least twenty by the time of the second? *Ramban* offers two brief answers: Either the number of deaths exactly equaled the number of new twenty-year-olds, or the first census included Levites while the second did not: "Only you shall not number the tribe of Levi" (ibid. v. 48). Offset by the exclusion of Levi was the increased population of the other tribes.

Ramban also explains the nature of "the holy shekel" (*Sh'mos* 30:13). When Moshe, as king, issued a pure silver coin and labeled it *"shekel hakodesh,"* he meant not "holy shekel," but "shekel used toward holy ends." The shekel was used to pay for valuation endowments to the Temple (*Vayikra* 27), the redemption of firstborn and the shekels of the Tabernacle. In the same way, Hebrew is called *lashon hakodesh*, not, as *Rambam* (*Moreh Nevuchim*) thinks, because of its holy nature or its absence of profanity, but because it is the language used for *Tanach*. Were *Rambam* right, Hebrew should have been called not *lashon hakodesh*, but *lashon nekiyah* — "the clean tongue." The holiness of Hebrew lies only in its sacred applications, just as the *shekel hakodesh* is a plain shekel used to measure holy weights.

Ramban, who states that for every census a half shekel must be collected, is puzzling to later commentaries. *Levush Orah* asks whether King David could possibly have erred in something stated explicitly in the Torah: "So the census will not lead to plague."

The *acharonim* mention a contradiction within *Ramban* himself. In *Bamidbar* 1:3, *Ramban* states that King David did collect a sum of atonement when he took his tally. He could not possibly have been ignorant of the words "so the census will not lead to plague." Hashem became angry at him only because he counted the Israelites needlessly. David had not just returned from war. He took a tally only to boast his reign over a large nation. Alternatively, Hashem's anger could have been because King David commanded that all males over age thirteen be counted when the Torah stipulated only age twenty. This source contradicts *Ramban* on our *parashah* who states that David erred, thinking it permissible to count the Israelites without requiring the payment of a sum for atonement.

Levush Orah resolves the contradiction by stating that in *Bamidbar*, *Ramban* is probably retracting his earlier statement. King David knew full well that our duty to collect shekels with the census is a *mitzvah* for all time. His error was in thinking he could count the Israelites when there was no real need, and for this he was punished.

Kli Chemdah wonders why *Ramban* does not bring support from *Yoma* 22. There, the *Mishnah* states that in choosing *Kohanim* to remove the ashes after burnt offerings, candidates would "display their fingers to be counted." The Talmud comments:

> Why must their fingers, and not they, themselves, be counted? This supports R' Yitzchak who said it is forbidden to count the Jewish people even for the sake of a *mitzvah* ... R' Elazar said, "Whoever counts the Jewish people violates a prohibition: 'The

population of the Israelites shall be like the sand of the sea, which cannot be measured' (*Hoshea* 2:1)." R' Nachman bar Yitzchak says, "Two prohibitions are involved. For the verse states: 'Which cannot be *measured* or *counted*.' "

This source teaches a number of separate laws regarding tallies:

(a) Any type of census of the entire Jewish people violates the double prohibition of "which cannot be *measured* or *counted*."

(b) A census of part of the Jewish people avoids these prohibitions, but is still forbidden lest plague result. All this applies to a head count, but a "finger count" of part of the Jewish people is permissible.

Thus, we find support here for *Ramban's* view that counting the entire Jewish people for no reason is forbidden, even if accompanied by a collection of shekalim.

Ultimately, *Kli Chemdah* concludes that this source is no proof for *Ramban*. Even if King David counted thirteen-year-olds, he still was not counting the entire Jewish people, hence "which cannot be measured or counted" does not apply. *Ramban*, therefore, must have arrived at his understanding through logic: If the Torah requires the half shekel for counting those twenty and older, it means that those thirteen and older must constitute the entire Jewish people, and to count them even with a shekel collection, is forbidden.

◆§ A Warning for All Time

The Vilna Gaon holds that the warning about tallies precipitating plagues (*Sh'mos* 30:12) applies for all time. Even so, unlike *Ramban* and *Rashi*, he holds that no census is commanded here, and none is commanded until *Parashas Bamidbar*. Unlike *Rashi* and *Ramban*, the Vilna Gaon holds that there was only one census, not two. The half shekel of verse 13 was collected for the Temple sockets: "Now they shall contribute." The word זֶה (normally translated as "this") is understood here as "now," as in וַיַּעְקְבֵנִי זֶה פַעֲמַיִם — "He has fooled me now twice" (*Bereishis* 27:36). There is no *mitzvah* for all time to give specifically a half shekel during each census, but only to conduct each census in such a way that no plague occurs. Thus, when King Shaul counted the Israelites, rather than counting heads he collected lambs (*I Shmuel* 15:4) or shards (ibid. 11:8).

In support of *Rashi's* and *Ramban's* view that a census was held here, *HaKesav VeHaKabalah* quotes several *Midrashim* which state that the Israelites were counted following the Golden Calf episode. Yet, *HaKesav VeHaKabalah* also quotes the *Yerushalmi* which supports the

Vilna Gaon: "First came the contribution to the Temple: 'It came to pass on the first day of the first month of the second year, the Tabernacle was erected' " (*Sh'mos* 40:17). *Rambam* explains that with the erection of the Tabernacle on the first day of *Nissan* in the second year, the first collection was taken.

HaKesav VeHaKabalah adds that *Yoma* 22 seems to agree with the Vilna Gaon that there was only one census. *Chazal* there state that even for the sake of a *mitzvah* it is forbidden to count the Jewish people, because regarding Shaul we read "He counted them with lambs" (*I Shmuel* 15:4). If *Rashi* and *Ramban* are correct in understanding the beginning of *Ki Sisa* as permitting a census taking through collection of a sum, why do *Chazal* in *Yoma* neglect this Torah verse in favor of a verse from *Shmuel*? The answer must be that the Vilna Gaon is correct, and that at the beginning of *Ki Sisa* there was no census, but only a warning to take preventive measures against plague when counting the Jewish people.

In the end, *HaKesav VeHaKabalah* retracts this conclusion, saying that the *Gemara* in *Yoma* is no proof for the Vilna Gaon. *Chazal* could be deducing from what Shaul did, that even to count part of the Jewish people is forbidden. After all, Shaul counted only 300,000 people, yet he collected lambs and earthen vessels to avoid taking a head count.

While R' Eliyahu Mizrachi believes that no such prohibition exists, from *Chazal* it is clear that even part of the Jewish people may not be counted directly, but one must resort to counting fingers or earthen vessels. As for counting the entire Jewish people, there a sum must always be collected in atonement.

Abarbanel disagrees totally with *Ramban's* view that in verse 30:12, Hashem is commanding a census or that a half shekel must always be taken as atonement, and he offers several arguments: (a) Were it a command, it would have been stated in the imperative and not as, "When you count" (ibid). (b) If the half shekel applies to all future tallies, why would Hashem command Moshe to count the Jewish people in the Sinai Desert (*Bamidbar* 1:2) and the Plains of Moav (ibid. ch. 26) without collecting a half shekel? (c) Shaul counted the Jewish people one time by collecting lambs and a different time by collecting earthen vessels, but he took no half shekels. (d) Why, during the several times that the Levites were counted, was no half shekel ever collected?

Abarbanel therefore concludes that when Hashem commands a census, the Evil Eye is not aroused and no atonement is needed. Here, however, Moshe himself wished to count the Israelites to know how large their army would be, and also the Tabernacle needed silver. The Israelites, through contributions, had supplied all the Tabernacle's needs except for silver, which they kept for themselves to buy items from their neighbors. Hashem therefore commanded that the half shekel be collected, both to provide the Tabernacle with silver and to avoid problems resulting from Moshe's tally.

The Torah states that the silver collected was "a memorial before Hashem" (Sh'mos 30:16). Abarbanel understands this as announcing that henceforth, every year, donations of silver would be solicited to purchase animals for communal offerings, as in Ezra, which mentions donations of a third of a shekel.

How do we explain that at the time of Ezra a third — and not a half — was solicited? The answer must evidently be that the mitzvah of a half shekel was not for all time. (Chazal might respond that a third of a shekel in the time of Ezra was worth a half in the time of Moshe.)

ᏯᏕ Two Types of Tallies

The Torah states, "When you wish to take a census of the Israelites, each man should give a ransom for himself to Hashem so the census does not lead to plague" (Sh'mos 30:12). Rashi comments, "Do not take a head count. Rather, let everyone give a half shekel, and count those." This implies that even here, where money is being collected in atonement, the object contributed must be counted, and not the Israelites themselves. On verse 13, however, Rashi continues, "Those taking a tally customarily have the objects of the tally pass before them one by one, as with sheep beneath the shepherd's rod." This implies that the Israelites and not the shekels were counted.

Many deal with this discrepancy. Gan Raveh answers that according to Rashi there were two tallies. First, the half shekels were counted, thus providing a tally without risk of plague. Then a head count was taken. As this carried the risk of plague for those who had not given their half shekel, it was a good way to ensure that all would contribute the silver needed for the Tabernacle.

Divrei Chanoch employs this answer to solve a similar problem: The Torah tells us that the half shekel was meant "to atone for your souls" (v. 15), and Rashi comments, "to prevent your being smitten because of the census." If Rashi had already said in verse 12 that no headcount was taken, why should atonement have been needed? The answer must be that two tallies were taken.

Still another problem is solved in this fashion. The Torah states that when the Israelites are counted, if they each give a half shekel, then, "There will be no plague when they are counted" (30:12). What purpose is served by the phrase "when they are counted?" It teaches that after the shekalim were counted, a second tally was taken, of the Israelites themselves. The Torah here promised that those who had contributed their half shekel for the first tally would not be harmed by the second.

We can also employ *Gan Raveh's* answer to deal with a question raised previously: How could King David have counted the Israelites without collecting the sum explicitly required by the Torah? Hundreds of answers have been given, but according to *Gan Raveh*, there is no prohibition against counting people if a sum is given as atonement beforehand. King David thought that the sum given in the days of Moshe served as atonement for all tallies that followed, an idea which actually appears in *Tanchuma, Ki Sisa*. Hashem, anticipating that every future census would lead to deaths, decreed that a half shekel be collected one time as atonement, so that no plague would strike in future tallies.

Likewise, *Chazal* in *Berachos* 62 comment on the verse, "When He was about to destroy, Hashem saw and relented" (*I Divrei HaYamim* 21:15): "What did He see? R' Yitzchak Nafcha answered, 'The silver of atonement.' " *Rashi* explains that this refers to the silver given at the first census.

We see here that Moshe took precautions to ensure that plague would not strike in the time of King David. It was this that King David relied upon in taking his census.

⊷§ No Jew by Himself Is a Complete Unit

Censuses, in singling out individuals from a group, create division where there was unity, hence atonement is necessary. Yet, why was a half shekel chosen for this purpose? According to the Chassidic literature, it is to teach that no Jew can be complete without other Jews. Every individual Jew is an incomplete part of the whole.

As *Alshech* says, quoting R' Shlomo Alkabetz, we must realize the importance of unity. Let no Jew consider himself an independent unit. Until we unite, we are only half complete.

According to *Chasam Sofer* in his *Rosh HaShanah* sermons, this is a point Hashem taught Moshe. Moshe knew that when a community is divided into separate groups it leads to discord, and he wondered how the Israelites, composed of many small groups, would ever be transformed into one united mass. Hashem therefore showed him a fiery coin. This demonstrated to Moshe the essence of the Jewish people, proving that unity was basic to their nature, despite their division into separate groups.

R' Elimelech of Lizensk (*Noam Elimelech*) explains *Chasam Sofer's* allegory. When Moshe wondered how anything as insignificant as a half-shekel coin could stop a plague, Hashem showed him a coin made of fire. Fire possesses two qualities: It both burns and gives warmth. A coin, as well, can be used for good or for evil. It can even stop a plague. So the census does not lead to plague; it is divisiveness which leads to plague. If we learn from this, however, this episode of the Torah can be transformed from a curse into a blessing. A Jew is only half of a coin, and only by joining with others can he be transformed into a whole person, and an inseparable part of the Jewish people.

II.

The Golden Calf

It is hard to understand the episode of the Golden Calf. Having just experienced the Sinai Revelation and the miracles of the Exodus, how could the Chosen People have deteriorated so quickly as to trade Hashem's glory for an idol? *Chazal*, being experts in the human mind, knew very well how to answer this. Miracles cannot change habit. Only many years of constant education can create a new generation with a new spirit.

All the commentaries struggle to understand Aharon's role in this great crime. The Torah implies, albeit indirectly, that Aharon took part: "Hashem was very angry with Aharon" (*Devarim* 9:20). Yet, Aharon was not punished for doing so, and he remained the *Kohen gadol*.

There is much below the surface here. In the words of Chizkuni:

Heaven forbid that we should say that Aharon worshiped idols! He was holy to Hashem and a prophet of Israel, and many *mitzvos* were given through him and his brother Moshe. If he worshiped idols, how did he escape being killed by Moshe? How did he and his line become Israel's eternal agents of atonement? No sin is explicitly associated with him beside that of the water drawn from the rock (*Bamidbar* 20:11). If he truly were destined for idolatry, would Hashem have named him messenger?

In *Chazal* and the Midrash there are many views on the Golden Calf. Some say there was true idolatry. *Rashi* quotes this view: "Their desire for idolatry was great." Yet, most commentaries cannot accept this. We shall now present their rich store of novel ideas.

◆§ Paths to Serving Hashem

Kuzari (1:37) offers an interesting explanation for the Golden Calf: The Israelites only wished a special place where they could focus their prayers and concentrate on serving Hashem. Among the nations of that era, physical forms and symbols functioned as focal points for prayer and meditation, like our synagogues today: "Just as we do today in our places of worship, taking pride in their stones and mortar." The Israelite masses could not concentrate on serving Hashem except in a special place. They hoped Moshe would bring down something concrete from Heaven, to which they could direct their hearts, and they thought the Tablets would serve this purpose. When Moshe failed to appear, they reasoned, "Let us serve something tangible like the other nations, without denying Hashem who took us out of Egypt." They wished to turn their prayers to this concrete object the way we today turn our hearts to "Heaven," which is itself a concrete concept. In our day, says *Kuzari*, it is difficult to understand this, for all the concepts have changed. At the time, however, such worship was quite widespread among the nations. In fact, what they did was no different from the synagogues of our day. Only, in their time it was forbidden to build an altar wherever one wished. Offerings could be brought only in the Temple chosen by Hashem.

According to *Kuzari*, worshiping the Golden Calf was not a severe sin in and of itself. As proof, only three thousand people were killed as a result. During all this time, neither the manna, the pillar of smoke or prophecy ceased to exist for the Israelites. Their only sin was envisioning Hashem by means of a form, without being commanded to do so. We do find that physical forms have a place in Divine worship: "The Calf was like the *Cheruvim*, but those were commanded by Hashem."

In *Kuzari's* view, the worship involving the Golden Calf did not comprise rebellion against Hashem, but only against a few *mitzvos*. The Israelites had been commanded not to make physical forms. However, by making analogies to other forms Hashem had commanded, they deemed it permissible to make the Calf. They were like the medical quack who mixes together remedies by imitating expert physicians, and succeeds only in poisoning his patients.

Kuzari also justifies what Aharon did. Aharon wished to correct the people's error regarding unauthorized worship of physical forms. His first step in doing so was to have them spell out their heretical thoughts as actions. His intentions were good. He wished to educate them to serve Hashem truthfully.

Ibn Ezra's views are so consistent with *Kuzari's* that Abarbanel cannot tell who learned from whom. Ibn Ezra holds that Israel's sin was in viewing Hashem concretely, and he views Aharon as partner in the crime: "Hashem was very angry with Aharon" (*Devarim* 9:20).

Ibn Ezra does not accept the opinion of R' Sa'adiah Gaon that Aharon wished only to discover who among the Israelites were idolaters, like Yehu in his time (*II Melachim* 10). In Ibn Ezra's view, Aharon sinned. He also rejects the view that Aharon's actions were compelled by the fear that like Chur, he would be killed for opposing idolatry. Aharon could not have done that because idolatry is one of those sins we must shun at the cost of our own lives. Ibn Ezra therefore understands that the Israelites wished to serve Hashem concretely, because Moshe had disappeared from the scene, and there was no one to teach them the meaning of serving Hashem.

Aharon answered their call, thinking no great sin was involved. After all, the Israelites were not turning their hearts away from Hashem, only choosing a different form of service. Therefore Aharon said: "Tomorrow is a feast to Hashem" (*Sh'mos* 32:5). He mentioned Hashem's name, i.e., the spiritual content remained unchanged. Only, there was a small concession to concreteness of worship.

Yet, adds Ibn Ezra, this concession led to the sin of part of the nation, the mixed multitude, who abandoned the content and grasped only the form. For them, the Calf was true idolatry. The mixed multitude were a minute minority, three thousand people, only one half a percent of the population. Yet, the entire nation was held responsible for daring to create unauthorized forms of worship. They did not understand the meaning of "Do not make for yourself any carved idol or any likeness" (*Sh'mos* 20:4). The sin was therefore associated with them all.

This idea is succinctly expressed in *Beis HaLevi* by R' Yosef Ber of Brisk. Those who worshiped the Golden Calf knew that the Torah treated certain people (*Kohanim*) and a certain place (the Tabernacle) as special. They therefore believed they could engage in any form of adoration they wished, as long as it was ultimately directed to Hashem. Yet, they were wrong. Bound up with the Tabernacle and its vessels are countless secrets and mysteries, and the only way to serve Hashem properly is to follow His orders. The moment we worship Hashem in an unauthorized manner, we deserve punishment. This explains why regarding every detail of the Tabernacle's construction we read, "as Hashem commanded." This stresses that one may not create new, unauthorized forms of worship based on existing forms.

R' Yehonasan Eybeschutz (*Tiferes Yehonasan*) states that the people's mistake stemmed from their likening the Calf to the *Cheruv*, since both are part of the celestial chariot. They did not understand that only what was commanded is permissible. All else is deemed idol worship.

In accordance with this interesting idea, one may state that when the Torah says, "They have speedily left the path I commanded them" (*Sh'mos* 32:8), it explains both why the people sinned and why they deserved punishment. They sinned by creating a false analogy between forms of worship Hashem had commanded, and those He had not. Their sin originated with the mentality of their times, and the direction it led them.

◄§ False Beliefs Shattered

Meshech Chochmah applies an idea mentioned above, that Moshe shattered the tablets to shatter the nation's false but deep-seated beliefs:

Torah and faith are the axioms of the Jewish people. *Eretz Yisrael* and Jerusalem are holy only because the Torah says they are. The entire Torah is equally valid in every time and place, both in and outside of *Eretz Yisrael*, and equally valid for every Jew, the highest of the high, i.e., Moshe, and the lowest of the low. Even Moshe, an agent between Hashem and man, has no special status on a personal level where *mitzvah* observance is concerned. For us to exist the Torah must exist, for Hashem and the Torah are one, and the Torah depends only upon Hashem, the Prime Cause.

Likewise, Moshe cried out, "Am I so holy that in my absence you felt you had to make a Golden Calf? Heaven forbid! I am only a man like you. The Torah does not depend upon me ... Do not imagine that the Tabernacle and the Temple are holy in and of themselves. Their holiness derives only from Hashem's residing among His children, and if those children break their covenant, the holiness of the Temple and Tabernacle will be removed. They will be like mundane items destroyed by vandals."

Thus, when Titus entered the Temple with a harlot, he was not harmed, for the Temple's holiness had already been lifted. Even the tablets, the work of Hashem, have no holiness in and of themselves. When Hashem's new bride committed adultery during her wedding ceremony, those tablets reverted to mere potsherds. Their holiness derived from the Jewish people's watching over them, and they failed in this. Ultimately, nothing in the world deserves our devotion and submission but Hashem, for only He is inherently holy, and only to Him are praise and service acceptable.

The Tabernacle and Temples are holy only because Hashem decreed them to be so ... Thus, when Moshe approached the camp and saw the calf and the dancing, he realized the gravity of Israel's error, and conceding to their mood as Aharon had done, he broke the tablets. Moshe wished to show that nothing is Divine or holy besides Hashem. Had Moshe brought down the tablets, the Israelites would have exchanged the Golden Calf for the tablets without their misunderstanding being removed. By shattering them, he made the people realize that they had not reached their goal, faith in Hashem and in His pure Torah. Moshe did a wonderful deed by breaking the tablets and Hashem congratulated him for doing so. The breaking of the tablets was a lesson to the Jewish people in the essence of faith in Hashem.

✺§ A Leader to Replace Moshe

Ramban's view of the Golden Calf differs from that of *Meshech Chochmah*. *Ramban* rejects the idea that Aharon made concessions to those who wished to worship Hashem concretely. The severity of this sin rules out its being associated with Aharon. The Israelites did not seek to create changes in their worship of Hashem, but to find a replacement for Moshe: "Make us judges (*elohim*) who shall go before us" (*Sh'mos* 32:1). Here, *elohim* is translated "judges" as in *Sh'mos* 22:27. The Israelite message was, "Moshe took us out of Egypt and showed us the way. Now that we have lost him, let us appoint another Moshe over us." As this was all they sought, Aharon viewed the matter without much concern, and chose for them the physical likeness of an ox. The ox, which stands to the left of the celestial chariot, represents strict Divine justice, the very trait by which Hashem ruled Israel in the barren desert.

Other commentaries, such as Rabbenu Bachya and *Bechor Shor*, follow *Ramban's* path as well, yet omit the mystical element of a figure representing Divine justice replacing Moshe to lead the Israelites through the desert. They hold that Aharon refused a request made by the Israelites of a human replacement for Moshe. Aharon was afraid that if he appointed someone, Moshe would eventually return, those who had grown accustomed to the new leader would not wish to leave him and civil war would ensue. Aharon therefore created a statue representing leadership. His intention was to slow the proceedings until Moshe returned. He told the Israelites: "Break off the golden earrings which are in your wives' ears" (*Sh'mos* 32:2), knowing that the women would not easily part with their jewelry, and matters would be further postponed. Then, when they submitted their gold he declared: "These are your lords, O Israel" (v. 4), meaning their rulers and leaders. Aharon feared that the Israelites would quickly become convinced that such leadership was unreal, and would request a different leader. He therefore stalled until the morning saying, "Tomorrow is a feast to Hashem" (v. 5). He made them an altar, saying that the next day they would hold a feast dedicated to Hashem in Heaven, thanking Him for providing a leader to replace Moshe.

Ramban adds that immediately upon Moshe's return, when he saw the Calf and the dancing, the masses fled. Moshe took the Calf, burnt it and put its ashes into the drinking water, yet the masses did not object. This proves they did not believe the Calf was their god. Otherwise, they would have objected, perhaps violently. One thing is clear from the text: Aharon was accused only of causing the sin: "What did this people do to you that you have brought upon them such a great sin?" (v. 21). Aharon, Hashem's chosen priest, offered excuses for his deeds. Even so, the Torah does not spare his dignity, stressing that "Aharon had made the people wild" (v. 25) and referring to the calf "which Aharon had made" (v. 35). The Torah's limiting Aharon's punishment to condemnation proves that he did not personally take part in the worship. Otherwise, the Torah would not have spared him at all. The Torah states: "Hashem was very angry with Aharon" (*Devarim* 9:20). The Torah does not hesitate to accuse Aharon of being partly responsible. Yet, his punishment ends with rebuke. The fact is, the only reason he deserves rebuke is that Hashem is extremely strict with the righteous.

III.

My Face Shall Not Be Seen

n *Sh'mos* 33:12-16, Moshe requests that the Israelites be led by Hashem and not an angel. Yet, he expresses himself unclearly. In fact, at first he seems only to want to know the name of the angel Hashem is sending: "You have not let me know whom You will send with me" (v. 12). Also, he first bases his request upon his having pleased Hashem: "If I find favor in Your eyes" (v. 13). Then upon Hashem's closeness to Israel: "Observe that this nation is Your People" (v. 13). At last he secures Hashem's promise: "My Presence will go and lead you" (v. 14). Yet, no sooner has he done so, than he begs further: "If Your Presence does not go, do not take us up out of here" (v. 15). Then he raises additional demands: "Let Your nation and myself be distinct from all other nations" (v. 16); and, "Please show me Your glory" (v. 18). Hashem responds to his urging, but refuses just one request, answering, "You cannot see My face" (v. 20).

These verses can be understood in various ways. We can only offer a minute portion of the sea of existing interpretations.

Rashi understands Moshe's first request, "You have not let me know whom You will send with me," as "You have not let me know what I wish to hear." Hashem had told him that He would send an angel, but this was not the information Moshe sought.

Ramban rejects this as not fitting the text. At the same time he wonders why Moshe suddenly protests, "If Your Presence does not go, do not take us up out of here," when Hashem announced before the incident of the Golden Calf that He would send an angel. After that sin, do the Israelites deserve the reward of Hashem's personally leading them instead of an angel? Why was Moshe silent when Hashem first announced He was sending an angel (v. 23:20)? *Ramban* also rejects Ibn Ezra's view that Moshe wished only to know if the angel that was announced in verse 33:2 is the same one promised in verse 23:20, believed by Ibn Ezra to be Michael. As *Ramban* puts it: "Ibn Ezra logically deduces that Michael would be suitable for Moshe and Israel. Yet, he has no way of knowing that this is what Moshe is asking, because he is no prophet and did not hear this idea anywhere."

For *Ramban*, these verses can only be understood on a kabbalistic level. Hashem planned to lead the nation with a mixture of strict justice and mercy, while Moshe wanted Hashem's relationship to be entirely "face to face," i.e., merciful.

Maharal in *Gur Aryeh* deals with *Ramban's* question of why Moshe did not react immediately to Hashem's announcement of an angel before the incident of the Calf. *Chazal* state that Moshe was told that the Israelites were going to sin, and Hashem would then hand over the reins to an angel. Knowing this, however, did not enable Moshe to protest it, because there was a chance that Israel would not sin, and the reins would not be handed over. Because man has free will, "knowing" that a person will sin is no guarantee that he will. Moshe therefore waited until the Israelites had actually sinned, and then he made his petition.

Tosafos and other *rishonim* state that Moshe's lack of clarity stemmed from his caution. Moshe was afraid to state clearly his wish that Hashem, and not an angel, lead the people. After Hashem said, "I will not go up in your midst lest I consume you on the way" (*Sh'mos* 33:3), Moshe investigated Hashem's ways. He wished to understand Hashem's conduct to know whether he could risk such a petition. Thus, he expressed his request vaguely: "You have not let me know whom You will send with me."

S'forno, paraphrasing verses 12-16, presents a different picture: Moshe told Hashem, "According to my understanding, You have appointed me to be Your messenger to lead the Israelites into the Land. I must therefore know Your wondrous ways." Hashem answered that He would walk before the People, but would not dwell in their midst. Shocked, Moshe responded, "If Your Presence does not go up among us, do not take us out of here. Otherwise, how will it be known that we are remarkably different from other nations? By the very fact that we conquer the Land? Will we be the only nation to engage in successful conquest?"

S'forno's explanation is actually a small fragment taken from the great investigation carried out by *Akeidah* on our *parashah*. *Akeidah* states that there are three levels of Divine Providence in Creation. One applies generally to the entire universe, the second specifically to the Jewish people and the third even more specifically to the pious and observant. This hierarchy parallels the relationship between man and man. Everyone feels close to his friends, closer still to his relatives and closest still to his own family. Moshe suspected that because of the Golden Calf, Hashem had lowered Israel from their special level to be like all the other nations. He therefore stressed, "Observe that this nation is Your people" (v. 33:13). Moshe felt confident enough about Israel's status to risk their not being taken out of the desert. Only when promised that nothing had changed was he appeased. Hashem was to remain as merciful and kind to Israel as before, for these traits are basic to His nature.

◆§ If I Have Pleased You, Show Me Now Your Way

Rashi explains that Moshe asked Hashem to reveal to him in what sense Hashem was pleased with him, and how He would express this concretely. Moshe immediately added, "Observe that this nation is Your People" (v. 13). According to *Maharal* on *Rashi*, Moshe meant he would never accept Hashem's making him a great nation to the Jewish people's exclusion: "This nation is Your people, not I. That is my starting point when I ask You to inform me how I have pleased You." Hashem's answer was not long in coming: "I personally will lead you" (v. 14). Moshe now responded, "If Your Presence does not go, do not bring us up out of here," which *Rashi* understands as, "That is my wish; if it will be by an angel, we are better off not going up at all."

Ramban asks: After Hashem promised to lead them Himself, how could Moshe once more mention the possibility that an angel might lead them? *Tosafos* and Ibn Ezra hold that Hashem's answer, "I personally will lead you," relates only to Moshe. Hashem promised that he would guide Moshe on the route. In this sense, אִם אֵין פָּנֶיךָ הֹלְכִים (v. 33:15) means, "If You do not go before the nation." This idea is supported by the fact that in "I personally will lead you," the word "you" is singular, whereas Moshe's "Do not lead us" is in the plural.

Ramban rejects this explanation as well, proving from the text that no importance can be attached here to number. Moshe said, "If I have pleased You, show me now Your way' " (v. 13). *Rashbam* understands Moshe to have asked Hashem to show him the way to please Him. Hashem responded, "I will walk before you until all your enemies around you leave you alone."

According to *Rashbam*, Moshe had yet another request: "That the nation as a community and Moshe as an individual be distinct from all other nations. Then, in verse 18 Moshe asked, הַרְאֵנִי נָא אֶת כְּבֹדֶךָ. Literally translated, this means, "Show me Your glory," but the verse is actually no more than a continuation of verse 16, "Let Your nation and myself be distinct from all other nations," and a prayer that Hashem would forge a covenant with the Israelites making them distinct from others. It cannot be taken literally. How could Moshe, who hid his face from Hashem at the Burning Bush, now seek to bask in the Divine Light? Rather, Moshe petitioned Hashem to uphold His promises with a covenant as Avraham did "between the parts" (*Bereishis* 15:10). Hashem accepted his petition and forged a covenant: "Hashem passed before him . . . Behold, I make a covenant. Before all your people I will do marvels" (*Sh'mos* 34:6,10). This is in line with 33:16: "Let your nation and myself be distinct from all other nations." Hashem concluded by mentioning "the awesome act of Hashem that I will perform with you" (v. 10). This refers to the luster of Moshe's face, regarding which we read: "They were afraid to approach him" (v. 30).

◦§ Show Me Your Glory

Zohar asks a question widely treated by the *rishonim* and *acharonim*: "How did Moshe dare ask to see this?" *Zohar* answers: "Since Moshe rose so high that he neither ate nor drank for forty days and nights and was nourished by Heavenly light, he thought himself worthy to ask this." What was Hashem's answer? "You will not be able to see My face" (v. 20). Moshe had undergone a great spiritual ascent and considered himself fit to see Hashem. He was answered, however, that as long as his soul was attached to his body, this was impossible.

There is an entire literature devoted to Moshe's quest for the unattainable. *Radbaz*, in his *teshuvos* (1:615), states that Moshe requested only that henceforth he would hear Hashem's voice directly, and not by means of an angelic translator. Hashem answered that this, too, was impossible. Had Hashem's voice reached him directly, his soul would touch the Heavenly source and would never return to the physical world.

The *rishonim* find much material here upon which to base their views of Hashem and man's perception of Him.

According to *Rambam* (*Hil. Yesodei HaTorah* 1:10), Moshe wished to know Hashem in a manner distinct from human perception. He wished to know his Maker as distinct from the beings He had made, just as he knew of man as distinct from other beings. Hashem therefore answered that no living man can grasp such a thing clearly. Hashem opened before Moshe the gates of light and informed him of everything no man before or after him would ever know. Even so, this knowledge was limited in that Hashem showed only His "back" (*Sh'mos* 33:23). It was not the thorough familiarity Moshe sought.

Through several chapters of *Moreh Nevuchim*, *Rambam* develops and expands this idea in depth. In 1:45 he states that Moshe had two requests of Hashem, and was answered regarding one but not the other. He asked to know Hashem's essence and being, and this was not granted. He asked to know Hashem's conduct and attributes, and this was granted. Moshe attained an understanding of Hashem's conduct in the universe so that he too would know how to lead the nation according to the Torah, the embodiment of Hashem's way in the universe.

Rabbenu Bachya elaborates in this direction as well. Regarding Moshe's two requests we read: "It is the glory of Hashem to conceal a thing, but the honor of kings is to search out a matter" (*Mishlei* 25:2). It is perfectly acceptable to investigate "the honor of kings," i.e., Hashem's regal conduct of the world, but it is unacceptable to investigate Hashem's very being and essence. It is possible to learn about the sun by examining its movements, but if someone looks directly at the sun he will hurt his eyes. How much more is this true regarding the shining light of Hashem's glorious throne:

"You shall see My back" (*Sh'mos* 33:23). We can learn about Hashem from Creation, but not by studying Hashem Himself.

According to *Akeidah*, we can know Hashem by reflecting on our own faults and shortcomings. Anything we lack, Hashem has. Hashem is the climax of perfection, but perfection can only be fathomed by studying its absence: "You shall see My back" refers to studying the converse of Hashem's attributes, whereas Hashem's "front" refers to studying Hashem's attributes positively, regarding which Hashem said: "No man will see Me and live" (ibid.). We can know of Hashem's attributes and of His conduct regarding our world in the sense of "I will make all of My goodness pass before you" (v. 19), but a person clothed in a physical body cannot grasp Hashem's physical attributes. Moshe grasped most of what there was to know about the absence of Hashem's attributes. He knew and understood everything that is not Divine. In this manner, he reached the exalted level of being acquainted with Hashem's "back."

Akeidah illustrates this explanation with a parable from *Moreh Nevuchim* 60:1. Some seafarers wished to investigate the nature of the ship in which they were traveling, without being able to see it from the outside. One grasped that the ship was not connected to the Earth, another that the ship is not a globe, a third that it is inanimate, a fourth that it is not concave and so on. By studying what the ship was not, they were eventually able to deduce everything humanly deducible about the ship. What was left to know? Only to see it and to know what it is. This they could not do, for all were inside the ship. They could see what the ship was not, just as Moshe could see Hashem's "back."

The philosophical works also elaborate on the concept of *tzimtzum* — "self-contraction."

Toldos Yaakov Yosef (Parshas Va'eschanan) states:

> I heard from my teachers that our world, and every other world, is created through *tzimtzum*, for the Divine Light contracts itself to human dimensions so that the inhabitants of that world can receive that light and can grasp its greatness, each according to his own understanding.

According to *Malbim*, Moshe wished to know what caused this process, but that was denied him. Hashem placed him at the boundary between the physical world and Heaven to see the transition point: "I will put you in a cleft of the rock" (*Sh'mos* 33:22). This is knowledge no mortal man can grasp. Yet, Moshe grasped it. Even so, He saw only Hashem's "back," i.e., what followed from Hashem's existence, but not Hashem's essence itself.

⮬ Why Do the Righteous Suffer?

Chazal (*Berachos* 7) state that Moshe wished to know why there are righteous people who suffer, and wicked people who seem to be rewarded. The *tanna'im* argue over the results of his query. R' Meir holds he received no answer, while R' Yehoshua holds he did. R' Samson Raphael Hirsch suggests the novel thought that the two were not arguing. Hashem told Moshe that no mortal man can ever know who is righteous and who is wicked, what is good and what is bad: "Behold, there is a place by Me, and you shall stand by a rock" (*Sh'mos* 33:21). Hashem was saying, "Only if you stand alongside Me and investigate the world by My standards will you understand." It turns out that while Hashem did answer Moshe, in practical terms Moshe remained ignorant of the reason, for he remained limited by his humanness.

By such means does the author of *Kanfei Nesharim* explain the verse, "You will not be able to see My face" (v. 20). This is not a negative utterance. Rather, Hashem, having told Moshe all, now informed him of one more fact: that no man can have absolute knowledge of Hashem.

Chafetz Chaim offers a telling parable in this regard. A *Shabbos* guest noticed how the *shammas* distributed honors to members seated all over his host's synagogue. Puzzled, he asked the *shammas* why he did not distribute the honors in a more orderly fashion. The *shammas* answered, "How do you know there is no order to my system? What do you know about our synagogue anyway? Do you know who was honored in previous weeks?" This is just what Hashem told Moshe. "You ask Me why the righteous suffer and the wicked enjoy reward. Yet, do you really know when reward begins and when it ends? Do you have any idea what was yesterday? Do you have any idea of what events happened in the past, and who the righteous and evil were in former incarnations?"

Everything we see, says *Chasam Sofer*, we see vaguely. A person does not know beforehand what present events will lead to in the future, as is demonstrated by the miracle of Purim. "You shall see My back" (*Sh'mos* 33:23) can be figuratively read, "You shall see My ending." Only in the end do we grasp the purpose of any act. "My front shall not be seen," i.e., we cannot know the reason for an event "up front" before its conclusion.

Vayakhel – ויקהל

I.

Contributions for the Building of the Mishkan

our *parashios*, *Terumah*, *Tetzaveh*, *Vayakhel* and *Pekudei*, deal with the construction of the *Mishkan* (Tabernacle) and its vessels. The Lubavitcher Rebbe (*Sichos*, 5721) deals at length with the differences between each *parashah*. In essence, he says, we find here an ordered sequence of events leading up to a flow of Divine inspiration to the Jewish people. In *Terumah* and *Tetzaveh*, we read of Hashem's command for the fashioning of the *Mishkan*, its vessels and the priestly garb. This is אִתְעָרוּתָא דִּלְעֵילָה — excitation from above. It is followed by אִתְעָרוּתָא דִּלְתַּתָּא — excitation from below, in *Parashas Vayakhel*, where the commands are channeled through Moshe to the Jewish people and executed by them. Finally comes the actual "flow," the supreme emanation of Divine Light from Heaven to earth: "Hashem's glory filled the *Mishkan*" (*Sh'mos* 40:34).

Let us follow the holy and majestic construction of the *Mishkan*, the last step before the spiritual climax, as revealed to us in our *parashah*.

◄§ Contribution of the Spirit

The language used in this *parashah* holds the key to a vast storehouse of ideas on the concept of generosity, the basis for the construction of the *Mishkan*.

Various commentaries struggle to understand the verse, "Take from among you an offering to Hashem. Whoever is generous of heart shall bring the offering of Hashem" (v. 35:5). Here, the first half seems to imply an obligation, whereas the second half implies a freewill contribution. Later we find repetitiveness: "And they came, everyone whose heart stirred him up, and everyone whose spirit made him willing, and they brought Hashem's offering" (v. 21).

Regarding verse 5 above, *Ramban* considers the text entirely uniform. Our *parashah* deals exclusively with a voluntary offering, whereas the compulsory half shekel is dealt with elsewhere. On a kabbalistic note, *Ramban* explains the second half of the verse as referring to a Divine "offering" to the Jewish people in return for the offering they make to Hashem: "Whoever is generous shall bring the offering from Hashem." Hashem sheds His light upon Israel in return for their generosity. As for the repetitiveness of verse 21 ("everyone whose heart stirred him up, and everyone whose spirit made him willing"), *Ramban* states that the expression "everyone whose heart stirred him up" refers to the wise men and artisans of the Jewish people whose hearts stirred them up to offer technical assistance in executing the work. The Torah defines their offer as a "stirring of the heart," for they were not trained in such work specifically and did not know if they were capable of it. Yet their hearts were filled with longing to put their natural talent to practical use, and it was with this longing that they approached Moshe. Moshe told them that according to Hashem's command, only Betzalel and Eliav were appointed to the operation. Yet, when the offering was completely collected, Moshe put these volunteers, together with the collected funds, at the disposal of Betzalel and Eliav, telling them to oversee the volunteers' work and to supervise the practical application of their talent.

Abarbanel, as well, holds that the selection of candidates to work as artisans was based on nothing more than the eagerness of those candidates themselves, for in Egypt they had had no experience in such work. Whoever's heart was "stirred up" with confidence to attack such work came and presented himself.

By contrast, *Kli Yakar* explains verse 5 as alluding to two distinct collections. "Take from among you" refers to the compulsory half shekel of *Parashas Terumah*, whereas "anyone generous of heart shall bring it" refers to a voluntary offering.

S'forno likewise sees two types of offerings denoted, but explains "Take from among you" as commanding the appointment of officials to collect the two types of offerings, the voluntary one brought by the "generous of heart," and the compulsory one, called an "offering of Hashem."

The Pressburger Gaon (*Sha'arei Simchah*), explaining why two types of collections were made together, says that the one had what the other lacked. The compulsory offering precluded gifts given for ulterior motives, for there was no honor to be gained by giving it. The voluntary offering provided the chance to show generosity and good will, but carried with it the possibility of insincerity, for some people donate money to win glory and honor. Only the two together create avenues for both generosity and sincerity.

Other commentaries understand verse 21, regarding those willing to give donations, as teaching that two types of people brought voluntary offerings.

Or HaChaim states that one kind of donor gives according to his means — "Everyone whose spirit made him willing." The other kind gives beyond his means — "Every man whose spirit stirred him up." To distinguish between them, the Torah adds the word "man" to the latter.

R' Yaakov Tzvi Meklenburg (*HaKesav VeHaKabalah*) views verse 21 as referring to two types of people. The first gives his donation wholeheartedly, without internal struggle. The second one's heart is not a partner to his deed, but he has the spiritual strength to overcome his emotions. The first is the one "whose heart stirred him up," and the second is the one "whose spirit made him willing."

Interestingly, one of the great figures of the *Mussar* movement of the last generation views the gift accompanied by internal struggle as more important than the one given without psychological impediments. R' Dessler, in *Michtav Me'Eliyahu* (vol. 1), explains the words "Take from among you" (*Sh'mos* 35:5) as referring to something taken by force, where the spirit overpowers the body. He quotes R' Yerucham as saying that with every *mitzvah* there is resistance by the Evil Impulse, and this must be overcome. The purpose of *mitzvah* observance is to expose us to this struggle. During the collection for the *Mishkan*, there was fear that the Israelites would give complacently without experiencing any internal resistance. Moshe therefore told them, "Take from among you," i.e., seek out only the element that hinders you. Without a doubt there is an Evil Impulse hidden in your hearts. In giving your donation, you must vanquish that element. Then, your gift will represent a satisfying victory of freewill, and not just the product of an inspired soul.

Other commentaries view the word מֵאִתְּכֶם — "from among you" — as implying devotion of body and soul. *Kli Yakar* interprets "Take from among you" as if we had sacrificed ourselves to Heaven. This situation, he says, exists regarding the poor, for their donation involved tremendous self-sacrifice.

R' Simcha Zisl of Kelm interprets the phrase "Whoever is generous of heart shall bring it" (ibid.) in like manner. In offering one's donation, one must offer one's heart. At the same time, and to the same degree, the Torah stresses the importance of action: "Every wise-hearted man among you shall come and do" (v. 35:10). In the *Mishkan* donations, heart and deed were intertwined. Both were linked to Hashem's command. As the verse concludes, "all that Hashem has commanded" (ibid.). Such "excitation from below" draws forth great emanations from above: "Hashem's glory filled the *Mishkan*" (v. 40:34). As is known, the gold of the *Mishkan* served to atone for the Golden Calf. Yet, greater than the gold itself was the remarkable generosity associated with it, for it emphasized that the holiness of the Jewish people shone even after their sin. This holiness rose up out of the ashes of sin and failure. It filled hearts with great love and powerful longing for spiritual ascent and attachment to Hashem, as expressed through the *Mishkan* contributions. This repentance out of love turned intentional sins into merit and raised the soul from the realm of sin to the throne of glory.

This, according to the kabbalists, is the mystical essence of the word תְּרוּמָה, donation, whose root means "to lift up." The donations to the *Mishkan* raised the Israelites' souls from the lowly level mirrored in "Go descend, for your people have become corrupt" (v. 32:7), returning them once more to their holy origins: "Whoever is generous of heart shall bring the offering of Hashem (תְּרוּמַת ה')" (v. 35:5).

◈§ The Wisdom of Women Builds Her House

All the Israelites, women as well as men, were swept away in a great wave of volunteering. Several times in this *parashah* the Torah stresses that the women took part, bringing their jewelry and spinning the goat wool. This is explained by the commentaries as serving to stress the holiness of the entire House of Israel. The women did not wish to give up their jewelry to the Golden Calf, but eagerly donated it to the *Mishkan*, even preceding their husbands.

We read, "They came, both men and women" (v. 35:22). *Ramban* understands from this that the women outshone the men. The women immediately removed their jewelry, and the men followed after.

Pirkei D'Rebbi Eliezer states that women merited to be joyous at the New Moon and to be absolved from work at that time, because they did not give their jewelry to the Golden Calf. *Da'as Zekeinim MiBa'alei HaTosafos* adds that they merited this because while they gave nothing to the Golden Calf, they gave joyously to the *Mishkan*. This addition is a logical one. In and of itself, the women's failure to give up their rings proves nothing. Perhaps they wished only to hold on to their valuables, as *Rashi* actually explains in *Ki Sisa*. Yet, their eager and joyous donations to the *Mishkan* proved that their failure to give to the Golden Calf was a matter of conscience, not miserliness.

King Shlomo said: "One man among a thousand have I found, but a woman among all those have I not found" (*Koheles* 7:28). *Rabbenu*

Bachya comments that King Shlomo was referring to the Golden Calf, informing us that among those who sinned, there was not one woman. Yet, women played a major role in erecting the *Mishkan*. One commentary explains "They came, both men and women" as meaning that the women accompanied their husbands. They wished to see with their own eyes that this time their husbands would give their jewelry to the *Mishkan* and not the Calf.

By contrast, the author of *Be'er Mayim Chaim* explains that here the Torah is demonstrating the righteousness of the men. The husbands took their wives' jewelry to the *Mishkan* by force, something they had not done with the Calf. With the Golden Calf they were in turmoil, for their love of their jewelry was stronger than their love of the Calf. The only reason they physically removed their wives' jewelry for the Golden Calf was to show that they were giving their wives permission to donate it. Without her husband's permission, a woman has no right to make more than minimal contributions (*Bava Kama*, Ch. 10).

Many deepen or broaden this explanation. R' Yaakov Tzvi Meklenburg in *HaKesav VeHaKabalah* notes that if a husband gives his wife jewelry, or if she brings any from her father's house, neither she nor her husband has the right to give it away. Besides their jewelry, the wives contributed their handiwork too: "All the women who were wise hearted did spin with their hands" (*Sh'mos* 35:25). Here too, by Jewish law, they were forced to receive their husbands' permission, because by law a wife's handiwork belongs to her husband.

Similarly, *Rashi* — commenting on the women spinning with their hands — notes that spinning requires extraordinary (יְתֵרָה) skill. *Yalkut HaUrim* explains that with these words *Rashi* wished to answer why the women did not require their husbands' permission. יְתֵרָה can be interpreted as "extra," i.e., in addition to the work the women did for their husbands. By law, the extra work performed by a woman belongs to her, and she is permitted to contribute it wherever she sees fit.

R' Yehonasan couches the spinning in halachic terms as well. Some of the women were menstrually impure, yet wished to participate in the construction of the *Mishkan*. They therefore did their weaving on the goats, i.e., before they were shorn, because living animals cannot be made impure through touch.

Meshech Chochmah adds that two verses refer to the women's spinning. One reads, "all the women" (v. 26), and the other reads, "every woman" (v. 25). The latter verse refers to the spinning of sky-blue and dark-red wool. Because these can be made impure through touch, not every woman could work with them, hence the use of the singular אִשָּׁה — "woman." Yet, regarding the former verse, which dealt with the spinning of the goat wool, all women could take part, hence the plural נָשִׁים is used. In any event, the women filled a prominent role in the construction of the *Mishkan*.

The Torah mentions women several times in this *parashah*, which serves to exalt and glorify them. The women did not lend a hand to the fashioning of the Golden Calf, but they did help generously with the construction of the *Mishkan*. At the same time, the *parashah* stresses the woman's role as housewife. Female wisdom deals only with one area of expertise, spinning, whereas male wisdom deals with many other areas, such as stone hewing, etc. It is true that *Chazal* state (*Yoma* 66), "There is no wisdom for a woman except at the spinning wheel." Yet, this statement is said only in reference to women studying Torah, a point stressed by Rabbenu Bachya: "From here we see that a woman's wisdom is in spinning, in the speed with which she can handle household chores and in the respect she shows her husband. *Chazal* therefore forbade the teaching of Torah to women."

This division of tasks in no way lessens the women's value as ethical, humane individuals, who withstood the test of the Golden Calf better than the men. The women's innocence saved them from sin. Perhaps because women do not study Torah, they did not seek a license to deviate from what is right and did not stray from the path of the Torah which commanded us not to fashion any statue or graven image. Perhaps this is also why women did not accept the arguments their husbands used regarding the Golden Calf, as explained in *Ki Sisa*. On the other hand, the women's righteousness and generosity stand out in their having volunteered for the work of the *Mishkan* when they required no atonement for the Golden Calf.

Chazal state that "Hashem gave women greater understanding than He gave men." This statement proves that they did not view women as inferior beings. Quite the contrary, they assessed women as being gifted with superior understanding, thus they did not participate in the sin of the Golden Calf. Even so, they designate this understanding as applying to household tasks, with the intention of making the woman the foundation of the family unit, and the mother of the home and family. This direction stems from the outlook and the recognition that women by their very nature are designed for these tasks. This is their purpose and that of their daughters in the world. Whoever sees this as degrading is mistaken. The woman's role is the most exalted and important in Creation. Not in vain does the wise king in *Mishlei* (31:10-31) praise the Jewish woman of valor who employs her wisdom toward exalted ends, for which purpose she was sent down to earth.

We read: "The wisdom of women builds her house" (*Mishlei* 14:1).

The holy house the women erected has stood the Jewish people in good stead from its inception until this very day.

II.

Shabbos and the Mishkan Construction

In *Vayakhel*, *Chazal* find an allusion to the thirty-nine categories of work prohibited on Shabbos. The Torah states: "These are the words which Hashem has commanded us to do" (*Sh'mos* 35:1), and R' Yehudah HaNasi comments (*Shabbos* 97b):

דְּבָרִים — "Words; הַדְּבָרִים — the words; אֵלֶּה הַדְּבָרִים — these are the words" (*Sh'mos* 35:1). This refers to the thirty-nine work prohibitions handed down to Moshe at Sinai. דְּבָרִים, being plural, implies at least two. The prefix ה of הַדְּבָרִים adds one, making three. The numeric value of אֵלֶּה is thirty-six, for a total of thirty-nine.

Paane'ach Raza finds an interesting allusion to this matter from the word לַעֲשֹׂת — "to do" — in the verse. This word is a combination of the letter ל, which is equal to thirty, and the remaining letters form the word תֵּשַׁע, nine. There were thirty-nine categories of work in building the *Mishkan*, and the Israelites were forbidden to perform them on Shabbos.

HaKesav VeHaKabalah offers yet another explanation. Linguistically, the words עֲבוֹדָה and מְלָאכָה differ from each other, although in English both are translated as "work." Any act can be called עֲבוֹדָה, even if it involves no skill, and changes or improves nothing. Such acts include carrying stones, running, bringing clothing to the bathhouse for one's teacher and dressing him — the sort of acts performed by servants.

By contrast, מְלָאכָה applies only where change is effected for the purpose of improvement. Such acts include building, destroying in order to rebuild and erasing in order to write. Study and knowledge must precede מְלָאכָה. We must know when and with what tool to work. It includes every means of improving the world Hashem created. Purposeless ruining is not included. Therefore, *Chazal* state that the

Torah forbade only creative work. Hashem's acts during the six days of creation were מְלָאכָה. Such acts are forbidden on Shabbos, "for then Hashem rested from all his מְלָאכָה" (Bereishis 2:3). The Torah prohibited only מְלָאכָה, not עֲבוֹדָה. That is why on Shabbos we may carry tables and chairs on our shoulders, and perform all servile work even if burdensome.

All מְלָאכָה can be shown to advance civilization except for one type, carrying (between private and public domains). Within a private domain we may carry anything, even a table, whereas between domains even something as small as a needle may not be carried. Although this particular מְלָאכָה does not fit the definition given, Hashem still decreed it. Therefore, regarding this act the Talmud asks, "Where does the Torah write that carrying is forbidden?" i.e., where does the Torah define it as a מְלָאכָה to make it forbidden on Shabbos? The Talmud answers: "Moshe commanded . . . let neither man nor woman do any more מְלָאכָה for the holy offering. The people ceased bringing" (Sh'mos 36:6). Now, while "carrying" is considered to be מְלָאכָה, it is the only form of מְלָאכָה that is not also עֲבוֹדָה. Hence, on Shabbos, regarding which we read "Do not do any מְלָאכָה" (v. 20:10), "carrying" is forbidden, but on Yom Tov, regarding which we read: "You shall do no servile work" (Vayikra 23:7), carrying between domains is permitted. Only regarding Yom Kippur do we read: "Do not do any מְלָאכָה" (ibid. 16:29). Likewise, Chazal declared in Rosh HaShanah 29: " 'You shall do no servile work' (ibid. 23:7) — this excludes blowing the shofar and removing bread from the oven. Both involve skill, but since they effect no physical change, they are not מְלָאכָה."

If only עֲבוֹדָה was forbidden, these too would be forbidden, but since מְלָאכָה is mentioned, they are not forbidden.

⋅§ Shabbos: Atonement for the Calf

The thirty-nine categories of work involved in building the Mishkan were forbidden on Shabbos. According to the commentaries, the connection between the Mishkan and Shabbos expressed in our parashah is an atonement for the sin of the Golden Calf. We read: "These are the things which Hashem has commanded us לַעֲשׂת to do" (Sh'mos 35:1), and Or HaChaim interprets לַעֲשׂת as "to rectify." We also read: "Happy is the man who does this" (Yeshayahu 56:2), and Chazal comment that if someone keeps Shabbos properly, even if he worships idols like the generation of Enosh, he will be forgiven. This is why the discussion of Shabbos immediately follows the chapter dealing with the atonement for the Golden Calf.

R' Zalman Sorotzkin expands this idea in his *Oznayim LaTorah*. Shabbos deepens our faith in the God of the universe, Who renews Heaven and earth. It serves to uproot the mistaken belief that Hashem had any Divine partner in Creation, expressed by the Israelites' words: "These are your gods, O Israel, who took you out of Egypt" (*Sh'mos* 32:8). Israel also sinned in viewing Hashem concretely: "These are your gods." Because of these sins, they were commanded to build the *Mishkan*, which concentrates Hashem's holiness in a set place, and to keep Shabbos, which concentrates holiness in a set time. The time-oriented holiness of Shabbos takes precedence over the space-oriented holiness of the *Mishkan*, for time was sanctified, i.e., Shabbos already existed, even before the world was created. One may not say that since we are here commanded about a holy place, which is holy for all times, that one is thereby exempt from the holiness of time. The Torah shows us that such a belief is not valid, by mentioning the holiness of Shabbos before that of the *Mishkan*.

This is actually a Chassidic idea, quoted by *Sefas Emes*. Shabbos is a time offering to Hashem, the *Mishkan* is a space offering, and the *kohanim* and the wise hearted are a human offering. All three are interwoven together in our *parashah* to sanctify the House of Israel and atone for their sins.

◆§ Building the Mishkan Does Not Take Precedence over Shabbos

Rashi states that *Vayakhel's* warning about Shabbos (35:1-3) precedes the section on the *Mishkan* to teach that the building of the *Mishkan* does not take precedence over Shabbos. Now, in *Parashas Kedoshim* we read: "Let every man fear his mother and father, and keep My Shabboss" (*Vayikra* 19:3), and *Rashi* comments, "If your father tells you to profane Shabbos, do not listen to him." In other words, in *Kedoshim*, the same point is made without the Torah needing to mention Shabbos first. Why does *Rashi* say that the Torah needed to do so here?

Kli Yakar answers this. To show that Shabbos takes precedence, it is placed first, but in *Kedoshim*, as the Torah uses the plural, "and (you — plural) keep My Shabboss," we learn that both a man and his father must keep Shabbos. The deduction is as follows: The Torah clause begins in the singular, "Let every man," and concludes in the plural, "fear (תִּירָאוּ — the plural form of the verb) his father and mother", to teach us that this rule applies to both men and women. The Torah needs to tell us that this rule applies to women as well, because otherwise one might have thought that as a married woman is now under the jurisdiction of her husband, the rule to honor her parents would no longer apply. Thus the use of the plural teaches us that honoring one's parents applies to women as well. This explanation does not, however, explain the plural use in the second part of the verse: "and you (plural) shall observe my Shabboss," where we would have had no logical reason to exclude women from Shabbos observance. From this use of the plural we deduce that both you and your father are required to observe Shabbos.

Similarly, we find in *Mechilta*:

> Why are we admonished about Shabbos in this *parashah* (35:1-2)? It is because "Let them make Me a sanctuary" (*Sh'mos* 25:8) implies that the construction of the *Mishkan* must continue on Shabbos. Logically, if the Temple service, which was made possible only by the construction of the *Mishkan*, takes precedence over Shabbos, surely the construction of the *Mishkan* itself should take precedence over Shabbos. The Torah therefore warns us that this is not so.

R' Yosef Tzvi Dushinsky questions the need for this lesson here when *Rashi* in *Parashas Ki Sisa* has already commented on the verse, "You must still keep My Shabboss" (v. 31:13) — "Despite your eagerness regarding the Temple service, do not let it take precedence over Shabbos." Furthermore, the tentative argument for Temple construction taking precedence over Shabbos was faulty to begin with. The only reason Temple offerings take precedence over Shabbos is that they provide atonement. Building the *Mishkan* is different, however, for this is but a preliminary step to atonement. R' Dushinsky answers the question by means of a point made earlier. The donations to the *Mishkan* were themselves an atonement for the Golden Calf, and hence were offerings. One might therefore think they would take precedence over Shabbos like any other offering. We therefore require the deduction from the verse in *Vayakhel* that the building of the *Mishkan* does not take precedence over Shabbos.

As for the question of why this lesson could not be learned from *Ki Sisa*, that verse preceded the incident of the Golden Calf and the Temple contributions were not yet considered to be an atonement.

What was the law regarding anyone who engaged in building the *Mishkan* on Shabbos? *Likutei Basar Likutei* brings a view that while a death sentence would be incurred, it would be one ordained by Heaven, and not one which an earthly court could impose. This is deduced as follows: We read here, "Whoever does work on it (i.e., Shabbos) shall be put to death (יוּמָת)" (Sh'mos 35:2), whereas, regarding the death sentence incurred in human courts we read, "he shall surely be put to death (מוֹת יוּמָת)."

R' Yehonasan Eybeschutz, on the other hand, states the opposite. יוּמָת — "he shall be put to death" — serves to teach that the individual who builds the Mishkan on Shabbos incurs death here on earth, yet still has a portion in Heaven. Ultimately, his intentions were for the sake of Heaven, for he sought to build the Mishkan. By contrast, wherever we read מוֹת יוּמָת — "he shall surely be put to death" — it means death both on earth and in Heaven.

R' Eliyahu Mizrachi (following the lead of Tosafos and others) questions Rashi's previously quoted words. Why should we require a special verse to teach that building the Mishkan does not take precedence over Shabbos? After all, the former is only a positive commandment and Shabbos is both a positive and a negative commandment, and how could we think that building the Mishkan could take precedence? Different commentaries offer various answers, of which we shall mention a few.

Yismach Moshe answers by suggesting that the positive commandment (in addition to the negative commandment) that we have prohibiting Shabbos work is in reality a negative commandment. Hence the prohibition is but a single negative commandment, in two different forms, as it were. One would therefore think that the halachah requiring building the Mishkan should take precedence over the prohibition of working on Shabbos, in accordance with the principle that a positive commandment takes precedence over a negative commandment, and one should thus be permitted to build the Mishkan even on Shabbos.

Divrei Shaul answers quoting the grammarian R' Zalman Henna: Any verb in the Torah starting with the letter ת applies both to men and to women. In accordance with this, the Mishkan construction, regarding which we find the word תַּעֲשֶׂה — "You shall do" — should apply to both sexes, and indeed we find, "They came, both men and women" (Sh'mos 35:22). Tosafos on Kiddushin 34 notes that R' Yosef of Eretz Yisrael raised the following hypothesis (which he subsequently rejected): Since time-bound positive mitzvos do not apply to women, therefore time-bound mitzvos which have both positive and negative aspects should be considered, with regard to women, as simple negative mitzvos. Now, the construction of the Mishkan was a positive commandment that applied to all, including women. Shabbos, however, has both a positive and negative commandment, but only the negative commandment applies to women. One might think, therefore, that women would be able to engage in the construction of the *Mishkan*, even on Shabbos. The Torah therefore states: "Whoever does work on it shall be put to death," letting us know that any negative prohibition carrying a death penalty cannot be thrust aside by a positive commandment; hence women are also forbidden from constructing the *Mishkan* on Shabbos.

While the previous answer serves chiefly to sharpen our wits, *Paane'ach Raza* answers in a more straightforward manner. The whole idea that a positive commandment cannot take precedence over a negative and a positive commandment comes from the fact that the *Mishkan* construction does not take precedence over Shabbos. Without this very case, we would not know this principle. This answer is not too satisfactory. From logic alone we would understand that one positive commandment cannot take precedence over a positive and negative commandment combined.

A more acceptable explanation appears in *Raza Deme'ir*, the commentary on *Paane'ach Raza*. The Talmud in *Bava Metzia* 32 states: Because honoring one's parents has been compared in importance to honoring Hashem, one might have thought that it would take precedence over any action which involves both a positive and negative commandment. And if this is true about honoring one's parents, it should be all the more true with honoring Hashem. And we know that Hashem Himself is honored in the building of the *Mikdash*, as it states: "They shall make for Me a sanctuary and I shall dwell among them" (*Sh'mos* 25:8). One would therefore think that the *Mishkan* may be built on Shabbos, and that is why the Torah had to tell us differently.

⊷§ Six Days Shall Work Be Done

R' Aharon Levin of Reisha (*HaDrash VeHaIyun*) applies the present discussion to our outlook on life. He notes that wherever the Torah warns us about Shabbos observance, it first says, "for six days, work shall be done." Such a pattern appears here, and in *Yisro*, *Va'eschanan*, *Ki Sisa* and *Emor*. In accordance with this, it stands to reason that working for six days each week is a duty. *Chazal* state in *Avos* (Ch. 1), "Love work," and in the *Yerushalmi Kiddushin*: " 'Choose life' (*Devarim* 30:19): This refers to having a trade." *Sifri* also states: " 'Hashem your God shall bless you in all you do' (ibid. 15:18). How do we know this does not apply if we sit idle? From the words, 'In all you do.' "

Chazal abound with utterances in praise of those who support themselves by their own labors. When the Torah commanded us to rest on Shabbos, it wished to alert us to this. Shabbos is a time for rest, but one should not sit idly with hands folded all week. Hashem said, "Behold, I will rain bread for you from Heaven" (Sh'mos 16:4), but with one condition: that the people go out and collect a certain portion every day. Just because one's food falls from Heaven does not mean he must remain helpless. Rather, he must do his share and be a partner in Creation.

Other commentaries explain this in an opposing fashion. The verse reads: "Six days shall work be done," rather than "shall you do work." The passive refers to work done for you by others. By contrast, in *Yisro* and *Va'eschanan* we find, "You shall do work." Moreover, here, as well as in *Ki Sisa* and in *Emor*, Shabbos is called "שַׁבַּת שַׁבָּתוֹן — a Sabbath of Sabbaths" — whereas in *Yisro* and *Va'eschanan* it is called simply "Sabbath." Various commentaries offer an explanation meant to sharpen our wits. They begin with a quote from *Chazal*: When the Jewish people perform Hashem's will, their work is performed by others: "Strangers shall rise and herd your flocks" (*Yeshayahu* 61:5). When the Israelites do not perform Hashem's will, they perform their own work. Our *parashah*, as well as *Ki Sisa* and *Emor*, where the passive form "shall be done" is employed, which refers to our work being performed by others, surely deals with a situation in which Hashem's will is being performed. Then it is Shabbos the entire week, for we rest from our work, and on Shabbos it is "Shabbos of Shabboss." *Yisro* and *Va'eschanan*, on the other hand, which say, "You shall do work," refer to us doing our own work ourselves. Then, the seventh day is called "Shabbos," and the weekdays are days of activity. This explanation is creative, but it is hard to imagine that the Ten Commandments were addressed to people who did not perform Hashem's will, and who therefore had to perform their own work. In any event, the various attitudes of the commentaries to work and labor are reflected in these explanations.

What R' Aharon Levin views as a command to work and toil, others view in just the opposite manner. R' Aharon Levin's view of שַׁבַּת שַׁבָּתוֹן differs as well. He sees it as implying not an enhanced Shabbos, but a diminished one, when one does not work the whole week. This is based upon *Radak* (*II Melachim* 18:4), who states that certain suffixes act as diminutives. Thus a small נָחָשׁ, snake, is called a נְחֻשְׁתָּן, and the pupil of the eye is called אִישׁוֹן because it reflects the image of a small אִישׁ, man. Similarly, שַׁבָּתוֹן is a diminutive form of שַׁבָּת.

According to *Chazal*, שַׁבָּתוֹן implies the encroachment of the profane upon the holy. Whenever a person does his own work all week, Shabbos is called שַׁבָּת. By contrast, wherever a man's work is done by others, Shabbos is merely שַׁבָּתוֹן.

This controversy regarding the importance of physical toil and activity is present in all rabbinic discussions up to the present day. The various views find expression in the interpretations of the commentaries on our *parashah*, and in countless other places as well.

Or HaChaim states that the mention of weekday work in the context of Shabbos serves to stress that if Shabbos is preserved properly, our work will be performed automatically during the week.

R' Chaim Vital, on the other hand (*Eitz HaDa'as Tov*), reminds us that *Chazal* said, "Torah study combined with work is a fine thing," and "Any Torah not accompanied by work ultimately leads to idleness." When the Torah said, "Six days shall you work," it meant that for six days it is proper to work towards supporting one's wife and children. Now one might say, "If so, let me work on Shabbos as well so I can support myself from my own labor." Therefore, the Torah said, "The seventh day shall be holy for you" (*Sh'mos* 35:2). Shabbos must be devoted only to Torah study, which is called "holy".

III.

Hashem's Selection of Betzalel

ayakhel is one of the few Torah portions with an explicitly positive attitude toward professional skill and artistic talent, as expressed in the enumeration of Betzalel's virtues. True, Betzalel did not advance by his own efforts, but through a "Divine spirit" which filled him so he could accomplish a set goal.

According to *Chazal* in *Sanhedrin*, Betzalel was only thirteen years old at the time. At such an age, he could not have attained his wondrous expertise unless Heaven had blessed him at birth with a brilliant mind, capable of absorbing everything (R' Eliyahu Mizrachi questions Betzalel's being so young, and his question is that of *Chazal* in *Sanhedrin* 69). Yet, the fact that the man designated for the exalted mission of constructing the *Mishkan* was prepared beforehand with these artistic and professional talents, proves that these talents have value in day to day life, and must be viewed as a Divine gift.

Moshe's words in verses 35:30-35 are quite similar to what precedes them in verses 31:2-5, where Hashem stresses the importance of Betzalel's virtues. Here Moshe simply passes on Hashem's words to the

Israelites. However, one virtue is added to those listed above: Betzalel is competent to teach, to pass on his knowledge to others.

Let us address each of Betzalel's virtues, as viewed by the commentaries. The commentaries contrast Hashem's words: "Observe! I have selected Betzalel" (v. 31:2), with those of Moshe here: "Observe! Hashem has selected Betzalel" (v. 35:30). The latter seem to hint at conflict, as if there are people who doubt he was selected, and must be convinced. It is also interesting that in introducing Betzalel, the Torah mentions his father and grandfather, Uri and Chur, whereas regarding Oholiav, only his father, Achisamach, is mentioned.

◄§ Observe! Hashem Has Selected Betzalel

Ramban interprets the phrase "Observe! Hashem has selected Betzalel" (v. 35:30) as expressing admiration. Hashem has alerted Moshe to an unusual phenomenon. "Observe this wonder," Hashem says. Here is remarkable talent revealed, destined from birth to construct the *Mishkan*: "Before I formed you in the belly I knew you, and before you came out of the womb I sanctified you" (*Yirmiyahu* 1:5). Besides a lofty knowledge of the secrets of creation, Betzalel was blessed with a broad knowledge of the disciplines of his times, remarkable when one takes into account the circumstances in which the nation lived: The Israelites in Egypt slaved with bricks and mortar. They did not learn how to work with silver, gold or precious gems, never having seen them. It is therefore remarkable that among them was found a man who was a master artisan of silver, gold, wood, stone, embroidery and weaving. Even among people who have studied from accomplished artisans, one will never find a man skilled in all these areas, and the Israelites had spent their lives in mud and mire. Where would they have mastered such precise disciplines?

S'forno interprets the verse similarly. Hashem informs Moshe that no simple craftsman stands before him, but someone who has been readied for the task by means of Divine inspiration: "An essential element of the work in the Sanctuary was that it be performed by one chosen by Hashem, a master of his field, so that Hashem's word could be carried out."

The Rogatchover Gaon (*Tsofnas Paane'ach*) explains the verse, "I have filled him with the spirit of Hashem" (*Sh'mos* 31:3), along similar lines. This verse is Hashem's support for the idea that work which no one else is capable of performing should be done by Betzalel, whose talents make him capable.

The Torah states, "In whom Hashem put wisdom and understanding to know how to perform all manner of work for the service of the Sanctuary" (*Sh'mos* 36:1). *Be'er Mayim Chayim* explains this as emphasizing that the work was earmarked exclusively for a holy, not a secular, purpose.

According to the Rogatchover Gaon, Betzalel lost all his wisdom once the *Mishkan* construction was complete. Oholiav, by contrast, was an artisan to begin with, and he passed his trade on to his sons (*Eruvin* 16). Betzalel was an artisan through Divine inspiration, for a specific purpose. Once that purpose was achieved, his inspiration ceased. On this basis, the Rogatchover Gaon suggests a novel idea. Generally, if an artisan finds an object and employs his talents to enhance it, he can lay claim to it. This did not apply to Betzalel, however, because his talent was an unnatural gift of Hashem. It was not his to use for his own purposes.

Abarbanel interprets both announcements of Betzalel's selection (vs. 31:2 and 35:30) as meant to authoritatively remove all doubts, including those of Moshe, about Betzalel's position. With so many volunteers, Moshe did not know who would be chosen to fashion the *Mishkan* vessels, and the Israelites had their own preferences. Some thought Oholiav was more worthy. Others wondered whether any Jew could be fit for such work. Having spent so much of their lives with bricks and mortar, they were unaccustomed to handicraft. Still others grumbled that Moshe had chosen only members of his own family for chief positions, even handing over the silver of the *Mishkan* to the grandson of his sister Miriam. Hashem's decisive announcement of Betzalel's name, and that of his father and grandfather, quelled all doubts. His specifying Betzalel's special virtues served notice that Betzalel was His choice for this exalted task. Moshe accomplished the same later on when he passed Hashem's words on to the Israelites. The word "Observe!" is a decisive expression. Hashem's message was not open to misunderstanding. It was Betzalel He had chosen.

According to *Midrash Rabbah*, Hashem's choice of Betzalel was based on the outstanding self-sacrifice of his grandfather, Chur, when he interceded at the Golden Calf incident. The Torah details Betzalel's lineage going back to his grandfather to stress this innate family quality. *Chazal* compare this to the case of a king whose troops rebel against him, while his top general remains at his side. When the rebellion is quelled, the king will make the general's children dukes and governors. Not simply a reward, this is the natural outcome of the grandson's guarding the great flame lit by his grandfather. This fire gave birth to the Divine spirit in Betzalel's heart so he could perform the work of the *Mishkan*.

Sometimes a person sacrifices himself for a cause without seeing the outcome of his sacrifice. Yet, says R' Yaakov of Alexander (*Beis Yaakov*), sometimes, after several generations, this flame burns anew, and achieves the object for which the person at the head of the chain sacrificed himself. Betzalel drew his holiness from two parts of his family tree that had excelled in self-sacrifice. First, he was from the tribe of Yehudah, which at the splitting of the sea jumped into the water before any other tribe. Second, he was the grandson of Chur. These virtues, says *Meshech Chochmah*, prepared him to serve Hashem with self-sacrifice, subjugating his heart to serve Hashem without second thoughts.

The Sefardic sage Ya'avetz states that during the Spanish Inquisition, it was not the intellectually outstanding who withstood the test, but those of pure faith. Betzalel was chosen because his grandfather had sacrificed his life to sanctify Hashem's name. The self-sacrifice of Betzalel's family contributed to the atonement inherent in the *Mishkan*'s construction. Just as its gold atoned for the gold of the Calf, transforming an exhibit for the prosecution into an exhibit for the defense, so too did having a grandson of Chur build the *Mishkan* achieve the same end.

The *Mishkan* and its gold, states R' Yaakov Etlinger, atone for the sin of the Calf. Yet, Chur's murder required atonement as well. This was accomplished by having the victim's grandson be the one to build the *Mishkan*, and thus defend the accused (*Minchas Ani*).

This idea is emphasized in the Midrash:

> "Observe! Hashem has selected Betzalel": This verse is in harmony with "I will heal their backsliding; I will love them freely" (*Hoshea* 14:5). First we read "The Israelites brought a freewill offering to Hashem" (v. 35:29), and then "Hashem has selected Betzalel." Hashem said to Moshe, "When the Israelites fashioned the Calf, Aaron asked them to bring him their wives' earrings, and they did so (*Sh'mos* 32:2). When they built the *Mishkan*, donations were solicited as well, and we read: "The generous of heart brought bracelets and earrings" (v. 35:22). With earrings did they sin, and with earrings did they find atonement. The Holy Spirit cries out, "It shall come to pass that instead of that which was said to them, 'You are not My people,' it shall be said to them, 'You are the sons of the living God' " (*Hoshea* 2:1).

This Midrash shows that even Betzalel's selection was itself a means of rectifying the sin of the Calf. It also explains why the Torah mentions his grandfather Chur.

❧ He filled Him with the Spirit of Hashem, with Wisdom, Understanding and Knowledge

Numerous virtues and talents are ascribed to Betzalel and Oholiav. Ibn Ezra, quoting "the Gaon," states that their selection had a tribal basis as well. Betzalel was from Yehudah, and Oholiav from Dan, two tribes described by Yaakov and Moshe as lions. Since the *Beis HaMikdash*, according to *Chazal*, was shaped like a lion, these two tribes were chosen to build the *Mishkan*, the forerunner of the *Beis HaMikdash*.

Ibn Ezra, though, rejects this explanation. In his opinion, they were selected for this mission only because they were the best of the artisans. Betzalel knew science, mathematics, engineering, and all kabbalistic knowledge involving the soul and creation. In his breadth of knowledge he surpassed all his contemporaries. Many wise men, says Ibn Ezra, do not know even one craft. Betzalel could devise plans like no other artisan. Unlike some artisans, who are experts with gold but not silver, wood but not stone, Betzalel was a master of them all. Beyond that, he knew how to teach this to others.

Abarbanel points to Betzalel's practical knowledge. When wise men concentrate on abstract disciplines, their grasp of the practical world weakens and they become "fools in worldly matters." This is why the prophet Yeshayahu testified that regarding *Mashiach*, "The spirit of Hashem shall rest upon him, a spirit of wisdom and understanding" (*Yeshayahu* 11:2), i.e., a combination of abstract wisdom and practical understanding. Such competence is rare in our world, yet Betzalel shone in this regard, attaining mastery even in the kabbalistic secrets of creation. Beside all this, Betzalel knew every craft, with a skill lacking to other abstract thinkers: "As the wise philosopher said, 'Those blessed with great intelligence have poor motor skills.' Hence, most wise men are physically awkward, and among them are found no fast and efficient artisans."

The Torah (*Sh'mos* 31:2) lists all of Betzalel's talents: (a) a Divine spirit, (b) wisdom, (c) understanding, (d) knowledge, (e) mastery of all crafts, (f) talent at conceiving designs for working with gold, silver and copper, (g) cutting stones to be set, (h) carpentry, (i) all other skilled work, (j) teaching skills. Every one of his talents has practical application, and is interpreted by the *rishonim* and *acharonim* according to their understanding and inclinations. *Rashi* explains each one: wisdom: what one learns from others; understanding: what one deduces himself from things he has learned; knowledge: prophetic inspiration; to conceive designs: skilled weaving; cutting: skilled stone cutting; to be set: to fit each stone fully in its setting, tailoring the setting to the dimensions of the stone.

R' Sa'adiah Gaon interprets "wisdom" as does *Rashi*, but he explains "understanding" as the knowledge one acquires on one's own and "knowledge" as the empirical knowledge one attains from research and investigation.

Numerous interpretations are offered of these traits, ranging from the surface level to the mystical, and incorporating all science and knowledge.

Netziv (Haamek Davar) views the three preparatory stages of "wisdom, understanding and knowledge," as cornerstones in building the world: "Hashem by wisdom founded the earth; by understanding established the Heavens; by His knowledge the depths were broken up" (*Mishlei* 3:19-20). Later in *Mishlei* these three elements reappear as foundations of the "house:" "Through wisdom a house is built; by understanding it is established; by knowledge are the chambers filled" (ibid. 24:3-4).

Hashem commanded that the *Mishkan* and Temples be constructed of materials from which the world is composed. *Chazal* had this in mind when they said that Betzalel knew how to manipulate the letters in the words from which Hashem created Heaven and earth, to create other things. "Not only man and his world, but the *Mishkan* and its vessels are a shadow of the Divine." So says *Malbim*, following the path of the kabbalists. This is why Hashem called on Betzalel, whose name means "in the shadow of Hashem." Betzalel knew how to combine the letters from Hashem's commands during the Creation, and to use them to enter the spirit world. We read "I have filled him with a spirit of Hashem, with wisdom" (*Sh'mos* 31:3), and this refers to prophecy and *ruach hakodesh*. "To conceive designs" means to coordinate one's plans here on earth with those conceived in Heaven.

"And I, behold, have given with him Oholiav" (ibid. v. 6). Betzalel was so blessed with wisdom that it could overflow to others. Sometimes a man is Divinely influenced so that he becomes wise or the Presence rests upon him. Yet other times he is Divinely inspired so that he can inspire others: "Hashem appeared again in Shiloh, for He revealed Himself to Shmuel in Shiloh" (*I Shmuel* 3:21). The overflow of Betzalel's wisdom went to Oholiav as well. Later the fountain increased its flow into the tributaries, and "the flocks were watered."

‌‌ Hashem Made Him Able to Teach

Chassidic literature finds still other virtues in Betzalel's personality, in accordance with the pathways of the great lights of Chassidism. "To conceive designs:" Betzalel knew the thoughts of every single Israelite donor when the person contributed his or her gift, and he used each contribution for something suitable in terms of the thoughts and intent of the donor. A contribution made with sincerity was earmarked for the Ark. A contribution based on ulterior motives was earmarked for the sockets, etc.

Sefas Emes interprets "to make all manner of artistic work" (*Sh'mos* 35:33), as meaning that in the case of Betzalel, there was nothing which interrupted between his thoughts and his deeds. Rather, his thoughts and deeds were one, all holy to Hashem.

"Hashem made him able to teach" (v. 35:34). One more outstanding virtue is mentioned. As *Chasam Sofer* notes, some people, despite their great wisdom, are not good teachers. The ability to teach is a unique gift.

Or HaChaim, as well, states that being able to share one's wisdom with others is a special gift. Yet, to do so one needs not only talent, but a generous spirit. Not everyone can teach. Some wise men are on so high a plane that they cannot descend to the people to speak their language.

Of King Shlomo we read, "More than a wise man, Shlomo was a wise teacher." (*Koheles* 12:9). In his *Tosefes Berachah*, R' Baruch Epstein explains this verse as praise of King Shlomo for his skill in teaching the people what he had learned, just as the Torah here praises Betzalel.

Betzalel had every gift. He was the paragon of virtue and perfection. *Ramban* defined him well in calling him "an inspiring wonder," who both understood man and was a master of science and philosophy. "Observe! Hashem has selected Betzalel." What a rare wonder he must have been!

Pekudei – פְקוּדֵי

I.

The Mishkan Audit

All the commentaries seek to explain the beginning of this *parashah*, which on the surface seems unclear. The word פְקוּדֵי, meaning "account," refers to the account taken of how the donated gold, silver and copper were used in building the *Mishkan*. In listing the amounts collected of silver and gold, the verses (38:25-31) also specify for what they were used. Yet in counting the gold (v. 24), no mention is made of how the gold was used.

The commentaries are also puzzled by the *Mishkan's* being labeled מִשְׁכַּן הָעֵדֻת — "the *Mishkan* of Testimony" (v. 38:21). Also puzzling is the expression: "the work of the Levites, in the hands of Isamar the son of Aharon the *Kohen* (ibid.). What work is being referred to? Why is only one son of Aharon mentioned, and why are Betzalel and Oholiav omitted? Through excerpts of the commentaries we shall attempt to sketch a picture of the accounting taken in our *parashah*.

Ramban quotes the view of several commentaries that the expression אֵלֶּה פְקוּדֵי, which begins the *parashah*, refers back to *Vayakhel*. In *Vayakhel*, we find details concerning the outer structure, the courtyard and other items listed in *Bamidbar* as being in Isamar's charge. According to this, the words אֵלֶּה פְקוּדֵי do not mean "This is the account," but rather "These were the responsibilities."

Ramban rejects this view. True, the outer structure and courtyard were under Isamar's supervision, but the holy vessels, Altars, Ark and Table were under the supervision of Aharon's son Elazar. Why then does the Torah mention only Isamar, when Elazar's responsibilities were more important? *Ramban* explains that the verse relates to what follows and not to what precedes this section. What follows are details of how the hundred silver talents were used for the sockets, the pillar hooks and their settings and joints, and how the seventy talents of copper were used for the copper altar, its screen and utensils, etc. All these were weighed and handed over to Isamar.

By contrast, no account is given of how the gold was used. Some of this gold, such as that used to coat the boards and bolts, was Isamar's responsibility, and some, like that used for the Ark, the gold Altar and the Ark covering, was Elazar's. As it was not known the exact amount of gold used for plating each of the vessels and boards, the Torah did not quantify this for us. The copper and silver, on the other hand, were given by exact weight, and were entirely in Isamar's charge, except for the copper Altar which was in Elazar's charge. Yet, because the copper Altar was made from the donated copper, it too is mentioned here.

Abarbanel offers a simpler explanation. The Levites, headed by Isamar, were auditors. In every audit there are three essential parties: (a) the one who orders the audit; (b) the auditor; and (c) those being audited, who provide figures. The Torah here mentions all three: (a) "As they were counted according to Moshe's command" (*Sh'mos* 38:21) — Moshe ordered the audit; (b) "by the hand of Isamar" (ibid.) — Isamar was the auditor; (c) "Betzalel ... and Oholiav" (v. 22) — they provided the figures. After this declaration, the audit itself follows.

Malbim follows Abarbanel's view. He adds that the expression "*Mishkan* of Testimony" is used here as proof of the audit's accuracy. The word "testimony" is used because Hashem's presence coming to rest over the *Mishkan* testifies that none of the materials of which the *Mishkan* was composed had been associated with any sin.

Meshech Chochmah holds that the expression "*Mishkan* of Testimony" relates to later in the verse: "the work of the Levites" (v. 38:21). It is true that as *Chazal* say, the *Mishkan* was "testimony" for the Israelites that the sin of the Calf was forgiven. Even so, henceforth the worship would be carried on by the Levites instead of the firstborn.

On the surface, at least, the expression "the work of the Levites" implies that the Levites were in charge of carrying out the audit. This parallels *Ezra* 8, where the Prophet Ezra appointed Levites to handle such responsibilities.

⋙ Gold, Silver and Copper

We have mentioned *Ramban*'s reason why no inventory was taken of the gold the Israelites contributed. R' Yonasan Eybeschutz offers a fine explanation of his own. The silver was collected as a compulsory offering, in which all took part, whereas only great philanthropists contributed gold. Large contributors do not demand an account of how their gift will be used the way small contributors do. Some add that although the copper was not a compulsory offering, it was brought by the stingy or the poor, who demand an accounting.

Abarbanel offers a different view. The copper of Egypt and the east was the finest in existence. This is why those who donated it demanded an accounting.

Pardes Yosef uses *Chazal's* statement that the Ark carried those who carried it. As it was weightless, there was no way to know how heavy was the gold it contained.

All the commentaries strive to explain why there is no account given of the gold vessels. *Meshech Chochmah* answers this. We read here of the "work of the Levites," but find nothing about what was handed over to the *Kohanim.* Later we read of the gold forehead plate, apron and breastplate, and of how the gold was beaten into thin plates, cut into wires, chains, rings and settings. For the present, however, the *Kohanim* had not yet been issued their priestly garments, so the gold is not discussed.

An original explanation, or more properly, moral exposition, of verse 38:21, is offered by S'forno. Unlike the *Batei HaMikdash* and their vessels, which fell into the hands of Babylon and Rome, the *Mishkan* and its vessels never fell into enemy hands. Why is this? Verses 21-22 answer this by stressing four unique virtues of the *Mishkan* which contributed to its longevity: (a) It was the *Mishkan* of Testimony — its tablets were written by Hashem's hand; (b) it was commanded by Moshe — Moshe was the greatest prophet of all times; (c) it was the work of the Levites; and (d) Betzalel ben Uri made all that Hashem commanded Moshe.

In Shlomo's *Beis HaMikdash,* however, the work was performed by non-Jews from Tyre; while in the Second *Beis HaMikdash,* not one of these four conditions was fulfilled. There were no tablets written by Hashem, its construction was at the command of Cyrus and no Levites participated in its construction: "There I found none of the Levites" (*Ezra* 8:15). For these reasons, the *Batei HaMikdash* did not last forever. The Torah informs us of the gold, copper and silver in the *Mishkan* to emphasize that it is not these materials which make the sanctuary last forever, but rather the behavior of Hashem's servants. After all, there was much more silver and gold in the *Batei HaMikdash* than in the *Mishkan,* as we find in *I Melachim,* and in the words of *Chazal.* Even so, the *Batei HaMikdash* did not last, but fell into enemy hands.

The *poskim* (*Bach, Yoreh Deah* 257) derive from this section that even the most trustworthy charity collectors are obliged to give an accounting, just as Moshe did with the contributions to the *Mishkan.* The Midrash calls Moshe "blessed and faithful" because he gave an accounting although he was trusted. We do not put public charity funds in the hands of one man. It is true that Moshe was an exception, serving alone as treasurer, but to place himself above suspicion, he presented his account for others to see: "This is the account of the *Mishkan*, ordered by Moshe." Moshe himself did not take the count. Rather, it was "ordered by Moshe, in the hands of Isamar." Moshe himself asked that an audit be taken. The Midrash concludes, "It was Moshe who requested the audit, not those who had contributed the silver."

Chasam Sofer says that by law Moshe was not bound to give an accounting, for *Chazal* state that "we do not put charity funds in the hands of one man, unless the public accepts him." Without a doubt, the public accepted Moshe as trustworthy. Yet, Moshe still wished to set an example for charity collectors in his wake. He therefore chose Isamar so there would be a second treasurer. Public trust may also explain why Moshe picked not just one, but two artisans, Betzalel and Oholiav (vs. 22-23).

In countless sources *Chazal* deal with the conditions for contributing to the *Beis HaMikdash*, and numerous laws exist regarding this in the halachic literature. The source of all these laws is in *Mishnah Shekalim*, 3:2. There it says that "whoever is assigned to withdraw funds from the *Beis HaMikdash* treasury must not come dressed in clothes in which money can be hidden, lest he later become rich and people say he stole the money from the *Beis HaMikdash* coffers." Just as a Jew must satisfy Hashem's laws, so must he satisfy man's laws as well: "Remain guiltless before Hashem and Israel" (*Bamidbar* 32:22).

Every commentary has something to add about the example set here for charity treasurers, guiding them in the laws of collection and keeping accounts. According to the author of *Panim Yafos*, Oholiav had no special task in the construction of the *Mishkan*. Even so, the Torah emphasizes his presence to teach future generations that a single treasurer must not be in charge of charity funds.

Abarbanel holds that the accounting taken here was not to guard against embezzlement, but to appease those who began to complain that their donations were not being accepted. Moshe sought to prove that enough had been donated to provide for constructing the *Mishkan* and its vessels, and that no more was needed. According to Abarbanel, it must not be suggested that the workers who volunteered their services to the *Mishkan* were suspected of stealing the materials with which they worked.

The rest of the commentaries, however, view the audit as serving to remove suspicion. According to a few, while neither Moshe, Betzalel nor

Oholiav, who were appointed by Hashem, were under suspicion, the workers who had volunteered were. *Kesav Sofer* even uses this idea to explain why there was no accounting of the gold, as only Betzalel and Oholiav dealt with it, and they were free of suspicion. The silver and copper, however, were dealt with by volunteers, and they were asked to give an account.

Chazal in the Midrash take the extreme position that even Moshe was under suspicion. Doubtless, their words are intended to teach us the practical law that even the very greatest among us are obliged to "remain guiltless before Hashem and Israel." No charity collector may handle funds on his own. All must give a detailed accounting of income and expenses.

✑ The Holiness of the Mishkan: A Reflection on Its Donors

In contrast to those commentaries who view the purpose of the account as to remove suspicion, we find other views in the Chassidic and sermonic literature. The holiness of the *Mishkan* came into being because those who had contributed to it were holy persons of pure intent. *Tiferes Shlomo* holds that the sign demonstrating this to be the case was the audit, which came out exact, leaving nothing unaccounted for. By calling this remarkable phenomenon to the Israelites' attention, Moshe showed them that their donations had been accepted willingly, and their own integrity was responsible for the *Mishkan* being sanctified.

The Dubno Magid explains Moshe's intentions regarding the accounting in a simpler fashion. Moshe wished to know each of the donors personally, to ensure that they had all come by their wealth honestly. Otherwise, he would have violated the rule that "money [which had been set aside] for [the purchase of] guilt and sin offerings was not brought into Hashem's house [i.e., used in the construction or repair of the Temple]" (*II Melachim* 12:17). By gathering all the donors together for the audit, Moshe could examine them to determine their character. This is the intention of the Midrash which states, "We do not read, 'The account which Moshe took,' but 'the account ordered by Moshe and taken by Isamar.'" Regarding Moshe we read, "No audit was done of those into whose hands they delivered the money to pay the workmen, for they were trustworthy. Money for guilt or sin offerings was not brought into Hashem's house" (ibid. v. 16). Here *Chazal* state explicitly that the purpose of the account was not to investigate those doing the work, for they were above suspicion. Rather, the account was a means of clarifying the character of the donors and their motives in contributing.

A pleasant idea is suggested by R' Yitzchak of Spinka. The donors wished to have an accounting, not out of suspicion, but out of eagerness to fulfill the *mitzvah* fully, and to be convinced that every penny was being used for the glory of Hashem. Jews, by nature, are not suspicious. At the Golden Calf, they requested no accounting. As *Chazal* state, "When the Israelites were solicited for the *Mishkan*, they contributed, and when they were solicited for the Calf, they contributed as well." Even so, there was a fundamental difference between the two givings. For the *Mishkan*, they demanded an accounting, for they wished to verify that their money was being spent for completely holy purposes. With the Golden Calf, they took no interest in this at all. What did it matter if their money was being stolen? Either way it was money lost. We thus see that their request for an audit was based on pure motives.

◆§ Of the Thousand . . .

"Of the 1,775 shekels he made hooks for the pillars" (*Sh'mos* 38:28). It is a known fact that the musical notes (טְעָמִים) on the Torah provide commentary. The note for the phrase וְאֶת־הָאֶלֶף — "of the thousand" — is *azla geresh*, and the sermonic literature associates this with an exposition of *Chazal* according to which Moshe forgot that 1,775 shekels were meant to be used for the pillar hooks: "Surprised, Moshe feared the Israelites would accuse him of theft. Finally Hashem enlightened him, showing him these shekels being used to make the hooks." The musical notes emphasize this point through accent and melody. The words *azla* and *geresh* mean "leave" and "expelled," implying absence, or in this case, mental omission. As for the tune of this combination, it expresses surprise.

Interestingly, *Midrash Rabbah* speaks of an "irreverent" group of Israelites who suspected Moshe of theft. Verse 33:8, "They stared after Moshe until he had gone into his tent," is interpreted as implying slanderous, scornful speech behind his back. R' Yochanan states that they said, "Happy is she who bore him." R' Chama states that they said, "Observe how obese is his neck." The Midrashic commentaries hold that R' Yochanan and R' Chama differ, with R' Yochanan saying that Moshe was not being scorned but praised. What they find difficult to understand is why *Chazal* refer to those who criticized Moshe, mentioned by R' Chama, as "irreverent" (לֵצָנִים), when they were not simply ridiculing Moshe, but seriously accusing him of becoming rich from the *Mishkan* treasury. Yet, a fine explanation appears in R' Aharon Levin's *HaDrash VeHalyun*: *Chazal* in several places say that the Israelites slandered Moshe, accusing him of nepotism: "Moshe is king, Aharon his brother is the *Kohen Gadol*, Aharon's sons are the assisting *Kohanim*, etc." Even regarding the *Mishkan* construction they found room for gossip over Moshe's appointment of Betzalel, Miriam's grandson. R' Yochanan holds that they said, "Happy is she who bore him," and what he meant was "Happy is anyone born a relative of Moshe." Thus, while both Moshe and Betzalel were accused of theft, there was also irreverent humor over Moshe's supposed nepotism.

II.

The Mishkan:
Unifier of the Jewish People

ver and over again throughout the description of the *Mishkan* construction we find repeated the expression "as Hashem commanded Moshe." R' Yosef Ber of Brisk (*Beis HaLevi*) states that this repetition serves to warn the Israelites not to create unauthorized forms and symbols based on analogies to what Hashem did command. Let them not think that just as they were commanded to make forms for the *Mishkan* service, so may they create new ones of their own.

Chazal stress several times that the *Mishkan* served to atone for the Golden Calf. Recent *darshanim* (homiletical expositors) have explained that the wonderful generosity of the Israelites in donating materials for the *Mishkan* put a stamp of love on their activity, and whoever repents out of love for Hashem will find even his intentional sins transformed to merit. Thus do the *darshanim* explain what Moshe said, according to *Chazal*, when he completed the *Mishkan* construction: "May it be Hashem's will to cause His Presence to rest upon your handiwork." Moshe prayed that even the Israelites' forbidden handiwork would be transformed to merit, and the Divine Presence would rest on all that they did.

One may, however, venture to say that this prayer also alludes to the sin of creating unauthorized forms of worship, as previously explained regarding the verse, "They have turned aside quickly from the path which I commanded them" (Sh'mos 32:8). After the Israelites made all the parts of the Mishkan "as Hashem had commanded," Moshe's blessing was fulfilled, and the Divine Presence came to rest on this work, which had been commanded by Hashem. Even to create unauthorized forms through analogy with existing ones is forbidden, for this ascribes physical traits to Hashem and is as great a sin as idolatry.

R' Meir Simchah of Dvinsk offers a remarkable idea of the same sort. Regarding the fashioning of every item in the Mishkan we read, "He made," yet regarding the Ark we read, "Betzalel made the Ark" (37:1). Why was Betzalel specifically mentioned in this regard? As the Ark was to house the two tablets, there was fear that the Israelites would attribute Divine significance to a mere shape and start to worship the Ark itself, when in fact the Ark was only the Torah's garb. Hashem therefore insisted that the Ark be fashioned by Betzalel, grandson of Chur. Previously Chur had been killed by the Israelites for refusing to treat a mere shape as Divine by making the Golden Calf. Hashem knew that a grandson of Chur would avoid straying from Hashem's intent. In making the Ark, Betzalel would not entertain the fallacious thought that a mere form possessed Divine character, but he would conform to Hashem's commands. Such a person would not do anything bordering on the idolatrous. His work would be carefully planned, pure and free of all blemish and devoid of any intent to create unauthorized physical forms for the worship of Hashem. The wisdom to distinguish between the sacred and the secular, between a holy form of worship and a profane one, was demanded of those who made the Mishkan and its vessels. The single tested means of acquiring this wisdom was total submission to Hashem's command, and the execution of His commands without question or challenge, without making analogies on one's own.

Ikarim, 3:21, explains at length why the two tablets were called tablets of "testimony." Just as the testimony of witnesses must not be distorted to mean something other than what was said, so too, must we not distort Hashem's mitzvos from their simple and clear meaning, neither on the straightforward or the kabbalistic level. Doubtless, every mitzvah contains secrets of profound importance, but our task is to perform the mitzvos as they are. Knowing the philosophical or kabbalistic background of a mitzvah does not empower us to alter our practical performance of it to the least degree, or to transform it into something similar. The foundation of a mitzvah is its simple performance "as Hashem commanded," without straying in action or intent, and without making false analogies. What makes a form of worship legitimate is Hashem's having commanded it.

Eighteen times in our discussion of the *Mishkan* construction do we find the expression, "as Hashem commanded." *Chazal*, in *Yerushalmi*, state that this number corresponds to the eighteen blessings of the *Shemoneh Esrei*. Interestingly, if we count the number of times this expression appears, we find a nineteenth: "Betzalel . . . did all that Hashem commanded Moshe" (*Sh'mos* 38:22). *Rashi* explains that this verse does not relate to Hashem's explicit commands. Rather, it serves to emphasize Betzalel's high spiritual level: Even things his teacher Moshe did not tell him, he intuitively understood just as they were explained to Moshe at Sinai.

Moshe told Betzalel to first make the vessels and then the *Mishkan*. Betzalel said to him, "Normally one first builds a house, and then introduces the furniture." Moshe responded, "Have you been in Hashem's shadow? (בְּצֵל אֵל — a play on Betzalel's name). That is exactly what I heard from Hashem — that the *Mishkan* must be made first and then the vessels."

Kli Yakar wonders where *Rashi* derived that there were discrepancies between what Betzalel did and what Moshe commanded him. Do we not find in both *Vayakhel* and *Ki Sisa* that Moshe commanded explicitly that the *Mishkan* be built before the vessels? Only in *Terumah* do we find the Ark mentioned before the *Mishkan*, and there the Torah is merely listing items in order of importance and not in what order they should be built. *Kli Yakar* offers a simple explanation. The Torah does not say that Moshe provided Betzalel with the order in which to construct the *Mishkan* and its vessels. Moshe gave Betzalel a general command to construct them. Yet Betzalel, on his own initiative, did just what Hashem had told Moshe, and he performed "just as Hashem had commanded Moshe."

One may still ask a question regarding *Kli Yakar's* explanation. Are not *Rashi's* words explicitly stated by R' Shmuel bar Nachmani, quoting R' Yehonasan, in *Berachos* 55a? *Tosafos* asks: "Does not *Parashas Terumah* mention the Ark before the *Mishkan*?" and answers that R' Yehonasan was referring to the command in *Parashas Ki Sisa*: "The Tent of Meeting and the Ark of Testimony" (*Sh'mos* 31:7). According to *Chazal*, Moshe switched the order and said the vessels should be first, whereas Betzalel did as Hashem had commanded Moshe.

We must look more deeply in *Chazal's* words. How do they know that Moshe switched the ordering? Why should he have done so? *Maharsha* attempts to explain that in *Vayakhel* no name is ever explicitly associated with the work. In every case we find only the anonymous "he made," except regarding the Ark, where we find "Betzalel made" (37:1). From this *Chazal* conclude that Betzalel made the Ark after completing the *Mishkan*, in contrast to the command that he had received from Moshe. Yet, *Maharsha's* explanation is problematic. In *Sh'mos Rabbah* 49 the Midrash derives from verse 37:1 exactly the opposite conclusion. There it states that Moshe told Betzalel he should first make the *Mishkan*, yet Betzalel made the Ark first to honor the Torah. The Midrash apparently differs with *Chazal* of *Berachos*, but can two diametrically opposed lessons be learned from one verse?

Maharal in his *Gur Aryeh* on the Torah struggles to understand the differences between what Moshe said and what Betzalel did. In his opinion, the differences are inherent in the difference between Moshe, the spiritual leader, and Betzalel, the technician. Moshe, teacher of Israel, handed over the building of the *Mishkan* in accordance with the spiritual value of each of its items. Using this order, the vessels, used to serve Hashem, precede the *Mishkan* frame, which is just meant to house the vessels. Betzalel, however, carried out the construction in accordance with technical considerations. First the dwelling is built, then the furniture is placed inside.

Turei Zahav, in his *Divrei David*, explains similarly, yet adds: In *Terumah*, Hashem Himself mentioned the vessels before the *Mishkan* because of their spiritual value. In *Ki Sisa* and *Vayakhel*, however, He mentioned the *Mishkan* first, following a technical ordering. In construction, a house is built before the furniture is introduced. Hashem wished to demonstrate to Moshe that Betzalel would manage on his own, and would know what to build first and what to build later, even though the Torah said one thing in one place and another thing elsewhere. When Moshe heard from Betzalel that one generally builds a house before its furniture, he did not hesitate to express his amazement: "Have you been in Hashem's shadow? So was I supposed to tell you." In other words, "Hashem told me to explain the order unclearly, so you could arrive at an understanding yourself. You stood the test and fulfilled Hashem's will."

I believe that *Rashi* was bothered by two questions regarding verse 38:22: "Betzalel did all that Hashem commanded Moshe." First, why did *Yerushalmi* not count this as a nineteenth occurrence of the expression "as Hashem commanded Moshe?" Second, why do we read here "all that Hashem commanded Moshe" when elsewhere the word "all" is missing? These two questions led *Rashi* to follow *Chazal's* lead, and to explain that not only did Betzalel carry out all the work on the *Mishkan* as Hashem had commanded, but he did so in the exact order Hashem had commanded. Now, Moshe did not give Betzalel clear instructions about the order of construction. One time he mentioned the Ark first, and another time the *Mishkan*. Yet, Betzalel, who made the *Mishkan* first, fulfilled Hashem's will even in this. Therefore, Betzalel truly did "all" that Hashem commanded Moshe.

Previously we mentioned *Chazal's* view that Betzalel did something different from what Moshe had told him, making the *Mishkan* before the Ark. In accordance with this, R' Sorotzkin (*Oznayim LaTorah*) explains why specifically regarding the Ark we find "Betzalel made," whereas regarding the other vessels we find simply "he made." After Betzalel told Moshe that the *Mishkan* should be made before the Ark, it seemed as though, God forbid, he was making light of the Ark's dignity. He therefore honored the Ark by making it himself. According to this, however, we would have to find Betzalel's name linked to the Ark cover, Table and Menorah as well, for in *Parashas Terumah*, they too precede the *Mishkan*. Only after Betzalel expressed his opinion did Moshe admit that he was right. Betzalel should, therefore, have had to make them himself to demonstrate that he did not view them lightly.

Ibn Ezra's opinion, in fact, is that the word "he made," said regarding each of the *Mishkan* vessels, refers to Betzalel in each case. *Ramban*, however, disagrees. According to *Ramban*, there is no reason to explain the way R' Sorotzkin does, unless we say that the Torah was more strict about the Ark's dignity than about that of other vessels.

◄§ Debate in the Chassidic Literature

The *rishonim* do little to explain the debate between Moshe and Betzalel over whether the vessels or the *Mishkan* should be made first. Even so, the Chassidic literature makes up for this, developing the debate as a metaphor. Moshe, who thought the vessels should be made first, intended to return the world to its primal state, before the sin of Adam, when goodness, which the Chassidim call "the holy core," was more powerful than evil, or "the impure shell." Betzalel, by contrast, recognized that in reality it is impossible, following the sin of the Calf, to turn back the clock. He therefore built the *Mishkan* first, as if to protect the core from what was outside.

In his *Eretz Chemdah*, *Malbim* develops and expands this idea. Moshe thought that the Israelites' repenting from the sin of the Calf totally erased that sin, and they could then be returned to Eden. Betzalel, however, held that our repentance hides beneath Hashem's throne, whereas out in the open, accusing angels abound, who have not come to terms with our sins. Eventually Moshe conceded to Betzalel, saying, "You must have been in Hashem's shadow," i.e., he agreed with Betzalel's view.

Today, despite the existence of repentance, we still live in a world of "shadows," in which the impure shell triumphs over the holy core. *Chasam Sofer* employs this idea as well, concluding that the world will be perfected only with *Mashiach's* arrival. Then, good will triumph over evil: "Be benevolent to Zion. Build the walls of Jerusalem" (*Tehillim* 51:20). In the Messianic era, Zion, i.e., holiness, will be protected from impurity by a "wall." Until then, Betzalel was correct in building the *Mishkan* first.

Sefas Emes offers a remarkable explanation of Betzalel's understanding Hashem's will without having heard it from Him. In this matter, Betzalel symbolizes the entire Jewish nation, who possess great spiritual power. The Jewish people, through their innocent faith, can intuitively sense the will of their Father in Heaven more than any of the prophets. Hence, we read of Moshe's surprise at their success: "Moshe saw all the work, and, behold, they had done it as Hashem commanded" (*Sh'mos* 39:43).

Or HaChaim, as well, is effusive in his praise of the Jewish people's holiness, yet expresses that praise by different means. The Torah states, "The Israelites did all that Hashem had commanded Moshe" (v. 32), and *Or HaChaim* comments:

> In Torah observance, Hashem created a bond to link the entire Jewish people. He showed them that every Jew can bring merit to his fellow Jews, for the Torah can only be fulfilled by the entire Jewish people working together. If all Jews do what they can, they will bring one another merit.

Perhaps when the Torah said, "Love your neighbor as yourself" (*Vayikra* 19:18), it meant "Love him through what he has in common with you," i.e., the *mitzvos*. Our neighbor's welfare is important to our own. Through him, we ourselves achieve perfection. In effect, a Jew's neighbor is really part of him. This should ease our minds. Hashem commanded 613 *mitzvos*, and it is impossible for one person to fulfill them all. Proof of this is the existence of categories such as *Kohanim*, Levites, Israelites and women, each of which performs *mitzvos* that the others cannot perform. How then is it possible for an individual to fulfill all 613 *mitzvos*? How can he bring perfection to the 613 units of his soul that correspond to the *mitzvos*? It must be that the Torah is meant to be fulfilled by the entire Jewish people working together, bringing each other merit: "The Israelites did all that Hashem had commanded." As

S'forno explains, "The complete act to its perfection was performed by the entire Jewish people. Some donated money and others volunteered to do the work, to fulfill Hashem's will." This same idea was developed by many Chassidic works which followed.